GREAT DEBATES IN AMERICAN HISTORY

*From the Debates in the British Parliament on the
Colonial Stamp Act (1764–1765) to the Debates
in Congress at the Close of the Taft
Administration (1912–1913)*

EDITED BY

MARION MILLS MILLER, Litt.D. (Princeton)

Editor of "The Life and Works of Abraham Lincoln," etc.

IN FOURTEEN VOLUMES

EACH DEALING WITH A SPECIFIC SUBJECT, AND CONTAINING A SPECIAL INTRODUC-
TION BY A DISTINGUISHED AMERICAN STATESMAN OR PUBLICIST

VOLUME EIGHT

CIVIL RIGHTS: PART TWO

With an Introduction by WALTER HINES PAGE, LL.D.
American Ambassador to the Court of St. James

CURRENT LITERATURE PUBLISHING COMPANY
NEW YORK

CONTENTS OF VOLUME EIGHT

PAGE

INTRODUCTION: Industry and Education: The True Factors of
Southern Reconstruction 1
By WALTER HINES PAGE

CHAPTER
I. RACE, EDUCATIONAL, AND SEX QUALIFICATIONS
FOR THE SUFFRAGE 8
Debate in the Senate on Manhood Suffrage in the District of
Columbia: in favor of educational qualifications, LOT M.
MORRILL (Me.); opposed, SAMUEL C. POMEROY (Kan.), B.
GRATZ BROWN (Mo.), JAMES W. GRIMES (Ia.); in favor of
Negro Suffrage, WAITMAN T. WILLEY (W. Va.); opposed,
GARRETT DAVIS (Ky.).
Debate in the Senate on Equal Suffrage (Manhood and Wom-
anhood) in the District: varying views by Senator MORRILL,
Senator WILLEY, HENRY WILSON (Mass.), Senator POMEROY,
EDGAR COWAN (Pa.), HENRY B. ANTHONY (R. I.), GEORGE
H. WILLIAMS (Ore.), BENJAMIN F. WADE (O.), RICHARD
YATES (Ill.), REVERDY JOHNSON (Md.), FREDERICK T. FREL-
INGHUYSEN (N. J.), Senator BROWN, Senator DAVIS, WIL-
LIAM SPRAGUE (R. I.), CHARLES R. BUCKALEW (Pa.), JAMES
R. DOOLITTLE (Wis.), JAMES DIXON (Ct.), WILLARD SAULS-
BURY (Del.), LAFAYETTE S. FOSTER (Ct.), THOMAS A. HEN-
DRICKS (Ind.), HENRY S. LANE (Ind.), CHARLES SUMNER
(Mass.).
Debate in the Senate on passing the bill over the President's
veto: in favor, JOHN SHERMAN (O.); opposed, Senator DOO-
LITTLE.

II. MILITARY RECONSTRUCTION BY CONGRESS . . 40
President JOHNSON's message on Reconstruction: reply by
Representative SAMUEL L. WARNER (Ct.).
Debate in the House on the Stevens Bill: varying views by
THADDEUS STEVENS (Pa.), AUGUSTUS BRANDEGEE (Ct.),
FRANCIS C. LE BLOND (O.), WILLIAM E. FINCK (O.), JOHN
A. BINGHAM (O.), WILLIAM LAWRENCE (O.), M. RUSSELL
THAYER (Pa.), SAMUEL SHELLABARGER (O.), HENRY L.
DAWES (Mass.), JOHN A. GRISWOLD (N. Y.), HENRY J.
RAYMOND (N. Y.), General JAMES A. GARFIELD (O.), General
NATHANIEL P. BANKS (Mass.), JOHN A. KASSON (Ia.),
JAMES M. ASHLEY (O.), GEORGE S. BOUTWELL (Mass.),
WILLIAM E. NIBLACK (Ind.), WILLIAM D. KELLEY (Pa.),
HORACE MAYNARD (Tenn.), WILLIAM B. ALLISON (Ia.),
JAMES G. BLAINE (Me.), BURT VAN HORN (N. Y.).

Debate in the Senate on the bill: varying views by GEORGE
H. WILLIAMS (Ore.), REVERDY JOHNSON (Md.), WILLIAM
M. STEWART (Nev.), LOT M. MORRILL (Me.), JOHN B. HEN-
DERSON (Mo.), JAMES R. DOOLITTLE (Wis.), THOMAS A.
HENDRICKS (Ind.), WILLARD SAULSBURY (Del.), GARRETT
DAVIS (Ky.), HENRY WILSON (Mass.), JOHN SHERMAN (O.).

Debate in the House on the amended bill: varying views by
Mr. STEVENS, Mr. BOUTWELL, WILLIAM B. STOKES (Tenn.),
Mr. BLAINE, JAMES F. WILSON (Ia.), JOHN F. FARNSWORTH
(Ill.), General ROBERT C. SCHENCK (O.), General GARFIELD,
GILES W. HOTCHKISS (N. Y.), HENRY H. P. BROMWELL
(Ill.), IGNATIUS DONNELLY (Minn.), Mr. LE BLOND, General
BANKS.

Debate in the House on passage of bill over President's veto:
in favor, Mr. STEVENS; opposed, CHARLES A. ELDRIDGE
(Wis.), Mr. LE BLOND.

Debate in the Senate on passage over President's veto: in
favor, Senator JOHNSON; opposed, Senator SAULSBURY, Senator HENDRICKS.

Debate in the Senate on pardoning power of the President: in
favor, Senator JOHNSON; opposed, LYMAN TRUMBULL (Ill.).

Third Annual Message of President JOHNSON on Reconstruc-
tion; Debate in the Senate on the Message: in favor,
CHARLES R. BUCKALEW (Pa.), Senator WILSON, JAMES
DIXON (Ct.); opposed, Jacob M. Howard (Mich.), SIMON
CAMERON (Pa.), CHARLES SUMNER (Mass.).

Denunciations of Military Reconstruction by HORATIO SEY-
MOUR (N. Y.), AUGUST BELMONT (N. Y.), General THOMAS
EWING (Kan.).

III. THE FIFTEENTH AMENDMENT (*Equal Manhood Suf-*
frage)   96

Debate in the Senate: varying views by JOHN B. HENDERSON
(Mo.), WILLIAM M. STEWART (Nev.), GARRETT DAVIS (Ky.),
HENRY WILSON (Mass.), THOMAS A. HENDRICKS (Ind.),
JAMES DIXON (Ct.), SAMUEL C. POMEROY (Kan.).

Debate in the House: varying views by GEORGE S. BOUTWELL
(Mass.), WILLIAM E. NIBLACK (Ind.), CHARLES A. ELD-
RIDGE (Wis.), JAMES BROOKS (N. Y.), SAMUEL SHELLABAR-
GER (O.).

Renewed debate in the Senate: ORRIS S. FERRY (Ct.), WIL-
LARD WARNER (Ala.), GEORGE H. WILLIAMS (Ore.), CHARLES
SUMNER (Mass.), GEORGE VICKERS (Md.), WAITMAN T. WIL-
LEY (W. Va.), HENRY W. CORBETT (Ore.), JAMES A. BAY-
ARD, JR. (Del.), FREDERICK T. FRELINGHUYSEN (N. J.),
EDMUND G. ROSS (Kan.), Senator DAVIS, JOSEPH S. FOWLER
(Tenn.), WILLARD SAULSBURY (Del.), ADONIJAH S. WELCH
(Fla.), Senator HENDRICKS, OLIVER P. MORTON (Ind.),
JAMES R. DOOLITTLE (Wis.), CHARLES D. DRAKE (Mo.),
FREDERICK A. SAWYER (S. C.), Senator WILSON, SIMON
CAMERON (Pa.), LYMAN TRUMBULL (Ill.), JAMES W. PAT-
TERSON (N. H.), ROSCOE CONKLING (N. Y.), JOHN SHER-
MAN (O.), CHARLES R. BUCKALEW (Pa.).

CONTENTS OF VOLUME EIGHT

CHAPTER   PAGE

IV. FEDERAL POWER TO SUPPRESS ABUSES AGAINST
CIVIL RIGHTS (*The Ku-Klux Outrages*) . . . 162
Debate on appointment of Senate Committee of Investigation:
in favor, OLIVER P. MORTON (Ind.), WILLARD WARNER
(Ala.), JAMES W. NYE (Nev.), ZACHARIAH CHANDLER
(Mich.); opposed, EUGENE CASSERLY (Cal.), THOMAS F.
BAYARD (Del.), ALLEN G. THURMAN (O.).
Debate on Sherman Bill to suppress the outrages: in favor,
JOHN SHERMAN (O.), JOHN SCOTT (Pa.), JOHN POOL
(N. C.), Senator MORTON; opposed, Senator BAYARD, General
FRANCIS P. BLAIR (Mo.).

V. THE SECOND CIVIL RIGHTS BILL 203
Debate in the House: in favor, JOHN R. LYNCH (Miss.),
General JAMES A. GARFIELD (O.), General BENJAMIN F.
BUTLER (Mass.); opposed, ALEXANDER H. STEPHENS (Ga.),
LUCIUS Q. C. LAMAR (Miss.), CHARLES A. ELDRIDGE (Wis.),
JOHN Y. BROWN (Ky.).

VI. THE SEMINOLE WAR 237
Debate in the House on Censure of General Andrew Jackson
for Barbarities toward Indians: in favor, THOMAS W.
COBB (Ga.), JAMES JOHNSON (Va.), HENRY CLAY (Ky.),
CHARLES F. MERCER (Va.), JOSEPH HOPKINSON (Pa.), JOHN
TYLER (Va.); opposed, JOHN HOLMES (Mass.), RICHARD
M. JOHNSON (Ky.), ALEXANDER SMYTH (Va.), LEMUEL
SAWYER (N. C.), GEORGE POINDEXTER (Miss.).

VII. INDIAN RIGHTS (*Removal of Southern Tribes to the West*) 261
President JACKSON's Message on the Removal.
Debate in the Senate on the Removal: in favor, JOHN FOR-
SYTH (Ga.); opposed, THEODORE FRELINGHUYSEN (N. J.).

VIII. REFORM OF OUR INDIAN POLICY (*Granting Lands in
Severalty, etc.*) 277
Representative IGNATIUS DONNELLY (Minn.) on "Reform of
the Indian System."
Messages of Presidents GRANT and HAYES on the subject.
Debate in the Senate on Removal of the Colorado Utes:
RICHARD COKE (Tex.) advocates grants of land in severalty;
opposed, HENRY M. TELLER (Col.); N. P. HILL (Col.) sup-
ports the bill; JOHN T. MORGAN (Ala.) would subject In-
dians to laws of the land; HENRY L. DAWES (Mass.) and
JAMES G. BLAINE (Me.) advocate their education; opposed,
PRESTON B. PLUMB (Kan.).

IX. WOMAN SUFFRAGE (*Debates connected with Fifteenth
Amendment*) 313
Debate in the Senate on Petition for Woman Suffrage from
Mrs. GERRIT SMITH (N. Y.), *et al.*: varying views by JOHN
B. HENDERSON (Mo.), WILLARD SAULSBURY (Del.), CHARLES
SUMNER (Mass.), RICHARD YATES (Ill.).

CHAPTER   PAGE

Debate in the House on Petition from Equal Rights Association: varying views by CHARLES A. ELDRIDGE (Wis.), RUFUS P. SPALDING (O.), THOMAS E. NOELL (Mo.).

Petitions of Mrs. VICTORIA C. WOODHULL (N. Y.), Dr. MARY E. WALKER, and others for Woman Suffrage.

Speech of Representative STEVENSON ARCHER (Md.) on ''The Reaction from Woman Suffrage.''

X. WOMAN SUFFRAGE (*Recent Debate*) 345

Debate in the House Committee on Judiciary on Constitutional Amendment granting Women the Suffrage: in favor, Miss JANE ADDAMS (Ill.), Miss LEONORA REILLY (N. Y.), Representative JOHN E. RAKER (Cal.), Mrs. JEAN NELSON PENFIELD (N. Y.), Representative EDWARD T. TAYLOR (Col.), Representative A. W. LAFFERTY (Ore.), Mrs. WILLIAM KENT (Cal.), Mrs. IDA HUSTED HARPER (N. Y.), Representative VICTOR L. BERGER (Wis.), Miss MARY E. McDOWELL (Ill.), Miss CAROLINE A. LOWE (Mo.), JAMES F. LAIDLAW (N. Y.), Mrs. ELSIE COLE PHILLIPS (Wis.); opposed, Mrs. GRACE D. GOODWIN (D. C.), Miss ELLA C. BRÉHAUT (D. C.), Mrs. FRANCIS W. GODDARD (Col.), Judge MOSES HALLETT (Col.).

XI. FEDERAL RECOGNITION OF POLYGAMY (*Polygamy and Slavery*) 401

Debate in the House to exclude polygamists from land grants: varying views by JOHN M. BERNHISEL (Utah), SOLOMON G. HAVEN (N. Y.), JOHN LETCHER (Va.), THOMAS DAVIS (R. I.), WILLIAM SMITH (Va.), WILLIAMSON R. W. COBB (Ala.), JOSHUA R. GIDDINGS (O.), PHILIP PHILLIPS (Ala.), LEWIS D. CAMPBELL (O.), ALEXANDER H. STEPHENS (Ga.), GERRIT SMITH (N. Y.), DAVID T. DISNEY (O.), JOHN S. MILLSON (Va.), GEORGE A. SIMMONS (N. Y.), SAMUEL PARKER (Ind.), SAMUEL P. BENSON (Me.), JOSEPH LANE (Ore.), MIKE WALSH (N. Y.), JOHN KERR (N. C.), JOHN C. GOODRICH (Mass.), NATHANIEL G. TAYLOR (Tenn.), CHARLES READY (Tenn.), LAWRENCE M. KEITT (S. C.), JAMES L. SEWARD (Ga.), HIRAM WALBRIDGE (N. Y.), CALEB LYON (N. Y.), CHARLES HUGHES (N. Y.), BISHOP PERKINS (N. Y.), WILLIAM W. BOYCE (S. C.), JOHN L. TAYLOR (O.).

Speech of Representative JUSTIN S. MORRILL (Vt.) on ''Polygamy a National Reproach.''

XII. POLYGAMY: CRIME, OR RELIGIOUS PRACTICE? (*Debate on the Cullom Bill*) 439

Debate in the House on the Cullom Bill to punish polygamists: in favor, SHELBY M. CULLOM (Ill.); opposed, WILLIAM H. HOOPER (Utah).

XIII. DEBARRING POLYGAMISTS FROM CIVIL RIGHTS (*The Edmunds Bill*) 456

Debate in the Senate on the Edmunds Bill: in favor, AUGUSTUS H. GARLAND (Ark.), GEORGE F. EDMUNDS (Vt.); opposed, GEORGE G. VEST (Mc.), JOHN T. MORGAN (Ala.), WILKINSON CALL (Fla.).

Messages of CLEVELAND and HARRISON on Polygamy.

ILLUSTRATIONS IN VOLUME EIGHT

PAGE

Andrew Johnson . . . . . . *Frontispiece*
Photogravure

The Great American Tanner [Grant] 87

An Impending Catastrophe 94
[Presidential Campaign of 1868]

The Great National Game 115
Our Colored Brother's Innings [The XVth Amendment]

Ku-Klux Warning to a "Scalawag" and a "Carpet-Bagger" 152

Reconstruction, or "A White Man's Government" . . 163

The Precarious Situation 171
[Grant Supported by Negro Supremacy]

Ku-Klux Costumes 175

"Go On!"—U. S. Grant 195
[Ku-Klux Snake Pierced by U. S. A. Bayonet]
Cartoon by Thomas Nast

"It Is Only a Truce to Regain Power" 200
[Greeley and Sumner on the Ku-Klux Issue]
Cartoon by Thomas Nast

The "Civil Rights" Scare Is Nearly Over 212
The Game of (Colored) Fox and (White) Goose
Cartoon by Thomas Nast

The Murder of Louisiana 226
[Caricature of President Grant]

Louisiana and the Nation 227

James A. Garfield 228
Photogravure

"Of Course He Wants to Vote the Democratic Ticket" . 236
[Southern Coercion of the Negro Voter]
Cartoon by A. B. Frost

"Move On!" 303
Has the Native American [Indian] No Rights That the Nat-
uralized American Is Bound to Respect?
Cartoon by Thomas Nast

PAGE

The Age of Brass 339
    Caricature of "Strong-minded Females"

The Woman Trumpeter 347
    [Herald of Woman Suffrage]

The Anti-Suffragist and the Pro-Vice Delegation . . 369

Mormon Breastworks and United States Troops . . . 437
    Caricature of the "Mormon War"

George F. Edmunds 456
    Photogravure

INTRODUCTION

Industry and Education: the True Factors of Southern Reconstruction [1]

THE problem of real reconstruction of the South is the most important that has been presented in our national life. It is not the education of a few millions of neglected persons; it is not the modernizing of a few picturesque institutions; least of all is it the task of imposing on these people the civilization that has been developed elsewhere (for this would be a fool's errand indeed and in no way desirable if it were possible); but the larger question is this:

Since democracy means constant social growth and social mobility, is Southern life becoming democratic or is it remaining stable, or going back to an essentially aristocratic structure? Are forces inside it asserting themselves that give promise of shaping this life in line with democratic growth? Or are the native forces reactionary? Is democracy there at last to be a failure? Is it equal to the task of assimilating the master race and the freed race?

There are thoughtful men who frankly deny the possibility of such a complete conquest by the democratic idea. I quote one such, a man of learning, if not of wisdom, who wrote this memorandum for me under the mistletoe in an old South Carolina mansion:

[1] Adapted from an article in the *Atlantic Monthly* for May, 1902, entitled "The Rebuilding of Old Commonwealths," afterward published (by Doubleday, Page and Company, New York) in a volume with this title.

1

"The dominant elements of society in the two sections of the country were different from the beginning. Slavery did not make the difference, it only emphasized it. The unconscious aims and ideals of the two peoples diverged. The abolition of slavery was a matter of force. So also was the suppression of secession. But these events did not change the essential character of the people. Superficially they are now one. But forty years are as nothing in the life of a people, nor fifty years nor a hundred. The South is to-day further from a willing acceptance of real democratic ideals than it was twenty years ago. The growth of such organizations as the Daughters of the Confederacy, the increasing celebration of the heroism of the Confederate soldier, the silent unwillingness of white men to tax themselves to educate the negro, the instinctive denial to the negro of any real standing in the most important matters of life—these things seem to me to point to a different genius, a different tendency, a different ideal, even a different necessity. How the divergence will work itself out, I do not know; but a century hence the South will be, in the essence of its civilization, further from the North than it now is. No outward forms of government can make two different peoples the same."

Another man of learning, if not of wisdom, used to say to me in Cambridge, Mass.: "The Southerners have always seemed foreigners to me. The Northern and the Southern people are different. I do not think they will ever work out the same ideals."

These opinions (which I have heard only in South Carolina and in Massachusetts and there in academic circles) strip the question of all side issues and of all temporary aspects. It is true that the same laws may not mean the same thing North and South (as the Fourteenth Amendment to the Federal Constitution does not); and fifty years have not essentially changed the negro's place in the community; and it is true that no exterior or temporary influence counts for much and the hereditary "essence of a civilization" is everything. No man of thought has ever regarded laws enacted at Washington against the consent of the Southern people as a primary force in shaping their life, nor outside aid to education or to anything else as revolutionary if it ran counter to the native "genius"; preaching is of no avail;

alms-giving is an estranging force; in a word, if Southern life have not in it the seed and the necessity of a
true democratic development, then a democratic order
cannot be thrust upon it and it were useless to try.

But, if I understand the great forces of our time,
and if I know the history of the people of the Southern
commonwealths (which to the obscuring of the whole
large matter remains unwritten), my friends from whom
I have quoted have made a radical misinterpretation of
all the large facts and of all dominant present tendencies. There is no undemocratic trait in the Southern
people that is not directly accounted for by slavery and
by the results of slavery. The most conspicuous insti-
tutional results were the political machines that were
built on race differences first by one political party and
then by the other, and the ecclesiastical machines that
are the direct result of popular ignorance and isolation.
The country people that I have described are men of
good mettle, men to make free commonwealths of. The
very strongest impulse they have is patriotic and democratic. The contrary tendencies are clearly survivals
of a deflection of their development. So strongly have
I been impressed with the democratic quality of Southern character that I believe, if a democracy existed nowhere in the world, Southern life would now evolve one,
perhaps even of a radical type.

These old commonwealths were arrested in their development by slavery and by war and by the double
burden of a sparse population and of an ignorant alien
race. When the weight of these burdens is considered,
the progress made these thirty years in the development
of the innate democratic tendency is without parallel in
our history. The present backwardness of Southern
life in rural communities and in old academic or social
circles is but a picturesque reminder of the distance we
have traveled. Descriptions of these may entertain us,
as the charm of the obsolete appeals to all cultivated
minds, but they give no hint except by contrast of the
real forces of the period in which we live.

The process that has been going on in the upland

South in particular is a process of conscious and natural
State-building, constructive at every important step.
Reactionary influences have been respectable, but they
are spent impulses. There are two great constructive
forces. The first is *industry,* which has already given
the essential power over to a class of men that bring
mobility to social life and opportunity to them that can
take it. This industrial development would finally work
out the inherent democratic tendency of the people if
no other force were brought into play. But no man who
knows the gentleness and the dignity and the leisure of
the old Southern life would like to see these qualities
blunted by too rude a growth of sheer industrialism.

The other great force that frankly recognizes the arrested development of the people and is taking hold of
the problem of their natural growth is the new impulse
in *public education.* This is native, and it is nothing
different from Jefferson's creed and plan. So strong is
it that its manifestation may fairly be called a new chapter in our national history. In the presence of this revolutionary force, fear of reaction and doubt about the
democratic "essence" of Southern civilization fall away.
Besides this all other forces except the force of industrial
life count for nothing.

The situation has been discouraging enough, Heaven
knows. In the ten cis-Mississippian Southern States the
proportion of illiterate white voters was as large at the
beginning of the century as it had been in 1850. But it
is precisely because the situation was so bad that it has
since become so hopeful. The leaders of the best Southern opinion began work in a new way with results which
have already proved most gratifying. They discovered
that the schools must do something more than teach the
three R's, for a people without diversified occupations
and without training do not care for the three R's, nor
do the three R's profit them greatly. An idle and unpro-
ductive man is no less useless because he can read and
write.

It was this fundamental fact that General Armstrong
saw when he worked out the system of training toward

occupations at Hampton Institute for the negroes; and it is this fundamental fact that the present leaders of popular education in the Southern States understand. They are training hand and mind together. The experience in every rural community where a school of this kind has been established is that the people who cared nothing for what they called "education" are so eager for this training that they will make any sacrifice to obtain it. Herein is the beginning of a complete change in neglected village and rural life. Here, too, is proof that the people are not "in the essence of their civilization" different from the people of the other parts of the country. The "way out" has been found. The problem that the South now presents has at last become so plain that thoughtful men no longer differ about it. It is no longer obscured by race differences, nor by political differences. It is simply the training of the untrained masses. As slavery and war and an isolated life arrested their development and held them in a fixed social condition, so the proper training of them to helpful occupations will release them to usefulness in a democracy.

The new movement is revolutionary for another reason. The old notion of education was that it meant the training of a few. It is now understood that none can be well educated unless all are trained.

The men and women of both races who are leading this great popular movement work with an inspiration that puts conventional teachers to shame. For example: A young agricultural chemist several years ago began with enthusiasm a campaign of education among the farmers. He put much faith in bulletins and leaflets which were sent broadcast. "I soon found out," said he, "that sending out literature did little good as long as many farmers could not read, and many more would not." He left his laboratory and became an educational statesman, and there are few men in America whose influence in building up the people is greater than his. Out of a comparatively small acquaintance, I know many similar experiences. A well-trained preacher, for example, who has had much to do with the administration of the churches of his sect in rural regions, lately gave up his work and became a superintendent of public schools. "Till the country people are educated," said he, "church work will not stick."

Educational work in these States is, therefore, something more than the teaching of youth; it is the building of a new social order. The far-reaching quality of the work that the energetic educators in the South are doing lifts them out of the ranks of mere school-masters and puts them on the level of constructive statesmen. They are the servants of democracy in a sense that no other public servants now are; for they are the rebuilders of these old commonwealths.

Any man who has the privilege to contribute even so small a thing as applause to this great movement feels the thrill of this State-building work so strongly that he is not likely to take a keen interest in such tame exercise as historical speculation. Yet it would be interesting to speculate on the effects of Jefferson's plan for public education if it had been carried out. Would the public schools not have prevented the growth of slavery? True, public schools and slavery, as well as most other human institutions, are the results of economic forces; but, if the masses of the Southern population had been educated, or trained to work (and such training is education), a stronger economic impetus might have been given to diversified pursuits than cotton culture gave to slavery, and the whole course of our history might have been changed. But, whatever may have been the results of Jefferson's educational policy if it had been worked out in Virginia, the development of Southern life in the next hundred years will be determined by the success with which it shall now be worked out. The nature of the problem is clear. The work will be slow and the recovery from these last effects of slavery may require as long a time as it required to abolish slavery; but of the ultimate result no man who can distinguish dominant from incidental forces can have a doubt.

The Southern people were deflected from their natural development. They are the purest American stock we have. They are naturally as capable as any part of our population. They are now slowly but surely working out their own destiny; and that destiny is a democratic order of society which will be an important contribution to the republic that their ancestors took so large a part in establishing. Rich undeveloped resources of American life lie in these great rural stretches that are yet almost unknown. The foremost patriotic duty of our time is to hasten their development.

Walter H. Page

CHAPTER I

RACE, EDUCATIONAL, AND SEX QUALIFICATIONS FOR THE SUFFRAGE

[EQUAL MANHOOD SUFFRAGE IN THE DISTRICT OF COLUMBIA]

Benjamin F. Wade [O.] Introduces in the Senate Bill Granting Equal Male Suffrage in the District of Columbia—Debate on Educational Qualification: in Favor, Lot M. Morrill [Me.]; Opposed, Samuel C. Pomeroy [Kan.], B. Gratz Brown [Mo.], James W. Grimes [Ia.]; the Qualification Is Omitted—Debate on Negro Suffrage: in Favor, Waitman T. Willey [W. Va.]; Opposed, Garrett Davis [Ky.]—Bill Postponed—Debate Resumed in the Next Session—''Equal Suffrage (Manhood and Womanhood) in the District of Columbia''; Varying Views by Sen. Morrill, Sen. Willey, Henry Wilson [Mass.], Sen. Pomeroy, Edgar Cowan [Pa.], Henry B. Anthony [R. I.], George H. Williams [Ore.], Sen. Wade, Richard Yates [Ill.], Reverdy Johnson [Md.], Frederick T. Frelinghuysen [N. J.], Sen. Brown, Sen. Davis, William Sprague [R. I.], Charles R. Buckalew [Pa.], James R. Doolittle [Wis.], James Dixon [Ct.], Willard Saulsbury [Del.], Lafayette S. Foster [Ct.], Thomas A. Hendricks [Ind.], Henry S. Lane [Ind.], Charles Sumner [Mass.]; Congress Passes Bill for Equal Manhood Suffrage in the District, and the President Vetoes It with Remarks; Debate in Senate on Passage Over Veto: in Favor, John Sherman [O.]; Opposed, Sen. Doolittle; Congress Passes Bill Over Veto—Congress Decrees Equal Manhood Suffrage in the Territories, Admits Nebraska into the Union with This Suffrage, Abolishes Peonage in New Mexico, and Establishes Howard University for Negroes.

THE controversies of 1866 developed the fact that the majority opinion of the people of the country was in favor of extending the elective franchise to the negro. Accordingly, upon Congress reassembling in December of that year, the dominant Radicals, who had heretofore acted with great caution upon the issue, resolved to take the District of Columbia (as they had done in the case of emancipation) as the first

8

subject of legislation embodying the principle of equal manhood suffrage, which, it was contemplated, should afterwards be extended by Federal power throughout the Union.

Negro Suffrage in the District of Columbia

Senate, December 4, 1865-June 27, 1866

A bill was already before Congress upon the subject. On the opening day of the previous session (December 4, 1865) Benjamin Wade [O.] had brought forward in the Senate a bill "to regulate the elective franchise in the District of Columbia." On December 6 it was referred to the Committee on the District. On January 10, 1866, it was brought forward in the Committee of the Whole. As amended by the committee it granted the elective franchise to every male person without distinction of race who was twenty-one years of age and upward and had not been convicted of crime, and was not a pauper or under guardianship, and was able to read the Constitution in English, and write his name. Those who should disturb any lawful elector in his exercise of the franchise were, at the discretion of the court, to be fined not over $1,000, or imprisoned and fed only on bread and water for not over thirty days, or suffer both penalties.

Samuel C. Pomeroy [Kan.] objected to the educational requirements. Not to speak of the fact that many well-educated persons, such as Germans, could not read English, it was wrong to exclude the franchise from those who, like the negroes, had never had any educational opportunities.

After having legislated them away from schools and science and everything else, to thrust in their faces a law saying, "If you can read and write, you can vote," I think is adding insult to injury.

All the amendments proposed by the committee but the educational one were accepted, and this was deferred for future consideration. The bill was taken up for discussion on January 16. Garrett Davis [Ky.] scouted the educational test proposed as ineffectual. In a short time every negro should be able to spell through the Constitution to the satisfaction of partial judges of election, and really would be no more capable of taking part "in the trivial matter of government" than he had been before.

Senator Davis then discussed the general principles of negro suffrage.

The right to vote is not a natural, but an artificial, right, as well in our country as in all others wherever it has been exercised, and in the countries where it has been most diffused it never was allowed to one-fourth of the people, the women and minors and many other small classes not being permitted to vote under the most popular governments. From our systems the negro has been always shut out, except in a few localities; and in a majority of them for a short period only was this mischievous anomaly tolerated.

How many States allow negro suffrage? Massachusetts, Vermont, Rhode Island, and New York. All the others forbid it, and, notwithstanding the extreme acme to which the negro-mania has risen in the free States since the rebellion broke out, Connecticut, Wisconsin, Minnesota, Nevada, and Colorado have voted against negro suffrage. In this District one-fourth of the whole population are negroes? Of the States which allow negro suffrage, Vermont has 709 negroes and 314,380 whites; Rhode Island has 3,952 negroes and 170,668 whites; Massachusetts has 9,602 negroes and 1,221,464 whites, and New York has 49,005 negroes and 3,831,730 whites, and requires each negro to own real estate of the value of $250 to qualify him to vote. A healthy man may take into his stomach one, or two, or three drops of arsenic without serious detriment to his health, but if he were to swallow one, two, or three hundred drops it would destroy his life. Negro suffrage is political arsenic. If it is not, why do not the free States open wide their throats and gulp down the grateful and invigorating draught? Why does not California give the right of suffrage to her Chinamen; Michigan and many other States to their Indians; and Pennsylvania to her gypsy gangs, that are perpetually vibrating between her plains and mountains?

If the negro population ran upon the white population

the free States in the same proportion as it does in this District and the Southern States, in some of them being from thirty to fifty, and in South Carolina more than fifty per cent., would any of the free States, under such a condition of things, accept negro suffrage? A successful effort to force it upon them would very speedily inaugurate another rebellion.

But, Mr. President, the question whether a few thousand negroes of this District shall vote in its elections is of very trivial importance to the people of the United States, and to that portion of them who are so exercised by it, and who are making such strenuous efforts to bring it about. This contest is but an experiment, a skirmish, an entering wedge to prepare the way for a similar movement in Congress to confer the right of suffrage on all the negroes of the United States, liberated by the recent amendment of the Constitution, the power to be claimed under its second clause. It is following up the tactics of the party four years ago, when the assault upon slavery in this District heralded the general movement that was to be made against it.

Senator Davis argued that the peace and freedom of a country depended upon the homogeneity of its people. The various branches of the Caucasian race, if not brought together too suddenly, mingled without serious antagonism, none of the stocks degrading the others.

But in our country a race of people that is essentially inferior to the Caucasian race in its physical, mental, and moral structure, and that no cultivation can bring to an approximation of that high standard; that has by nature so low an organization as to be wholly incapable of self-civilization, or organizing a self-government, or maintaining a civilization and form of government which had been bestowed upon it by a superior people— a race which could take no part in the great business of government, to improve or uphold it, but only to obstruct, thwart, confound, and break it up, should never have any political power conferred on it. I hold that the negro is such a race; that he is the lowest and the Caucasian is the highest of the races of man, and the others are intermediate; and that he cannot be mingled with the blood, or in the management of the affairs, of the white man without degradation and mischief to him.

The word "negro," as an ethnological term, does not comprehend all the black, much less the dusky families of man; it refers to that race which Cuvier describes as being "marked by a black complexion, crisped or woolly hair, compressed cranium, and a flat nose. The projection of the lower parts of the face and the thick lips evidently approximate it to the monkey tribe." The great naturalist might have added, as other distinctive characteristics of the negro: first, that his skin exhales perpetually a peculiar, pungent, and disagreeable odor; second, that "the hollow of his foot makes a hole in the ground."

Copeland, Chambers, Dr. Moseley, White, Dr. Prichard, Smith, and Vrolih, of Amsterdam, name many other distinctions between the white and the negro race, such as low nervous irritability, all of which mark their approach toward the lower form of animals.

Camper, Soemmering, Lawrence, Virey, Ebel, and Blumenbach agree that the brain of the negro is smaller; and Gall, Spurzheim, and Combe, that it is so distributed as to denote less capacity for reasoning and judging than the Caucasian.

Thomas Carlyle thus addresses himself to the emancipated negroes of the West Indies:

"You are not slaves now, nor do I wish, if it can be avoided, to see you slaves again; but decidedly you will have to be servants to those who are born wiser than you, that are born lords of you—servants to the whites if they are (as what mortal man can doubt they are?) born wiser than you. That, you may depend on it, my obscure black friends, is and was always the law of the world, for you and for all men to be servants, the more foolish of us to the more wise. Heaven's laws are not repealable by earth, however earth may try."

Mr. Jefferson's passionate denunciation of slavery has been often and exultingly quoted by its opponents, yet this is his testimony as to the capability of the negro race:

"Never yet could I find that a black had uttered a thought above the level of a plain narration; never saw even an elementary trait of painting and sculpture."

Theodore Parker, as quoted by Nott, in his work, "Types of Mankind," declares that:

"The Caucasian differs from all other races. He is humane, he is civilized, he progresses. It is intellect, after all, that conquers, not the strength of man's arm. The Caucasian has often been the master of other races, never their slave. Republics are Caucasian. All the great sciences are of Caucasian origin. All inventions are Caucasian. Literature and romance come from the same stock."

Even Prichard, one of the few writers on the natural history of man who does not frankly concede the inferiority of the negro race, admits that:

"By the animality or degradation of the forms of the pelvis, peculiar to the negress and the Bushman and the Hottentot, is implied an approach toward the forms of the chimpanzee and the orang-outang."

The freedman tends to revert to barbarism. Sir Archbald Alison in his "History of Europe" says:

"By the expulsion of the French from San Domingo it has been nominally independent; but slavery has been far indeed from being abolished, and the condition of the people anything but ameliorated by the change. The industrious habits, the flourishing aspect of the island, have disappeared; and the inhabitants, reduced to half their former amount, and bitterly galled by their republican task-masters, have relapsed into the indolence and inactivity of savage life."

All the other races of men were also once benighted savages, but they had been created with a higher and more perfect organism and endowed with superior faculties and powers. More excellent in complexion, form, action, and innate grace; the nicest sensibilities; deep reflection, with long forethought, exhaustless invention, the most complex ratiocination; an active and insatiable desire for progress and perfectibility; the workings within him of a higher divinity; a readier, freer, and closer communion with nature and God, lifted him up and propelled him from his primal and ignoble ignorance and destitution to the achievements of his present civilization, which, grand and affluent as they be, are but the prelude of his vast and incomprehensible future.

But during the long period in which the other races have been moving on with their wonderful creations, almost a continent of negroes have been fixed as a fossil under the weight of the barbarism and ignorance of untold centuries, because their Creator had not endowed them with the faculties and energies to emerge from it. So He made the progenitors of our negroes, the freedmen of the United States, and they can never break away from the essential nature of their parent stock. Individual property in the African slave may have ceased forever, but his involuntary labor, his slavery, in some form, in the fields of the South, is his destiny. The God of nature hath so ordained, and man cannot thwart it.

The Senator declared that negro suffrage, with the attendant element of miscegenation, had been adopted by the Northern Radicals, especially those of New England, as a means of continuing themselves in power.

For that power to be enthroned in Boston, and by its imperial will to direct how more than six hundred thousand negro votes, spread over fifteen States, should be cast in every election, is a great stake, for which a bold and desperate game is being played, and, if won, it may save the fate and fortunes of the daring political gamblers who are playing it. With the aid of their negro allies, constituting more than half of the whole vote of South Carolina and Louisiana, nearly half of that of several other States, forty thousand in the State of Kentucky, and a heavy proportion in the remainder of the late slave States, and possessed of the Government, and wielding its vast powers and patronage singly to their own ends, they would be omnipotent, and, standing in the name and according to its forms upon our subverted Constitution, they would be the absolute masters of the people.

But their aim is to embody the miscegenation of the races in the Southern States as part of their system. They have noted the permanent national degeneracy and weakness produced in other countries by this blighting curse, and they contemplate similar results in the Southern States. Without those results they know that a regenerated South would soon break away from the base thralldom with which they are seeking to envelop her, but with miscegenation and those results they might make the vassalage of the South to the North permanent. Massachusetts & Co. know that the negro has an invincible aversion to the cold Northern States. They know that so soon as the few negroes resident in the Northern States have the option the most of them will fly back to the sunny South, and the process will be expedited by the vexations and injustice of the "Freedmen's Bureau." The cotton, rice, sugar, and coffee plantations are the theater to which the negro laborer has been allotted by nature; everywhere beside he will be met and vanquished by his white competitor, but there this meeting will never take place. From all these causes the aggregation of the mass of the negroes of the United States in the Southern States will progress rapidly.

Miscegenation would be encouraged by large numbers of the two races inhabiting the same country, and every law and regulation in favor of the white being broken down: by the white race becoming poor and broken in spirit, and cut off from position and office and political power, and the negro race being elevated as the other is depressed, and becoming the ruling power of the country. The white man is to be driven from his lands, and they are to be given to the negro and the negro's guardian angel, the Yankee. The white man finds the malaria of the country fatal—to the negro it is innoxious. The one can labor in the fields if he will; the other it would speedily transfer to the grave. But wherever money is to be made there is the omnipresent Yankee. He steps in and forms associations with the negro; he engrosses the cotton and rice and sugar lands, and by the agency of the Freedmen's Bureau, and often with its officers as his secret partners, seduces the negro laborers from the employment of the resident landholders, if any of that class should be left, and himself monopolizes the entire labor of the country.

Thus the white resident is excluded from all part or lot in the cultivation and production, and eventually the ownership, of the lands, and all their avails that can pass through the hands of the Yankee proprietor go to the negro laborer. Poverty, destitution, and squalid want await the white residents and their families; and the men who devised this cruel and revolting system knew full well what cogent motive to miscegenation such a deplorable condition of the white race would offer to it. These august architects are gloating over the success of their crude and hastily tried scheme, and the misery it has even now brought on the Southern people, and they are in haste to perfect it by supplementary and new measures of legislation. The whole scheme was concocted after long reflection, by able men, for mischief and oppression, and it was devised with diabolical forecast. The original proposition to amend the Constitution by abolishing slavery throughout the United States was the first section; the succeeding sections rapidly followed: the organization of the oppressive and infamous Freedmen's Bureau, with the object to degrade the white man and elevate the negro; the pending bill "to enlarge its power"; the bill "to protect all persons in the United States in their civil rights, and furnish the means of their vindication"; the pending measure, and the numerous bills to extend the right of suffrage, not to all the free negroes of the United States, but to those recently liberated in the late slave States, all are harmonious parts of a huge system of tyranny and iniquity, built up not only without any rightful power, but in all their essential features against the plainest and most vital constitutional restrictions of power.

The purpose is to bring the South to such a condition of weakness and abasement that it shall have neither the spirit nor resources to throw off the galling yoke of the North; that it shall become a permanent colony, and be made to pay tribute under measures and laws passed by the North to build up its own sectional interests; that it shall become so much Mexicanized as to be incapable of self-government, and its government by the North become a necessity.

Mr. President, throughout his whole history the negro has been found in but two conditions: living separately to himself as an ignorant savage, or with some other race of people as a slave or dependent. Freedom, with ignorance and barbarism, or slavery with civilization, is his destiny.

The bill did not come again before the Senate until June 27.

Lot M. Morrill [Me.] argued for the educational qualification. This was opposed by B. Gratz Brown [Mo.]. He said:

I do not wish the suffrage restricted by any educational qualifications, nor do I wish it restricted by any property qualifications. I want it simple and absolute, a right of human nature, which is as much a right as any other of self-defence in political communities or out of political communities.

Senator Pomeroy again opposed the requirement that the voter should be able to read English.

I have yet to learn that a man is any more of a patriot by writing in English than he would be by writing in German or some other language. I have believed that a man was an American as truly when he became so from choice as though he was so from necessity. The Senator from Maine and myself were born here, but we could not help it. There is no great merit in that. But the man who becomes an American from choice, who looking over the ocean and seeing America, learning of our institutions, breathing somewhat of our freedom, longing to identify himself with us in this great struggle for self-government, comes here and voluntarily assumes the duties of a citizen, enters our army, and carries our flag to victory; I say such a man, if he cannot write a word in English, is an American; he is a patriot; he is loyal, and he should be entitled to vote.

Senator Morrill insisted on the requirement of a knowledge of English.

It is the language of this country. There is none other
recognized in the publication of the laws of Congress. The
Constitution of the United States is not furnished by Congress
to anybody except in the English language. The five years'
quarantine, within which a foreigner is to have an opportunity
to learn our institutions, are sufficient, if he is intelligent, to
learn the English language, and to enable him to read the Constitution, and therefore it is no hardship. I believe for the
sake of unity, unity in our civilization, unity in our language,
unity in our sentiments and opinions, that we ought to inculcate
as a standard and a formula that the laws should always be
printed in the English language; and, so far as any qualification
is concerned, certainly our civilization is worth but little in its
influence and its effect upon aliens and foreigners if at least
we do not require them to speak our language. That is the
reason that influences me more than anything else, and leads
me to desire the adoption of some such proposition. At the
same time, I do not think it of importance enough to divide
our friends upon that subject, and in order to accommodate
the question to the views of gentlemen I am perfectly willing
to modify the amendment by striking out the words "in the
English language," so that it will read, "and who can read
the Constitution and write his name."

James W. Grimes [Ia.] thought that reading the Constitution in a foreign language was an impracticable
test owing to the fact that the Constitution had not
been printed in one-half of the languages spoken in the
United States. The entire educational qualification was
stricken out by a vote of 15 yeas to 19 nays.

Waitman T. Willey [W. Va.] supported the bill. He
admitted that suffrage was not a natural right; "the
universal law of self-defence, belonging to communities
no less than to individuals, involves the principle of restricted suffrage."

On this principle our naturalization laws are based, and
these laws imply that no person belonging to any one of these
communities has the right to incorporate himself into the body-
politic of any other community without its consent and without
complying with such conditions as shall be prescribed for his
admission. On this foundation, too, has been erected the whole
superstructure of international law. Every nation or com-

VIII—2

munity, therefore, has the absolute right to regulate its own affairs and govern its own people.

But, said Senator Willey, the nation or community has no right to exercise this power *arbitrarily, or in derogation of the principles of justice and equity toward all or toward any of its people.*

These principles, he said, required us to extend the suffrage to the negro. He is here by no fault of his own, and here to stay. Having freed him, we must extend to him equal civil rights to enable him to preserve that freedom.

This protection involves, on his part, obedience to the law; the same obedience that the white man renders. Enjoying the full benefit of this relation to civil government, he must also bear its burdens, the same burdens which the white man bears. He must pay taxes. He must render military service. He must work upon or pay for keeping in repair the public highways. He must, in short, respond to all the obligations and duties which rest upon the white man. Does the mere color of his skin constitute any rational disability? Surely not in the mind of any Christian statesman.

What is the logical inference from these statements? Can it be true that a class of men may be justly entitled to all the civil rights and privileges of the citizen, and still be wholly unworthy of all political rights? Is not the relation between civil and political rights intimate, if not indissoluble? How can they be logically separated? Does not civil obligation imply political right unless some motive of the public welfare and safety intervenes to justify the exclusion? The fundamental principle of our political institutions is that all rightful government must rest on the consent of the governed. If the freedmen are to be subject to the laws, are they not, therefore, entitled in justice and equity to some authority in the appointment of those who are to make the laws? There is another fundamental principle of American liberty involved in the question. It was the cardinal complaint of our revolutionary fathers that they were taxed without representation. Upon this issue they went to war. Upon this issue the revolutionary war was fought. How can we consistently tax the freedmen and wholly exclude them from representation? And upon what principle of justice or American liberty, I ask, can a freedman be compelled to perform military service, and yet be excluded from having any voice in the Government which sends him to the field? Is he to be intrusted with the bayonet and not with the ballot? Is he worthy to die for his country, and yet necessarily unworthy of the elective franchise?

Should we fear to give the ballot to him who is ready to give his life for his country? His country, sir! He who is morally and intellectually qualified to vote, and to whom the privilege is denied, can hardly be said to have a country. He is virtually still a slave. Sir, we have seen the blood of the black man and the blood of the white man during the late terrible rebellion mingling undistinguishably together as a common libation to liberty on the altar of their country. Is not such a sacrifice sufficient to propitiate the favor of a magnanimous race, and to merit the boon of political enfranchisement? For myself, sir, I should be ashamed to deny it wherever there is capacity to appreciate it and use it discreetly, and where I have the right to bestow it.

Again, Mr. President, what is the legitimate effect on the status of the freedman of the constitutional amendment abolishing slavery? If he was not a citizen before that amendment took effect, is he not now? According to the spirit of our institutions, if not according to the letter of our Constitution, it appears to me that he is. I can conceive of no intermediate state between slavery and citizenship among the natives of our soil and within our jurisdiction, unless there be an exclusion in express terms. Why were negroes born on our soil heretofore ruled not to be citizens? Was it simply because they were of African descent? I suppose not—no more than it would be competent to exclude on account of German descent or French descent. It was because the negro belonged to an enslaved race; it was on account of slavery; it was because their ancestors were brought to this country as chattels and not as persons. But slavery being now abolished, and all men born on our soil being now made free by our organic law, the reason of the original exclusion no longer exists. With the extinction of slavery, its incidents and disabilities are necessarily extinguished. I know it is said that the sole effect of the constitutional amendment was to release him from the control of his master—nothing more. But it seems to me that this is a narrow view of the subject. Freedom is a fact if it is anything—a reality, not a mere shadow without substance.

But the freedman is not the only party interested in this question. I consider the political enfranchisement of such of the freedmen as shall become capable of a judicious and intelligent use of the right of suffrage as very materially connected with the welfare of the white man and of the nation. The great argument against emancipation was the danger to be apprehended from the want of homogeneity between the two races. I shall not attempt to deny that there was force in the argument. But the deed is done. Slavery has been abolished. It is for the future we are required to provide. Four million colored slaves have been emancipated—forever emancipated. They are in our midst, and we cannot help it. There may be danger in giving to them the elective franchise, but is there not equal if not greater danger in withholding it from them? They may not be homogeneous as voters, but will they be any less so as freedmen deprived of the right to vote? Is there not more danger in the want of homogeneousness in the endowment of political rights than in race or color? May they not claim the right to vote at some time? Is there no danger here? If we tax them, will they always peaceably submit to it without representation? Will they always yield unresisting obedience to a government imposed upon them without their consent? Will they have courage enough to bear arms in our defence, and to die in our defence, as they have done recently, and yet be incapable of exerting equal courage and determination in asserting their own rights, real or imaginary? Remember, they are four millions now—more in numbers than our fathers were when they fought the battles of the Revolution and established our independence as a nation. There may be danger in the direction indicated, but is there not, I repeat, equal, if not greater, danger in the contrary direction?

Now, I know that it has been said that any attempt to elevate the negro to an equality with the white man at the polls will certainly provoke a conflict with the white voter; that the white man will submit to no such humiliation. Where is the humiliation? Can there be any humiliation in granting to any and to every human being what he is worthy of receiving or what he is entitled to receive? Nay, sir. The degradation, I think, would consist in withholding it from him. Besides, sir, I suppose the white man would be no more humiliated by the equality of the negro at the ballot-box than he would be by equality at the bar of a court of justice. There ought to be, there is in truth, no good reason why justice to the negro should provoke the hostility of the white man, but there would be reason in the revolt of the former if the latter should be guilty of injustice to him. It may be impossible sometimes to give practical effect to abstract principles of right and justice, but wherever it is possible to do so we ought not to fear evil consequences from doing it. What is right is always expedient if it is practicable.

But, Mr. President, I may as well notice this outcry against negro equality a little more particularly. It is an unmeaning clamor, addressed to the passions and prejudices of the un- thinking rather than the respectful consideration of the states- man. Will you, it is frequently asked, will you make the negro equal to the white man? Well, sir, what does that mean? If it were possible to make the negro fully equal to the white man—equal in virtue, in knowledge; equal in all the attributes of our common human nature—why should it not be done? And, if he were really and truly made our equal, what would we have to complain of? It would take away the grounds of complaint. And, if the elective franchise really had any such wondrous power of transmutation and refinement of the negro, why should it not be bestowed upon him? If the power to vote would really make the negro equal to us, we ought to desire it to be given to him, for it is his inequality with us of which we complain. It would at once remove the apple of discord which has been so long disturbing the peace of the nation. But unfortunately it could have no such effect. Equality of civil and political rights could have but little influence on the social relations of the races.

Why, sir, the negro has an equal right to breathe the same vital air which we do; and he does breathe it equally with us; and it is equally necessary to the life of us all. Does that prove the social equality of the races? The right of suffrage is the vital principle of republican institutions, but its equal enjoyment by the white man and the black man does not and cannot in any wise change the personal identity of either or affect their social relations. Social relations cannot be regulated by law. They are beyond its power. They are not the legitimate subject of legal regulation. Social equality is a matter of taste, of feeling, and of every man's unfettered sense of propriety. The idea that because a negro can vote he is thereby placed on a social equality with the white man is supremely ridiculous. The idle, vicious, dissolute, dishonest white man votes; am I thereby placed under any obligation to acknowledge his social equality, or any other kind of personal equality? Is he, there- fore, my equal? I may not and ought not to associate with him at all, nor will the law compel me to do it. Mr. President, such arguments are intended for other ears than ours. I am willing they shall go to those for whom they are intended, assured that the good sense of the people will readily distinguish between what is artfully addressed to their prejudices and passions and what shall justly challenge their enlightened judgment.

Akin to this class of objection is another even more trivial. I allude to the intermarriage and miscegenation of the races. It admits of the same reply. These also are matters of taste and feeling. And I have this further remark to make about it, that if any white man should ever so far forget all the instincts of nature and all sense of propriety as to intermarry with a negress, I would say, Heaven help the negress! She would certainly have the harder part of the bargain. But how could the elective franchise affect this matter? It imposes no obligation on the races to intermarry. It holds out no inducements to do it. There is no possible relation between the elective franchise and such intermarriage. It leaves the two races, in that respect, precisely where they now are. Moreover, it creates no barrier to the interposition of legislative prohibitions against such intermarriage. Every State, I suppose, has statutory provisions inhibiting the marriage relation between persons within certain degrees of kindred. The same policy might be observed in reference to these races, if the good of society should render it necessary. On the question of illegitimate miscegenation I need only refer to the census. The Southern mulatto furnishes a conclusive answer to the argument on miscegenation. There has been brutality in both races. But in proportion as we shall elevate the negro, and increase his self-respect by extending to him the rights of man, these instincts and evidences of lechery and brutality will disappear. In my judgment, one of the most beneficial results of the abolition of slavery will be the decline of miscegenation.[1]

Slavery has been abolished, not by the will or the wisdom of man, but by the folly of its friends and the providence of God. Shall we superinduce a repetition of the sanguinary history of the last five years in another form? Shall we lay the foundation of another insurrection? I think I may confidently anticipate increasing agitation in this hall, and in all the councils of the country, and through every avenue reaching the public mind until the political enfranchisement of the negro in this District is accomplished. "The tide has set that way." It may ebb, but it will flow again as ceaseless as the sea. For the sake of the public peace, therefore; to avoid a conflict as

[1] This prophecy has been strikingly fulfilled.

irrepressible as that through which we have passed; to prevent the sorrows and desolations of another civil war; to complete the harmony and symmetry of our political system, and reconcile the logical demands of our cherished principles of civil and political liberty by exhibiting a practical recognition of the Declaration of Independence, let the experiment be made. Our race can well afford to make it. It imperils none of our rights. It curtails none of our privileges or power. It cannot appeal to our fears, but it does challenge our magnanimity. If it fail, then the strife will be ended and the question forever settled. If it succeed, who is there so basely recreant to the high behests of his own humanity as to say he would not rejoice?

Sir, we are admonished against the radicalism of the times. Perhaps there is some necessity for the admonition. But let us not be so cautious as to err in the opposite direction. This is an age of progress—progress of ideas, of science, of philosophy, of civilization, of law, of liberty. The truth does not change, the fundamental principles of government as proclaimed by our fathers may not change, but their application may be made more complete. It would be unwise, it would be ludicrous, to stand still, steadfastly adhering to the same policies and measures which were appropriate to the radically different condition of affairs existing a century ago. Slavery is abolished. It is forever prohibited by our organic law. Shall our feelings, our prejudice, our policy, our laws relating to the freedman be the same now as when he was a slave?

"Tempora mutantur, et nos in illis mutamur."[1]

The only worthy interpretation of the tremendous conflict which has just convulsed the nation, but which has been crowned with such resplendent victory, is progress—progress especially in the principles of human freedom. Let us not refuse the providential hand extended to lead us onward and upward toward a more exalted destiny. The great rebellion proclaimed that slavery was to be the chief corner-stone of its treasonable organization. And thus it was a revolt not only against legitimate human authority, but it was also a rebellion against the law of God. The result is announced by a fundamental decree of universal emancipation. This revolution will not stop there. It has awakened a spirit that will never slumber again until all laws and all statesmen shall recognize the authority of the precept which was uttered by the divine Law-giver on the mount more than eighteen hundred years ago in tones that, however

[1] "Times change and we change with them."

gentle and sweet, have sounded along down through the suc-
cessive centuries, commanding an eager responsive echo from
every liberal human heart: "Therefore, all things whatsoever
ye would that men should do to you, do ye even so to them";
which was republished, in effect, by the great apostle in the
midst of Mars hill: "And hath made of one blood all nations
of men for to dwell on the face of the earth," and which, at
last, was essentially incorporated into the great national charter
of American independence at Philadelphia. In America this
Christian principle of humanity and freedom first received a
legal definition and found a practical political recognition. In
America let it have its complete and glorious consummation.

Action on the bill was postponed owing to the illness
of Senator Morrill, who had the bill in charge, and the
radical leaders, knowing that the President would reject
the measure, and fearing that they would not be able
to override the veto, deferred its consideration until
the next session, by which time they hoped that the voice
of the people in the elections to the succeeding Congress
would have given a clear mandate to the national legislature to take this forward step toward removing race
disability in the United States.

This question came immediately to the front in the
following session of Congress. As soon as the organization of the Senate was completed (December 3, 1866)
Charles Sumner [Mass.] brought forward the bill which
had been postponed from the previous session. Discussion upon it, however, was postponed.

EQUAL SUFFRAGE IN THE DISTRICT OF COLUMBIA [1]
[Including Negro and Woman Suffrage]

SENATE, DECEMBER 10, 1866-JANUARY 8, 1867

On December 10 Senator Morrill introduced the
measure in a speech of considerable length. He called
attention to the fact that since the last session had closed
a vote had been taken to find the sentiment of the citizens

[1] Compiled from the "History of the Thirty-ninth Congress" by
William H. Barnes, 1868.

of the District on the question with the result that some 6,500 ballots had been cast against it, and only 30 or 40 in its favor.

"But," said the Senator, "this is a matter affecting the capital of the nation, one in which the American people have an interest, as indirectly, at least, touching the country at large. What the national Congress pronounce here as a matter of right or expediency, or both, touching a question of popular rights, may have an influence elsewhere for good or for evil. We can not well justify the denial of the right of suffrage to colored citizens on the protest of the voters of the corporation of Washington. Our action should rest on some recognized general principle, which, applied to the capital of the nation, would be equally just applied to any of the political communities of which the nation is composed."

In closing his speech Senator Morrill remarked:

"In a nation of professed freemen, whose political axioms are those of universal liberty and human rights, no public tranquillity is possible while these rights are denied to portions of the American people. We have taken into the bosom of the Republic the diverse elements of the nationalities of Europe, and are attempting to mold them into national harmony and unity, and are still inviting other millions to come to us. Let us not despair that the same mighty energies and regenerating forces will be able to assign a docile and not untractable race its appropriate place in our system."

Waitman T. Willey [W. Va.] wished to restore the educational qualification.

"There ought to be some obligation, either in our fundamental laws in the States, or somewhere, by some means requiring the people to educate themselves, and if this can be accomplished by disqualifying those who are not educated for the exercise of the right of suffrage, thus stimulating them to acquire a reasonable degree of education, that of itself, it seems to me, would be a public blessing."

"I am against this qualification of reading and writing," said HENRY WILSON [Mass.]. "I never did believe in it. I do not believe in it now. I voted against it in my own State, and I intend to vote against it here. There was a time when

I would have taken it, because I did not know that we could get anything more in this contest, but I think the great victory of manhood suffrage is about achieved in this country.''

''Reading and writing, as a qualification for voting,'' said SAMUEL C. POMEROY [Kan.], ''might be entertained in a State where all the people were allowed to go to school and learn to read and write, but it seems to me monstrous to apply it to a class of persons in this community who were legislated away from school, to whom every avenue of learning was shut up by law.''

EDGAR COWAN [Pa.] proposed to amend the bill by striking out the word ''male'' before the word ''person,'' that females might enjoy the elective franchise. ''I propose to extend this privilege,'' said he, ''not only to males, but to females as well; and I should like to hear even the most astute and learned Senator upon this floor give any better reason for the exclusion of females from the right of suffrage than there is for the exclusion of negroes.

''If you want to widen the franchise so as to purify your ballot-box, throw the virtue of the country into it; throw the temperance of the country into it; throw the purity of the country into it; throw the angel element—if I may so express myself—into it. [Laughter.] Let there be as little diabolism as possible, but as much of the divinity as you can get.''

On the following day, Henry B. Anthony [R. I.] advocated Mr. Cowan's amendment.

''I suppose that the Senator from Pennsylvania introduced this amendment rather as a satire upon the bill itself, or, if he had any serious intention, it was only a mischievous one to injure the bill. But it will not probably have that effect, for I suppose nobody will vote for it except the Senator himself, who can hardly avoid it, and I, who shall vote for it because it accords with a conclusion to which I have been brought by considerable study upon the subject of suffrage.''

After having answered objections against female suffrage, Senator Anthony remarked in conclusion:

''I should not have introduced this question; but as it has been introduced, and I intend to vote for the amendment, I desire to declare here that I shall vote for it in all seriousness, because I think it is right. The discussion of this subject is not

confined to visionary enthusiasts. It is now attracting the attention of some of the best thinkers in the world, both in this
country and in Europe; and one of the very best of them all,
John Stuart Mill, in a most elaborate and able paper, has declared his conviction of the right and justice of female suffrage.
The time has not come for it, but the time is coming. It is coming with the progress of civilization and the general amelioration of the race, and the triumph of truth, and justice, and
equal rights.''

George H. Williams [Ore.] opposed the pending
amendment.

''To extend the right of suffrage to the negroes in this
country I think is necessary for their protection; but to extend
the right of suffrage to women, in my judgment, is not necessary for their protection. Wide as the poles apart are the conditions of these two classes of persons. The sons defend and
protect the reputation and rights of their mothers; husbands
defend and protect the reputation and rights of their wives;
brothers defend and protect the reputation and rights of their
sisters; and to honor, cherish, and love the women of this country is the pride and the glory of its sons.

''When the women of this country come to be sailors and
soldiers; when they come to navigate the ocean and to follow
the plow; when they love to be jostled and crowded by all sorts
of men in the thoroughfares of trade and business; when they
love the treachery and the turmoil of politics; when they love the
dissoluteness of the camp, and the smoke of the thunder, and
the blood of battle better than they love the affections and en-
joyments of home and family, then it will be time to talk about
making the women voters; but, until that time, the question
is not fairly before the country.''

Benjamin F. Wade [O.], who had introduced the
original bill, putting it upon the most liberal principle
of franchise, said:

''The question of female suffrage had not then been much
agitated, and I knew the community had not thought sufficiently
upon it to be ready to introduce it as an element in our political
system. While I am aware of that fact, I think it will puzzle
any gentleman to draw a line of demarcation between the right
of the male and the female on this subject. Both are liable to

all the laws you pass; their property, their persons, and their lives are affected by the laws. Why, then, should not the females have a right to participate in their construction as well as the male part of the community? There is no argument that I can conceive or that I have yet heard that makes any discrimination between the two on the question of right.

"I shall give a vote on this amendment that will be deemed an unpopular vote, but I am not frightened by that. I have been accustomed to give such votes all my life almost, but I believe they have been given in the cause of human liberty and right and in the way of the advancing intelligence of our age; and, whenever the landmark has been set up, the community have marched up to it. I think I am advocating now the same kind of a principle, and I have no doubt that sooner or later it will become a fixed fact, and the community will think it just as absurd to exclude females from the ballot-box as males."

Richard Yates [Ill.] opposed the pending amendment, deeming it a mere attempt on the part of the Senator from Pennsylvania to embarrass this question.

"Logically, there are no reasons in my mind which would not permit women to vote as well as men, according to the theory of our government. But that question, as to whether ladies shall vote or not, is not at issue now. I confess that I am for universal suffrage, and, when the time comes, I am for suffrage by females as well as males."

"While I will vote now," said SENATOR WILSON, "or at any time, for woman suffrage as a distinct, separate measure, I am unalterably opposed to connecting that question with the pending question of negro suffrage. The question of negro suffrage is now an imperative necessity; a necessity that the negro should possess it for his own protection; a necessity that he should possess it that the nation may preserve its power, its strength, and its unity."

Reverdy Johnson [Md.] opposed the pending amendment.

"I think if it was submitted to the ladies—I mean the ladies in the true acceptation of the term—of the United States, the privilege would not only not be asked for, but would be rejected. I do not think the ladies of the United States would agree to enter into a canvass and undergo what is often the degradation of seeking to vote, particularly in the cities, getting up to the polls, crowded out and crowded in. I rather think they would feel it, instead of a privilege, a dishonor.''

Senator Johnson was unwilling to vote for the amendment with a view to defeat the bill.

''I have lived to be too old, and have become too well satisfied of what I think is my duty to the country to give any vote which I do not believe, if it should be supported by the votes of a sufficient number to carry the measure into operation, would redound to the interests and safety and honor of the country.''

''The women of America,'' said FREDERICK T. FRELINGHUY-SEN [N. J.], ''vote by faithful and true representatives, their husbands, their brothers, their sons; and no true man will go to the polls and deposit his ballot without remembering the true and loving constituency that he has at home. More than that, sir, ninety-nine out of a hundred, I believe nine hundred and ninety-nine out of a thousand, of the women in America do not want the privilege of voting in any other manner than that which I have stated. In both these regards there is a vast difference between the situation of the colored citizens and the women of America.

''The learned and eloquent Senator from Pennsylvania said yesterday with great beauty that he wanted to cast the angel element into the suffrage system of America. Sir, it seems to me that it would be ruthlessly tearing the angel element from the homes of America; and the homes of the people of America are infinitely more valuable than any suffrage system. It will be a sorry day for this country when those vestal fires of piety and love are put out.''

On the next day, December 12, the discussion being resumed, B. Gratz Brown [Mo.] advocated the amendment.

''I stand for universal suffrage, and, as a matter of fundamental principle, do not recognize the right of society to limit it on any ground of race, color, or sex. I will go further and say that I recognize the right of franchise as being intrinsically a natural right; and I do not believe that society is authorized to impose any limitation upon it that does not spring out of the necessities of the social state itself.''

Believing "that the metaphysical always controls the practical in all the affairs of life," Senator Brown gave the "abstract grounds" upon which he deemed the right of woman to the elective franchise rested. Coming finally to the more practical bearings of the subject, he answered the objection, that, "if women are entitled to the rights of franchise, they would correspondingly come under the obligation to bear arms."

"Are there not large classes, even among men in this country, who are exempt from service in our armies for physical incapacity and for other reasons? And, if exemptions which appertain to males may be recognized as valid, why not similar exemptions for like reasons when applied to females? Does it not prove that there is nothing in the argument so far as it involves the question of right? There are Quakers and other religious sects; there are ministers of the Gospel; persons having conscientious scruples; indeed, all men over a certain age who, under the laws of many of the States, are released from service of that character. Indeed, it is the boast of this Republic that ours is a volunteer military establishment. Hence, I say, there is nothing in the position that, because she may not be physically qualified for service in your army, therefore you have the right to deny her the franchise on the score of sex."

In closing his extended speech Senator Brown remarked:

"Even though I recognize the impolicy of coupling these two measures in this manner and at this time, I shall yet record my vote in the affirmative as an earnest indication of my belief in the principle, and my faith in the future."

Garrett Davis [Ky.] made a protracted speech against both the amendment and the original bill.

"The great God who created all the races, and in every race gave to man woman, never intended that woman should take part in national government among any people, or that the negro, the lowest, should ever have coördinate and equal power with the highest, the white race, in any government, national or domestic."

"When it is necessary," said WILLIAM SPRAGUE [R. I.], "that woman shall vote for the support of liberty and equality

I shall be ready to cast my vote in their favor. The black man's vote is necessary to this at this time. Do not prostrate all the industrial interests of the North by a policy of conciliation and of inaction. Delays are dangerous, criminal. When you shall have established, firmly and fearlessly, governments at the South friendly to the Republic; when you shall have ceased from receiving terms and propositions from the leaders of the Rebellion as to their reconstruction; when you shall have promptly acted in the interest of liberty, prosperity will light upon the industries of your people, and panics, commercial and mercantile revolutions will be placed afar off; and never, sir, until that time shall have arrived. And, as an humble advocate of all industrial interests of the free people of the North, white and black, and as an humble representative of these interests, I urge prompt action to-day, to-morrow, and every day until the work has been completed. Let no obstacle stand in the way now, no matter what it may be. You will save your people from poverty and free principles from a more desperate combat than they have yet witnessed. Ridicule may be used in this chamber, calumny may prevail through the country, and murder may be a common occurrence South to those who stand firmly thus and who advocate such measures. Let it be so; for greater will be the crowning glory of those who are not found wanting in the day of victory. Let us, then, press to the vote; one glorious step taken, then we may take others in the same direction.''

"The objection," said CHARLES R. BUCKALEW [Pa.], "which I have to a large extension of suffrage in this country, whether by Federal or State power, is this: that thereby you will corrupt and degrade elections, and probably lead to their complete abrogation hereafter. By pouring into the ballot-boxes of the country a large mass of ignorant votes, and votes subjected to pecuniary or social influence, you will corrupt and degrade your elections and lay the foundation for their ultimate destruction.''

"After giving some considerable reflection to the subject of suffrage," said JAMES R. DOOLITTLE [Wis.], "I have arrived at the conclusion that the true base or foundation upon which to rest suffrage in any republican community is upon the family, the head of the family; because in civilized society the family is the unit, not the individual.''

The vote being taken on Senator Cowan's amendment conferring the elective franchise upon women the result was: yeas, 9; nays, 37.

James Dixon [Conn.] then moved to amend the bill by adding a proviso:

"That no person who has not heretofore voted in this District shall be permitted to vote unless he shall be able, at the time of offering to vote, to read and also write his own name."

"I would deny to no man," said SENATOR DIXON, "the right of voting solely on account of his color; but I doubt the propriety of permitting any man to vote, whatever his race or color, who has not at least that proof of intelligence which the ability to read and write furnishes."

"What is the test?" asked WILLARD SAULSBURY [Del.]. "A person who can read and write. Is it his name, or only read and write?"

"His name," said one.

"Read and write his name!" continued SENATOR SAULSBURY. "A wonderful amount of education to qualify a man for the discharge of the high office and trust of voting! Great knowledge of the system of government under which we live does this impart to the voter!"

"If this were really an intelligence qualification," said MR. COWAN, "I do not know what I might say; but of the fact that the ability of a man merely to write his own name and read it, is intelligence, I am not informed. To write a man's name is simply a mechanical operation. It may be taught to anybody, even people of the most limited capacity, in twenty minutes; and to read it afterward certainly would not be very difficult."

"I understand the amendment to include," said SENATOR WILLEY, "the qualification of reading generally, and also of writing his name! two tests, one the reading generally, and the other the writing of his own name."

"Where is its precision?" asked SENATOR COWAN; "where is it to end, and who shall determine its limits? I will put the case of a board belonging to the dominant party, and suppose they have the statute amended by my honorable friend from Connecticut before them, and a colored man comes forward and proposes to vote. They put to him the question: 'Can you write your name and read?' 'Oh, yes.' 'Well, let us see you try it.' He then writes his name and he reads it, and he is admitted if he is understood to belong to that party. But suppose, as has recently happened, that this dark man should come to the conclusion to vote on the other side, and it were known that he meant to vote on the other side, what kind of a chance would he have? Then the man of the dominant party, who desires to carry the election, says: 'You shall not only write your name and read it, but you must read generally. I have read the senatorial debates upon this question, and the honorable Senator from West Virginia, who originated this amendment, was of opinion that a man should read generally. Now, sir, read generally, if you please.' 'Well,' says he, 'what shall I read?' 'Read a section of the "Novum Organum," or some other most difficult and abstruse thing, or a few sections from Okie's "Physiology." ' "

On the 13th of December, the last day of the discussion, Senator Anthony occupied the chair during a portion of the session, and Lafayette S. Foster [Conn.], the President *pro tem.*, took the floor in favor of the amendment proposed by his colleague.

"The honorable Senator from Pennsylvania, from the manner in which he treats this subject, I should think, was now fresh from his reading of 'Much Ado about Nothing,' and was quoting Mr. Justice Dogberry, who said: 'To be a well-favored man is the gift of fortune, but to read and write comes by nature.' The Senator from Pennsylvania and others seem inclined to say: 'Away with writing and reading till there is need of such vanity.' I believe that the idea of admitting men to the elective franchise who can neither read nor write is going backward and downward.

"Who are the men who come forward to deposit their ballots in the ballot-boxes? They are the people of this country, to whom all questions must ultimately go for examination and correction. They correct the mistakes which we make, and which Congress makes, and which the Supreme Court makes. The electors at the ballot-boxes are the grand court of errors for the country. Now, sir, these Senators propose to allow men who cannot read and write to correct our mistakes, to become members of this high court of errors.

"The honorable Senator from Massachusetts [Mr. Wilson] says he wants to put the ballot into the hands of the black man for his protection. If he can not read the ballot, what kind of protection is it to him. A written or printed slip of paper is put into the hands of a man, black or white, and, if he can not read it, what is it to him? What does he know about it? What can he do with it? How can he protect himself by it? As well might the honorable Senator from Massachusetts put in the hands of

VIII—3

a child who knew nothing of firearms a loaded pistol with which to protect himself against his enemies. The child would be much more likely to endanger himself and his friends by the pistol than to protect himself. A perfectly ignorant man who cannot read his ballot is much more likely to use it to his own detriment, and to the detriment of the country, than he is to use it for the benefit of either.''

''The argument in favor of making the right to vote universal,'' said SENATOR FRELINGHUYSEN, in making a second speech upon the question, ''is that the ballot itself is a great education; that, by its encouraging the citizen, by its inspiring him, it adds dignity to his character, and makes him strive to acquire learning. Secondly, that, if the voting depended on learning, no inducement is extended to communities unfavorable to the right of voting in the colored man to give him the opportunity to learn; they would rather embarrass him to prevent his making the acquisition, unless they were in favor of his voting; while, if voting is universal, communities, for their own security, for their own protection, will be driven to establish common schools, so that the voter shall become intelligent.''

Senator Wilson pursued a similar line of thought:

''Allow the black men to vote without this qualification and they will demand education, school-houses will rise, schoolteachers will be employed, these people will attend the schools, and the cause of education will be carried forward in this District with more rapidity than at any other period in its history. Give the negro the right of suffrage, and before a year passes round you will see these men, who voted that they should not have the right to vote, running after them and inquiring after the health of their wives and children. I do not think the Senator from Kentucky [Mr. Davis] will be examining their pelvis or shins, or making speeches about the formation of their lips, or the angle of their foreheads on the floor of the Senate. You will then see the Democracy, with the keen scent that always distinguishes that party, on the hunt after the votes of these black men [laughter]; and, if they treat them better than the Republicans do, they will probably get their votes, and I hope they will.

''And it will be just so down in these rebel States. Give the negroes of Virginia the right to vote, and you will find Wise and Letcher and the whole tribe of the secessionists undertaking to prove that, from the landing at Jamestown in 1607, the first families of the Old Dominion have always been the champions and the special friends of the negroes of Old Virginia, and that there is a great deal of kindred between them [laughter] ; that they are relations, brethren; that the same red blood courses in the veins of many of them. They will establish all these things, perhaps by affidavits. [Laughter.] And I say to you, sir, they will have a good opportunity to get a good many of their votes, for in these respects they have the advantage of us poor Republicans."

Of the pending amendment Thomas A. Hendricks [Ind.] said:

"I propose to vote for it, not because I am in favor, as a general proposition, of an intelligence qualification for the right to vote, but because in this particular instance I think it to be proper to prescribe it."

"I shall vote," said HENRY S. LANE [Ind.], "to enfranchise the colored residents of this District because I believe it is right, just, and proper; because I believe it is in accordance with those two grand central truths around which cluster every hope for redeemed humanity—the common fatherhood of God above us and the brotherhood of universal mankind."

"The bill for impartial suffrage in the District of Columbia," said CHARLES SUMNER [Mass.], "concerns directly some twenty thousand colored persons, whom it will lift to the adamantine platform of equal rights. If it were regarded simply in its bearings on the District it would be difficult to exaggerate its value; but when it is regarded as an example to the whole country under the sanction of Congress, its value is infinite. It is in the latter character that it becomes a pillar of fire to illumine the footsteps of millions. What we do here will be done in the disorganized States. Therefore we must be careful that what we do here is best for the disorganized States.

"When I am asked to open the suffrage to women, or when I am asked to establish an educational standard, I can not, on the present bill, simply because the controlling necessity under which we act will not allow it. By a singular Providence we are now constrained to this measure of enfranchisement for the sake of peace, security, and reconciliation, so that loyal persons, white or black, may be protected and that the Republic may live. Here, in the District of Columbia, we begin the real work of reconstruction by which the Union will be consolidated forever."

The question was taken upon Mr. Dixon's amendment, which was lost, eleven voting for, and thirty-four against, the proposition. The vote was then taken upon the bill to regulate the elective franchise in the District of Columbia. It passed the Senate, 32 voting in the affirmative, and 13 in the negative.

On the following day, December 14, the bill came before the House of Representatives and passed without discussion, 118 voting in the affirmative and 46 in the negative.

On the 7th of January, 1867, President Johnson returned the bill to the Senate with his objections. The veto message was immediately read by the Secretary of the Senate.

The President's first objection to the bill was that it was not in accordance with the wishes of the people to whom it was to apply, they having "solemnly and with such unanimity" protested against it.

It seemed to the President that Congress sustained a relation to the inhabitants of the District of Columbia which was analogous to the relation of a legislature to the people of a State, and therefore that Congress "should have a like respect for the will and interests of its inhabitants."

Without actually bringing the charge of unconstitutionality against this measure the President declared "that Congress is bound to observe the letter and spirit of the Constitution as well in the enactment of local laws for the seat of government as in legislation common to the entire Union."

The Civil Rights bill having become a law it was, in the opinion of the President, a sufficient protection for the negro. "It can not be urged," said he, "that the proposed extension of suffrage in the District of Columbia is necessary to enable persons of color to protect either their interests or their rights."

The President argued that the negroes were unfitted for the exercise of the elective franchise, and "can not be expected correctly to comprehend the duties and responsibilities which pertain to suffrage."

"It follows, therefore, that, in admitting to the ballot-box a new class of voters not qualified for the exercise of the elective franchise, we weaken our system of government instead of adding to its strength and durability. It may be safely assumed that no political truth is better established than that such indiscriminate and all-embracing extension of popular suffrage must end at last in its destruction."

The President occupied a considerable portion of his message with a warning to the people against the dangers of the abuse of legislative power. He quoted from Judge Story that the legislative branch may absorb all the powers of the government. He quoted also the language of Mr. Jefferson that one hundred and seventy tyrants are more dangerous than one tyrant.

The statements of the President in opposition to the bill were characterized by Senator John Sherman [O.] as "but a *résumé* of the arguments already adduced in the Senate," hence but little effort was made by the friends of the measure to reply.

Senator Sherman, in noticing the President's statements in regard to the danger of invasions by Congress of the just powers of the executive and judicial departments, said:

"I do not think that there is any occasion for such a warning, because I am not aware that in this bill Congress has ever assumed any doubtful power. The power of Congress over this District is without limit, and, therefore, in prescribing who shall vote for mayor and city council of this city, it cannot be claimed that we usurp power or exercise a doubtful power.

"There can be but little danger from Congress; for our acts are but the reflection of the will of the people. The recent acts of Congress at the last session, those acts upon which the President and Congress separated, were submitted to the people, and they decided in favor of Congress. Unless, therefore, there is an inherent danger from a republican government, resting solely upon the will of the people, there is no occasion for the warning of the President. Unless the judgment of one man is better than the combined judgment of a great majority, he should have respected their decision, and not continue a controversy in which our common constituency have decided that he was wrong."

The last speech before taking the vote was made by Senator Doolittle.

"Men speak of universal negro suffrage as having been spoken in favor of in the late election. There is not a State in this Union, outside of New England, which would vote in favor of universal negro suffrage. When gentlemen tell me that the people of the whole North, by anything that transpired in the late election, have decided in favor of universal, unqualified negro suffrage, they assume that for which there is no foundation whatever."

The question being taken whether the bill should pass over the President's veto, the Senate decided in the affirmative by a vote of 29 yeas to 10 nays.

The next day, January 8, 1867, the bill was passed over the veto by the House of Representatives, without debate, by a vote of 113 yeas to 38 nays. The Speaker then declared that, notwithstanding the objections of the President of the United States, the act to regulate the elective franchise in the District of Columbia had become a law.

EQUAL RIGHTS IN THE TERRITORIES

An act forbidding denial of the elective franchise in the Territories to any citizen on account of race, color, or previous condition of servitude was passed by Congress on January 14, 1867. Not being approved by the President, it became a law on the expiration of ten days, excluding Sunday.

ADMISSION OF NEBRASKA

An act admitting Nebraska into the Union on condition that there be in the State no denial of the elective franchise to any person, by reason of race or color, except Indians not taxed, was passed by Congress. This was vetoed by the President, and was passed over his veto by the Senate on February 8, and by the House on February 9, 1867.

Abolition of Peonage

An act abolishing peonage in New Mexico was approved by the President on March 2 1867.

Howard University

An act incorporating Howard University in Washington, D. C., an institution intended for the normal, collegiate, professional, and agricultural education of negroes, was approved on the same day.

CHAPTER II

MILITARY RECONSTRUCTION BY CONGRESS

President Johnson, in His Second Annual Message, Treats of Reconstruction; Reply to It by Representative Samuel L. Warner [Ct.]—Thaddeus Stevens [Pa.] Reports Military Reconstruction Bill in the House—Debate: Mr. Stevens, Augustus Brandegee [Ct.], Francis C. LeBlond [O.], William E. Finck [O.], John A. Bingham [O.], William Lawrence [O.], M. Russell Thayer [Pa.], Samuel Shellabarger [O.], Henry L. Dawes [Mass.], John A. Griswold [N. Y.], Henry J. Raymond [N. Y.], Gen. James A. Garfield [O.], Gen. Nathaniel P. Banks [Mass.], John A. Kasson [Ia.], James M. Ashley [O.], George S. Boutwell [Mass.], William E. Niblack [Ind.], William D. Kelley [Pa.], Horace Maynard [Tenn.], William B. Allison [Ia.], James G. Blaine [Me.], Burt Van Horn [N. Y.]; the Bill Is Passed—Debate in the Senate: George H. Williams [Ore.], Reverdy Johnson [Md.], William M. Stewart [Nev.], Lot M. Morrill [Me.], John B. Henderson [Mo.], James R. Doolittle [Wis.], Thomas A. Hendricks [Ind.], Willard Saulsbury [Del.], Garrett Davis [Ky.], Henry Wilson [Mass.], John Sherman [O.]; the Bill Is Passed with Amendments—Debate on the Amended Bill in the House: Mr. Stevens, Mr. Boutwell, William B. Stokes [Tenn.], Mr. Blaine, James F. Wilson [Ia.], John F. Farnsworth [Ill.], Gen. Robert C. Schenck [O.], Gen. Garfield, Giles W. Hotchkiss [N. Y.], Henry H. P. Bromwell [Ill.], Ignatius Donnelly [Minn.], Mr. Le Blond, Gen. Banks; the House Refuses to Concur in the Senate Amendments, and the Senate Refuses to Recede from Them; the House Partially Concurs and the Bill Is Passed by Both Chambers—The President's Veto—Debate in the House: Charles A. Eldridge [Wis.], Mr. Le Blond, Mr. Stevens; Bill Is Passed over Veto—Debate in the Senate: Sen. Johnson, Sen. Saulsbury, Sen. Hendricks; Bill Is Passed over Veto— Act Is Amended in Next Congress—Debate in the Senate on the Pardoning Power of the President: in Favor, Sen. Johnson; Opposed, Lyman Trumbull [Ill.]; Congress Repeals the Power; the President Ignores the Repeal—Congress Passes over the President's Veto Supplementary Legislation to the Military Reconstruction Act: Opinion of Attorney-General Henry G. Stanbery against the Supplementary Legislation; the Legislation Is Modified by Congress, and Passed over the President's Veto—Work of Military Reconstruction—Third Annual Message of President Johnson, Dealing with Reconstruction—Debate in the Senate on Printing Extra Copies of the Message: in Favor, Charles

R. Buckalew [Pa.], Sen. Wilson, James Dixon [Ct.]; Opposed, Jacob
M. Howard [Mich.], Simon Cameron [Pa.], Charles Sumner [Mass.];
Motion Carried—Acts of Congress: Appropriations for Reconstruction;
Admission to Congress of Representatives from All Southern States but
Virginia, Mississippi, and Texas—The Reconstruction Issue in the Presi-
dential Contest of 1868—Denunciations of Reconstruction by Horatio
Seymour [N. Y.], August Belmont [N. Y.], Gen. Francis P. Blair
[Mo.], and Gen. Thomas Ewing [Kan.]—Election of Gen. Ulysses S.
Grant as President—Charges of Southern Frauds and Outrages.

I N his annual message at the opening of Congress on
December 3, 1866, President Johnson spoke as follows upon the burning subject of reconstruction.
The address, contrary to expectations, was moderate and
judicially impartial in tone.

BENEFICENCE, NOT POWER, THE TRUE STRENGTH OF GOV-ERNMENT

SECOND ANNUAL MESSAGE OF PRESIDENT JOHNSON

After rehearsing his actions in regard to reconstruction of the States lately in rebellion, and deploring the
non-concurrence of Congress in them, leading to the continued absence from the national legislature of the representatives of ten States, more than one-fourth of the
whole number, and the consequent perpetuation of dis-
content in the outlawed section, he combated the idea
that there was any danger in restoring these States without any further guaranties, the two ideas, secession and
slavery, which had divided the Union, having been forever destroyed, both practically by the war, and the
latter legally by the Thirteenth Amendment.

In the admission of Senators and Representatives from any
and all of the States, there can be no just ground of apprehension that persons who are disloyal will be clothed with the
powers of legislation; for this could not happen when the Constitution and the laws are enforced by a vigilant and faithful
Congress. Each House is made the "judge of the elections,
returns, and qualifications of its own members," and may, "with
the concurrence of two-thirds, expel a member." When a
Senator or Representative is refused admission as a member

for want of due allegiance to the Government, and returned to his constituents, they are admonished that none but persons loyal to the United States will be allowed a voice in the legislative councils of the nation, and the political power and moral influence of Congress are thus effectively exerted in the interests of loyalty to the Government and fidelity to the Union. If this anomalous condition is right now—if, in the exact condition of these States at the present time, it is lawful to exclude them from representation, I do not see that the question will be changed by the efflux of time. Ten years hence, if these States remain as they are, the right of representation will be no stronger; the right of exclusion will be no weaker.

The admission of loyal members from the now unrepresented States would consummate the work of restoration, and exert a most salutary influence in the reëstablishment of peace, harmony, and fraternal feeling. It would tend greatly to renew the confidence of the American people in the vigor and stability of their institutions. It would bind us more closely together as a nation, and enable us to show to the world the inherent and recuperative power of a Government founded upon the will of the people, and established upon the principles of liberty, justice, and intelligence. Our increased strength and enhanced prosperity would irrefragably demonstrate the fallacy of the arguments against free institutions drawn from our recent national disorders by the enemies of republican government. The admission of loyal members from the States now excluded from Congress, by allaying doubt and apprehension, would turn capital, now awaiting an opportunity for investment, into the channels of trade and industry. It would alleviate the present troubled condition of those States, and, by inducing emigration, aid in the settlement of fertile regions now uncultivated, and lead to an increased production of those staples which have added so greatly to the wealth of the nation and the commerce of the world. New fields of enterprise would be opened to our progressive people, and soon the devastations of war would be repaired, and all traces of our domestic differences effaced from the minds of our countrymen.

In our efforts to preserve "the unity of government which constitutes us one people," by restoring the States to the condition which they held prior to the rebellion, we should be cautious, lest, having rescued our nation from perils of threatened disintegration, we resort to consolidation, and, in the end, absolute despotism, as a remedy for the recurrence of similar troubles. The war having terminated, and with it all occasion for the exercise of powers of doubtful constitutionality, we should hasten to bring legislation within the boundaries prescribed by the Constitution, and to return to the ancient landmarks established by our fathers for the guidance of succeeding generations. ''The Constitution, which at any time exists until changed by an explicit and authentic act of the whole people, is sacredly obligatory upon all.'' ''If, in the opinion of the people, the distribution or modification of the constitutional powers be, in any particular, wrong, let it be corrected by an amendment in the way in which the Constitution designates. But let there be no change by usurpation; for'' ''it is the customary weapon by which free governments are destroyed.'' Washington spoke these words to his countrymen when, followed by their love and gratitude, he voluntarily retired from the cares of public life. ''To keep in all things within the pale of our constitutional powers, and cherish the Federal Union as the only rock of safety,'' were prescribed by Jefferson as rules of action to endear to his ''countrymen the true principles of their Constitution, and promote a union of sentiment and action equally auspicious to their happiness and safety.'' Jackson held that the action of the general Government should always be strictly confined to the sphere of its appropriate duties, and justly and forcibly urged that our Government is not to be maintained nor our Union preserved ''by invasions of the rights and powers of the several States. In thus attempting to make our general Government strong, we make it weak. Its true strength consists in leaving individuals and States as much as possible to themselves; in making itself felt, not in its power, but in its beneficence; not in its control, but in its protection; not in binding the States more closely to the center, but leaving each to move unobstructed in its proper constitutional orbit.'' These are the teachings of men whose deeds and services have made them illustrious, and who, long since withdrawn from the scenes of life, have left to their country the rich legacy of their example, their wisdom, and their patriotism. Drawing fresh inspiration from their lessons, let us emulate them in love of country and respect for the Constitution and the laws.

Most of the first two months of the session of Congress was occupied with discussion of the political condition of the South. The Radicals claimed that the spirit of rebellion still existed in the South, and pointed to numerous outrages against the loyalists, chiefly the

New Orleans "Massacre,"[1] as evidence of this. They
therefore demanded reconstruction in a more drastic
form than had hitherto been presented. With a majority sufficient to override every presidential veto, they
determined to ignore the executive department of government except as the agent of the legislative department. This determination was expressed in the strongest and most direct form by Samuel L. Warner [Conn.]
in a speech delivered in the House of Representatives on
January 18, 1867. It was high time, he said, that Congress should take the matter of reconstruction entirely
in its own hands. The work will never commence, he
told the House, until you have declared, in the language
of the Supreme Court, that the Executive, as commander-
in-chief of the army and navy, can not exercise a civil
function. He reviewed the reconstruction acts of the
President in the light of usurping such a function, and
plainly hinted at his impeachment if the usurpation continued.

Various drastic plans of reconstruction under the
supreme control of Congress were proposed, which were
referred to the Special Committee on Reconstruction.
This committee, through Thaddeus Stevens [Pa.], its
chairman, reported its bill on February 6. The bill, after
sundry amendments, became the leading measure of the
session. In its original form it declared:

"Whereas the pretended State governments of the late so-
called Confederate States afford no adequate protection for life
or property, but countenance and encourage lawlessness and
crime; and, whereas it is necessary that peace and good order
should be enforced in said so-called Confederate States until
loyal State governments can be legally established; therefore
be it enacted that said so-called Confederate States shall be
divided into military districts and made subject to the military
authority of the United States as hereinafter prescribed; and
for that purpose Virginia shall constitute the first district,
North Carolina and South Carolina the second district, Georgia,
Alabama, and Florida the third district, Mississippi and Arkansas the fourth district, and Louisiana and Texas the fifth district."

[1] See Volume VII, page 458.

The subordinate provisions of the bill are thus summarized by Mr. Blaine in his "Twenty Years of Congress":

It was made the duty of the general of the army to assign to the command of each of said districts an officer not below the rank of brigadier-general, and to detail a sufficient force to enable such officer to perform his duties and enforce his authority within the district to which he was assigned. The protection of life and property, the suppression of insurrections, disorders, and violence, the punishment of all criminals and disturbers of the public peace, were entrusted to the military authority, with the power to allow civil tribunals to take jurisdiction and try offenders; and, if that was not sufficient in the officer's judgment, he was authorized to organize military commissions, "anything in the constitutions and laws of these so-called Confederate States to the contrary notwithstanding." It was further declared that all legislative acts or judicial processes to prevent the proceedings of such tribunals, and all interference by "said pretended State governments with the exercise of military authority under this act, shall be void and have no effect." The courts and judicial officers of the United States were forbidden to issue writs of *habeas corpus,* except under certain restrictions which further established the military authority over the people. Prompt trials were guaranteed to all persons arrested, cruel and unusual punishments were forbidden, and no sentence could be executed until it was approved by the officer in command of the district.

MILITARY RECONSTRUCTION [1]

HOUSE OF REPRESENTATIVES, FEBRUARY 7-13, 1867

On the following day, February 7th, Mr. Stevens introduced the discussion with a brief speech.

"This bill provides that the ten disorganized States shall be divided into five military districts, and that the commander of the army shall take charge of them through his lieutenants as governors, or you may call them commandants if you choose, not below the grade of brigadiers, who shall have the general supervision of the peace, quiet, and the protection of the peo-

[1] This and the two succeeding debates in the chapter are compiled from the "History of the Thirty-ninth Congress" by William H. Barnes.

ple, loyal and disloyal, who reside within those precincts; and that to do so he may use, as the law of nations would authorize him to do, the legal tribunals wherever he may deem them competent; but they are to be considered of no validity *per se,* of no intrinsic force, no force in consequence of their origin, the question being wholly within the power of the conqueror, and to remain until that conqueror shall permanently supply their place with something else.''

"Of all the various plans," said AUGUSTUS BRANDEGEE [Conn.], "which have been discussed in this hall for the past two years, to my mind it seems the plainest, the most appropriate, the freest from constitutional objection, and the best calculated to accomplish the master aims of reconstruction. It begins the work of reconstruction at the right end, and employs the right tools for its accomplishment.

"The American people demand that we shall do something, and do it quickly. Already fifteen hundred men have been massacred in cold blood whose only crime has been loyalty to your flag. Thousands of loyal white men, driven like partridges over the mountains, homeless, penniless, to-day throng this capital. They crowd the avenues, they gather in these marble corridors, they look down from these galleries, and, with supplicating eye, ask protection from the flag that hangs above the Speaker's chair—a flag which has thus far unfurled its stripes but concealed the promise of its stars.''

Francis C. LeBlond [Dem.], of Ohio, declared that the bill struck down every important provision in the Constitution.

"You have already inaugurated enough here to destroy any government that was ever founded. I do not predict anything; I do not desire war, but, Mr. Speaker, as one American citizen I do prefer war to cowardly submission to a total destruction of the fundamental principles of our Government.''

William E. Finck [Dem.], of Ohio, talked in a similar vein.

"I declare it as my solemn conviction that no government can long continue to be free when one-third of its people and one-third of its States are controlled by military power.''

John A. Bingham [O.], a moderate Republican, begged that the House "make haste slowly in the exercise of this highest possible power conferred by the Constitution upon Congress.''

"For myself, sir, I am not going to yield to the proposition of the chairman of the committtee for a single moment, that one rood of the territory within the line of the ten States enumerated in this bill is conquered territory. The Government of the United States does not conquer any territory that is under the jurisdiction of the Constitution.''

William Lawrence [O.] said:

"For myself I am ready to set aside by law all these illegal governments. They have rejected all fair terms of reconstruction. They have rejected the Constitutional amendments we have tendered them. They are engines of oppression against all loyal men. They are not republican in form or purpose. Let them not only be ignored as legal governments but set aside because they are illegal.''

M. Russell Thayer [Penn.] said:

"This measure will be of brief duration, and will be followed, as I am informed, by other measures which will secure the permanent and peaceful restoration of these States to their proper and just position in the Union, upon their acceptance of such terms as are necessary for the future security of the country. When that is done, and when order is restored, and permanent protection is guaranteed to all the citizens of that section of the country, this measure will be abrogated and abandoned.''

Samuel Shellabarger [O.] said:

"This measure, taken alone, is one which I could not support unaccompanied by provisions for the rapid and immediate establishment of civil government based upon the suffrages of the loyal people of the South. I could not support a military measure like this if it was to be regarded as at all permanent in its character. It is because it is entirely the initiative, because it is only the employment of the army of the United States as a mere police force, to preserve order until we can establish civil government based upon the loyal suffrages of the people, that I can support this measure at all. If it stood by itself I could not, with my notions of the possibility and practicability of establishing civil governments in the South, based upon loyal suffrage, vote for this bill.''

Henry L. Dawes [Mass.] inquired:

''After the general of the army has, under this bill, assigned a competent and trustworthy officer to the duties prescribed is there anything to hinder the President of the United States, under virtue of his power as commander-in-chief, from removing that officer and putting in his place another of an opposite character, thus making the very instrumentality we provide one of terrible evil?''

John A. Griswold, who became the Republican candidate for Governor of New York the ensuing year, earnestly opposed the bill.

''By it we are proceeding in the wrong direction. For more than two years we have been endeavoring to provide civil governments for that portion of our country, and yet, by the provisions of this bill, we turn our backs on our policy of the last two years, and by a single stride proceed to put all that portion of the country under exclusively military control. For one, I prefer to stand by the overtures we have made to these people, as conditions of their again participating in the government of the country. We have already placed before them conditions which the civilized world has indorsed as liberal, magnanimous, and just. I regret exceedingly that those very liberal terms have not been accepted by the South, but I prefer giving those people every opportunity to exhibit a spirit of obedience and loyalty.''

Henry J. Raymond [N. Y.] opposed the bill in a vigorous speech.

''Because we cannot devise anything of a civil nature adequate to the emergency it is urged that we must fly to the most violent measure the ingenuity of man could devise. Let me remind gentlemen that this has been the history of popular governments everywhere, the reason of their downfall, their decadence, and their death.''

James A. Garfield [O.] indicated his support of the measure if it could be amended.

"But I call attention to the fact that from the collapse of the Rebellion to the present hour, Congress has undertaken to restore the States lately in rebellion by coöperation with their people, and that our efforts in that direction have proven a complete and disastrous failure."

Alluding to the fact that the Fourteenth Amendment had been submitted as the basis of reconstruction, General Garfield continued:

"The constitutional amendment did not come up to the full height of the great occasion. It did not meet all I desired in the way of guaranties to liberty, but, if the rebel States had adopted it as Tennessee did, I should have felt bound to let them in on the terms prescribed for Tennessee. I have been in favor of waiting to give them full time to deliberate and to act. They have deliberated. They have acted. The last one of the sinful ten has, at last, with contempt and scorn, flung back in our teeth the magnanimous offer of a generous nation. It is now our turn to act. They would not coöperate with us in building what they destroyed. We must remove the rubbish and build from the bottom."

Nathaniel Banks [Mass.] asked for deliberation and delay in the discussion.

"We might reach a solution in which the two Houses of Congress will agree, which the people of this country will sustain, and in which the President of the United States will give us his support. And, if we should agree on a measure satisfactory to ourselves, in which we should be sustained by the people, and the President should resist it, then we should be justified in dropping the subject of reconstruction and considering the condition of the country in a different sense."

·The allusion of General Banks, says Mr. Blaine, though thus veiled, was understood to imply the possible necessity of impeaching the President.

John A. Kasson [Ia.] objected that the bill was too sweeping in its provisions, that it affected the loyally disposed in the South with the same severity as it did the disloyally disposed.

VIII—4

"Instead of erecting this great military power over people of some portions of the South who are, in fact, at peace and observing law and order, our rule should be so flexible that we may apply martial law wherever peace and law and order do not prevail, without imposing it upon people whose subordination to the law renders military rule unnecessary."

He therefore proposed, as a substitute for the pending measure, "A bill to establish an additional article of war for the complete suppression of the insurrection against the United States." This provided for a division of the rebel territory into military districts, as did the original bill, and authorized commanders to declare martial law wherever it should be necessary for the "complete suppression of violence and disorder."

James M. Ashley [O.] moved an amendment providing for the restoration to loyal owners of property confiscated by the rebel government, and providing that military government should cease so soon as the people of the rebel States should adopt State constitutions securing to all citizens equal protection of the laws, including the right of the elective franchise, and should ratify the proposed amendment to the Constitution.

Mr. Raymond thought that on account of the great diversity of opinion the whole subject should be referred to a select committee who should be instructed to report within three or four days a bill which should "provide temporarily for the protection of rights and the preservation of the peace in the States lately in rebellion, and also for the speedy admission of those States to their relations in the Union upon the basis of the constitutional amendment." Thus he hoped a result could be reached which "would command the support of Congress and of the country, and the approval, or at least the assent, of the Executive."

George S. Boutwell [Mass.] remarked that, previous propositions having been referred to the Committee on Reconstruction, they had agreed upon the bill before the House with a unanimity which no other report had ever obtained, nor had any bill submitted by that committee ever been so carefully considered as this.

"To-day there are eight millions and more of people, occupying six hundred and thirty thousand square miles of the territory of this country, who are writhing under cruelties nameless in their character—injustice such as has not been permitted to exist in any other country in modern times; and all this because in this capital there sits enthroned a man who, so far as the executive department is concerned, guides the destinies of the Republic in the interest of rebels; and because, also, in those ten former States rebellion itself, inspired by the executive department of this Government, wields all authority, and is the embodiment of law and power everywhere. Until, in the South, this obstacle to reconstruction is removed, there can be no effectual step taken toward the reorganization of the Government."

William E. Niblack [Dem.], of Indiana, said:

"A well man needs no remedies; it is only when he is sick that you can require him to submit to medicinal applications. A country at peace does not need and ought not to allow martial law and other summary remedies incident to a state of war. The highest and dearest interests of this country are made subordinate to party exigencies and to special and particular interests. No wonder, then, that trade languishes and commerce declines."

On the 12th of February Mr. Bingham proposed an amendment making the restoration of the rebel States conditional upon their adoption of the constitutional amendment, and imposing upon them, meanwhile, the military government provided by the pending bill.

William D. Kelley [Pa.] advocated the bill as reported from the committee.

"This is little more than a mere police bill. The necessity for it arises from the perfidy of the President of the United States. Had he been true to the duties of his high office and his public and repeated pledges, there would have been no necessity for considering such a bill."

Said HORACE MAYNARD [Tenn.]: "Throughout the region of the unreconstructed States the animating, life-giving principle of the rebellion is as thoroughly in possession of the country and of all the political power there to-day as it ever has been since the first gun was fired upon Fort Sumter. The rebellion is alive. It is strong—strong in the number of its votaries, strong in its social influences, strong in its political power, strong in the belief that the executive department of this Government is in sympathy and community of purpose with them, strong in the belief that the controlling majority of the supreme judiciary of the land is with them in legal opinion, strong in the belief that the controversy in this body between impracticable zeal and incorrigible timidity will prevent anything of importance being accomplished or any legislation matured.''

WILLIAM B. ALLISON [Ia.] said: ''It is because of the interference of the President of the United States with the military law which exists in those States that this bill is rendered necessary. In my judgment, if we had to-day an Executive who was desirous of enforcing the laws of the United States to protect loyal men in those States, instead of defending the rebel element, this bill would not be needed.''

James G. Blaine [Me.] submitted an amendment providing that any one of the ''late so-called Confederate States'' might be restored to representation and relieved of military rule when, in addition to having accepted the constitutional amendment, it should have conferred the elective franchise impartially upon all male citizens over twenty-one years of age. Mr. Blaine maintained that the people in the elections of 1866 had declared in favor of ''universal, or, at least, impartial suffrage as the basis of restoration.''

On the 13th of February the discussion was continued. Said Burt Van Horn [N. Y.]:

''That the spirit of rebellion still lives and now thrives in the South no sane man can deny; that the determination exists to make their rebellion honorable and the loyalty of the South a lasting disgrace and a permanent badge of dishonor is equally true and cannot be denied. The leaders of the rebellion, being in power in all the ten States unreconstructed, still defy the authority of the United States to a great extent, and deny the power of the loyal millions of the country, who have saved our nation's life against their treason and rebellion, to prescribe terms of settlement of this great controversy, and deny also that they have lost any rights they had before the war or committed any treason against the Government.''

Mr. Stevens said that the measure before the House, as it came from the Committee on Reconstruction, "was not intended as a reconstruction bill."

"It was intended simply as a police bill to protect the loyal men from anarchy and murder, until this Congress, taking a little more time, can suit gentlemen in a bill for the admission of all those rebel States upon the basis of civil government."

The various amendments proposed were designed by their authors to add a plan of reconstruction to the pending bill. Of these Mr. Boutwell remarked:

"Without examining into the details of the amendments, I have this to say: that any general proposition for the restoration of these States to the Union upon any basis not set forth in an act of Congress is fraught with the greatest danger to the future peace and prosperity of the Republic."

The amendments of Mr. Bingham and Mr. Blaine were finally combined by their authors. The combination made an amendment providing that the "States lately in insurrection" should be restored and relieved of military rule upon their ratification of the constitutional amendment and adoption of impartial suffrage. In order to "disentangle what seemed so much entangled," it was moved that the bill be recommitted to the Judiciary Committee, with instructions to report back immediately the amendment of Messrs. Blaine and Bingham.

Mr. Stevens then addressed the House, promising that in his state of health a few words must suffice. He felt a moral depression in viewing the condition of the party responsible for the doings of Congress.

"For the last few months Congress has been sitting here, and, while the South has been bleeding at every pore, Congress has done nothing to protect the loyal people there, white or black, either in their persons, in their liberty, or in their property."

Of his previous bill, which had been consigned to its tomb in being referred to the Committee on Reconstruction, Mr. Stevens said:

"I thought it was a good bill; I had labored upon it in conjunction with several committees of loyal men from the South for four months; I had altered and realtered it, written and rewritten it four several times, and found that it met the approbation of numerous societies and meetings in all the Southern States. It was, therefore, not altogether my fault if it was not so good a bill as might be found; but I did think that, after all, it was uncivil, unjust, indecent, not to attempt to amend it and make it better, to see whether we could do something to enable our friends in the Southern States to establish institutions according to the principles of republican government."

Mr. Stevens deprecated a disposition among his friends to be hypercritical in relation to mere verbal details.

"If I might presume upon my age, without claiming any of the wisdom of Nestor, I would suggest to the young gentlemen around me that the deeds of this burning crisis, of this solemn day, of this thrilling moment will cast their shadows far into the future and will make their impress upon the annals of our history, and that we shall appear upon the bright pages of that history just in so far as we cordially, without guile, without bickering, without small criticisms, lend our aid to promote the great cause of humanity and universal liberty."

The question being taken on the motion to refer to the Committee on the Judiciary it was decided in the negative—yeas, 69; nays, 94. The question was then taken on the passage of the bill. It passed the House— 109 voting in the affirmative, and 55 voting in the negative.

When the vote was announced Mr. Stevens said:

"I wish to inquire, Mr. Speaker, if it is in order for me now to say that we indorse the language of good old Laertes, that Heaven rules as yet, and there are gods above."

The bill reached the Senate on the 13th of February. On the 14th George H. Williams [Ore.], who had the bill in charge, gave notice that he would offer an amendment which was almost literally the same as that offered by Mr. Blaine in the House, but fearing that it might obstruct the passage of the bill he withdrew it. Reverdy Johnson, of Maryland, renewed the amendment with the remark that if it should be adopted it would make the bill very much less objectionable than it then was. Upon the Johnson amendment the debate then proceeded.

MILITARY RECONSTRUCTION

SENATE, FEBRUARY 13-18, 1867

William M. Stewart [Nev.] sustained the amendment. He said that the history of military bills was that they were always represented in the beginning as temporary measures.

"But suppose the President of the United States approved it, or the next President, if you please, should like the bill, and should veto your measure repealing it, or suppose a bare majority in either House of Congress should like it, then you could not repeal it. It may be years after you desire to get rid of it before you can. I say, when you use the military for temporary purposes you should give the people of the South a chance to comply with all the requirements which you propose to make. If, in the Blaine amendment, as it is called, there are not sufficient guaranties, not enough conditions, then put in more and make it sufficient."

Lot M. Morrill [Me.] thought Senator Stewart was unnecessarily troubled about military governments in the South.

"Are we, who have stood here for five long, bloody years and witnessed the exercise of military power over these rebel States, to be frightened now by a declaration of that sort? That is not the temper in which I find myself to-day. I have got so accustomed to the exercise of this authority——"

SENATOR STEWART.—"That is the trouble."

SENATOR MORRILL.—"It has not been our trouble that we have exercised power; that has been the salvation of the nation. The trouble has arisen from our hesitation to exercise authority when authority was required."

John B. Henderson [Mo.] thought that the remedy proposed by him long before would be found the only cure for the ills of the nation.

"I offered twelve months ago a proposition, as a constitutional amendment, that was to give political rights to the negroes. Some Senators said it was a humbug, that it was Jacob Townsend's Sarsaparilla, or something to that effect; that it would amount to nothing. Now, I will ask what other protection can you give to a Union man in the Southern States than the ballot?"

On February 15 Senator Williams was anxious that the bill be passed at once so that, if it were vetoed by the President, time would remain before the close of the session to pass it over the veto.

James R. Doolittle [Wis.], an Administration Republican, protested against this haste in a measure of so great importance: "a bill that proposed to establish a military despotism over eight million people and a country larger than England, France, and Spain combined is to be pressed to a vote in this Senate the first day it is taken up for consideration."

Thomas A. Hendricks [Ind.] said:

"If the measure will not bear argument then let it be passed in the dark hours of the night. When despotism is established in this free land, that the best blood that ever ran in mortal veins was shed to make free, it is becoming that it be done when the sun does not shed its bright light upon the earth. It is a work for darkness and not for light."

Said Senator Henderson:

"Why, sir, the Southern States have presented nothing but a despotism for the last six years, and, since the rebel rule ceased, the President of the United States certainly has governed the Southern States without ever consulting Congress on the subject."

The Senate held an evening session for the consideration of the bill. Mr. Hendricks proposed to modify the pending amendment so as to provide for impartial rather than universal suffrage. He thought that States should be allowed to limit suffrage. Willard Saulsbury [Del.] would not vote for this amendment because he was unwilling to "touch, taste, or handle the unclean thing." On the other hand Garrett Davis [Ky.] could vote for it because he preferred a "little unclean thing" to "a big one." Mr. Hendricks finally withdrew his amendment.

Mr. Doolittle hoped that the majority would seriously weigh this question because on it might depend whether the people of the South would accept the constitutional amendment, and accept the proposition necessary to get rid of military despotism.

"Make them," said Henry Wilson [Mass.].

SENATOR DOOLITTLE.—"I ask, if that is the true language of a statesman to say to a people who have been educated in the largest liberty, a people in whose veins the Anglo-Saxon blood is flowing, which, for a thousand years, has been fighting against despotism of every form: 'You must accept this position at the point of the bayonet or forever live with the bayonet at your throats'? Is that the way to make peace?"

SENATOR WILSON.—"I think it is statesmanship to settle this question of reconstruction upon the solid basis of the perfect equality of rights and privileges among citizens of the United States. Colored men are citizens, and they have just as much right as this race whose blood has been fighting against oppression for a thousand years, as he says, and any settlement of this civil war upon any other basis than perfect equality of rights and privileges among citizens of the United States is not statesmanship; it is mere trifling; only keeping open questions for future controversy. Nothing is settled unless it is settled upon the basis of justice."

SENATOR JOHNSON.—"The amendment is objectionable to me only upon the ground that it denies to those States the right of coming into the Union entitled to representation until they extend the suffrage, because I believe the right of suffrage is a matter with which the Congress of the United States has no concern."

The opponents of the bill, by making long speeches, kept it from coming to a vote, the Senate adjourning at three o'clock the next morning (Saturday, February 16).

Reassembling at the usual hour, the Senate was addressed by Senator Doolittle. Saying that the measure was founded on heresies which originated in Massachusetts, and had for their chief advocate Senator Charles Sumner, he acknowledged that these were now dominant in the country, and that he would be crucified by his former political associates for opposing them; yet nevertheless he would fight to the last against the bill since he believed that it was destruction of that spirit which gave life to the Republic.

The session lasted until six o'clock Sunday morning.

John Sherman [O.] offered a substitute for the whole bill, embodying the Blaine amendment of the House, and giving the President power to control assignments of army officers in the military districts. This was passed by a vote of 29 to 10.

Debate on the Sherman Substitute

House of Representatives, February 18-March 2, 1867

The bill as amended by the Senate returned to the House on Monday, February 18. Mr. Stevens moved that the amendments be not concurred in. and that the House ask a Committee of Conference.

He asked: "What has the Senate done? Sent back to us an amendment which contains everything else but protection. It has sent us back a bill which raises the whole question in dispute as to the best mode of reconstructing these States by distant and future pledges which this Congress has no authority to make and no power to execute. What power has this Congress to say to a future Congress: When the Southern States have done certain things, you shall admit them, and receive their members into this House? Our friends, who love this bill, love it now because the President is to execute it, as he has executed every law for the last two years, by the murder of Union men, and by despising Congress and flinging into our teeth all that we seek to have done."

Mr. Stevens thought that in two hours a Committee of Conference could frame a bill and report it to the House free from all these difficulties—free from all this extraneous matter—which would protect every loyal man in the Southern States, and do no injustice to the disloyal.

Mr. Boutwell supported the motion of Mr. Stevens. He objected to the bill on the ground that it proposed to reconstruct the rebel State governments at once through the agency of disloyal men, and that it gave additional power to the President when he had failed to use the vast power which he already possessed in behalf of loyalty and justice.

William B. Stokes [Tenn.] saw in the bill the principle of universal amnesty and universal suffrage.

"I would rather have nothing if these governments are reconstructed in a way that will place the rebels over Union men."

Mr. Blaine supported the bill as it came from the Senate.

"Congress no more guarantees, under this bill, the right of any rebel in any State to vote than did Congress guarantee to the rebels in Tennessee the right to vote."

Said JAMES F. WILSON [Ia.]: "Although this bill does not attain all I desire to accomplish, it does embrace much upon which I have insisted. It reaches far beyond anything which the most sanguine of us hoped for a year ago. It secures equal suffrage to all loyal men; it sets aside the pretended governments which now abuse power in the rebel States; it insists on the ratification of the constitutional amendment, under the operation of which all the rebels who now occupy official position in the States affected by this bill will be rendered ineligible to office, State or national; it presents an affirmative policy, on the part of Congress, hostile to that of the President; it demonstrates the ability of Congress to agree upon a given line of future action; and, finally, it reserves to Congress jurisdiction over the whole case when the people of any Southern disorganized State may present a Constitution and ask for admission to this body as a part of the governing power of the nation. There is too much of good in this to be rejected. I will vote to concur in the amendment of the Senate."

John P. Farnsworth [Ill.] supported the bill.

"It provides a platform ten steps in advance of the platform upon which we went to the people last fall. We then only expected the ratification of the amendment to the Constitution proposed by Congress at its last session, and the formation of Constitutions, republican in form, which should give the people there the right to send loyal men here as Senators and Representatives. But by this bill we extend impartial suffrage to the black man—universal suffrage."

ROBERT C. SCHENCK [O.].—"I believe we ought to declare to these rebel States, as we do by this bill, that they shall be put under martial law, and held by the strong hand to keep the peace until they have complied with whatever conditions are imposed upon them. But, while we do this, I think it equally important to announce to them, to announce to the country, to announce to our constituents as the completion of the whole platform upon which we go before the nation the terms which we require of them."

General Garfield favored the Senate amendment.

"There are some gentlemen who live among the eagles on the high mountain peaks, beyond the limit of perpetual frost, and they see the lineaments in the face of freedom so much clearer than I do; whenever any measure comes here that seems almost to grasp our purpose, they rise and tell us it is all poor and mean and a surrender of liberty."

Giles W. Hotchkiss [N. Y.] opposed the bill as amended.

"If you allow this bill to go into operation as it now stands without making any amendment of its provisions, and permit these elections to be held, as they must necessarily be held under this bill, under the authority, control, and regulation of the rebel governments in those States, there will be no security whatever, and you will have the elections in New Orleans held under the control of Mayor Monroe and the mob which he used to such fell purpose last summer. That is the entertainment to which this bill invites us."

HENRY H. P. BROMWELL [Ill.].—"I regard this as a flank movement by which is to be brought about that darling scheme of certain politicians—universal amnesty and universal suffrage. Whether it end in universal suffrage or not one thing is certain, it is universal amnesty."

IGNATIUS DONNELLY [Minn.].—"It would be emphatically a government of rebels. I say a government of rebels because, although the amendment which has reached us from the Senate contains the words, 'Except such as may be disfranchised for participation in the rebellion,' that disfranchisement has to come from the rebels themselves, and, surely, there is no man upon this floor weak enough to suppose that they will so disfranchise themselves."

Mr. LeBlond opposed both bills. Of the one before the House he said:

"This bill is quite as infamous, quite as absurd, as the bill that the distinguished gentleman from Pennsylvania [Mr. Stevens], who is chairman of the Committee on Reconstruction, contends for and hangs so tenaciously to. It confers all the powers that that bill gives; it confers all the powers that the most radical could claim consistently."

GENERAL BANKS.—"If this bill be passed in my belief there will be no loyal party known and no loyal voice heard in any of these States, from Virginia to Texas."

Many members subsequently presented arguments and opinions for and against the bill in speeches limited to fifteen minutes in length. This occupied a session protracted until near midnight.

On the following morning, February 19, a vote was taken and the House refused to concur in the amendments of the Senate and asked a Committee of Conference. The Senate immediately proceeded to consider a motion made by Mr. Williams that they insist on their amendment and agree to the conference. The vote was finally taken after a prolonged discussion. The Senate insisted on its amendment, and refused to appoint a Committee of Conference.

The bill having gone back to the House of Representatives they resolved by a vote of 126 to 46 to recede from their disagreement to the amendment of the

Senate, and to concur in the same with amendments
providing that no person excluded from holding office by
the recently proposed constitutional amendment should
be eligible for membership in the convention to frame
a constitution for any of the rebel States, nor should
any such person be allowed to vote for members of such
convention. Another amendment proposed by the House
was the addition of a section (sixth) to the bill providing that, until the rebel States should be admitted to
representation in Congress, any civil governments existing therein should be deemed provisional only, and subject to the paramount authority of the United States,
who may at any time abolish, modify, control, or supersede them.

This qualified concurrence on the part of the House
having been announced in the Senate, that body proceeded immediately to consider the question of acquiescence.

After an extended discussion the vote was taken upon
the final passage of the bill as amended by the House;
it passed the Senate—yeas, 35; nays, 7.

The bill "to provide for the more efficient government
of the rebel States" having thus passed both Houses
of Congress on the 20th of February, it was immediately
submitted to the President for his approval. On the
second of March the President returned the bill to the
House in which it originated with his objections, which
were so grave that he hoped a statement of them might
"have some influence on the minds of the patriotic and
enlightened men with whom the decision must ultimately
rest." The veto message was immediately read by the
clerk of the House of Representatives. The following
were the President's principal objections to the measure:

"The bill places all the people of the ten States therein
named under the absolute domination of military rulers.

"It is not denied that the States in question have, each of
them, an actual government, with all the powers—executive,
judicial, and legislative—which properly belong to a free State.
They are organized like the other States of the Union, and, like
them, they make, administer, and execute the laws which concern

their domestic affairs. An existing *de facto* government, exercising such functions as these, is itself the law of the State upon all matters within its jurisdiction. To pronounce the supreme law-making power of an established State illegal is to say that law itself is unlawful.

"The military rule which it establishes is plainly to be used, not for any purpose of order or for the prevention of crime, but solely as a means of coercing the people into the adoption of principles and measures to which it is known that they are opposed, and upon which they have an undeniable right to exercise their own judgment.

"I submit to Congress whether this measure is not, in its whole character, scope, and object, without precedent and without authority, in palpable conflict with the plainest provisions of the Constitution, and utterly destructive of those great principles of liberty and humanity for which our ancestors on both sides of the Atlantic have shed so much blood and expended so much treasure.

"The power thus given to the commanding officer over all the people of each district is that of an absolute monarch. His mere will is to take the place of all law. The law of the States is now the only rule applicable to the subjects placed under his control, and that is completely displaced by the clause which declares all interference of State authority to be null and void.

"I come now to a question which is, if possible, still more important. Have we the power to establish and carry into execution a measure like this? I answer certainly not, if we derive our authority from the Constitution, and if we are bound by the limitations which it imposes. This proposition is perfectly clear; that no branch of the Federal Government—executive, legislative, or judicial—can have any just powers except those which it derives through and exercises under the organic law of the Union. Outside of the Constitution we have no legal authority more than private citizens, and within it we have only so much as that instrument gives us. This broad principle limits all our functions and applies to all subjects. It protects not only the citizens of States which are within the Union, but it shields every human being who comes or is brought under our jurisdiction. We have no right to do in one place more than in another that which the Constitution says we shall not do at all. If, therefore, the Southern States were, in truth, out of the Union, we could not treat their people in a way which the fundamental law forbids.

"If an insurrection should take place in one of our States

against the authority of the State government, and end in the overthrowing of those who planned it, would they take away the rights of all the people of the counties where it was favored by a part or a majority of the population? Could they, for such a reason, be wholly outlawed and deprived of their representation in the legislature? I have always contended that the Government of the United States was sovereign within its constitutional sphere; that it executed its laws, like the States themselves, by applying its coercive power directly to individuals; and that it could put down insurrection with the same effect as a State, and no other. The opposite doctrine is the worst heresy of those who advocated secession, and cannot be agreed to without admitting that heresy to be right.

"This is a bill passed by Congress in time of peace. There is not, in any one of the States brought under its operation, either war or insurrection. The laws of the States and of the Federal Government are all in undisturbed and harmonious operation. The courts, State and Federal, are open and in the full exercise of their proper authority. Over every State comprised in these five military districts life, liberty, and property are secured by State laws and Federal laws, and the national Constitution is everywhere enforced and everywhere obeyed.

"Actual war, foreign invasion, domestic insurrection—none of these appear, and none of these in fact exist. It is not even recited that any sort of war or insurrection is threatened."

Upon this question of constitutional law and the power of Congress the President gave quotations from "a recent decision of the Supreme Court *ex parte* Milligan." Having commented upon this question, the President proceeded with his objections:

"I need not say to the Representatives of the American people that their Constitution forbids the exercise of judicial power in any way but one; that is, by the ordained and established courts. It is equally well known that, in all criminal cases, a trial by jury is made indispensable by the express words of that instrument. I will not enlarge on the inestimable value of the right thus secured to every freeman, or speak of the danger to public liberty, in all parts of the country, which must ensue from a denial of it anywhere, or upon any pretence.

"The United States are bound to guarantee to each State a republican form of government. Can it be pretended that this obligation is not palpably broken if we carry out a measure like this, which wipes away every vestige of republican government in ten States and puts the life, property, liberty, and honor of all the people in each of them under the domination of a single person clothed with unlimited authority.

"The purpose and object of the bill—the general intent which pervades it from beginning to end—is to change the entire structure and character of the State governments, and to compel them by force to the adoption of organic laws and regulations which they are unwilling to accept if left to themselves. The negroes have not asked for the privilege of voting; the vast majority of them have no idea what it means. This bill not only thrusts it into their hands, but compels them, as well as the whites, to use it in a particular way. If they do not form a constitution with prescribed articles in it, and afterward elect a legislature which will act upon certain measures in a prescribed way, neither blacks nor whites, can be relieved from the slavery which the bill imposes upon them. Without pausing here to consider the policy or impolicy of Africanizing the Southern part of our territory, I would simply ask the attention of Congress to that manifest, well-known, and universally acknowledged rule of constitutional law which declares that the Federal Government has no jurisdiction, authority, or power to regulate such subjects for any State. To force the right of suffrage out of the hands of the white people and into the hands of the negroes is an arbitrary violation of this principle.

"This bill imposes martial law at once, and its operation will begin so soon as the general and his troops can be put in place. The dread alternative between its harsh rule and compliance with the terms of this measure is not suspended, nor are the people afforded any time for free deliberation. The bill says to them: Take martial law first, then deliberate.

"The bill also denies the legality of the governments of ten of the States which participated in the ratification of the amendment to the Federal Constitution abolishing slavery forever within the jurisdiction of the United States, and practically excludes them from the Union.

"That the measure proposed by this bill does violate the Constitution in the particulars mentioned, and in many other ways which I forbear to enumerate, is too clear to admit of the least doubt.

"I am thoroughly convinced that any settlement, or compromise, or plan of action which is inconsistent with the principles of the Constitution will not only be unavailing, but mis-

chievous; that it will but multiply the present evils instead of
removing them. The Constitution, in its whole integrity and
vigor, throughout the length and breadth of the land, is the
best of all compromises. Besides, our duty does not, in my
judgment, leave us a choice between that and any other. I
believe that it contains the remedy that is so much needed, and
that, if the coördinate branches of the Government would unite
upon its provisions, they would be found broad enough and
strong enough to sustain, in time of peace, the nation which
they bore safely through the ordeal of a protracted civil war.
Among the most sacred guaranties of that instrument are those
which declare that 'each State shall have at least one Representative,' and that 'no State, without its consent, shall be
deprived of its equal suffrage in the Senate.' Each House is
made the 'judge of the elections, returns, and qualifications of its
own members,' and may, 'with the concurrence of two-thirds,
expel a member.'

"And is it not far better that the work of restoration should
be accomplished by simple compliance with the plain requirements of the Constitution than by a recourse to measures which,
in effect, destroy the States and threaten the subversion of the
general Government? All that is necessary to settle this simple
but important question, without further agitation or delay, is a
willingness, on the part of all, to sustain the Constitution, and
carry its provisions into practical operation. If, to-morrow,
either branch of Congress would declare that, upon the presentation of their credentials, members constitutionally elected and
loyal to the general Government would be admitted to seats in
Congress, while all others would be excluded and their places
remain vacant until the selection by the people of loyal and
qualified persons; and if, at the same time, assurance were given
that this policy would be continued until all the States were
represented in Congress, it would send a thrill of joy throughout
the entire land, as indicating the inauguration of a system which
must speedily bring tranquillity to the public mind.

"While we are legislating upon subjects which are of great
importance to the whole people, and which must affect all parts
of the country, not only during the life of the present generation
but for ages to come, we should remember that all men are entitled at least to a hearing in the councils which decide upon the
destiny of themselves and their children. At present representation is denied to ten States, and, when the Fortieth Congress as-
sembles, on the fourth day of the present month, sixteen States
will be without a voice in the House of Representatives. This

grave fact, with the important questions before us, should induce us to pause in a course of legislation which, looking solely to the attainment of political ends, fails to consider the rights it transgresses, the law which it violates, or the institutions which it imperils.''

House Debate on the Veto

March 2, 1867

After the reading of the message the question came up, ''Shall the bill pass, the objections of the President to the contrary notwithstanding?''

Mr. Eldridge declared it was the duty of the minority if it were within their physical power to defeat the bill.

''But we are conscious that no effort of ours can prevent its passage, and the consequent accomplishment of a dissolution of the Union, and the overthrow and abandonment of our constitution of government. We can only, in the name of the Constitution, in the name of the Republic, in the name of all we hold dear on earth, earnestly, solemnly protest against this action of this Congress.''

Mr. LeBlond said that ''the passage of this bill would be the death-knell of republican liberty upon this continent.'' He declared his willingness, if a sufficient number on his side of the House would stand by him, to resist to the utmost extremity of physical exhaustion the passage of this bill which would ''strike a death-blow to this Government.''

Mr. Stevens would not be discourteous to those who were opposed to this bill. ''I am aware,'' said he, ''of the melancholy feelings with which they are approaching this funeral of the nation.'' He was unwilling, however, to lose the opportunity to pass the bill at once, and send it to the Senate, that the House might proceed to other matters.

The vote was taken and the House passed the bill over the President's veto—yeas, 135; nays, 48. The announcement of this result was followed by great applause on the floor and in the galleries.

The veto message having been read in the Senate by the secretary, the pending question at once became whether the bill should pass notwithstanding the objections of the President.

Senator Johnson advocated the passage of the bill over the veto.

"The President's message contains some legal propositions which are unsound, and many errors of reasoning. I lament the course he has thought it his duty to pursue, because I see that it may result in continued turmoil and peril, not only to the South, but to the entire country. I see before me a distressed, a desolated, country, and, in the measure before you, I think I see the means through which it may be rescued and restored ere long to prosperity and a healthful condition, and the free institutions of our country preserved."

The Senator urged upon the people of the South their acceptance of the terms proposed by Congress. In view of the probability these overtures should be rejected, harsher measures would be resorted to.

Senator Saulsbury expressed his admiration for the wisdom of the President in "vetoing the most iniquitous bill that ever was presented to the Federal Congress."

"I hope that there may be no man within the limits of these ten States who will participate in his own disgrace, degradation, and ruin: let them maintain their honor. If there be wrath in the vials of the Almighty, if there be arrows of vengeance in His quiver, such iniquity and injustice cannot finally prove successful."

Senator Hendricks disagreed with the Senator from Delaware that the people of the South, at once and without consideration, must turn their backs upon the proposition now made them in order to maintain their honor. He hoped they would bring to the consideration of the subject the coolest judgment and the highest patriotism. He was still opposed to the bill; he approved of the President's veto. His judgment against the measure had been "fortified and strengthened by that able document."

The question being taken, the bill was passed over the veto by a vote of 38 to 10.

The Fortieth Congress, meeting on the 4th of March, immediately upon the close of its predecessor, proceeded without delay to perfect and pass over the President's veto a bill supplementary to the act to provide for the more efficient government of the rebel States. By this act it was provided that the commanding general of each district should cause a registration to be made of the male citizens twenty-one years of age in his district, qualified to vote under the former act. In order to be registered as a voter under this act a person was required to swear that he had not been disfranchised for participation in any rebellion or civil war against the United States, nor for felony; that he had never been a member of any State legislature, nor held any executive or judicial office in any State and afterward engaged in insurrection or rebellion against the United States, nor given aid or comfort to the enemies thereof; that he had never taken an oath as a member of Congress of the United States, nor as a member of any State legislature, nor as an executive or judicial officer of any State, to support the Constitution of the United States, and afterward engaged in insurrection or rebellion against the United States, nor given aid or comfort to the enemies thereof; and that he will faithfully support the Constitution and obey the laws of the United States, and encourage others to do so.

Persons thus qualified might vote at elections held for the purpose of selecting delegates to the conventions for framing constitutions for the States.

A majority of voters so qualified should determine whether constitutional conventions should be held in the several States, and vote for delegates who should be as numerous as the members of the most numerous branch of the legislature of such State in the year 1860. This convention having framed a constitution, it should be submitted to the people, and, if ratified by a majority of the qualified voters, it should be forthwith transmitted to Congress. If this constitution was satisfactory to

Congress, and found to be in accordance with the provisions of the act of which this is supplementary, the
State should be declared entitled to representation. All
elections were required to be by ballot, and all officers
acting under the provisions of this act were required to
take the test oath.

During this session Congress repealed section 13 of
the Confiscation Act of July 17, 1862. Not being approved by the President, to whom it was presented on
January 9, 1867, it became a law on the expiration of
ten days, excluding Sunday.

Pardoning Power of the President

The section referred to gave the President power to
extend pardon and amnesty to former rebels. The bill
was intended to remove an abuse which had arisen in
the sale of pardons in Washington by various persons,
including women, who had influence with the Administration. It was passed by the House on the first day of
the session (December 3, 1866).

James G. Blaine, in his "Twenty Years of Congress," thus describes the course of the bill through the
Senate and its enactment over the President's veto:

The repeal of the clause did not take from the President his constitutional power of pardoning, but in the
judgment of Lyman Trumbull [Ill.], who had charge of
the bill in the Senate, it took from him the power to
pardon by proclamation and confined him to his right
of issuing individual pardons. The difference between
pardon and amnesty was defined by Senator Trumbull.
Pardon is an act of mercy extended to an individual.
It must be by deed. It must be pleaded. According
to Chief-Justice John Marshall, it is essential to its
validity that it be delivered to the person pardoned.
But an amnesty is a general pardon by proclamation.
Senator Trumbull thought the repeal would be a "valuable expression of opinion on the part of Congress that
general pardons and restoration of property will not
be continued, and, if the President continues to pardon

rebels and restore their property by individual acts under
the Constitution, let him do so without having the sanction of Congress for his act.''

Reverdy Johnson took issue with Senator Trumbull.
He maintained that the President's power to grant
pardons, as conferred by the Constitution, had not been
affected by the provision of law whose repeal was now
urged. He declared that the power of the President ''to
grant reprieves and pardons for offences against the
United States'' was as broad, as general, as unrestricted
as language could make it. He could find no logical
ground for the distinction made by Senator Trumbull
between individual pardons and general amnesties by
proclamation—in illustration of which he said President
Washington had by proclamation pardoned the offenders
engaged in the Whiskey Insurrection. The enactment
of the provision had not, in Mr. Johnson's opinion, enlarged the President's pardoning power, and its repeal
would not restrict it.

A majority of the Senate concurred in Mr. Johnson's
interpretation of the Constitution, but they passed the
bill as a rebuke to the scandalous sale of pardons by
a class of ''middle men'' who had in some form the
opportunity to secure the interposition of men who
could reach the ear of the President or the Attorney-
General. It is hardly necessary to add that neither of
those high officials was in the remotest degree reflected
upon even by their bitterest opponents. It was believed
that the nefarious practice was stopped by this bill. Exposure made public men careful to examine each application for pardon before they would consent to recommend it to the President.

The President obviously took the view that had been
advanced by Senator Johnson, and did not take the
trouble to sign it, much less to veto it. It was *brutum
fulmen,* and the President used his constitutional power
to pardon by proclamation just as freely after its enactment as before.

The old Congress was so distrustful of what the
President might do in the usual recess that it summoned

the new Congress (the Fortieth) to convene immediately at the close of the session. Accordingly it assembled on March 4, 1867. It sat until March 30, on which date the House took a recess, and the Senate immediately convened in a special session which lasted until April 19. Both chambers reassembled on July 3, and sat until July 20. Reassembling on November 21 they sat until December 1.

The House of Representatives elected Schuyler Colfax [Ind.] Speaker; in his speech accepting the office he clearly intimated that the Radicals would take no steps backward in their reconstruction policy, and that they would further advance to negro suffrage extending throughout the Union.

The chief business of Congress in 1867 was the passage of supplementary legislation to the Military Reconstruction act. On March 19 Congress passed an act prescribing the mode of registering voters and for calling constitutional conventions in the ex-rebel States in order that Congress might know if the constitutions adopted were approved by a majority of the qualified (*i. e.,* loyal) citizens of these States. The President immediately vetoed the bill on the ground that the oath it required of voters rendered them liable to uncertain penalties, the region affected by the act being under martial law. "If ever the American citizen," he said, "should be left to the free exercise of his own judgment, it is when he is engaged in the work of forming the fundamental law under which he is to live."

Congress passed the act over the President's veto on March 23: the House by 114 ayes to 25 nays, and the Senate by 40 ayes to 7 nays.

During the spring recess (on March 24 and June 12) Henry Stanbery, Attorney-General, gave forcible opinions of the supplementary Reconstruction act calculated to nullify its execution. Accordingly, when Congress reassembled in June, it set to work to remedy the defects of the act by framing another supplementary bill. This was passed on July 13, and was vetoed by the President on July 19. In his veto message he said:

"The military commander is, as to the power of appointment, made to take the place of the President, and the general of the army the place of the Senate, and any attempt on the part of the President to assert his own constitutional power may, under pretence of law, be met by official insubordination. It is to be feared that these military officers, looking to the authority given by these laws, rather than to the letter of the Constitution, will recognize no authority but the commander of the district or the general of the army. While I hold the chief executive authority of the United States, while the obligation rests upon me to see that all laws are faithfully executed, I can never willingly surrender that trust or the powers given for its execution. I can never give my assent to be made responsible for the faithful execution of laws, and at the same time surrender that trust and the powers which accompany it to any other executive officer, high or low, or to any number of executive officers."

The Radicals construed these words of the President as a threat to assume sole direction over the military officers in charge of the ex-rebel States, and thus to frustrate the plans of Congress. In the debate in the House on the message there were veiled threats of impeaching him, which his supporters characterized as "mere bluster." On the same day Congress passed the bill over the veto: the House by 108 ayes to 25 nays, the Senate by 30 ayes to 6 nays.

During these sessions of Congress the work of reconstruction under military authority proceeded with expedition. Distinguished Union generals were placed at the heads of the departments with veteran troops at their command, and as a result no attempt was made to resist or nullify the provisions of the act. Qualified voters were registered with no discrimination against negroes, and elections to the constitutional conventions were held without disorder. The State conventions assembled and formed constitutions calculated to be acceptable to Congress, and the people duly ratified these. State governments were organized, legislatures were elected, and the Fourteenth Amendment was ratified in virtually the same manner and form in all the ex-rebel States.

Unconstitutionality and Impracticability of Military Reconstruction

Third Annual Message of President Johnson

In his third annual message to Congress at the beginning of the regular session on December 3, 1867, the President presented a doleful view of the condition of the country. He said that there was no Union in the sense in which the fathers used that term, for many of the States were deprived of their constitutional rights. Disregard of the Constitution if persisted in would inevitably be followed by disaster.

"We can look forward only to outrages upon individual rights, incessant breaches of the public peace, national weakness, financial dishonor, the total loss of our prosperity, the general corruption of morals, and the final extinction of popular freedom."

He reiterated that his policy of reconstruction was the only true one, and that military reconstruction was utterly unconstitutional.

The acts of Congress in question are not only objectionable for their assumption of ungranted power, but many of their provisions are in conflict with the direct prohibitions of the Constitution. The Constitution commands that a republican form of government shall be guaranteed to all the States; that no person shall be deprived of life, liberty, or property without due process of law, arrested without a judicial warrant, or punished without a fair trial before an impartial jury; that the privilege of *habeas corpus* shall not be denied in time of peace; and that no bill of attainder shall be passed even against a single individual. Yet the system of measures established by these acts of Congress does totally subvert and destroy the form as well as the substance of republican government in the ten States to which they apply. It binds them hand and foot in absolute slavery, and subjects them to a strange and hostile power, more unlimited and more likely to be abused than any other now known among civilized men. It tramples down all those rights in which the essence of liberty consists, and which a free government is always most careful to protect. It denies the *habeas corpus* and the trial by jury. Personal freedom, property, and life, if assailed by the passion, the prejudice, or the rapacity of the ruler, have no security whatever. It has the effect of a bill of attainder, or bill of pains and penalties, not upon a few individuals, but upon whole masses, including the millions who inhabit the subject States, and even their unborn children. These wrongs, being expressly forbidden, cannot be constitutionally inflicted upon any portion of our people, no matter how they may have come within our jurisdiction, and no matter whether they live in States, Territories, or districts.

I have no desire to save from the proper and just consequences of their great crime those who engaged in rebellion against the Government; but, as a mode of punishment, the measures under consideration are the most unreasonable that could be invented. Many of those people are perfectly innocent; many kept their fidelity to the Union untainted to the last; many were incapable of any legal offence; a large proportion even of the persons able to bear arms were forced into rebellion against their will; and of those who are guilty with their own consent the degrees of guilt are as various as the shades of their character and temper. But these acts of Congress confound them all together in one common doom. Indiscriminate vengeance upon classes, sects, and parties, or upon whole communities, for offences committed by a portion of them against the governments to which they owed obedience was common in the barbarous ages of the world. But Christianity and civilization have made such progress that recourse to a punishment so cruel and unjust would meet with the condemnation of all unprejudiced and right-minded men. The punitive justice of this age, and especially of this country, does not consist in stripping whole States of their liberties and reducing all their people, without distinction, to the condition of slavery. It deals separately with each individual, confines itself to the forms of law, and vindicates its own purity by an impartial examination of every case before a competent judicial tribunal. If this does not satisfy all our desires with regard to Southern rebels, let us console ourselves by reflecting that a free Constitution, triumphant in war and unbroken in peace, is worth far more to us and our children than the gratification of any present feeling.

I am aware that it is assumed that this system of government for the Southern States is not to be perpetual. It is true this military government is to be only provisional, but it is through this temporary evil that a greater evil is to be made perpetual. If the guaranties of the Constitution can be broken provisionally to serve a temporary purpose, and in a part only of the country, we can destroy them everywhere and for all time. Arbitrary measures often change, but they generally change for the worse. It is the curse of despotism that it has no halting place. The intermitted exercise of its power brings no sense of security to its subjects; for they can never know what more they will be called to endure when its red right hand is armed to plague them again. Nor it is possible to conjecture how or where power, unrestrained by law, may seek its next victims. The States that are still free may be enslaved at any moment; for, if the Constitution does not protect all, it protects none.

It is manifestly and avowedly the object of these laws to confer upon negroes the privilege of voting, and to disfranchise such a number of white citizens as will give the former a clear majority at all elections in the Southern States. This, to the minds of some persons, is so important that a violation of the Constitution is justified as a means of bringing it about. The morality is always false which excuses a wrong because it proposes to accomplish a desirable end. We are not permitted to do evil that good may come. But, in this case, the end itself is evil as well as the means. The subjugation of the States to negro domination would be worse than the military despotism under which they are now suffering. It was believed beforehand that the people would endure any amount of military oppression for any length of time rather than degrade themselves by subjection to the negro race. Therefore they have been left without a choice. Negro suffrage was established by act of Congress, and the military officers were commanded to superintend the process of clothing the negro race with the political privileges torn from white men.

The blacks in the South are entitled to be well and humanely governed, and to have the protection of just laws for all their rights of person and property. If it were practicable at this time to give them a government exclusively their own, under which they might manage their own affairs in their own way, it would become a grave question whether we ought to do so or whether common humanity would not require us to save them from themselves. But, under the circumstances, this is only a speculative point. It is not proposed merely that they shall govern themselves, but that they shall rule the white race, make and administer State laws, elect Presidents and members of Congress, and shape, to a greater or less extent, the future destiny of the whole country. Would such a trust and power be safe in such hands?

The peculiar qualities which should characterize any people who are fit to decide upon the management of public affairs for a great State have seldom been combined. It is the glory of white men to know that they have had these qualities in sufficient measure to build upon this continent a great political fabric, and to preserve its stability for more than ninety years, while in every other part of the world all similar experiments have failed. But, if anything can be proved by known facts—if all reasoning upon evidence is not abandoned, it must be acknowledged that in the progress of nations negroes have shown less capacity for government than any other race of people. No independent government of any form has ever been successful in their hands. On the contrary, wherever they have been left to their own devices they have shown a constant tendency to relapse into barbarism. In the Southern States, however, Congress has undertaken to confer upon them the privilege of the ballot. Just released from slavery, it may be doubted whether, as a class, they know more than their ancestors how to organize and regulate civil society. Indeed, it is admitted that the blacks of the South are not only regardless of the rights of property, but so utterly ignorant of public affairs that their voting can consist in nothing more than carrying a ballot to the place where they are directed to deposit it. I need not remind you that the exercise of the elective franchise is the highest attribute of an American citizen, and that, when guided by virtue, intelligence, patriotism, and a proper appreciation of our free institutions, it constitutes the true basis of a democratic form of government in which the sovereign power is lodged in the body of the people. A trust artificially created, not for its own sake, but solely as a means of promoting the general welfare, its influence for good must necessarily depend upon the elevated character and true allegiance of the elector. It ought, therefore, to be reposed in none except those who are fitted morally and mentally to administer it well; for, if conferred upon persons who do not justly estimate its value, and who are indifferent as to its results, it will only serve as a means of placing power in the hands of the unprincipled and ambitious, and must eventuate in the complete destruction of that liberty of which it should be the most powerful conservator.

The plan of putting the Southern States wholly, and the general Government partially, into the hands of negroes is proposed at a time peculiarly unpropitious. The foundations of society have been broken up by civil war. Industry must be reorganized, justice reëstablished, public credit maintained, and order brought out of confusion. To accomplish these ends would require all the wisdom and virtue of the great men who formed our institutions originally. I confidently believe that their descendants will be equal to the arduous task before them, but it is worse than madness to expect that negroes will perform it for us. Certainly we ought not to ask their assistance until we despair of our own competency.

The great difference between the two races in physical, mental, and moral characteristics will prevent an amalgamation or fusion of them together in one homogeneous mass. If the inferior obtains the ascendency over the other, it will govern with reference only to its own interests—for it will recognize no common interest—and create such a tyranny as this continent has never yet witnessed. Already the negroes are influenced by promises of confiscation and plunder. They are taught to regard as an enemy every white man who has any respect for the rights of his own race. If this continues, it must become worse and worse, until all order will be subverted, all industry cease, and the fertile fields of the South grow up into a wilderness. Of all the dangers which our nation has yet encountered none are equal to those which must result from the success of the effort now making to Africanize the half of our country.

I would not put considerations of money in competition with justice and right. But the expenses incident to ''reconstruction'' under the system adopted by Congress aggravate what I regard as the intrinsic wrong of the measure itself. It has cost uncounted millions already, and, if persisted in, will add largely to the weight of taxation, already too oppressive to be borne without just complaint, and may, finally, reduce the treasury of the nation to a condition of bankruptcy. We must not delude ourselves. It will require a strong standing army and probably more than two hundred million dollars per annum to maintain the supremacy of negro governments after they are established. It is vain to hope that negroes will maintain their ascendency themselves. Without military power they are wholly incapable of holding in subjection the white people of the South.

We cannot be too cautious of a policy which might, by possibility, impair the confidence of the world in our Government. That confidence can only be retained by carefully inculcating the principles of justice and honor on the popular mind, and by the most scrupulous fidelity to all our engagements of every sort. If we repudiate the Constitution we will not be expected to care much for mere pecuniary obligations. The violation of such a pledge as we made on the 22d day of July, 1861, to wage the war solely to preserve the Union, without impairing the rights of the States, will assuredly diminish the market value of our other promises. Besides, if we now acknowledge that the national debt was created, not to hold the States in the Union, as the taxpayers were led to suppose, but to expel them from it and hand them over to be governed by negroes, the moral duty to pay it may seem much less clear.

I therefore urge you to repeal the reconstruction laws. The great interests of the country require immediate relief from these enactments. Business in the South is paralyzed by a sense of general insecurity, by the terror of confiscation, and the dread of negro supremacy. The Southern trade, from which the North would have derived so great a profit under a government of law, still languishes and can never be revived until it ceases to be fettered by the arbitrary power which makes all its operations unsafe. That rich country—the richest in natural resources the world ever saw—is worse than lost if it be not soon placed under the protection of a free constitution. Instead of being, as it ought to be, a source of wealth and power, it will become an intolerable burden upon the rest of the nation.

On December 4, upon a formal resolution to print the President's message and the reports of the Cabinet ministers, with 3,000 additional copies for the use of the Senate, certain Radical Senators seized the occasion to denounce the message.

ON THE PRESIDENT'S MESSAGE

SENATE, DECEMBER 4, 1867

JACOB M. HOWARD [Mich.].—I cannot vote for the printing of the President's message. I do not think it is worthy of that attention, especially as to the extra number which the resolution calls for. I will not be instrumental in publishing to the world what I regard as a most singular and wanton libel on the two Houses of Congress who enacted the reconstruction laws, and a libel on the laws themselves. I look upon that document as an insidious but unmistakable invitation to the people of the rebel States to use violence in resistance of that legislation, and, of course, as such it is an act on the part of the President entirely unconstitutional and revolutionary in its character.

SIMON CAMERON [Pa.].—Mr. President, there was one part of the President's message which we heard read yesterday which I approved; it was the suggestion recommending economy in our expenses. We cannot begin at a better time than now, and, therefore, I oppose the printing of these extra numbers.

CHARLES SUMNER [Mass.].—There is really a reason, independent of economy, why we should not circulate extra copies of the President's message. It has already been characterized as a libel; unquestionably it is a libel; it is an incendiary document, calculated to stimulate the rebellion once more and to provoke civil war. It is a direct appeal to the worst passions and the worst prejudices of those rebels who, being subdued on the battlefield, still resist through the aid of the President of the United States. It is the evidence of a direct coalition between the President and the former rebels. If Jefferson Davis were President of the United States he could not send to this chamber a message different in character. I have often said that Andrew Johnson was the successor of Jefferson Davis, and this message is a complete confirmation of all that I have heretofore said. I move to strike out the words relating to the President's message.

CHARLES R. BUCKALEW [Pa.].—As to the amendment which the Senator from Massachusetts has proposed, it would be giving undue or untimely prominence to the differences of opinion which exist concerning the message to adopt his motion. Be it remembered, sir, that this message proposes to Congress the repeal of certain laws which were enacted in the month of March and in the month of July last. The President, under his clear constitutional power to recommend to Congress such measures as he may think important to the public interest, recommends the repeal of those laws, and, as a reason for that repeal, he goes on at length to submit an argument against their constitutionality. Now, sir, all that is perfectly legitimate; and to describe that argument of his as a libel on Congress or as a libel on those laws is an abuse of terms. There is certainly no impropriety in the fact that he denounces those laws as unconstitutional when he appeals to us to repeal them, because it is in the legitimate course of the argument which arises upon his recommendation. If we disagree with him in opinion we shall meet him in debate; we shall be heard by the country, and the people to whom we are both responsible will judge between us.

HENRY WILSON [Mass.].—Mr. President, nothing, I am sure, is to be gained by refusing to print the President's message according to the usual custom of the Senate. I go quite as far as any one in condemnation of the tone, temper, and doctrines of the message, but I think we are not justified in departing from the ordinary practice of this body. The message is an assault of the President of the United States upon the Congress of the United States for attempting by legislation to take the governments of the rebel States out of the control of traitors into whose keeping he had placed these governments. The writer of this message seems to have forgotten that we ever had any rebellion at all. The message remembers to forget that President Johnson, in the summer and autumn of 1865, assumed and exercised constitutional powers for the exercise of which he now condemns the legislative branch of the Government. If the President's reconstruction policy was within the provisions of the Constitution surely the reconstruction policy of Congress is within the provisions of the Constitution. If the President without the authority of law could fix the terms and conditions for the reconstruction of the rebel States surely Congress, the lawmaking power of the Government, could determine the terms and conditions of reconstruction.

From those once conquered States, restored by Andrew Johnson to the control of rebels, there came to us a cry of agony, a voice of supplication, demanding the interposition of Congress and the protection of the national Government. Congress heard that cry; the country heard it; the world heard it; the God of the Universe heard it; but President Johnson could not hear it. Congress, after giving the President's policy a trial of nearly two years, adopted the policy of reconstruction against which the President now hurls his denunciations. This reconstruction policy of Congress immediately carried peace and comparative law and order into and through the rebellious States. The President's policy has failed, has been abandoned, and will not be revived. The policy of Congress is progressing, will be inflexibly adhered to, and will be consummated.

The statement of the President in this message that the black men of the South, enfranchised by Congress, knew only enough to deposit their votes where they were told to deposit them is a libel upon the seven hundred thousand black men whose hands have been weaponed with the ballot. Sir, how stands the great fact? These enfranchised black men without property, without homes, surrounded by the great landholders, the cultivated, the intellectual men, sometimes called the "natural leaders" of the South—men who had held them and their ancestors in bondage, who owned their humble cabins, the ground they trod upon, in whose employment they are, were in positions to be swayed and controlled by love, authority, interest, and fear. When Congress passed the reconstruction acts the rebel presses and leaders appealed with the utmost confidence to these enfranchised black men. We were told quite as confidently as we were told in other days that the black men would not fight against their old masters, that the black men of the South would vote as they were directed by their old masters. The rebel leaders, the great landholders, the old slave-masters, uttered honeyed words and brought to bear every seductive influence they were masters of to win a controlling influence over the enfranchised black men. Even Wade Hampton, the representative of the white aristocracy of South Carolina, led off with Beverly Nash, the black man. He graciously admitted that the colored people ought to have the right of suffrage, and he appealed to them to unite with him and the men of his class. Others joined in these appeals; the black men were told on the stump in public speeches by these men, the great landholders and late slave-masters, that they had played together in childhood, that they had fished and hunted together, and they were invoked to give their votes to the conservatives; yet all those influences utterly failed. When flattery, persuasion, and cajolery failed they were threatened. They were told that there might be a war of races, that they might be turned out of employment, their families driven from their cabins. Thousands of these poor men without property have been turned from their homes, dismissed from employment for the votes they gave, and yet that body of enfranchised men, in spite of every oppression brought to bear upon them, have voted as patriotism, liberty, justice, and humanity dictated. These black men into whose hands Congress has put the ballot, never to be wrenched from them by President or rebel, with the loyal white men and the few repentant rebels, will bring the rebel States back into these chambers and thus rebuke this assault of the President of the United States upon Congress for attempting to save that section of the country from rebel domination.

JAMES DIXON [Ct.].—The Senator from Massachusetts [Mr. Sumner] says the President is the successor of Jefferson Davis and equally guilty, and still he complains that the President has been guilty of a libel. It struck me at the time that if there was any competition of vehement language between the President and that Senator it would be very easy to decide who, in vituperation had the advantage.

Now, sir, what is this message? Is it a libel? Is it violent in language? Does it show, as the Senator from Massachusetts says, bad temper? In the first place, what is the duty of the President? The Constitution says that he shall from time to time give to the Congress information of the state of the Union, and recommend to their consideration such measures as he shall judge necessary and expedient. He has now done so. I confess that I can see nothing of violence or ill temper, much less of a libelous character, in this message. He expresses strong opinions —with regard to what? With regard to the constitutionality of certain laws now on the statute-book.

The statute-book is full of laws of questionable constitutionality in the opinion of some men; and certainly if a law is supposed to be unconstitutional no better reason can be given for its repeal; nor is it any reflection upon Congress to say that a bill is unconstitutional. The President says that he has the misfortune to differ from Congress. That, too, has been my severe misfortune; I have been compelled to differ from Congress. I objected to the passage of this very bill on the ground that it was so palpably unconstitutional that for me to vote for it would be a violation, a conscious, known violation of my official oath. Did anybody say that was criminal? Have we come to that that the opinions of a Senator or a President with regard to the unconstitutionality of a measure cannot be expressed in earnest language?

If the President is too sanguine, if he believes too readily that Congress will bow to the will of the nation as expressed at the ballot-box, certainly it is not matter of condemnation and is not disrespectful. I confess I have no hopes, for one, that Congress will retrace its steps; but, if the President sees fit to express a hope to the contrary, I am not prepared to condemn him, nor am I prepared to say that in that there is anything disrespectful to Congress.

Will Senators say that the President's remark that reconstruction was done "with a view to the ultimate establishment of negro supremacy" is disrespectful to Congress? Has not the Senator from Massachusetts [Mr. Wilson] to-day declared in express language that "we put the destinies of that portion of the country in the hands of the blacks"?

SENATOR WILSON.—The Senator will certainly find that I included in my remark the loyal white men of that part of the country, and I spoke also of repentant rebels, because many of the rebels are working and toiling for the reconstruction policy of Congress as hard as any other class of men. Some of them who were in the military service and attained the position of major-general in the rebel army have used all their influence this year to carry out our policy, and, in some of the States, men who have been leaders, who have been compromised by the rebellion, and cannot vote or hold office, have done this.

SENATOR DIXON.—Well, sir, with regard to that question, whether those States are under the control of the black population, it is unnecessary to make any remark. It is a notorious, acknowledged fact. How is it that seven hundred thousand black men govern the South; how is it that they govern the white population, ten millions in number, of that country, unless your law has provided that they, and they alone, shall control the ballot-box?

Is it a crime for the President of the United States to say that he is a defender of the Constitution? Certainly I have thought sometimes that it was a crime in the minds of some men, that it was not only proof of guilt but guilt itself to advocate the Constitution and to defend it.

SENATOR HOWARD.—I think the expression as used by the President in his message is arrogant and unauthorized; that it is not constitutional language. He is no more the defender of the Constitution than I am here in my place. He is invested with more powers, to be sure, but his obligation is precisely the same, and I think, therefore, it is in very bad taste for the President of the United States to assume that he is "the elected defender" *par excellence* of the Constitution. It is an assumption on his part by which he seeks to place himself above the law-making power and to become its dictator.

SENATOR DIXON.—The Senator says it is "arrogant," "presumption," "in bad taste" on the part of the President of the United States to call himself the defender of the Constitution: that it is unconstitutional language. Let us see the oath which he is required by the Constitution to take:

"I do solemnly swear (or affirm) that I will faithfully execute the office of President of the United States, and will, to the best of my ability, preserve, protect, and *defend* the Constitution of the United States."

It is a very different form of oath from that which the Senator himself takes. The Constitution requires a Senator only to swear to support the Constitution. Why was the oath in the two cases expressed in different language? If the President of the United States sees fit to declare himself, after having sworn to defend the Constitution, its "elected defender," I can see nothing in that disrespectful to Congress, nor can I see anything arrogant in it.

He says that "if the legislative department should pass an act" to abolish a coördinate department of the Government, "the President must take the high responsibilities of his office, and save the life of the nation at all hazards."

Does any Senator doubt that? Are there not cases when the President of the United States is bound to assume high responsibilities to save this nation? If anything which President Lincoln ever did endeared him to the hearts of the American people it was his taking the responsibility in April, 1861, of defending the Constitution of the United States against rebels who attacked it, although he was not then sustained and supported by the proper laws. We actually made the laws afterward. We legalized his acts, although at that time technically illegal, and we sustained and justified him. Now, I think nobody will deny that if it were possible to suppose that Congress could under any circumstances be guilty of passing an act to abolish the office of President of the United States, one of the coördinate departments of this Government—a thing which I do not suppose possible, and which the President of the United States only hypothetically states in his message—it would be the duty of the President to resist it.

Sir, I have said this much because the President has been charged with ill temper, with disrespect, and with arrogance in this message. I think he is not liable to that charge. I think the message is respectful in its form and correct in its reasoning, as it is acknowledged to be of unsurpassed ability. I know that the President expresses himself warmly. He is a man of earnest convictions, and believing what he says to be true he declares it in earnest and expressive language; and no doubt he is somewhat strengthened—and it is natural that it should be so—by the fact that the people of the United States in their recent elections have stamped on this reconstruction policy their condemnation in the clearest and most explicit manner.

I am aware that Senators may consider it their duty to persevere in what they regard to be right without reference to what may seem to be popular or unpopular. I have done that myself; I may do it again. But this I say: that when the question is asked, what is the opinion of the American people? no man who looks at the recent elections can doubt that it is against the policy of Congress.

And the unanimous voice of the country is that this message and the entire series of messages which have come from President Johnson since he has been in office have never been surpassed in ability by the State papers of any administration since

the adoption of the Constitution. Such papers can never be
suppressed or concealed by refusal of the Senate to print them.

On December 5 the resolution to print the extra
copies of the President's message was adopted by a vote
of 36 to 9.

ACTS OF CONGRESS

During this session Congress passed two acts making
appropriations for reconstruction: the first received by
the President on January 31, 1868, and, not being returned by him, becoming a law ten days thereafter, excluding Sundays; the second received by him on May 19
and treated in similar fashion.

Acts were passed admitting Arkansas, North Carolina, South Carolina, Louisiana, Georgia, Alabama, and
Florida to representation in Congress; they were vetoed
by the President and passed over his veto June 20-25.
These acts required that negro suffrage, with which these
States were admitted, should never be repealed. Georgia
was compelled to repeal an act of her legislature which
virtually outlawed debts of her citizens to creditors outside of the State. The Senators and Representatives admitted from these States were Republicans. About half
were natives of the South, and half were "carpet-
baggers"—Northern adventurers, who had packed their
grips and gone South to take advantage of the anomalous
political situation there.

In the Presidential contest of 1868 General Ulysses
S. Grant [Ill.] and Schuyler Colfax [Ind.], the Speaker
of the House, were nominated by the Republicans as candidates respectively for President and Vice-President,
and ex-Governor Horatio Seymour [N. Y.] and General
Francis P. Blair [Mo.] were nominated by the Democrats, the latter gaining the nomination by a letter read
at the convention declaring himself in favor of complete
overthrow of congressional reconstruction.

In the Democratic platform the reconstruction acts
of Congress were declared to be "usurpations, unconstitutional, revolutionary and void." General Wade
Hampton [S. C.], a member of the Committee on Resolu-

THE GREAT AMERICAN TANNER

From the collection of the New York Historical Society

tions, subsequently stated that he was the framer of this sweeping declaration. In the Democratic convention and overflow meetings denunciations of military reconstruction were indulged in by Mr. Seymour, August Belmont [N. Y.], and General Thomas Ewing [Kan.].

Mr. Belmont characterized the rule of Congress over the South as a "ruthless tyranny" such as even Russia did not dare inflict on conquered Poland. And this was but the beginning of a military despotism which would extend over the Union if it should be permitted Congress to seat as President the one who now was commanding general of the armies of the United States. Then congressional usurpation of all the branches of government would be enforced by the bayonet.

MILITARY RECONSTRUCTION DEFEATS THE PURPOSE OF THE WAR

GENERAL EWING

General Ewing reviewed the history of reconstruction. He praised the spirit with which the South had accepted the results of the war, amending their State constitutions so as to abolish slavery and the harsh codes founded upon it; abandoning the doctrine of secession, and repudiating the rebel debt.

The Republican party was bound in honor to accept this submission by admitting the Southern States to representation in Congress, since it had declared during the rebellion that the war was waged solely to effect the unconditional restoration of the Union upon the submission of the rebels. And the people suppressed the rebellion on this understanding.

But the Republican party, upon the submission of the South, repudiated this pledge, not desiring to increase the power of the Democratic party.

Yet, with the prestige and moral power resulting from a successful prosecution of the war, and a prompt and cordial restoration of the Union, it could have retained power until this generation of voters had passed away or had forgotten the anti-

war follies of the Democratic party. But it took counsel of its
fears, doubted its own destiny, forgot the inextinguishable love
in the hearts of the Northern people for the Constitution and
the Union, and therefore refused to take what the war was
alone waged to get—a prompt and cordial pacification and re-
union under the Constitution. It did this in the vain hope of
controlling the Southern States by making voters of the negroes, and proscribing all the intelligent white men whom Congress and the Freedmen's Bureau could not bribe, or coax, or
kick, or cuff into republicanism. But, while destroying the ten
Southern States, and building in their stead ten rotten boroughs,
to be represented in Congress in the interests of the Northern
radicals by white adventurers and plantation negroes, the party
is losing its strong hold on the *Northern* States, and, like the
dog in the fable, drops the substance to snatch at the shadow.
[Laughter and applause.]

Having adopted the rebel theory that the Southern States
were out of the Union, and unsheltered by the broad ægis of
the Constitution, Congress declared invalid the governments
chosen by the electors of those States under the advice of Presidents Lincoln and Johnson, in conformity with State constitutions and laws, and established over them military dictator-
ships, through which to inaugurate the rule of the negroes and
their Northern allies. But here a new rent in their program was discovered, requiring to be patched by a newly invented dogma. The Calhoun-Stevens theory of the validity of
secession was good as far as it stretched; but, like a shelter tent,
was neither broad nor long enough. It took the States out, and
made them conquered provinces, but did not increase the power
of Congress, nor deprive the inhabitants of the conquered territory of those guaranties of life, liberty, and property which
the Constitution extends *to citizens and aliens alike* on every
foot of ground within the jurisdiction of the United States.
While these guaranties remained in the Constitution, and were
obeyed, the whole governing talent of the South could not be
disfranchised by a sweeping *ex post facto* law.

It was indispensable, therefore to get rid of these constitutional provisions, which are at once guaranties of the liberties
of the people and prohibitions of power to Congress. To avoid
an avowal of a purpose to trample on the Constitution, the
party, with decent hypocrisy, claimed a new derivation of congressional power. They said that a formidable rebellion was
never contemplated by the framers of the Constitution, and no
powers were conferred in anticipation of such an emergency.

Congress, therefore, was compelled, in the matter of reconstruction, to act *outside of the Constitution*.

As to Congress deriving power in any contingency outside of the Constitution, it is enough to say that Congress gets all its powers from the Constitution, and outside of it has no powers, and *is no Congress* [applause] : and that all its acts not authorized by the Constitution are mere usurpations, whether against express prohibitions or not. If you present this argument to Radicals, they will reply that the Constitution in not giving Congress such authority is therein defective, and Congress needs, and must exercise it. A French philosopher once propounded to Professor Faraday a new theory of the transmission of light, which the English philosopher heard patiently and then objected to it that the theory was inconsistent with certain established facts of natural science. ''So much ze worse for ze *facts*,'' was the ready answer of the confident Frenchman. So, if you prove the reconstruction plan unconstitutional, the Radicals, in effect, answer, ''So much the worse for the *Constitution*.'' [Great applause.]

Thus, to secure a reconstruction giving the Radicals of the North absolute control of the ten States of the South, not only were the State governments abolished and military despotisms built on their ruins, but every revered guaranty of life, liberty, and property, which the Southern people and ourselves inherited from a free ancestry, and which our forefathers and their forefathers placed in the Constitution to be beyond the reach of the rude hand of faction, was boldly destroyed. No civilized people on this earth are as wholly without legal protection from the capricious oppression of their rulers as the Southern people under these military despotisms. It is amazing how passively the people, North and South, have borne this gross, dangerous, insolent usurpation. But it has been quietly submitted to because of the belief—now, thank God! almost certainty—that the Northern people will, in November, seize this Radical party and its half-executed usurpations, and dash them to pieces [prolonged cheering] ; and because many of the military commanders have tempered the harsh rule they were sent to inflict out of that love for our ancient liberties which is born in every true American, and which so shone through the administration of at least one of those commanders as to cover with new and fadeless glory the twice-illustrious name of Winfield S. Hancock. [Tumultuous cheering and waving of hats.]

What a spectacle for gods and men does this reconstruction present! See the black laborers of the South, fed in idleness

out of moneys wrung from the toil of Northern white men
[applause], filled with ambition to rule the whites, and to grow
rich by confiscations, and becoming each year more utterly and
irreclaimably idle and thriftless.   The splendid sugar, cotton,
and rice plantations, at once the evidence and the product of a
century of civilization, overgrown with weeds; idle machinery
rusting in the sugar houses; the floods of the Mississippi sweeping over neglected levees and abandoned plantations, and the
boorish negro field hands sitting in conventions! Behold Virginia, the Niobe of States, the mother of Presidents and illustrious statesmen—her at whose call our great free Republic was
formed—her by whose free gift the Republic acquired the territory of the six great States of the Northwest! See the civil
government founded by her Washington [applause], Madison
[applause], Jefferson [applause], Lee [applause], the foremost
statesmen of their day on the earth, destroyed, supplanted by
a military despotism, and that, in turn, about to be supplanted
by a civil government framed by infamous whites like Hunni-
cutt, and a rabble of half-civilized negroes [hisses]. If this be
prosperity, progress, and liberty, God send us misfortune, reaction, and despotism forever! [Prolonged applause.]

The Radicals endeavor to smooth the hideous visage of this
reconstruction by asserting that it is indispensable to prevent
the Democracy getting power and repudiating the national debt.
In other words, to prevent repudiation, some device must be
arranged by which a majority of the legal electors of ten
States shall not be permitted to rule them. If that necessity
really exists, the dire event cannot be long postponed by devising in the interest of the national creditors a scheme of reconstruction which violates the Constitution and the fundamental theory of our Government; breaks pledges of infinitely
more sacred obligation than the money debt; cripples every industry of the land, and while reducing one-half every man's
ability to pay taxes doubles his share of the public burden—the
essential condition of which scheme is the perpetuation of
the rule of a party which now represents not one-third of the
white people of the nation. But, thank God, that necessity does
not exist! The credit of the Republic, as the union of the
States, rests secure *in the hearts of the people.* [Applause.]
A vast majority of all parties will preserve and defend it, as
they did the Union. But, if the national credit could be shaken,
it would be by the public creditors flocking into one party, and,
under the panoply of the national honor, scheming to perpetuate the power of that party at the cost of the established con-

stitutions and liberties of the States and the nation. [Great applause—cries of "That's so."]

To accomplish this scheme of reconstruction, the Constitution is not only abrogated so far as the Southern States are concerned, but the form of our Government is being destroyed by the absorption by Congress of the chief powers of the national Executive:

Congress has assumed to take from the President the control of the army which the Constitution gives him, and to commit that part of it employed in the South to General Grant and five district commanders [hisses], independent of the orders of the President. By this bold assumption of power, it has converted many high officers of the regular army to radicalism, and made them zealous instruments of its usurpations.

It has usurped the pardoning power, which the Constitution gives solely to the President, and, by sweeping bills of pains and penalties, proscribed the intelligent white men of the South, notwithstanding the pardons of the President. And it now shamelessly avows that it will give *congressional pardon* only to those who eat the leek of radicalism. [Hisses.] All such are *loyal*, though, like Governor Brown, of Georgia, they drove and dragged their people into rebellion, and, coward-like, seized our arsenals and navy yards while yet wearing the mask of loyalty; while men like George W. Jones, of Tennessee, who stood by the Union from the first, but who opposed negro suffrage and white disfranchisement, are stigmatized as *"heart malignants,"* deserving only proscription at the hands of the Sumners, and Kelleys, and Butlers of Congress. [Great hisses. Cries, "Who stole the spoons?" etc.]

> "Those pseudo privy-councilors of God,
> Who write down judgments with a pen hard-nibbed."

The Republican party represents no principle for which we fought. We thought not of negro suffrage [applause and cries of "No, no"], or of white disfranchisement; of forcing on the Southern States unequal fellowship in the Union ["Never, never"], of changing our beneficent form of government. ["No, never"], or of perpetuating the Republican party ["Never, never"]. Out of the five hundred thousand of Union soldiers, Democrats and Republicans, who sleep on fields washed by the waters of the Atlantic and the Gulf, not one laid down his life for any such end. Of the fifteen hundred thousand of their surviving comrades, not one will say he would have risked his life for either of these objects. And these measures of the Republican party are not only not the objects of the war, but are so prosecuted as to defeat those objects, and to inflict on the nation evils as great as those the war was waged to prevent. [Shouts, "That's so."]

The Democratic party is now the only party true to the Constitution and the Union. [Applause.] If we would accomplish the purposes of our service and sacrifice, if we would save the Union, the States, their liberties, and laws, we must unite with the Democracy. [Long continued applause.] We must not ask what men *have been*, but what they *are;* not who *lately* defended the Constitution, but who *now* defend it. [Great applause.] In the path which the Democratic party treads we see the footprints of Washington, Jefferson, Madison, Adams, and all the heroes of the Revolution; of Webster, Jackson, Clay, Wright, and all the giants of the generation just gone before us; and while it keeps that line of march, and bears the flag of the Constitution and the Union, we can follow it with pride and with unfaltering trust. [Immense applause, cheers, and waving of hats, followed by the band playing "Rally Round the Flag."]

In the beginning of the ensuing campaign General Blair took the lead of his party, forcing reconstruction to the front as the chief issue. But as the campaign wore on the October State elections showed by Republican victories that on this question the Democracy was doomed to defeat, and Blair was withdrawn from the stump and Governor Seymour put forward to win the battle, if it were possible. During October he made a speaking tour of New York, Pennsylvania, and the Central States, dwelling on economic subjects rather than constitutional ones. The change of program, however, was unavailing. General Grant was chosen President by 214 electoral votes to Governor Seymour's 80. Nevertheless the Republican popular majority was only 309,584, and, had Virginia, Mississippi, and Texas, which were still unreconstructed, voted, this would have been further reduced, the "black Republican" (a phrase which had now become literally true) majority of Mississippi being overbalanced by the white Democratic majorities of the two other States.

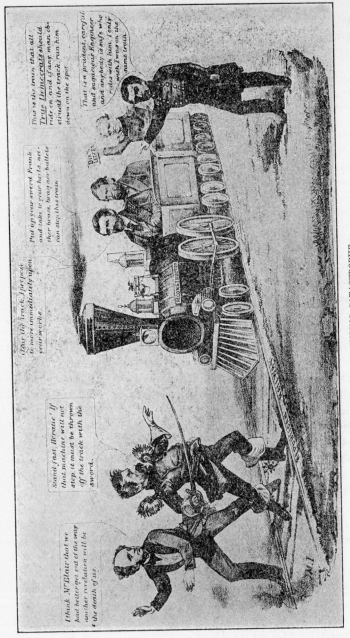

AN IMPENDING CATASTROPHE

From the collection of the New York Historical Society

94

The Republicans carried six of the eight reconstructed States (all but Georgia and Louisiana), owing to the negro vote, to which a considerable white vote was added in Tennessee and North Carolina, the mountains of which had been loyalist strongholds during the war. It was charged in Congress that negroes had been kept from the polls in Louisiana by violence and intimidation, and that there had been gross frauds in counting the vote. The fact that the Republicans had carried the spring election in the State by 12,000 majority, and that the Democratic majority was now reported as 47,000 gave color to these charges. There being no legal evidence before Congress as to the frauds, however, the returns from the State were accepted on their face. Various investigations of the charges were made later by Congress, one committee reporting that over 2,000 persons had been killed or wounded within the few weeks prior to the election; that the State had been overrun by midnight raids and open riots, Ku-Klux Klans hounding the Republicans through the swamps, and intimidating them by scattering through the city of New Orleans warnings not to vote. The committee reported that in one parish, where but a single vote for General Grant was recorded, the white Republican leaders had been either killed or driven away, and the negroes had been herded to the polls and compelled to vote the Democratic ticket, and that in another parish the entire registered vote (4,787) had been cast for the Democratic ticket, although in the spring election the Republicans had won by 678 majority.

CHAPTER III

The Fifteenth Amendment

[EQUAL MANHOOD SUFFRAGE]

Resolution of John B. Henderson [Mo.] Made the Basis of the Senate's Proposal of the Constitutional Amendment Establishing Equal Manhood Suffrage—Debate: William M. Stewart [Nev.], Garrett Davis [Ky.], Henry Wilson [Mass.], Thomas A. Hendricks [Ind.], James Dixon [Conn.], Samuel C. Pomeroy [Kan.]; Debate Postponed—George S. Boutwell [Mass.] Proposes a Similar Resolution in the House—Debate: Mr. Boutwell, William E. Niblack [Ind.], Charles A. Eldridge [Wis.], James Brooks [N. Y.], Samuel Shellabarger [O.]; Resolution Passed; Senate Substitutes It for Its Own Resolution—Debate: Orris S. Ferry [Conn.], Willard Warner [Ala.], George H. Williams [Ore.], Charles Sumner [Mass.], George Vickers [Md.], Waitman T. Willey [W. Va.], Henry W. Corbett [Ore.], James A. Bayard, Jr. [Del.], Frederick T. Frelinghuysen [N. J.], Edmund G. Ross [Kan.], Sen. Davis, Joseph S. Fowler [Tenn.], Willard Saulsbury [Del.], Adonijah S. Welch [Fla.], Sen. Hendricks, Oliver P. Morton [Ind.], James R. Doolittle [Wis.], Charles D. Drake [Mo.], Frederick A. Sawyer [S. C.], Sen. Wilson, Simon Cameron [Pa.], Lyman Trumbull [Ill.], James W. Patterson [N. H.], Roscoe Conkling [N. Y.], John Sherman [O.], Charles R. Buckalew [Pa.]; Resolution Amended and Passed; Joint Conference Committee Reports Resolution Without the Amendments, Which Is Passed by Both Chambers; Fifteenth Amendment Ratified by the States.

THE Fortieth Congress met for its third session on December 7, 1868. On that day Aaron H. Cragin [N. H.] introduced in the Senate a joint resolution to submit to the State legislatures what was in effect the present Fifteenth Amendment to the Constitution granting negro suffrage throughout the Union. Samuel C. Pomeroy [Kan.] also introduced what was virtually the same joint resolution. On the same day William D. Kelley [Pa.], John M. Broomall [Pa.], and William B. Stokes [Tenn.] introduced similar resolutions in the House of Representatives, which were referred to the Committee on Judiciary.

On the 9th both Chambers listened to the reading of the fourth annual message of President Johnson. In this the President reiterated his fixed opposition to military reconstruction and deplored its evil results in non-representation of States in Congress, and in "negro domination" in the South.

Late in the preceding session John B. Henderson [Mo.] had submitted what was virtually the present Fifteenth Amendment, forbidding any State to deny or abridge the rights of its citizens to vote or hold office on account of race, color, or previous condition of servitude.

Congress was not then ready to pass so sweeping a measure, affecting as it did the Northern States, in most of which the negro was disfranchised. Neither was the Republican party prepared to accept this policy in the ensuing presidential campaign. But the decisive victory of that campaign emboldened it to take the advanced position toward which the logic of emancipation and equal civil rights was indeed driving it. As we have noted, constitutional amendments embodying this principle were submitted in the Senate on the first day that it convened after the election. Being referred to the Judiciary Committee, they were laid aside, and the bill of Mr. Henderson was made the basis of the committee's bill. This was reported by William M. Stewart [Nev.], chairman, on January 18, 1869, in the form of a joint resolution submitting the following constitutional amendment to the State legislatures for ratification.

"The right of citizens of the United States to vote and hold office shall not be denied or abridged by the United States or any State on account of race, color, or previous condition of servitude."

The Amendment came up for discussion on January 28, 1869.

VIII—7

The Fifteenth Amendment

Senate, January 28-29, 1869

Senator Stewart.—This great question is the culmination of a contest which has lasted for thirty years. It is the logical result' of the rebellion, of the abolition of slavery, and of the conflicts in this country during and before the war. Every person in the country has discussed it; it has been discussed in every local paper, by every local speaker; it has been discussed at the firesides; and now we are to place the grand result, I hope, in the Constitution of the United States. And let me remind my fellow-Senators that it is well that this work be now done, for we have realized the force of the very pointed sentence which was read here from the Swiss address,[1] that "undetermined questions have no pity for the repose of mankind." This question can never rest until it is finally disposed of. This amendment is a declaration to make all men, without regard to race or color, equal before the law. The arguments in favor of it are so numerous, so convincing, that they carry conviction to every mind. The proposition itself has been recognized by the good men of this nation; and it is important, as the new Administration enters upon the charge of the affairs of this country, that it should start on this high and noble principle that all men are free and equal, that they are really equal before the law. We cannot stop short of this.

It must be done. It is the only measure that will really abolish slavery. It is the only guaranty against peon laws and against oppression. It is that guaranty which was put in the Constitution of the United States originally, the guaranty that each man shall have a right to protect his own liberty. It repudiates that arrogant, self-righteous assumption, that one man can be charged with the liberties and destinies of another. You may put this in the form of legislative enactment; you may empower Congress to legislate; you may empower the States to legislate, and they will agitate the question. Let it be made the immutable law of the land; let it be fixed; and then we shall have peace. Until then there is no peace. I want a vote. I will not occupy time. The proposition itself is more eloquent than man can be. It is a declaration too high, too grand, too noble, too just, to be ornamented by oratory.

[1] To Congress on the subject.

Garrett Davis moved to amend the joint resolution by having it and all future propositions of constitutional amendments submitted to the vote of the people of the States instead of to the State legislatures. The people, he said, had no idea that such an important proposition as this would come before the legislators when they had elected them. Consequently the legislators might not be truly representative of their constituencies. To the objection that this method of submission was not constitutional, he replied: "Then make it constitutional." The Republican party, he said, ought to live up to its professions of belief in popular government. "Are you afraid to trust your people? What does Republican mean? He who represents the will of his constituency." But he knew that the Republican politicians feared to submit this amendment to the people lest it be rejected. The State legislatures they could control. The evident purpose of the bill was to keep the Republican party in power.

Henry Wilson [Mass.] replied to Senator Davis.

For the sake of justice the Republican party had dared to endanger its political power, instead of seeking to maintain it. The struggle to give the negro his rights had cost the party a million and a quarter votes, so unpopular was, and still continues, the policy.

But no matter how unpopular the doctrine is, no matter what it costs, no matter whether it brings victory or defeat, our duty is to hope on and struggle on and work on until we make the humblest citizen of the United States the peer and the equal in rights and privileges of every other citizen of the United States. Sir, I do not intend to cease my efforts until that end is fully accomplished. Let us give to all citizens equal rights, and then protect everybody in the United States in the exercise of those rights. When we attain that position we shall have carried out logically the ideas that lie at the foundation of our institutions; we shall be in harmony with our professions; we shall have acted like a truly republican and Christian people. Until we do that we are in a false position, an illogical position —a position that cannot be defended; a position that I believe is dishonorable to the nation with the lights we have before us. Through all the contests of the past thirty-five years I have looked to the final consummation of the perfect equality of citizens of the United States in rights and privileges and the complete protection of all citizens in their rights and privileges. Peace can come in all its power and beauty only by the complete triumph of equality and justice.

This constitutional amendment, which, if it be submitted to the people and sustained by the States, is to crown the great work, to make every citizen equal in rights and privileges, will cost us the opposition of some of our political associates. But with an Administration coming into power pledged to liberty and equality of rights and privileges, pledged to peace, I believe before the four years pass away we shall become accustomed in all parts of the country to see all classes of our citizens peacefully exercising their rights. When the work is achieved all sections of the country will thank God that it is accomplished, and the people will wonder why it was that they ever made any opposition to its accomplishment.

THOMAS A. HENDRICKS [Ind.].—I call your attention to the election of last fall, honorable Senators, and I ask you now to stand upon the pledge of honor that your party made to the people in the election last fall.

The position of the Democratic party last summer, I presume, is not a question of doubt or of uncertainty. That the Democratic party, in casting its vote for Seymour and Blair, did not vote for negro suffrage is plain enough. That the Republican party last fall in voting for Grant and Colfax cast a vote against universal suffrage is as plain. You took the question away from the people. You said that they should not consider it last summer; and now I understand it to be proposed to submit it to legislatures that are not again responsible to the people, but that were elected before this question is submitted. The second section of the Chicago platform, not yet a year old, declared the doctrine of the Republican party, and I simply ask honorable Senators now to make the pledged and plighted faith of their party to the country good and true, and not in the face of the nation and of humanity to give it the lie. You say:

Not yet a year old is this political faith, declared by the grand council of your party, upon which Grant and Colfax stood before the people; and now you propose, without giving the people a voice or a hearing upon the question, to say that the right to control suffrage in the Northern States does not belong to the people of those States.

"While the question of suffrage in all the loyal States properly belongs to the people of those States."

Circumstances may change in a country so as that the policy of a party must change somewhat. I have heard much said about "the logic of events." I have heard inconsistencies in political action and conduct and faith apologized for upon the general proposition of "the logic of events." But since the 20th day of May last up to the present hour what events have occurred that change this question? The negroes were free then —as free as now; your understanding of the subject was as ample then as now; and you said that in Indiana the right to control suffrage properly of right belonged to the people of that State. Now you propose to take it away from them, and, whatever may be the voice of Indiana, if you can get the concurrence of three-fourths of the State legislatures you propose to say to the people of Indiana, "It is not properly your right to control suffrage; it does not belong to you; our Chicago platform was false upon that subject." Men may be untrue to their political faith elsewhere, where offices are to be obtained, where political power is to be held; but in the Senate of the United States may I not appeal to the representatives of great States to stand by pledged and plighted faith?

My appeal, then, is, that Senators will so amend this proposition as that it shall go to the people. Then, when they decide it, let it stand.

SENATOR STEWART.—The Constitution does not point out any mode of taking the popular vote. In neither of the modes prescribed by the Constitution do the people act directly. There is no way of amending the Constitution so as to let the people act directly on the amendment. As the Constitution is now, you can submit the question to the legislature or to a convention in the State—to no other body.

Sir, it is very strange that whenever the Constitution of the United States can be construed to deny rights it is sacred with some; but whenever it can be used to secure right and liberty we are complained of for following the Constitution. Does the Senator from Indiana suppose that the Republican party intended in the Chicago convention to change the Constitution or to limit the power of Congress to submit propositions to the several States under the Constitution? No such construction is fair; no such construction can be maintained. The people understood perfectly well that Congress had power to submit amendments to the Constitution and ask for the action of the several States. They did regard that as a pledge against legislation; and that is the embarrassment in the way of legislation; but they did not regard it as a pledge against submitting propositions to amend the Constitution in the ordinary way.

Discussion was resumed on January 29. James Dixon [Conn.] spoke.

It is not, perhaps, too much to say that this is the most important question in many of its bearings which has ever been presented to Congress in the shape of a proposed constitutional amendment.

What is the question? It is not merely a question of suffrage. That of itself is a subject of vast importance, and is now agitating the public mind of this country to a very great extent. The question whether the female sex should be permitted to participate in the privilege of suffrage, whether other restrictions should be removed, the question of age, the question of property, a multitude of questions are, or may be, raised which are vastly important and interesting in connection with the right of suffrage. But, sir, we are not now dealing merely with the qualification of voters. The question is not what shall be the qualifications of the voter, but who shall create, establish, and prescribe those qualifications; not who shall be the voter, but who shall make the voter.

In considering that question we ought to remember that it is utterly impossible that any State should be an independent republic which does not entirely control its own laws with regard to the right of suffrage. Nor does it make the slightest difference with regard to this that any abdication or abnegation of its power is voluntary. It may be said that it is proposed that the States shall voluntarily relinquish their power to control the subject of suffrage within their respective limits. Sir, suppose a State should voluntarily assume upon itself a foreign yoke, or declare by a majority of its own people, or even by a unanimous vote, that it would prefer a monarchy, would the fact of its being voluntary at all affect the question whether it was still an independent republic?

Now, sir, it may be that the people of this country in their present condition of mind are ready to relinquish the power in the States of regulating their own laws with regard to suffrage; and if it should so prove, and the result should show that your own State (Ohio) and my State (Connecticut), having once or twice voted against extending the right of suffrage to the negro race, should now consent that a contral power should regulate that question, and should do this voluntarily and freely, nevertheless they would by that action lose their character as republican governments. And, sir, that is the reason why it was that in the formation of the Constitution of the United States there was an entire neglect to interfere in the slightest degree with the question of suffrage in the several States. Look through the Constitution as it was formed, and you find no allusion whatever to the question of suffrage, except by reference to existing laws and qualifications in the then existing States. And why was that? We are not left in the dark upon that question. Was it because suffrage was not considered an important question? In No. 59 of "The Federalist," written by Alexander Hamilton, I find the following words:

"Suppose an article had been introduced into the Constitution empowering the United States to regulate the elections for the particular States, would any man have hesitated to condemn it both as an unwarrantable transposition of power, and as a premeditated engine for the destruction of the State governments?"

That was the objection taken by Alexander Hamilton to the interference of the general Government in State elections except so far as was necessary to protect the very existence of the National Government, which required that the National Government should have power to interfere in the choice of Representatives and Senators as to the time, place, and manner of choosing them, leaving the question of the qualifications of the electors wholly to the States. He says:

"The violation of principle in this case required no comment."

What was the principle that would have been violated? It was the principle that an independent republic must necessarily control the question of suffrage in its own elections. This lies at the very foundation of all government, and it is therefore wholly impossible for any state to be an independent republic or an independent government in which the right of suffrage is controlled by an external power, whether by the consent of that state or against its consent. For that reason when it is proposed to amend the Constitution of the United States in this respect it is very questionable whether it is not an amendment which subverts the whole foundation and principle of the Government. Suppose it were proposed to strike out the clause of the Constitution guaranteeing a republican form of government to each State, and instead of that to insert a guaranty of a monarchy to each State. If a proposition of that kind were made it might be objected "this goes to the foundation of your Government;

this is not amendment; it is revolution, it is subversion." Can
that not be said in this instance? Is the proposed amendment
any more a fair carrying out of the intendment of the Constitution when it provides for its own amendment than it would be
if it proposed directly to subvert the form of government, if it
be true that the right of exercising and controlling the power
of suffrage must necessarily exist in a state or it ceases to be a
republic?

The Senator from Massachusetts [Mr. Wilson] said yesterday that he had no doubt that the Republican party had lost, I
think he said, seven hundred and fifty thousand votes by this
question of colored suffrage. I will not contend with him as to
the number of votes they may have gained or lost, but I cannot
but think, as he said, that that possibly was a reason why, under
his guidance and control and that of other distinguished Senators, the Chicago Republican national convention not only ignored this question, but actually declared a doctrine utterly in
opposition to this proposed amendment. They were compelled
to meet this question. It would not do to say that suffrage
should be granted in accordance with the letter and spirit of the
Constitution, as they said the debt should be paid in accordance
with the letter and spirit of the law. They were obliged to say
something definite. It was true they could not satisfy my honorable friend from Massachusetts [Charles Sumner], nor the
Anti-Slavery Standard. In that paper their course was very
severely condemned, and I suppose my friend from Massachusetts would condemn it. But what did they say? Their resolution on this subject was read yesterday by the Senator from
Indiana [Mr. Hendricks].

The honorable Senator from Nevada [Mr. Stewart] attempted to show that the true intent and meaning of this was
that the subject should be left to the people of the States by a
constitutional amendment. Why, sir, if he will look at this
resolution for a single moment he will see that it makes a distinction which the proposed amendment to the Constitution does
not make and cannot make between the several States. There
was to be one mode of action as to the Southern States and one
mode as to the Northern States. Can you do that by a constitutional amendment? The fact that the two are separated and
divided conclusively proves that the convention had in view a
different mode as to the two. Congress was to interfere as to
the one, the people of the Northern States were to regulate as to
the other. The people of all the States? By no means. The
people of the States interested—the loyal States—had preserved

their powers and rights inviolate, whereas the Southern States had sacrificed theirs by rebellion, and it was therefore necessary for the general Government to interfere in their case. That was the plain meaning.

How was it understood in point of fact? In the discussions before the people in all the Northern States the ground was taken by all the orators of the Republican party, almost without exception, that the question of suffrage was to be left to the States for their separate action. It was never claimed anywhere, in any newspaper from the New York *Tribune* down to the humblest organ of the party, that the intent and meaning of the resolution to which I have referred was that Congress at this session should propose a constitutional amendment to legislatures chosen in November last. Why, sir, if it had been so your legislatures would have been of a very different character, in my humble judgment.

Therefore I say that, not only from the importance of this question as subverting the character of the Government, but also from the pledged faith of the great Republican party, acting in solemn council, declaring and promulgating its principles, stating to the people what would be its action in case it should receive a renewal of their confidence—in view of all this, I say that this Republican party is bound in solemn honor, at least, to submit this question, in fact, to the people; to give them an opportunity to be heard upon the subject. Your convention, at least, said that it should be left to the people of the States. If you say now that you meant by "people" existing legislatures, or legislatures to be chosen on the day when General Grant was chosen, do you suppose that if this had been so understood the result would have been precisely what it was? I do not speak of party results; but would legislators have been chosen, precisely such as were chosen, if the people had supposed that the great question of the right of the States to continue their existence as independent republics was to be decided—a question far greater than the question whether a negro or a Chinaman shall vote?

Sir, I do not wish to bring railing accusations against the leaders of the Republican party, but I beg leave to suppose a case. I beg leave to suppose that the Democratic party in national convention had pledged itself by a solemn resolution to carry out a certain line of policy; that upon that line of policy it had succeeded in carrying the popular vote, and had elected the honorable candidate for whom its members voted to the office of President of the United States. Suppose, for example, the pledge had been on the question of the national debt and the Democratic party had resolved in solemn convention that the debt should be paid in gold, and upon that pledge of their faith and honor the confiding people of the country had elected a President and a Congress and State legislatures in accordance with the views of the Democratic party; suppose they had met here to-day in the Senate of the United States, controlling it by more than a two-thirds vote, and controlling also the House of Representatives, and in violation of their pledge had passed a resolution repudiating the public debt. What would be said of them? Does it require a very great stretch of imagination to suppose that the leaders of a party who had thus violated their honor would have been held up to popular scorn and indignation; that they would have been stamped with infamy as violators of faith, as having obtained power by false pretences, and that the leaders who devised and suggested such a palpable breach of faith would have been expelled by the common sentiment of mankind from the association of honest and honorable gentlemen throughout the world? Nor would any quibbling gloss or subtlety of interpretation by the leaders of the Democratic party, by which the words of the pledge were claimed to be complied with while its true spirit and meaning were violated, render the proceeding any the less contemptible, any the less worthy of the detestation of honest men.

Sir, I have supposed the Democratic party to have been guilty of such an outrage. *Mutate nomine, de te fabula narratur.*

> "Change but the name ———
> Of thee the tale is told."

Or, in another form, more scriptural, "Thou art the man." Without insisting on this extreme view of the case, I only now say that you are at least under obligations to give the people an opportunity to say whether or not they are willing, by the adoption of this amendment, to subvert their old form of government and become subject provinces to an external power. There is no possible mode by which you can give them this opportunity except by submitting the question of the ratification of the amendment to conventions of the people, as proposed in the amendment which I shall offer.

Samuel C. Pomeroy [Kan.] opposed Senator Wilson's view that the Republican party had sacrificed popularity on the altar of principle. The strength of the party with the voters of the country, he said, "consists in its adherence to principle, and to that embodiment of its principles, equality of rights among men." This was all that made the party worth substaining.

He proposed an amendment to the amendment providing that no State nor the United States shall make any inequalities which are not equally applicable to all citizens. This would enact woman suffrage throughout the Union.

Gathering lessons from the past, it now becomes a most solemn duty to inquire how to lay the foundations of a government that will stand securely both as against its dissatisfied citizens within and its jealous and opposing enemies from without. To give strength and character to any form of government there must be entire fairness and equality among all its citizens subject to it. Injustice framed into law or put into the Constitution is destined to work its overthrow. You can make an edifice of granite and marble stand upon the drifting sand sooner and better than you can found and maintain a government whose foundations are not laid securely in impartial justice and in an equality of rights, obligations, and duties where the conditions are equal.

If the people are safer to guard the precious trust of government than any mere individuals, why not all the people? Why trust a part sooner than the whole? The safety of a government is secured when it rests near to the hearts of good men and women—the people—whether wise or unwise, whether learned or unlearned, in books or schools. The very instinct of virtue and a love of human kind, binding indissolubly the citizen in the one bond of equality of rights, where liberty is secured in the law and the law made, upheld, and executed by the citizen, now forms and cements to some extent this National Government, which will tower in its magnificence and stand forever, provided that in this work of reconstruction we allow no injustice, no inequality among citizens, no proscription of rights, either civil or political.

The irresistible tendency of modern civilization is in the direction of the extension of the right of suffrage, and not at all toward proscription. Seven hundred thousand colored men were enfranchised in a day, and they have not disappointed the reasonable expectations which were entertained of them. They were unlearned and, for the most part, ignorant men. But instinct is wiser than logic. The negro has blended and is lost sight of in the man. Suffrage is now held to be the native and the inherent right of every male citizen of a prescribed age. But is there no injustice in completing the work of reconstruction upon such a basis? Are not men and women citizens of the Republic alike? And how can there be in a just government an equality of citizens with a proscription of any of their rights?

As the strength of a chain is only equal to the weakest link, so the strength of this Government is tested to failure when any of its links are sundered and alienated. Any man who supposes that you can disfranchise any innocent citizen, with the lights of the past blazing in his face, has become blind, and will not, or cannot, read the lessons of experience. The ballot is its own instructor. It is an educator. It teaches, and it speaks a language, and that for human rights. It is the great vindicator and protector of individual and personal, no less than of national, honor and character. But human nature, claiming its rights, has no sex; the mind and the soul have no gender, and there is no blending of the responsibility of one citizen into that of another. Sir, the criminal for himself or herself goes alone to dungeon or scaffold. To his own master he standeth, falleth; and by no ingenuity or contrivance can the responsibility of one citizen be shifted upon the shoulders of another. In the primary and individual capacity must each speak, vote, pray, believe, love, hate, live, and die for himself or herself alone. Stamped upon every soul are an individual character and individual responsibilities which can neither be laid aside nor transferred to another. In this respect no one can have a representative character. In this ordeal each one stands for himself, and no one for another. These are the duties of this life which cannot be discharged by proxy. You are your own free agent, but you have no power of substitution, and it cannot be delegated. These are duties pertaining to oneself alone, and it is monstrous to talk of one person voting or representing another in the unorganized and primary state. As well may he live another's life, or die another's death.

Now, if this question of suffrage is to be settled, and settled by the law of the Constitution, it is of the highest importance that it be settled upon the right basis and upon one entirely in harmony with the genius and spirit of our Government and institutions. I only claim the logical sequence of our political organization. All other governments save ours have their privileged men or classes and their unprivileged; some are citizens, others are mere subjects; one class control public affairs, the other bear its burdens with voices silenced. But in this Government, ordained by the people, the citizens, their right to administer it should not be questioned. And how can this Government be administered but by the ballot? Laws are made and executed by the representatives of the ballot. An elective officer is but a consolidated ballot; one person exercising the voice and will of many.

And how did the citizen obtain this power in our Government, or how was it exercised by one class and denied to others? Citizenship was not obtained by colonial charters, for then would their rights have perished with the charters themselves; not by any hereditary right or title, for all such were forbidden in the Constitution; not by successfully wielding the sword in battle, for then would it have been confined to warriors alone. How, then, was it obtained? I answer: it was given in the fundamental law when the Government was ordained for "all men" who are possessed of the "inalienable right to life, liberty, and the pursuit of happiness." And the word "men" is as comprehensive as the word "people"; for they all had the same title to life, liberty, and the pursuit of happiness.

The right of self-government springs from the consent of the governed, and there can be no just mind that will consent that a part shall exercise the will of the whole. Such an act would be a palpable usurpation of power and only one step removed from the right of a king or despot to rule; because if you desert the principle of equality of rights and circumscribe them to a part, that principle would not be violated if you proscribed still more and lodged the power finally in one man. And if by virtue of citizenship all are not entitled to the ballot as the source of power and rights, then none are; for power to deprive one extended would deprive all; and if you admit the existence of the power you must not deny its exercise to any extent.

I now come to this point to say that to deprive any citizen of the right of suffrage is a violation of the principles of our Government as it was ordained, and is a blow direct at the Government itself. I have studied this form of government to no purpose if its logic does not lead me to universal and impartial suffrage. The Constitution places all the powers of the Government in the people who ordained it (and it resided in them in any event); but while they delegated the exercise of certain powers to departments, State and national, still they held the reins of modification of all that was delegated, and provided for the exercise of that right. Hence it is that I can say that this is not only no "white man's government," but it is no male government; and it is a historical fact that in the early days of our history both colored men and white women were admitted to the ballot upon precisely the same terms as white men. This was done in some instances, but their number being few does not affect the principle. If you admit but one woman to vote or one negro it is a confession that there is no legal bar to all.

Citizenship is of birthright or of choice in our form of Government, and the ballot is one of the rights admitted, ay, conceded, and cannot be conferred. Who gave any class the right to monopolize the elective franchise? If a majority, however large, can strike down one right not forfeited then they can another, and hence, as I have said, all. So that if you admit the doctrine of legal disfranchisement you cannot stop short of admitting that the power exists to strike down all rights. It may be said this will allow not only, but require that, minors and even children should be entitled to vote. To this I reply that a right may exist where the person is not entitled to the exercise of the right until a prescribed period. A child is entitled to the right of walking, marrying, and inheriting property; still it must wait for development to exercise that right. When we become members of society under an organized form we consent to the regulation of the exercise of our rights, but not to their extinction.

I will cheerfully comply with all regulations respecting the time, manner, and place of voting, as well as the age and residence required, when made equally applicable to all citizens; but a man who will not resist a law of disfranchisement has lost the spirit of his manhood. Such a one deserves to have no rights if he dare not maintain them. The citizen who will tamely submit to one robbery will soon be prepared to welcome all. When you have taken away the ballot you have left nothing secure.

Do not tell me that the rights of one class of citizens are safe in the hands of another, that the men will take care of the rights of the women. The rights of individuals allied to you may be or may not be safe, but of a class they never can be.

The property and character of your own wife and child may be safe in the hands of the husband and father; but would you trust the property and character of all other women and children in his hands? There are instances where one man may safely speak, vote, and act for a whole community; but would you organize and administer a government upon such a theory? Anything short of entire disfranchisement is as destructive of the theory of our Government as it is dangerous and destructive of individual rights. When one right is destroyed the way is prepared to lose all. I would urge all citizens, by all that is valuable in liberty and desirable in the pursuit of happiness, to maintain and demand that equality of rights and those means of their defence which to a free man are better than an army with banners. I urge it by all that is valuable in a republican form of Government and by all that is dear to human life under it. Citizens who will submit to disfranchisement tamely deserve their fate, no matter whether they be men or women; and the men who demand it and deny the ballot are only one step removed from tyrants. As I would not be a slave, so I would not make a slave; and the man who would do or be either under our form of Government does not merit the condition of a freeman.

But I maintain and defend the right of the ballot to be in the hands of the citizen by virtue of his manhood and not of sex. It was man who was created a ''little lower than angels,'' and not males! ''In the image of God created He him,'' ''but male and female created He them''; ''and He called their name Adam.'' By men is meant mankind, and of this one blood are all the nations; and these nationalized here have a right to all that inherits to a free American citizen. These rights, I repeat, inhere to his manhood and are as inalienable as his immortality. I care not if he may have come to us from the center of dark, fettered Asia, from the plains of long-abused Africa, from the snows of Siberia, or the heat of the tropics, he is a man, and hence a brother, entitled to all the rights that are inalienable in man and to all he can possess and attain by the honest labor of his hands or by the powers of his mind.

I ask the ballot for woman, not on account of her weakness or on account of her strength; not because she may be above or below a man; that has nothing to do with the question. I ask it because she is a citizen of the Republic, amenable to its laws, taxed for its support, and a sharer in its destiny. There are no reasons for giving the ballot to a man that do not apply to a woman with equal force. She may use it or neglect it, as many men do; still it should be hers whenever she chooses to exercise the right. This would tend to its elevation and purification; for when the sacredness of the ballot is preserved it would not soil a woman's heart, hand, or dress, or the place of voting any more than when she uses the Bible and the prayer-book in the congregation of humble worshipers. In all the walks of life, retired or public, she adds grace, elegance, and purity to every step of her pathway, to every work of her hand, and to every love of her heart. I am for the enfranchisement fully and without restrictions of every man in the land who has the rights and discharges faithfully the duties of a citizen of the Republic, no matter how depressed or oppressed he may have been. The way of his elevation is by the way of the ballot, and that should be as fixed and as settled as the fundamental law itself. But I would put in the form of law precisely the same provision for every woman in the land; for it is as safe in her hands as in his; it will be used with as much intelligence and with as good results. And, besides all that, the distinctive character of our republican Government on the basis of the original design can be perpetuated in no other way. The highest justice is the only safety. Let it come, then, by one comprehensive amendment striking out all inequalities among citizens, and the dream of the fathers of a free and pure Republic shall be realized, and there shall be peace throughout the land and good will among men.

Mr. President, when John Stuart Mill unrolled his petition in the British Parliament a few years since it was found to bear the names of those English men and women whose very thoughts were an inspiration to the civilization of the age. It asked for the enfranchisement of woman, and, upon a vote taken, seventy-three members voted for it. Thousands of our own countrymen and women have passed their petitions to the bar of this Senate, through me, that woman might have the ballot in this Government of the people; and in obedience to their ten thousand voices I ask a vote upon my amendment, and I shall move at a proper time a call for the yeas and nays upon it. I leave the wisdom of this vote to the judgment of history, and will cheerfully meet the verdict of posterity.

At this point other business intervened in the Senate and discussion upon the joint resolution was postponed.

THE FIFTEENTH AMENDMENT

HOUSE OF REPRESENTATIVES, JANUARY 11-30, 1869

Various constitutional amendments providing for equal manhood suffrage were proposed in the House of Representatives in the early days of this session and were referred to the Committee on Judiciary.

On January 11, 1869, George S. Boutwell [Mass.], chairman of the committee, reported a joint resolution to submit to the States the following constitutional amendment:

ARTICLE XV

Sec. 1. The right of any citizen of the United States to vote shall not be denied or abridged by the United States or any State by reason of the race, color, or previous condition of slavery of any citizen or class of citizens of the United States.

Sec. 2. The Congress shall have power to enforce by proper legislation the provisions of this article.

Mr. Boutwell brought the resolution for discussion on January 23. He showed that the Fifteenth Amendment was necessary to complete and guarantee the right proclaimed in the Fourteenth, which declared that

"All persons born or naturalized in the United States and subject to the jurisdiction thereof are citizens of the United States and of the States wherein they reside." "There are," said he, "citizens in Kentucky and Maryland eligible to-day to the office of President or Vice-President of the United States, yet who cannot vote for Representatives in Congress, or even for a State, county, or town officer. What is the qualification for the office of President? He must be a native-born citizen of the United States and thirty-five years of age. Nothing more!"

Mr. Boutwell discussed at length the constitutional power of Congress over suffrage in the States, concluding as follows:

What is the conclusion, then, of the whole matter upon the text of the original Constitution in reference to the question of suffrage? Why, first, that the power to make regulations concerning elections is vested in the States, and, secondly, that the power of the general Government upon the subject of the franchise is just as comprehensive as the power of the States, and that we may make regulations, and that we may alter such regulations as the States have made. This view is supported, first, by the necessary theory of the Government that it cannot exist independently of the States if this power in the general Government is denied. It is also supported by the debates in the convention that framed the Constitution itself. It is supported by the debates in the State conventions which ratified the Constitu-

tion, where the issue was distinctly made upon that question between the friends of the Constitution and its opponents.   The
opponents of the Constitution charged that it contemplated
precisely what we now say it means; the supporters of the Constitution did deny that it contemplated precisely what we say
it means, and upon that ground they advocated the provision.
The opponents of the provision in four of the States sought the
submission of an amendment to the people giving a different and
more limited construction to the article.   The Congress of the
United States refused to submit such an amendment.   This is
conclusive evidence that all the men who participated in framing
this Government were of opinion that the power to regulate elections was in the States, subject to the supreme control of the
general Government; and this without any inquiry into other
provisions of the Constitution which give us ample basis for all
the legislation we now propose, such as the provision by which
the United States are to guarantee to each State a republican
form of Government.

WILLIAM E. NIBLACK [Ind.].—I desire to ask the gentleman
this question: will not the position which he assumes require us,
in order to make a State government republican in form, to
confer suffrage also on females to the same extent that we do
upon males?

MR. BOUTWELL.—Well, Mr. Speaker, I have myself been
rather broad and generous in times past in maintaining the
right of people to vote. I see that there is a party coming which
promises to go very far in advance of myself, with more rapid
strides than I have been able to take. I am willing, for one, that
the gentleman from Indiana [Mr. Niblack] for the present
should maintain the doctrine which he suggests in the question
he puts to me, because I suppose it carries with it as an incident
the result which I seek by this bill. If he will go with me in
granting suffrage to all male citizens of this country twenty-
one years of age, without regard to race or color, I will listen
most attentively to any argument he shall make here, or anywhere else within my reach, in favor of the right of women to
vote.

CHARLES A. ELDRIDGE [Wis.].—The question is, will you
vote for it? We are doing precisely the same thing for you—
listening to your argument; but we do not propose to go with
you on this question, and we do not expect you will go with us
on the other question.

Mr. Boutwell evaded the question.

James Brooks [N. Y.] ironically moved "in order to carry out the principles of the gentleman from Massachusetts" to amend the amendment so as to read that "the right of any *person* to vote shall not be denied, etc., by reason of his *or her* race, *sex, nativity or age when over twelve years,* etc."

THE GREAT NATIONAL GAME

Our Colored Brother.—"Hi yah! Stan' back dar; it's dis chile's innin's now."

From the collection of the New York Public Library

On January 29 Samuel Shellabarger [O.] supported the constitutional amendment. He declared that it was necessary in order to make logical, impartial, and secure the power of Congress now exercised over the suffrage in ex-rebel States.

By our reconstruction laws—now accepted by the country as permanent—we have required the reconstructed States to submit to equal suffrage. We have done this mainly, I admit, because it was absolutely impossible to organize or guarantee republican governments down there at all unless we enabled the only loyal race there was there to vote. This fact, distinguishing the Northern from the Southern States, might, perhaps, justify us in requiring temporarily of them what we did not accept for ourselves. But, if this be so, it can only be temporarily so; if, indeed, as we all devoutly hope, general loyalty is ultimately to come back to the South. We must, therefore, speedily either let the South disfranchise its colored races if they will, or else enfranchise our own, or else compel a submission by sister States to a rule of elective franchise pronounced by ourselves dangerous and ruinous to us. To so compel them permanently to submit to what we refuse ourselves to accept is dishonor—a dishonor which will soon become revolting to the sense of fair play for which the American people are not undistinguished, and will shock the moral sense of mankind. This consideration has exceeding force in impelling us to at once make the law of enfranchisement national, universal.

But, Mr. Speaker, these reasons for the adoption of the amendment making the citizens equal in the enjoyment of the best right of citizenship, though each important in itself, become so trivial in contrast with the great reason for it that we hesitate at even naming them. The decisive argument for the amendment is that it is right. In determining whether it is right, what we have to consider and to debate and to adjudge are problems like these, and only problems like these: is the right to vote in a government where votes make the government's constitution, laws, and rulers, and unmake them, a right worth having for one's protection or elevation or self-defence? Or is it, on the other hand, better for all these that a privileged and proud and prejudiced class should do all the voting, and make and change and abolish all the constitutions and laws and rulers for me—me unconsulted but subject! The ballot being both the highest franchise and highest defence of a freeman, ought a free citizen who endures all the burdens of his Government be by it denied its highest means of defence merely because he is dark or light, poor or rich, high or lowly? Sir, I tell you that it is precisely true that only questions as plain, or, rather, absurd, as these are involved in determining the righteousness of this great measure. Others may if they will, but I cannot debate here. It may yet, in this nineteenth century of our Lord's grace, be a question in doubt and darkness whether a government ought to be contrived and made on purpose so as to impose its burdens upon the poor and lowly equally with the high, and then deny to the former the chiefest means to rescue themselves and children from being the poor, lowly, and suffering.

It may be yet, in political science, one of its unsolved problems whether these poor do not need their government's protection as much as do the opulent, the defenceless as much as do the powerful, those ready to perish as much as do the prosperous and mighty. It may be that the moral sciences which go into the structures of our Christian civilization have not yet found out whether it is magnanimous or pusillanimous, honor or dishonor, courage or cowardice, virtue or crime, for the powerful to so contrive their government's structure as to put upon the weak and lowly the common burdens of their government, and then to take from them and their children forever that supremest right of their citizenship which best secures their elevation, defence, and happiness. But, Mr. Speaker, if these be, indeed, yet questions in our moral or social or political or religious or legal science, or in any other science, which are unsolved, then its non-solution turns that science, where such questions are unknown things, into the monstrous, and we turn away from arguing them with the feeling that our very instincts of honor and manhood have been outraged by the invitation to such debate.

Mr. Speaker, it is absolutely plain that for the Republican party of America to-day the path of safety is the path of duty. All the instincts of our common loves of liberty, equality, and fair play; all the memories, histories, and glories of our great party of freedom; all the senses of magnanimity, of chivalry, justice, and merest decency, which make us revolt at robbing the lowly and their children of those rights and franchises of freemen to which they are entitled as much as we, and which they need far more than we, tell us where that path of duty is. Nay, nay, Mr. Speaker—God, who made of one blood all the nations—God who maketh it so that righteousness exalteth a nation—God who careth for his poor as he doth for his sparrow; God hath shown us which way goes the path of this nation's duty. To go in it is virtue, honor, and success. To go from it is crime, dishonor, and overwhelming disaster and defeat.

The joint resolution was passed on January 30 by 150 yeas to 42 nays. When the House amendment reached the Senate this body, in order to expedite matters, laid aside in its favor its own amendment. Various amendments of the amendment were proposed and referred to the Committee on Judiciary, which was entrusted with the entire subject.

THE FIFTEENTH AMENDMENT—*Concluded*

SENATE, FEBRUARY 4-9, 1869

The House amendment was brought before the Senate for discussion on February 4.

Orris S. Ferry [Conn.] declared that every Senator who had opposed the measure did so not upon its principle, but upon its mode of submission to the States, or other technicalities. He replied particularly to the argument of his colleague [Senator Dixon] that the object of the amendment was not to declare who should vote, but who should make voters.

Willard Warner [Ala.] spoke in behalf of woman suffrage.

In this land Government does not make voters, but voters make the Government. To vote, under every principle upon which our Government is based, is a right of man because of his manhood, and it comes to every citizen because of that truth in our fundamental charter which proclaims that "governments derive all their just powers from the consent of the governed." And herein lies the essential distinction between the European and the American social theories. By the former all political functions find their source in the governing authority, and descend from it to the subject. By the latter all political functions originate from the people, in whom alone is inherent sovereignty. The European petitions for franchises; the American asserts rights. This amendment only forbids the denial of these rights.

Sir, I thank God that I have lived long enough to witness the dawning of that day when these caste distinctions shall be obliterated all over this land. The amendment attains the accomplishment of that state of society toward which the nations have been struggling since the beginning of the Christian civilization. To the old pagan system of civilization the only law was the law of force. To the new Christian civilization, ushered in by Divine revelation, the foundation of all law is right. For eighteen centuries that civilization has been struggling through the nations amid insurrections and revolts and wars and overturnings of kingdoms, until here upon this western continent it at last is to attain that accomplishment which has been the hope of philosophers and statesmen and patriots of all ages. One thing only yet remains to restrain its full fruition, the prejudice of race.

Sir, there were two nations of antiquity in which that prejudice exerted a more potent influence than in any others. To the Greek, tracing his lineage back through heroes and demi-gods to the very deities of Olympus, all the world outside of Hellas was but a barbaric chaos. To the Hebrew the family of Abraham were the chosen of God, to whom the very touch of the Gentile was defilement to the Jew. And now, sir, roll back for a moment the curtain of history. On the Athenian Areopagus, in the very center of that brilliant Greek life, Paul the Hebrew is proclaiming "God hath made of one blood all nations of men for to dwell on all the face of the earth." Behold the realization of that which is contained in those Divine words rapidly approaching on these western shores! Three centuries have scarce elapsed since Europe poured forth her children out of all her diverse nationalities upon our Atlantic coast, and Africa in chains was dragged thither to be their servant; while now, in the midst of the growing glory of the nation, the Orient is sending its myriads eastward across the Pacific. Europe, Asia, Africa are blending here into a nationality such as the world has never seen; a nation where equal civil rights and equal political rights, under the benign operation of a Constitution broad in its humanity as the sway of the Republic, shall be the law for every individual; a nationality which shall realize the vision of the statesman, and, may we not hope, the aspiration of the Christian.

Mr. President, I would admit woman, the most beautiful, the purest, and best of God's creations, to an equal voice with us in the Government. As she is now the sharer of all our pleasures, the partner of all our joys, I would have her share with us the powers, the duties, and the responsibilities of government. Suppose, Mr. President, that one of the many sorrow-stricken women made widows by the late war should walk into this Chamber and say, "Senators, my husband and two sons lie in yonder na-

tional cemetery—their graves marked, cared for, cherished
gratefully and tenderly by the nation—as the last resting-place
of the heroic defenders of its life. I have no husband, no son,
no brother, no father, no man left to represent me. I pay taxes;
every law you pass affects me and mine, and I demand a voice
in this Government.'' What answer shall you give her?

But I know that woman's suffrage is not now attainable, and
I would not, as a practical legislator, jeopardize the good which
is attainable by linking with it that which is impossible. Besides, whenever the women of this country ask with anything
like unanimity for the ballot they will get it.

The irresistible drift of modern civilization is toward a larger
and larger enfranchisement of the people, and our end is a pure
democracy. Let us proceed to it with firm and decisive steps.
Then we will have no disfranchised, disaffected, clamoring classes
always ready and ripe for tumult, rebellion, and revolution.
Then the will of the people, legally and peacefully expressed,
will have a weight and a power which will command and insure
universal acquiescence and obedience.

We are relaying the very corner-stone of our temple of liberty. Let us see that its proportions are broad, true, and ample,
and its material indestructible. Our fathers laid the foundation
of our Government upon the rock of truth and justice when they
proclaimed to the world, in their immortal Declaration, that
''all men are created equal''—not made so by laws and constitutions, but by the Creator; but they built badly, though perhaps of necessity, when they countenanced slavery in the provision relating to fugitives. Let us profit by their error, and,
enlightened by the experience of eighty years, and warned by
that experience of the terrible retribution which surely and inevitably follows compromise of truth and justice, let us follow our principles to their logical conclusion and found this
nation on the rock of universal equal human rights, thus set-
tling forever the questions which, never settled aright, have
risen again and again to disturb and finally to desolate our
beautiful land.

George H. Williams [Ore.] spoke on February 5.
He proposed as a substitute for the amendment one
giving Congress the power to abolish or modify State
laws on suffrage. Then the various States could experiment in the matter under the safe control of the
national legislature.

Under this amendment as I propose it, if the State of Kansas, which appears to be the pioneer State upon all questions of this nature, should memorialize Congress to pass a law striking the word "male" from her constitution, and her two Senators here should support that memorial, as I have no doubt they would, Congress could try the experiment of female suffrage in that State, and it could then be determined whether or not it would be advisable to extend the law to every State in this Union. I cannot divest myself of the conviction at this time that the experiment would be an unfortunate one for all concerned. I cannot now persuade myself that even the women, if they were to try this experiment, would be fully satisfied with it and would meet with all that power and happiness which some of them so fondly anticipate from the exercise of such a right. Women, when they have tried this experiment, may come to feel like a romantic boy going to the war, dreaming of greatness and glory, but finding in the sufferings and sacrifices of the march, the camp, and the battle a strong desire to go back again to the quiet and happy home of his boyhood.

Senator Williams then referred to the immigration of Chinese.

Now, if a constitutional amendment is adopted to the effect that all political distinctions as to race and color shall be forever abolished in the United States, of course it will follow that the Chinese, who are coming here by thousands every year, will find no constitutional obstacle to the exercise by them of the elective franchise and to the right to hold office.

SENATOR STEWART.—I ask the Senator if that could be accomplished unless we allowed them to be naturalized? This applies only to citizens.

SENATOR WILLIAMS.—I know that would not follow unless the naturalization laws are changed; but if the Constitution of the United States can be changed so as to abolish all political distinctions on account of race and color, how easy, upon the same principle, will it be to change the naturalization laws. And would not consistency require us to change the naturalization laws and make them comformable upon principle to the provisions of the Constitution?

Now, sir, there are, I suppose, at this time about one hundred thousand Chinese in the Pacific States and Territories, and every ship that comes across the Pacific brings its hundreds and lands them upon our shores. They are a people who do not, or will not, learn our language; they cannot, or will not, adopt our manners or customs and modes of life; they do not amalgamate with our people; they constitute a distinct and separate nationality, an *imperium in imperio*—China in the United States; and, sir, they are, and continue to be, the ignorant and besotted devotees of absolutism in politics and the blind disciples of paganism in religion.

Sir, conceive the condition of things upon the Pacific coast if the governments of the States there were delivered into the hands of such a people. Suppose that the control of all our educational and religious institutions was transferred to the hands of these people, what would be the consequences to that portion of the Republic? Everybody has heard of the exhaustless populations of China, and if sufficient inducements are held out they may come to this country, not only by thousands, but by millions, and it would be a very easy thing if by coming they could obtain political power for the Chinese to take possession of every State and Territory on the Pacific coast and appropriate the productions of that beautiful, interesting, and valuable region of the Republic to their exclusive benefit and use.

I hope, sir, that this nation will not bind itself hand and foot, for all coming time, and deliver itself up to the political filth and moral pollution that are flowing with a fearfully increasing tide into our country from the shores of Asia.

Charles Sumner [Mass.] said that the old doctrine of State rights was being used to bolster up the doomed and despicable cause of caste as it had been employed to protect the scarcely more abhorrent cause of slavery, of which caste was the direct offspring.

I meet this odious imposture, as I met the earlier measure, with indignation and contempt, naturally excited by anything unworthy of this Chamber and of the Republic. How it can appear here and find Senators willing to assume the stigma of its championship is more than I can comprehend. Nobody ever vindicated slavery who did not lay up a store of regret for himself and his children; and permit me to say now nobody can vindicate caste, whether civil or political, as beyond the reach of national prohibition, without laying up a similar store of regret.

Do not complain if I speak strongly. The occasion requires it. I seek to save the Senate from participation in an irrational and degrading pretension.

It was in the name of State rights that slavery, with all its brood of wrong, was upheld; and it is now in the name of State rights that caste, fruitful also in wrong, is upheld. The old champions reappear, under other names, and from other States, each crying out that, under the national Constitution, notwithstanding even its supplementary amendments, a State may, if it pleases, deny political rights on account of race or color and thus establish that vilest institution, a caste and an oligarchy of the skin.

This perversity is easily understood when it is considered that the present generation grew up under an interpretation of the national Constitution supplied by the upholders of slavery. State rights were exalted and the nation was humbled, because in this way slavery might be protected. Anything for slavery was constitutional. Vain are all our victories, if this terrible rule is not reversed, so that State rights shall yield to human rights, and the nation be exalted as the bulwark of all. This will be the crowning victory of the war. Beyond all question the true rule under the national Constitution, especially since its additional amendments, is that *anything for human rights is constitutional.* Yes, sir; against the old rule, *anything for slavery,* I put the new rule, *anything for human rights.*

Sir, I do not declare this rule hastily, and I know the presence in which I speak. I am surrounded by lawyers, and now I challenge any one or all to this debate. I invoke the discussion. On an occasion less important, Lord Chatham, after saying that he came not with the statute-book doubled down in dog's ears to defend the cause of liberty; that he relied on a general principle, a constitutional principle, exclaimed, "It is a ground on which I stand firm; a ground on which I dare meet any man." In the same spirit I would speak now. No learning in books, no skill acquired in courts, no sharpness of forensic dialectics, no cunning in splitting hairs, can impair the vigor of the constitutional principle which I announce. Whatever you enact for human rights is constitutional. There can be no State rights against human rights; and this is the supreme law of the land, anything in the constitution or laws of any State to the contrary notwithstanding.

The State is local in its character, and not universal. Whatever is justly local belongs to its cognizance; whatever is universal belongs to the nation. But what can be more universal than the rights of man? Such they have been declared by our fathers, and this axiom of liberty nobody can dispute.

Listening to the champions of caste and oligarchy, I do not err when I say that this whole terrible and ignominious pretension is traced to a direct and bare-faced perversion of the National Constitution.

By the National Constitution it is provided, that "the electors in each State shall have the *qualifications* requisite for electors of the most numerous branch of the State legislature," thus seeming to refer the primary determination of what are called "qualifications" to the States; and this is reënforced by the further provision, that "the times, places, and manner of holding elections for Senators and Representatives shall be prescribed in each State by the legislature thereof; but the Congress may at any time by law make or alter such *regulations.*" This is all. On these simple texts, conferring plain and intelligible powers, the champions insist that "color" may be made a "qualification"; and that, under the guise of "regulations," citizens, whose only offence is a skin not colored like our own, may be shut out from political rights; and that in this way a monopoly of rights, being at once a caste and an oligarchy of the skin, is placed under the safeguard of the National Constitution.

Now, to this perversion I oppose a point-blank denial. These two words are not justly susceptible of any such signification, especially in a national constitution which is to be interpreted always so that human rights shall not suffer. A "qualification" is something that can be acquired. A man is familiarly said "to qualify" for an office. Nothing can be a "qualification" which is not in its nature attainable, as residence, property, education, or character, each of which is within the possible reach of well-directed effort. Color cannot be a "qualification." If the prescribed "qualification" were color of the hair or color of the eyes, all would see its absurdity; but it is none the less absurd, when it is the color of skin. Color is a quality derived from nature. But a "quality" is very different from a "qualification." A quality, inherent in man and a part of himself, can never be a "qualification" in the sense of the National Constitution.

The same judgment must be pronounced on the attempt to found this outrage upon the power to make "regulations," as if this word had not a limited signification, which renders such a pretension impossible. "Regulations" are nothing but rules applicable to a given matter; they concern the manner in which a business shall be conducted, and, when used with regard to elections, are applicable to what may be called incidents, in contradistinction to the principle, which is nothing less than the right to vote. A power to regulate is not a power to destroy or to disfranchise.

It is under the National Constitution that the champions set up their pretension; therefore, to the National Constitution I go. And I begin by appealing to the letter, which from beginning to end does not contain one word recognizing "color." Its letter is blameless and its spirit is not less so. Surely a power to disfranchise for color must find some sanction in the Constitution. There must be some word of clear intent under which this terrible prerogative can be exercised. This conclusion of reason is reinforced by the positive text of our Magna Charta, the Declaration of Independence, where it is expressly announced that all men are equal in rights, and that just government stands only on the consent of the governed. In the face of the National Constitution interpreted, first, by itself, and then by the Declaration of Independence, how can this pretension prevail?

But there are positive texts of the National Constitution, refulgent as the Capitol itself, which forbid it with sovereign irresistible power, and invest Congress with all needful authority to maintain the prohibition.

There is that key-stone clause, by which it is expressly declared that "the United States shall guarantee to every State in this Union a republican form of Government," and Congress is empowered to enforce this guaranty. The definition of a republican government was solemnly announced by our fathers, first, in that great battle-cry which preceded the Revolution, "taxation without representation is tyranny," and, secondly, in the great Declaration at the birth of the Republic, that all men are equal in rights and that just government stands only on the consent of the governed. A republic is where taxation and representation go hand in hand; where all are equal in rights and no man is excluded from participation in the government. Such is the definition of a republican government, which it is the duty of Congress to maintain. Here is a bountiful source of power, which cannot be called in question. In the execution of the guaranty Congress may—nay, must—require that there shall be no caste or oligarchy of the skin.

If in the original text of the Constitution there could be any doubt, it was all relieved by the amendment abolishing slavery and empowering Congress to enforce this provision. Already Congress, in the exercise of this power, has passed a *civil rights act*. It only remains that it should now pass a *political rights act*, which, like the former, shall help consummate the abolition of slavery. According to a familiar rule of interpretation, expounded by Chief Justice Marshall in his most masterly judgment, Congress, when intrusted with any power, is at liberty to select the "means" for its execution. The civil rights act came under the head of "means" selected by Congress, and a political rights act will have the same authority. You may as well deny the constitutionality of the one as the other.

The amendment abolishing slavery has been reënforced by another, known as Article XIV, which declares peremptorily that "no State shall make or enforce any law which shall abridge the privileges and immunities of citizens of the United States," and again Congress is empowered to enforce this provision. What can be broader? Colored persons are citizens of the United States, and no State can abridge their privileges and immunities. It is a mockery to say that, under these explicit words, Congress is powerless to forbid any discrimination of color at the ballot-box. Why, then, were they inscribed in the Constitution? To what end? There they stand, supplying an additional and supernumerary power, ample for safeguard against caste or oligarchy of the skin, no matter how strongly sanctioned by any State government.

But the champions anxious for State rights against human rights strive to parry this positive text by insisting that, in another provision of this same amendment, the power over the right to vote is conceded to the States. Mark, now, the audacity and fragility of this pretext. It is true that "where the right to vote is denied to the male inhabitants of a State, or in any way abridged, except for participation in rebellion or crime," the basis of representation is reduced in corresponding proportion. Such is the penalty imposed by the Constitution on a State which denies the right to vote, except in a specific case. But this penalty on the State does not in any way, by the most distant implication, impair the plenary powers of Congress to enforce the guaranty of a republican government, the abolition of slavery, and that final clause guarding the rights of citizens, three specific powers which are left undisturbed, unless the old spirit of slavery is once more revived and Congress is compelled again to wear those degrading chains which for so long a time rendered it powerless for human rights.

I am now brought directly to the proposed amendment of the Constitution. Of course, the question stares us in the face, why amend what is already sufficient? Why erect a supernumerary column?

So far as I know, two reasons are assigned. The first is that the power of Congress is doubtful. It is natural that those who do not sympathize strongly with the equal rights of all should doubt. Men ordinarily find in the Constitution what is in themselves, so that the Constitution in its meaning is little more than a reflection of their own inner nature.

Another reason assigned for a constitutional amendment is its permanent character in comparison with an act of Congress which may be repealed. On this head I have no anxiety. Let this beneficent prohibition once find a place in our statute-book, and it will be as lasting as the National Constitution itself, to which it will be only a legitimate corollary. In harmony with the Declaration of Independence and in harmony with the National Constitution, it will become of equal significance, and no profane hand will touch its sacred text. It will never be repealed. The elective franchise once recognized can never be denied; once conferred can never be resumed. The rule of equal rights once applied by Congress under the National Constitution will be a permanent institution as long as the Republic endures; for it will be a vital part of that republican government to which the nation is pledged.

GEORGE VICKERS [Md.].—I would ask the Senator from Massachusetts if the color of the hair added to the disqualification of the voter intellectually is not a power resident in the legislature? I would ask the honorable Senator if public virtue and public intelligence are not the very foundations of our Republic?

SENATOR SUMNER.—The point is not whether public intelligence and public virtue are essential to a republic, for there we are agreed; not whether they may not be recognized as qualifications, but the point is whether any inherent quality under Providence planted in the human form by God can be made by any vote of man a qualification for an elector?

SENATOR VICKERS.—There are five races of men, the red man, the yellow man, the white man, the black man, and the brown man. Now, I ask if it is not competent for a legislature to disfranchise or to withhold the elective franchise from any one of these races? Is not color the distinctive mark of the race? And because here is a distinct race, an inferior race, and, because this race has color, the race is disqualified. It is not altogether on account of the color of the skin. That is only one of the indications and marks by which you distinguish the race. Have we not a right to withhold the elective franchise from the Chinese, who are of a different color from us and from the negro? Would the Senator say that because the Chinese have a certain complexion therefore we have no right to disfranchise them because of that complexion? If they are a different race, if they are pagans, according to the speech of the Senator from Oregon

[Mr. Williams], have we not a right to disqualify them and withhold from them the elective franchise?

SENATOR SUMNER.—That is not the question. I do not say that they may not be disqualified for their paganism. That is a question of character. A man may cease to be a pagan; he may change; he may become a Christian; but a man cannot cease to be a colored man if he is so made by Providence. The Ethiopian cannot change his skin.

SENATOR VICKERS.—If the color of the skin, the color of the hair, or the color of the eye distinguishes one race from another, then I say color of skin, of hair, or of eye can make the disqualification, and the legislature has a right so to decree.

SENATOR SUMNER.—I see my honorable friend does not flinch from the conclusion.

SENATOR VICKERS.—Mr. President, I had never heard, until the honorable Senator from Massachusetts asserted it to-day, that when human rights and the Constitution came into conflict the Constitution was to yield to human rights. Why, sir, if that doctrine is to prevail, how many differences of opinion are there in reference to human rights? We should have no Constitution; it would be undefined, and there would be nothing tangible in reference to the fundamental law. But if the doctrine of the Senator from Massachusetts prevails, if human rights are to override the Constitution of the country, then does not the doctrine of human rights asserted by the Senator apply as well to females as to males? The Senator from Kansas would say it did; and I ask if human rights are not as applicable to woman as to man? And, if the doctrine of human rights is to be the rule by which the Constitution is to be construed, then it must be so construed as to admit female suffrage; and yet I suppose the Senator from Massachusetts would not support a measure of this kind. It is not unusual for Senators to lay down a general principle and argue upon that principle, and then in the practical application of it to come short of its results. It has been beautifully said that "we go to man for philosophy and to woman for consolation"; and, although I am no advocate for woman suffrage, I believe that if the Congress of the United States had been composed exclusively of women we should have had no civil war. We might have had a war of words, but that would have been all. [Laughter.]

I would rather concede the ascendency of any party for twenty years or more if the country could thereby be shielded from any infraction or change of the Constitution, and its wonted prestige be preserved and continued. The success of party is a paltry consideration when weighed against the principles of the Constitution, of public tranquillity, and happiness. Parties are changing; they have changed. Mutability is stamped upon human productions, and disappointment to human plans and hopes; new generations are to succeed us, and the passions and prejudices of to-day cannot impress their minds and regulate their conduct. It is only by adhering to constitutional rules; to the principles of our fathers, whose purposes were single and patriotism undoubted; by a conformity to right, to justice, and by doing to others as we would have others do unto us that we can expect to establish a party which shall "stand the test of human scrutiny, of talents, and of time." No legislation of Congress can elevate or improve the physical, moral, or intellectual condition of the negro; we cannot legislate into them any fitness or qualification which they do not now possess. We may descend from the high position in which the framers of the Constitution left us and place ourselves upon the common and degrading platform of negro suffrage and political equality.

Public virtue and intelligence are the foundations of a republic. It is a government of opinion, of principle; its officers and agents must be wise, capable, and patriotic. The people who select them must, to a great extent, possess the same elements; they must have some knowledge of statesmanship, of political economy, of trade, commerce, manufactures, agriculture, and mechanic arts, and of the resources and wealth of the country, and withal a fund of experience and common sense. Will the introduction of the negro into our political affairs add to the intelligence, statesmanship, wisdom, and judgment of the country? Will it not weaken our institutions and the confidence we have had in their stability and lay another and different foundation than that which was laid by our fathers? The negro as a class, as a race, is unfortunately ignorant and superstitious; with some exceptions, he cannot read nor understand your Constitution, is unacquainted with your laws, institutions, history, and policy; he at present lacks independence and that high sense of honor and integrity which every voter should possess to shield him from sinister or unworthy influences. If you had a house to build would you procure ignorant and unskillful hands to erect it? And yet, in so grave a matter as legislation, statesmanship, and the affairs, internal and external, of a great country, and in choosing Representatives and officers to discharge the most difficult and momentous duties, we are to call to our aid the power of numbers only, which possess not the moral or intellectual strength to render the slightest assistance. They may be made the dupes and instruments of interested persons, but it should be recollected that, like the elephants in battle, they will be as likely to trample upon friends as upon foes. No one political organization can long hold them, and they will become a *tertium quid* which will enervate rather than strengthen the body-politic.

Waitman T. Willey [W. Va.] summed up his reasons for voting for the amendment as follows:

1. All just government must rest on the consent of the governed.
2. Taxation without representation is tyranny. If negroes are to be taxed or compelled to bear arms justice requires that they should vote.
3. The welfare of the white race requires that the intellectual development of the negro and the improvement of his physical condition be accomplished as speedily as practicable. The vote will be the best incentive for the negro so to develop and improve himself.
4. The amendment will definitely settle the vexatious question of suffrage in the ex-rebel States.
5. It will prevent the negro from sinking into a state of hopeless despondency, and becoming a pest to society and a burden to the State.
6. It will remove the troublesome negro issue from politics.
7. The ballot will be a broader and safer shield to the negro than specific legislation.
8. The amendment will place all the States on an equality with respect to suffrage, and so remove the just indignation that prevails in the ex-rebel States because of present discrimination in the matter.
9. The spirit of justice, human liberty, and Christian civilization demands the amendment.
10. The amendment leaves the question to the people of the country, whose will is of right supreme.

On February 6 Henry W. Corbett [Ore.] offered an amendment to the amendment which specifically excluded the Chinese from suffrage.

With the experience of the past few years on the Pacific coast we have found that this class of people are not beneficial to the advancement of those Christian institutions that lie at the foundation of our Government. The presence of large numbers of them in our midst is not beneficial to the observance of the Sabbath day. It is not encouraging to the Sabbath-school, which is the nursery of our children, and which is to fit them for enlightened and powerful and good statesmen. The question now is whether for our own race, whether for the benefit of our posterity, we shall not make this exception as against the Chinese.

This question reaches beyond the common rights of man under a Christian nation such as was founded upon Plymouth Rock. It reaches the very foundation of our Christian institutions. Allow Chinese suffrage, and you may soon find established pagan institutions in our midst which may eventually supersede those Christian influences which have so long been the pride of our country.

Those nations that have worshiped heathen gods have been overthrown and superseded by Christian nations, and I think it is very fair to presume that the overruling providence of God may curse us in the same way, and that we may eventually be overthrown by that class of people who come to our Pacific shores if we do not guard the priceless legacy which has been intrusted to us.

James A. Bayard, Jr. [Del.] opposed the argument that suffrage was a natural right.

I have never been able to accede to the dogma that suffrage is a natural right, or that universal suffrage is essential or even conducive to permanent free government. It cannot exist in a state of nature; and when men form themselves into communities the governments they adopt must of necessity depend upon the condition and capacity of those over whom they are to be organized. I concede fully the soundness of the maxim that the just basis of all government is "the consent of the governed"; but in fact there never has been such specific consent given by each individual in the organization of any government, and there is no natural right violated when it is denied. A government may be organized on this maxim, and yet numbers subject to its control have no part and no voice in its organization.

The frailty of humanity and the tendency of power to corruption forbid its deposit in the hands of a single individual and his posterity, or in the hands of a few, for in either case this corrupting tendency of power would end in tyranny and be used at the expense of the happiness and welfare of the community. The powers of government, therefore, are most safely for the benefit of all intrusted to the people at large. But this general truth, like all other general propositions, must be modified in practice, and is subject to exceptions. As to the exercise of the franchise and trust of suffrage there are many exceptions; they vary in the different States of this Union. Idiots and lunatics in all States are excepted from incapacity; felons as a punishment for their crime. There is residence also required, for the obvious reason that to vote with an approximation to intelligence the voter must have had an opportunity to become acquainted with the condition and habits of the community in which the franchise is to be exercised, and also to acquire some knowledge of the character and general standing of those who may be candidates for office. The length of residence required varies in different States, and the people of each State can best determine that for themselves. In some the prepayment of taxes is requisite. Although that exists in my own State I have always been opposed to such a qualification, and have endeavored to have it modified, because the prepayment of taxes has a tendency toward corruption, which is the growing vice of our country. But that, also, is a question for the people of the States, and not a question for the general Government.

In a few States there is what is called an educational franchise. It is made a prerequisite to the exercise of the franchise that the voter shall be able to read the Constitution of the United States or of the State, or some other paper, and to write his name. I should never object to any State adopting such a franchise if such is the will of her people, for the right properly belongs to them to regulate suffrage within their own State, though I should be entirely opposed to the adoption of such a qualification of the franchise in the State of Delaware; because, though I have no doubt that the training of the people is necessary to enable them to sustain self-government, I do not believe that merely teaching a man to read and write is such a training as specially fits him for the exercise of the elective franchise. Moral culture, which depends mainly upon the mother, is far more effective and far more important in securing an intelligent performance of this trust of suffrage. The institutions of the common law requiring that all local business shall be transacted by the inhabitants of the locality all aid in training and instructing the people in habits of self-government. It was such training that formed the habits of the people of this country, implanted in them the love and the appreciation of civil liberty, and enabled them to sustain self-government and maintain a government of laws, in contradistinction to a government of will, when they threw off their political allegiance to Great Britain and declared their independence. Centralize the powers of Government now and degrade the suffrage, and the people will lose their capacity for self-government, and one or more despotisms will establish their ascendency, and thus all security of the citizen against the aggressions of power, essential for the preservation of free government, will cease beyond recovery.

Beyond the minor exceptions which I have stated to the maxim that the just basis of all government is ''the consent of the governed'' there are three general exceptions—age, sex, and race.

First, as to age. If suffrage were a natural right you would find it very difficult to justify the exclusion of boys of sixteen or eighteen, for in general they have quite sufficient mental capacity for its exercise. Indeed, were it a natural right any child old enough to be sworn and give evidence in a court of justice might claim it.

But the right is restrained universally throughout this country. Nay, the age is fixed arbitrarily at twenty-one, founded no doubt upon the principle that the human passions develop more rapidly than the intellectual and the reflecting powers, and that the control over the passions is not sufficient under the age of twenty-one to trust men with the exercise of the franchise. The result would be personal conflicts and riots at elections becoming so general that, to avoid anarchy the people would accept despotism. There are boys of eighteen who might be safely intrusted with suffrage, but no tribunal could be possibly organized to determine fairly on the individual exceptions. The question of boyhood suffrage has not, however, yet become a hobby, and it is useless to discuss this exception further. To use the slang of the day, the community has not yet been educated up to the idea because some boys of eighteen may have more intellect and self-control than the average man of forty, and be quite competent to exercise the franchise of voting, that therefore all boys of eighteen ought to enjoy the franchise. But in this age of progress, according to the ideas of the honorable Senator from Indiana [Mr. Morton], no prediction can be made as to when this question will seriously arise. He has told you that the Democratic party is not a party of progress. That honorable Senator should recollect that there are two kinds of progress, and that progress down hill is much more easy and rapid than progress upward. To the *''facilis decensus averni,''* [1]

[1] ''Easy is the descent of hell.''

exemplified in the headlong career of the Republican party, the Democratic party has been opposed. Whether that opposition can yet save the country and preserve civil liberty rests with the people to determine.

The next exception is that of sex. I will not argue this question either with communists or socialists, nor with the woman's rights party, because the folly of this species of fanaticism, though it has made great progress lately, is not sufficiently widespread to need an elaborate refutation. The general objections may, however, be stated. Inordinate vanity and the love of notoriety may have tempted some women to unsex themselves, both in their dress and their pursuits; but woman's heart and the instincts of maternity will keep her true to the greatest of her duties in life, the culture and formation of the character of her offspring, the implanting of that second nature, which can only be done early in life, which influences and controls the happiness and welfare not only of her own generation, but that of her posterity. No higher or holier duty could be imposed upon humanity; and this duty rightfully performed is enough to occupy the head and the heart of any human being. There may be exceptional cases of individual women resembling men more than their own sex in their mental and moral organization, who thirst after direct power and revel in notoriety. They must be *great* women. My answer to them is: I have seen it somewhere written that there are three orders of *great* men, the worshippers of power, the worshippers of fame, but, for the last and greatest, those who are content with happiness in the performance of duty, history inscribes no tablet. Surely, a wise woman should be content to be enrolled in this last and greatest order. Let it not be supposed, Mr. President, in stating these objections to female suffrage, that I mean to characterize the sex as inferior to man. In their combined mental and moral organization I hold them to be quite our equals, if not our superiors. But there is a difference in the physical, mental, and moral structure of the sexes which fits them for the performance of different duties, and the pursuit of different avocations. Sir, it would perhaps be well for the country if duties were a little more considered, as well as so-called rights.

If I desired an illustration of the fallacy of the idea that the ballot, as it is called, is essential for the purpose of protection, I should select the condition of woman in this country. I feel proud and gratified that in this, our own America, there is a chivalrous devotion to the sex which has been equaled in no other age or country. I yield to none in my deference to the sex, and desire to secure and protect woman in all her rights; but suffrage is not a right, but a trust and a franchise.

Can there, Mr. President, be a doubt that the possession of the franchise of suffrage is entirely unnecessary for the protection of woman in all her rights? Has not the observation and memory of every Senator satisfied him that, in controversies between man and woman in this country, whether in courts of justice or elsewhere, the general sympathy and the bias are always, though she has no vote, with the woman, and not infrequently even at the expense of justice, such and so great is her influence? Sir, with all my deference for the sex, I believe there is truth in the advice supposed in one of the "imaginary conversations" to have been given by Roger Ascham to Lady Jane Grey, that "women, like the plants of the woods, derive their sweetness and tenderness from the shade." In my belief, if the sex is dragged down into the political arena, the coarse and selfish, and too often brutal, struggle for place and power and spoils will impair its influence and demoralize woman's nature, and that deference which now exists, and her real influence over man will gradually but certainly fade and be lost, and with that loss we shall, as a people, retrograde in civilization.

The third exception, Mr. President, to the general proposition that the consent of the governed is the just basis of government is that of race. I hold it to be a truth and a fact uncontradicted by history that where two races of men exist in the same country in large relative numbers so dissimilar in organization as to prevent the fusion of races, equality of political power can only end in the conflict of races. Look at the condition of Mexico with her sixteen different crosses of the Indian, negro, and European. The experiment of self-government with such a population has been tried there, and what has been the result? One revolution has followed another, and one military despotism another, until a country with high natural advantages and great sources of wealth has sunk into a state of insignificance and chronic anarchy, and advancement in civilization has become impossible from the insecurity of protection for either life, person, or property. Elevated as the people of this country now are, social fusion with an inferior race will be followed by the same results to our posterity.

Our own Indians afford another illustration. Numerous as they were at the first landing of the white man, they have perished before his onward pathway, and, though humanity may earnestly desire to prevent their ultimate destruction, it cannot be doubtful that to confer upon them political power would only hasten that destruction, and it is at least questionable whether they can be preserved under any circumstances from extinction in contact with so dissimilar and so superior a race.

Senators are aware that we have in one portion of the country—in California and may have in Oregon—the *effête* civilization of the Chinese. They are not yet citizens of the United States, but the professed principle of this amendment authorizes, sanctions, and demands their admission to political power, and when that power is granted to them the conflict of races on your Pacific coast becomes inevitable. The Senator from Oregon desires to avoid this. The Senators from California solace themselves under the delusion that the Chinese are not and will not become citizens. They will yet find that the injury they are so willing to inflict upon the people of other States in regard to a different race will recoil upon their own constituents, for, by the operation of this amendment, if adopted, and on its principle, the Chinese will be entitled to become, and will become, citizens and voters. They have a higher grade of intelligence than the negro. They have more capacity for persistent labor than the negro, and, when they exist in sufficiently large numbers to aspire to political power, you will have the conflict of the Asiatic and Caucasian races in California, and perhaps in Oregon.

The relations between the Chinese and the Americans in California is but another instance of the antagonism of race in the struggle for power. If I am correctly informed, in California the Chinaman is not even admitted as a witness in their courts of justice, except, perhaps, in special cases, and much less will the people of that State suffer political power to be conferred upon such a population against their consent without resistance.

The discussion was resumed on the next morning (February 8). It lasted until 11:35 a. m. the following day (the 9th).

Frederick T. Freylinghuysen [N. J.] spoke. He said that if negro suffrage were not adopted, ex-rebel States such as Kentucky and Missouri would increase that unjust advantage in national representation which the Southern States held over the Northern States in the days of slavery, when only three-fifths of the negro population were counted in apportioning such representation.

Edmund G. Ross [Kan.] demanded the amendment as the final blow to slavery.

The disqualification of the free negroes of the country before the war was one of the strong adjuncts of slavery, without the aid of which it could not have lived a day. It is now the last prop upon which its friends depend for its future reëstablishment. Remove that and all hope for them is forever gone. Slavery is not dead, however, until all its supports are removed. It will never die until the negro is placed in a position of political equality from which he can successfully bid defiance to all future machinations for his enslavement. Until he is clothed with the ballot he is without that power, and is in constant danger from the cupidity of men who have been and expect again to be his masters. Without the ballot he is the slave of public prejudice and public caprice—the football of public scorn. He is powerless to secure the redress of any grievance which society may put upon him. There is not a single argument in favor of his liberation from physical servitude which does not apply with equal force in favor of his enfranchisement. In no other way can he be disenthralled from the meshes of impotency and public contempt in which he is now cast and made a respectable and useful citizen than by his investiture with the rights of manhood, which will make him, as he was designed by his Maker to be, our peer in the State.

There are many races of people in the world quite as distinctive in their characteristics as the negro and quite as dissimilar from each other, yet none of them are excluded from the ballot on account of those dissimilarities. The wild Indian of the plains, whose hands are red with the blood of murdered women and children, may become a citizen and cast a vote which shall affect the public weal equally with that of the most enlightened and humane among us; yet the negro, who is vastly his superior in intelligence, in humanity, in industry, and in all that pertains to good citizenship, is deemed unworthy to have a voice in affairs of the State in which he was born and reared and which concern him as nearly as any of us. What democracy is there in that?

It is objected that the passage of this resolution would be an act of bad faith toward the States; that the issue of negro suffrage was not made in the election of the members of the several legislatures which will be called to act upon it, and, therefore, that it should be postponed until that issue can be tried before the people in some future election of their State legislatures.

Gentlemen forget that this has been a standing issue in every State of the Union for the past three years; that it has been actively and everywhere discussed during that time. It has been voted upon in several States, and already adopted in two.

There is another point, Mr. President, which gentlemen forget, in speaking of the observance of good faith. It may be a pertinent inquiry whether we have kept faith with the negro in this matter. Has he not, after all, more to complain of than anybody else, in the continued deprivation by the States of a right, privilege, or immunity, whichever you choose to call it, guaranteed to him in the most solemn and binding form by the Constitution itself? Personal liberty is of little moment to him without the power to maintain it by the ballot. In ten States, in the District of Columbia, and in the Territories we have decreed to him the ballot. Are not his rights as sacred in all the other States as in these ten? Is he any less a man in those ten States than in the others whose representatives here have enacted him a voter there? Every man who voted for the enactment of negro suffrage in those ten States and the Territories stultifies himself unless he also votes to enact it in his own State. His enfranchisement in the South was an implied pledge, at least so regarded by me at the time, given in the name and with the approbation of the people we represent, that the same thing should be done everywhere under the jurisdiction of the Federal Government. That pledge yet stands unredeemed, and the people of the States now withholding this right should be the last to complain of bad faith in the adoption of the pending proposition.

Senator Davis, on February 8, made a long speech in opposition to the amendment in which he repeated the familiar constitutional objections to the measure and told the movers of it that they were fighting against nature as well as the Constitution—that their hope to educate the Southerner out of what they called race prejudice was an idle dream, and the attempt to fulfill it by force would result in fearful disaster. Closing, he referred to woman suffrage. He called this one of "those evidences of derangement and disordered intellect and morals" which New England furnished to every generation. He repeated the familiar sentiments about woman being "the priestess of the altar of the household" and the degradation of her sex and the deterioration of the race which would ensue were she "dragged" to the polls "amid the influences of passion and liquor, vulgarity," etc.

No, Mr. President; a good and a pure woman would turn with loathing and disgust from any such contact, and bad women ought never to be allowed to have a vote. It will be a day of woe, of incomparable woe, when the ballot is forced upon American women.

Joseph S. Fowler [Tenn.] replied to Senator Davis upon the subject of woman suffrage.

In a time like the present, when it is thought best to make an amendment to the Constitution, let it not be said the American Congress has been influenced to such a step, not by the universal love of mankind, not by an enlarged patriotism, but from suspicion and distrust of our own race and fellow-citizens. Let it embrace all, not a part. Let it protect the white man as well as the colored. I would go still further, and embrace all who are the subjects of law. I would found it on the spiritual worth and inviolability of the individual. It should embrace women as well as men. There is no argument in favor of the suffrage of men that will not apply equally as well to women. She is equally well fitted to decide what measures are calculated to promote her own interests. If any man were asked whose advice was the wisest and truest on all matters of business and politics he would unhesitatingly answer his wife's, his mother's, or his sister's. It is all a delusion and a sham to talk of excluding women from the ballot and admitting all the civilized and uncivilized men of the world.

When men base their support of suffrage upon the natural rights of man, upon the worth of the individual, and then exclude woman, they do not believe the doctrine they assert. It is a direct contradiction of terms. When they admit the African and the Indian, and exclude their mothers and sisters, it is a startling exhibition of prejudice and the force of custom.

If elections are conducted improperly and rudely it is because the refining and humanizing influence of woman has not been brought to purify them. Let the husband and father go with his wife and daughters to the polls as he does to church, and the rudest men will be taught self-respect and integrity of purpose. It will make the polls as refined and solemn as the lecture or the school.

Willard Saulsbury [Del.] opposed the amendment in an extended speech at the close of which he summed up as follows:

To justify any amendment of the Constitution these facts must be made to appear:
1. Authority to make it.
2. Necessity of its being made, arising from evils suffered from its not having been made.
3. That these evils would not exist if the amendment should be made, and that those evils are greater than would result from the making of the amendment.
4. That society and government would be improved by its being made.

Apply these four tests to the resolution under consideration and what honest man can give it his support?

Mr. President, this proposition has its origin in the supposed necessity of party, not in the necessity of good or wise government. This is so manifest from the uniform action of Congress in relation to kindred subjects, as well as to the proposition itself, that no artifice can conceal the fact and no denial of it is worthy of credit.

Sir, I protest against the passage of this resolution. I protest against it in the name of the Constitution of the United States of America. I protest against it in the name of the constitution of my State. I protest against it in the name of civil liberty, which is dear and should be dear to the heart of every American citizen. I protest against it in the names of our departed heroes and sages. Pause, Mr. President. Pause, Senators. The destruction of the Federal Union, the destruction of the State governments, the destruction of civil liberty are to be the consequences of your inconsiderate action.

Adonijah S. Welch [Fla.] addressed himself to refuting the charge that "the African race in this country is inferior in respect to intelligence and virtue," and so should not have the right to vote.

Intelligence and virtue are not the distinctive characteristics of races; they are not peculiar to any race; they are not monopolized by nor wholly excluded from any people on the round earth. Intelligence and virtue are individual possessions, inconstant qualities, varying *ad infinitum* among the individuals of every people. Those constant qualities which mark the different races are mainly physical, consisting of peculiarities of color, feature, figure, and the like; but, as these peculiarities are not the qualifications for the voter, nor indicate the presence or absence of such qualifications, they cannot, without absurdity, be assumed as the ground for withholding or bestowing the right of suffrage. I do not share the prejudice of Senators against race; my prejudices are for or against individuals according to their merits or demerits.

But suppose the question of the inferiority or superiority of races be admitted as possible or pertinent to this discussion, we need not shrink from such conclusions as can be reached. In what respects, let us ask, are the Southern negroes, for example, inferior to the Southern whites? They are certainly in social position far below a large class of white citizens, but they are, on the other hand, the social peers of another class found everywhere throughout the South. But social distinctions, whatever they are, do not confer political privileges in this free land; otherwise American women, who are our social superiors, would outrank us all. Then, again, as to intelligence the freedman holds the same relative position as in regard to social standing. We grant that he is inferior intellectually to the educated whites. It is the legitimate fruit of slavery and not a defect of race. But, if he be inferior to one class, he is most assuredly equal or even superior to that other class known as the poor whites; and, if his intelligence in general be limited, it is encouraging to know that there are many exceptions, instances of learning and culture, which indicate capacity. The present Secretary of State of Florida is a gentleman of talent and learning, and yet he is an African pure and simple. The important question, however, is not as to the comparative, intellectual, or social status of the negro, for intelligence and refinement and social elevation alone do not avail to make the genuine American citizen. The crowning virtue of American citizenship is patriotism. Nothing is more clearly written in the history of the immediate past than that intellect becomes the instrument of treason when patriotism is wanting. Just here the Southern negro appears to decided advantage. He possesses this indispensable virtue. Intellectually and socially below the dominant class, but equal, at least, to the poorer class of Southern whites, he is, if we except the Southern loyalists, who are limited in number, infinitely superior to them all as a patriot; and I weigh my words well when I say that, if his ignorance were as rayless as the darkest midnight, if he never had a dozen thoughts in all his life and never changed their course, his steady, unflinching love of this Union would render him a far safer depositary of the right of suffrage than he who has compassed all knowledge and all science and hates his country.

Senator Hendricks replied to Senator Welch.

The Senator said that intelligence and virtue were essential to the safe exercise of the suffrage. I think the negro does not now bring to the mass of the intelligence of this country an addition. I do not think he ever will. That race in its whole history has furnished no evidence of its capacity to lift itself up. It has never laid the foundation for its own civilization. Any elevation that we find in that race is when we find it coming in contact with the white race. While the tendency of the white race is upward, the tendency of the colored race is downward; and I have always supposed it is because in that race the physical predominates over the moral and intellectual qualities.

SENATOR WELCH.—May I ask the Senator, are the qualities of the voter—which are qualifications—in the individual or in the race? Is the white villain, if there is such a character, qualified to vote, while the intelligent negro—for there are intelligent negroes—is unqualified to vote?

SENATOR HENDRICKS.—The amendment that is pending before the Senate is not considering the race in regard to the individuals that make it. This is a proposition to extend the suffrage to an entire race. I am speaking of that race, whether it is a wise thing to bring into the political government of this country this race, which has shown in its history an incapacity to elevate itself or to establish a civilization for itself.

Can you tell me of any useful invention by the race, one single invention of greater importance to the world than the club with which the warrior beats to death his neighbor? Not one.

There are some Senators here who do not want the Chinese to vote. The Senators from Oregon and California, I think, are all opposed to the Chinese voting; and I think the Senator from Nevada [Mr. Stewart] is; and why? I believe they said they were pagans; but they are not such pagans as we find in Africa. China is the original home of a civilization that the world honors to this day. Why, sir, in China they had many of the rare and useful inventions long before they were known in Europe, and one of their great writers is as immortal as the classics of Athens, with a morality that comes nearer the morality of Jesus Christ than that of any ancient writer. But these Chinese, who are capable of a very high civilization, who have sustained their own civilization, to some extent at least, if they come to our country are not to be voters. They are in the way, I suppose, of the State of Nevada and of party hopes in California! I do not know why. Are they not prepared to give as intelligent a vote as the negro? Do they not understand our form of government as well as the negro? Are they not likely to become as well informed?

But it is said that they are pagans. Is it the business of this Government to prescribe what God or in what form men shall worship? He says that we are a Christian people. Not altogether, sir. We have no such test as that. It is not a test that obtains in any of the States now that a man shall be a Christian in order to be a voter. The Jew, a man who is not a Christian, is a voter. You do not exclude the infidel, who recognizes no God at all.

SENATOR STEWART.—I should like to ask the Senator if he is in favor of naturalizing Chinese and pagans who acknowledge no allegiance to the Government of the United States?

SENATOR HENDRICKS.—Of course I am in favor of naturalizing no such man as that. But that, I take it, is the pretext and not the reason for excluding the Chinese. It does not suit the Senators from the Pacific coast to have the Chinese vote, for some reason or other. I guess it is not popular out there to have the Chinese vote, and they are opposed to it. I would not wish to force the Chinese vote upon the people of the Pacific coast unless they wanted it themselves; and, if I desired to amend the Constitution so as to force the Chinaman to vote in California, I would say: "Let the people of California have a chance to express their wish on that subject"; and if they voted it down I would not attempt to force it upon them. They are the best judges of the interests of their society and that which will contribute to the strength and purity of their State government. And the same is true in Indiana.

OLIVER P. MORTON [Ind.].—Mr. President, we have just heard from my distinguished colleague, we heard it this evening from the Senator from Kentucky [Mr. Davis], and this afternoon from the Senator from Delaware [Mr. Saulsbury], the argument against this constitutional amendment that the African is an inferior race, incapable of development, and a race that never invented anything. Suppose we admit this statement to be true; suppose we confess this argument in its length and breadth; I ask if it is an argument against this amendment or in its favor?

It is admitted by all these Senators at the same time that the negro is a kindly race; it is not a savage race; and it is a Christian race in this country, as much so as the white people; but they say that they are of inferior intellectual power, not capable of the same development and progress as the whites. Suppose we grant all this; I ask if it is not a reason why these men should have the ballot put into their hands by which they may protect and take care of themselves? The strong can protect themselves; the weak require to be furnished with the means of protection. In this country there is no protection for political and civil rights outside of the ballot. If men have a natural right to life, liberty, and the pursuit of happiness, they have a natural right to the use of the means by which life, liberty, and the pursuit of happiness can be enjoyed.

We are told, as an evidence of the inferiority of the race, that they have never invented anything. My colleague would seem to wish to establish a new test or qualification of suffrage, that no man shall be allowed to vote who has not invented something. I wonder how many inventors there are here in this body to-night.

SENATOR SAULSBURY.—I ask whether the historical references that I made were not true references; and whether the facts in relation to the formation of the Federal Constitution are not evidenced by the records of the convention which framed it?

SENATOR MORTON.—Mr. President, I might admit the Senator's references, but I should deny his deductions. The Senator told us to-day frankly that we were not one people. He said in the Senate of the United States, after the culmination of a war that cost this nation six hundred thousand lives, that we were not a nation. He gave us to understand that we were as many separate nationalities as we have States; that one State is different from another as one nation in Europe is different from another. He denied expressly that we were a nation. He gave us to understand that he belonged to the tribe of the Delawares, an independent and sovereign tribe living on a reservation up here near the city of Philadelphia [laughter], but he denied his American nationality. The whole argument from first to last has proceeded upon that idea, that this is a mere confederacy of States; to use the language of the Senator to-day, a partnership of States. What is the deduction? If that is true there was the right of secession; the South was right and we were wrong. He did not draw that deduction, but it is one that springs inevitably from his premises.

Sir, the heresy of secession is not dead; it lives. It lives after this war, although it ought to have been settled by the war. It exists even as snow sometimes exists in the lap of summer when it is concealed behind the cliffs and the hedges and in the clefts of the rocks. It has come forth during this debate. We have heard the very premises, the very arguments, the very historical references upon which the right of secession was urged for thirty years. The whole fallacy lies in denying our nationality. I assert that we are one people and not thirty-seven different peoples; that we are one nation, and as such we have provided for ourselves a national Constitution, and that Constitution has provided the way by which it may be amended.

Mr. President, much has been said in regard to the inconsistent position of the Republican party, and a clause has been read from the Chicago platform in support of that charge. That clause was put into the platform not with reference to an amendment of the Constitution, not estopping the party from amending the Constitution; but with reference to an understanding throughout the country that Congress might attempt to regulate the subject of suffrage in the States. It was with reference to congressional regulation that that clause was put in the platform, but it was not declared directly or by implication that we should not amend the Constitution so as to limit the States in the exercise of that power.

Mr. President, the Republican party has its errors; it has committed its faults; and yet but for that party this Capitol would now be the Capitol of a hostile slaveholding confederacy.

One word in regard to the so-called Democratic party. The Democratic party for more than twenty years has lived upon the negro question. It has been its daily food, and, if the negro question shall now be withdrawn from politics, the Democracy, as a party, will literally starve to death. We need not, therefore, be surprised to find them resisting this constitutional amendment which will forever withdraw the subject from politics, and will strike down that prejudice to which the Democratic party has appealed for years. The Democratic party has not for years appealed to the reason of the people, but it has appealed to their prejudices upon the subject of race. It has sought, and, to some extent obtained, power upon that subject. It is still following the fortunes of slavery after slavery is dead. It cherished slavery while it lived, and now that slavery is dead it has taken to its embrace its odious and putrescent corpse. The Democratic party is now performing the office of Old Mortality by trying to revive inscriptions upon the moldering and dishonored tomb of slavery.

JAMES R. DOOLITTLE [Wisc.].—The Senator from Indiana
seems to think that no statesman can bear in mind two ideas at
the same time; that there can be no such thing as State rights
maintained by anybody under the Constitution unless that person is a secessionist; and that, on the other hand, no man can
maintain that there is any such thing as rights in the Federal
Government under the Constitution without being in favor of an
absolute concentrated government at Washington.   Sir, these
two ideas must go together in our system of government, and the
time is coming when they must be discussed, when the rights
of the States under the Constitution must be acknowledged.   It
is just as much a war on the Constitution to deny the States the
rights which belong to them as it is a war on the Constitution
to maintain the doctrine of secession.

SENATOR MORTON.—I have always denied State sovereignty;
and I do now.   I deny the doctrine that the States are separate
and independent nations.   We are one people.   But, sir, the
States have certain rights, rights that are guaranteed to them by
the Constitution of the United States, just as we have rights secured to us both by the Federal and State Constitutions.   We
have State rights, but have no State sovereignty, and never had.

SENATOR DOOLITTLE.—Mr. President, the honorable Senator
says there is no State sovereignty.   I contend that by every decision of the Supreme Court of the United States, by every
declaration made by every writer upon our system of government in the beginning, whether a Federalist or Republican, it
was always maintained that the States had an attribute of sovereignty, not absolute, but under the Constitution, because under the Constitution they have parted with their absolute sovereignty; nor has the United States Government any sovereignty
under the Constitution which is absolute.   All the power which
the United States Government has under the Constitution is
limited.   Sovereignty is limited by the Constitution.   State sovereignty is limited by the Constitution; the United States sovereignty is limited by the Constitution; and the great difficulty
of our times is that men cannot think or will not think that the
two sovereignties exist at the same time under our government,
the one limited by the other.

Why, Mr. President, from earliest childhood every man in
this body has been taught that we live in the solar system where
the planets that revolve around the sun are controlled by two
forces: one a force tending toward the center by the force of
gravitation—the centripetal force; and the other is the centrifugal force, by which they are driven in their orbits around

the center. Mr. President, if either one of these forces were taken away it would absolutely destroy the system. In our solar system, if the centrifugal force were taken away and nothing but the centripetal force left to act, every planet would be drawn to the center, to the sun. On the other hand, if the centripetal force were destroyed in our solar system, and no force permitted to operate but the centrifugal force, all the planets would be driven in a tangent away from our system into illimitable space. Sir, it is the operation of these two forces, the one which tends to the center, the other which tends to the circumference, which keeps these planets moving in their orbits, which maintains our system, which keeps it from destruction; and the destruction of either of these forces is the destruction of the solar system.

Now, sir, come to our system of government; these two forces are planted in it of necessity. These two ideas have been here from the beginning. There have been men who represented the one and represented the other from the beginning. There have been men who have contended always for the absolute sovereignty of this central Government, and other men who have contended always for the absolute sovereignty of the States; and both of them have contended for a falsehood from the beginning. There is no absolute sovereignty in this Government; nor is there any absolute sovereignty in the States; but, under the operation of our system, devised by our fathers, wise as if they had been inspired from on high and had wisdom almost like Him who created the solar system under which we live, these two grand ideas, two great forces in government, were put in operation at one and the same time, each limiting the other, each operating upon the other, both working together, and working out that harmonious system in which alone we live and move and have our being; and that man or statesman, call himself what he may, whether a fire-eating secessionist of the South who comes into this body or elsewhere and maintains the absolute sovereignty of the State, with its right to withdraw from the Union, to retire from the system, to overturn the Government; or that other statesman, Republican though he may call himself, who comes into this body or elsewhere and maintains that this Government only has absolute sovereignty, and that it has the power to seize to itself all the powers of the Government—whichever one of these men undertakes to do this is making war on the Government and war on the system under which we live.

Mr. President, without going into a detailed history, what

has occurred since the close of the war? In my judgment, in many of the acts which have been entered upon, the Constitution of the United States has itself been violated. I believe, as much as I believe in my existence here, that in the law which was passed establishing military tribunals and military government in the States of the South, abolishing all civil government, denying all right of trial by jury, this party in power in the Congress of the United States have just as much violated the Constitution in that regard as it ever was violated by any party in the history of the Government.

CHARLES D. DRAKE [Mo.].—Mr. President, the whole argument of the gentleman and of all the other Senators on the other side who have spoken on this subject proceeds upon the doctrine that George H. Pendleton laid down in 1864, that, if every State in this Union should unite in ratifying the constitutional amendment abolishing slavery except one, slavery would not be abolished in that one State. They limit the power of amendment in the Constitution in that way.

SENATOR DOOLITTLE.—The Senator will allow me to interrupt him. I hope the honorable Senator does not mean to include me in that category from anything I have said. I believe that I made the first speech in this body in favor of the amendment abolishing slavery.

SENATOR DRAKE.—I say, Mr. President, that the whole doctrine of the opponents of this measure in this debate has been to the purport that, let any number of States ratify this amendment, it would have no binding force upon the other States, but only upon those States that ratify it. I say to the gentlemen who talk so about the rights of States, that there is not a State in this Union that has one single right but that which it derives from the Constitution, and there is not one right except that of equal senatorial representation which cannot be taken away from any State by a constitutional amendment passed by two-thirds of Congress and ratified by three-fourths of the States.

Frederick A. Sawyer [S. C.] replied to the charge that the negro was incapable of becoming an intelligent citizen. Were the Senators who made this charge to go to a reconstructed State they would, in spite of their prejudices, find evidences that the negro, although not the political equal of the white man, although not the intellectual equal of the Anglo-Saxon race, yet has in him that germ of development of character which in due process of time and with the genial sun of American institutions may make him a good citizen and an equal before the law with any other citizen.

We have, thank God, in South Carolina, in Alabama, in North Carolina, no class of men who propose at this time to deprive the negro of the right of suffrage, or to deny that he has a claim to it. During the late political campaign, when the late rebels of the Southern States expected the election of the Democratic candidates for President and Vice-President, they did not go before their people with a proposition to take away from the negro the right of suffrage. On the contrary, some of the most distinguished advocates of the platform of the Democratic party as laid down in the national convention expressed their entire willingness to grant suffrage to the negro.

SENATOR DAVIS.—Will the honorable Senator permit me to make a single remark? There was just a race between the parties which should secure the negro suffrage that had been forced upon the country.

SENATOR SAWYER.—Then I understand the doctrine of the Senator to be that, if the negro can be made to vote the Democratic ticket, he is an intelligent man and entitled to become a citizen.

SENATOR DAVIS.—Not at all. It is only because the suffrage of the negro has been enforced by power and by fraud and violence, and at the cannon's mouth, upon the people of the Southern States that any considerable portion of them consent to accept it.

SENATOR SAWYER.—Mr. President, I hold it to be a fact which cannot be disputed that to-day, were the question put to the white men of the lately reconstructed States whether the ballot should be taken out of the hands of the negro, the answer would be an almost universal negative; and, if the Government of the United States had not, as he says, at the point of the bayonet and by violent assumption of unconstitutional authority put that ballot into the hands of the negro, there would, to-day, yes, there would two years ago, have been a strong negro suffrage party in every one of those States. More, I believe that in his own State of Kentucky, while the honorable Senator himself, maintaining his peculiar views, might hesitate to put the ballot in the hands of the negro, the majority of his party would not hesitate one moment to do it if they believed he would throw his ballot in favor of the doctrines of the Democratic party.

Mr. President, it has been distinctly asserted by several Sen-

ators that the negro in contact with the white race has gained
a great degree of civilization since he was brought from his
native barbarism in Africa. If he has shown himself competent
to a certain degree of development, if, in the process of time,
he has come to that condition whereby he can be rendered a
freeman with safety to the State, I ask if that does not lead
logically and naturally to the inference that his development
may be still further carried on, and that he may be capable of
making a good citizen, carrying intelligently a ballot? I ask
if that citizen who has been able to carry a bayonet in defence
of his Government is not likely to be competent to carry a ballot
to protect the liberties which his rifle has helped to win?

SENATOR DAVIS.—Will the Senator permit me to ask him a
question? Does he believe that there could be found in the State
of South Carolina enough capable negroes to take charge of
the government of that State and of its polity, and of all its
interests and of all the city and town governments and of all
the corporations in the State, and manage them with any skill,
judgment, or success?

SENATOR SAWYER.—I will answer the question of the honorable Senator by asking another. I will ask him if he believes
that, if the white race of South Carolina had for two centuries
been the slaves of the black race, had been by statute and by
usage deprived of every means of cultivation and self-develop-
ment, if they had been shut out of all the relations of the citizen, if they had been the hewers of wood and the drawers of
water for two centuries, there could be found upon a sudden
emancipation of that white race probably men enough to assume
and perform all the duties which belong to civilized society in
the highest and most statesmanlike manner?

SENATOR DAVIS.—The answer of the honorable Senator I regard as equivalent to an answer in the negative. He puts to me
a question that involves an impossibility that the white race
should have been subjected for two centuries to the negro race.
The negro race has never enslaved any other race itself. It has
been, in all of its phases of existence, incapable of acquiring a
mastery over the other races, much less maintaining a mastery.

SENATOR SAWYER.—Mr. President, the danger of admitting
the negro vote because a portion of the negroes are ignorant, the
danger of admitting the votes of any class of men because
some of that class of men are ignorant, is a danger which is
incident to the possession of the ballot by all men. I suppose it
will not be claimed by any Senator that one-half of the white
men in any country exercise the vote on all occasions intelli-

gently; but on that account, because a man happens to be weaker
in intellect than his neighbor; because he happens not to have
the capacity for administration, the capacity for filling the offices
of the counties and towns and of the State, does anybody propose to deprive him of the ballot? No; but, when we get to a
man whose skin is a little darker than ours, whom we can mark
out as belonging to a class, we can assume that his color is a
badge of inferiority, notwithstanding the numerous exceptions
which we see even under the adverse circumstances under which
these people labor. Then, when we can establish that mark of
color as the mark of a class, men wish to discriminate against
them and deprive them of the rights of other citizens.

Now, Mr. President, the war has made all the slaves citizens.
Now, whatever class of men we make citizens of the United
States, it is, in my opinion, a public danger to keep from partici-
pation in the active powers of government.

SENATOR DAVIS.—Are not women citizens?

SENATOR SAWYER.—Women are represented through their
husbands or brothers.

SENATOR DAVIS.—Are not our negroes represented?

SENATOR SAWYER.—Through their masters. I know that the
theory is that the negroes should be represented by those who
have so long represented them in providing for their animal
wants and taking the proceeds of the labor of their muscle.

I do not propose to continue these remarks. I should not
have said anything on this question but for the strangeness of
the doctrines which have been announced here. Those doctrines,
it seems to me, are precisely the doctrines which led to the rebellion itself. More than that, they will, in my opinion, produce another revolution.

SENATOR DAVIS.—The Senator from South Carolina charges
myself and the Senators who occupy my position with discriminating against the negro from prejudice. I retort the charge
upon the honorable Senator and his friends and his supporters
in this chamber and elsewhere. I ask the honorable Senator to
tell me if he, or a single one of them, has ever taken a sable
Dinah to his bosom as a wife; and I ask if that is not a discrimination as distinct and quite as comprehensible as the distinction
we make that the negro is incapable of self-government?

SENATOR SAWYER.—Mr. President, I did not mean to cast any
reflection upon the gentleman in speaking of his prejudice. I
know my own observation has justified me in believing, that it is
almost an impossibility or next to an impossibility for a man
to have been born and brought in contact with the institution of

African slavery and look at the question with a fair, unbiased judgment. I have lived for ten years in a State where the system of slavery existed. I have seen the negro as a slave; I have seen him as a freeman; I have seen him as a voter. I have never had the taste to select any colored Dinah, to quote his language, as the companion of my social hours. I leave that to those who are "to the manner born" [laughter]; and I have the satisfaction of knowing that even that has become disreputable in re-

A Prospective Scene in the "City of Oaks," 4th of March, 1889.

KU-KLUX WARNING TO A "SCALAWAG" AND A "CARPET-BAGGER"

From the "Independent Monitor," Tuscaloosa, Ala., Sept. 1, 1868

constructed communities, and that it is only those people who, though they do not bear in the popular acceptation down there the name of scalawags, deserve eminently to have it.[1]

Senator Doolittle declared that, if political equality of blacks and whites were to be forced on States containing a majority of negroes, the end would be social equality.

If negroes can vote they can be voted for; if they can be voted for they can be elected members of the legislature, as

[1] "Scalawag" was a term applied to a native-born white man in the South who acted with the Republican party in order to gain political preferment. A "Carpet-bagger" was a Northern born man who so acted.

they are members of State conventions and legislatures, as they may be members of Congress, and I believe one was said to be elected to the other House; members of the Senate of the United States; generals in your army; and, if by possibility they could hold the balance of power and get our Republican brethren of the North, in their zeal to demonstrate that there is no distinction between the races, to nominate for the President of the United States a negro, they might perhaps in the end elect some negro as President of the United States, and live on social equality here in Washington, as well as in the States of the South. If negroes are to be elected Senators to this body you cannot refuse to meet them at your receptions, at your inauguration balls, at the President's table, and their wives with them, and their children also; and your children must meet them side by side, upon a footing of equality. Face the music, gentlemen; acknowledge the truth that this is the necessary, direct tendency, and the inevitable result which must come, in States where a majority of the population are colored, if you force upon the States unrestricted and unqualified negro suffrage.

While I admit that there are some white men who are utterly incapacitated to perform the high office of taking part in the government of the country, they are exceptions to the general rule, whereas with the African it is directly the contrary. There are but a few of them that are capable of taking part in the Government, and they are exceptions to the general rule. A few among them, if by any legislation you could select those few, might take part without danger in the government of the country.

But, sir, to give that power to the race, to give it to them as a mass, is to demoralize your Government; it is to sap it at the foundations; it is to strike down the bulwark upon which liberty rests; it is to do what has been done in other ages and countries of the world—to demoralize the ballot by making it so universal among the weak, the degraded, the ignorant, the demoralized, that a designing and ambitious man comes at last and rules the empire with a rod of iron. It is so in France; it was so in Greece; it was so in Rome. Are we to follow their example? Are we to cherish it, and to shout at the top of our voices, "Universal suffrage without distinction of race or color, to the negro, to the Indian, and to the Asiatic"? Sir, extend your suffrage among such a number of ignorant, demoralized masses of men and your whole liberties, Constitution, and Government will go down together.

On February 9 Senator Sumner proposed to strike the words "of citizens of the United States" from the amendment. Senator Morton objected, saying that this would admit to the suffrage the Chinese, who were debarred because of the word "white" in the naturalization requirements, a test case in the courts of California having resulted in the decision that a Chinaman was not of the white race and so could not become a citizen. Senator Sumner then declared that, following the principles of the Declaration of Independence, the word "white" should be stricken from the statute book.

Senator Williams said that the Chinaman had no more regard for the obligation of a Christian oath than he had "for the whistling of the idle wind."

Hundreds and thousands of them might come under such circumstances to be naturalized and take the oaths prescribed by law, and at the same time to all intents and purposes be foreigners. While I will go as far as any reasonable man in this country to give to the citizens of the United States, naturalized and native born, equal political rights, I say that this country has the absolute power to protect itself from Chinamen or any other sort of foreigners by such legislation as in its judgment is necessary for the purposes of protection. And in protecting itself from these hordes of foreigners, who may come here either from selfish or hostile motives; in protecting itself from these people living on the other side of the ocean, it does not in any respect violate the Declaration of Independence.

Senator Sumner withdrew his amendment. Senator Wilson then proposed the following substitute for section 1 of the amendment:

No discrimination shall be made in any State among the citizens of the United States in the exercise of the elective franchise or in the right to hold office in any State on account of race, color, nativity, property, education, or religious creed.

Senator Corbett wished that it might specifically exclude foreigners not of the white race, because he feared that Senator Sumner might succeed later in securing the excision of the word "white" from the naturalization laws.

Senator Cameron supported Senator Wilson's substitute.

I am in favor of the proposition of the Senator from Massachusetts because it invites into our country everybody; the negro, the Irishman, the German, the Frenchman, the Scotchman, the Englishman, and the Chinaman. I will welcome every man, whatever may be the country from which he comes, who by his industry can add to our national wealth. Our friends from the Pacific coast are afraid of that simple, frugal people, lest they should destroy their liberties. I have no such fears. These Senators tell us, at the same time, that Chinamen will never become citizens. If they will not become citizens, what harm will they do us under this amendment to the Constitution? We are told that they come here and labor and send all the result of their toil to their own country. They do send a great deal; but what they send is not a tithe of the wealth which they give to us by their industry and their frugal habits.

Mr. President, I must express my surprise at this talk about the poor Chinaman. I never heard of his doing any harm to anybody in America. He has enriched the Pacific slope by his toil. He has made that great railroad which is the miracle of the world by his patient industry. Whoever heard before of a people doing so much work in so short a space of time and getting so little reward for it as they have done? We might just as well say that the Irishmen who came into Pennsylvania and New York and Indiana and Illinois and Iowa, and gave their labor to make the canals and the railroads which have enriched those States, should be prevented from becoming citizens. The Chinese who are now here will probably return to their own country; most of them, however, in their coffins, for their bodies are always carried away after their dissolution; but their children, who remain here, will after a while imitate our people, adopt our institutions, and become citizens of our country, and by their toil add to the wealth of the country.

Lyman Trumbull [Ill.] opposed Senator Wilson's substitute. It would, he said, overturn, ruthlessly and without cause, the constitutions of perhaps all the States in the Union, since these contained such requirements as that the governor should be a natural-born citizen, which the people of each State, following the example of the Constitution as well as its permission, had an unimpeachable right to impose.

Senator Morton defended the substitute.

Mr. President, we are now about to amend the fundamental law in regard to suffrage. The amendment, as it is proposed by the House of Representatives and as it is reported by the committee on the judiciary of the Senate, confines the limitation upon State power to the single subject of race or color, just as if that was the only subject upon which there could be an abuse. Now, sir, that we are at work on this subject, can we stand justified before the people of this nation if we do not make this limitation apply to other possible abuses? I think there is no more principle, there is no more justice, in requiring a man to have a certain amount of property before he shall be allowed to exercise this right that is indispensable to the protection of his life, liberty, and happiness than there is in requiring him to have a white skin. If the right of suffrage is a natural right, if it belongs to all men because they have a right to have a voice in the government that controls their action, if it is necessary to all men as a means of protecting other acknowledged natural rights, how can you make it depend upon property?

The same may be said in regard to educational tests. I believe all educational tests in this country are humbugs. When you come to consider the question of voting as a natural right, what right have you to take it from a man because he cannot read and write? He may be, nevertheless, a very intelligent man, and he has his rights to defend and preserve just like other men, and the right of suffrage is just as important to him as it is to anybody else. What right have you to say that he shall not have it because he cannot read and write?

The same is true in regard to the qualification of religious faith. The State of New Hampshire now excludes any man from her House of Representatives unless he belongs to the Protestant faith. That exclusion is contrary to the whole spirit of our institutions; and, now that we are at work on this subject, and the question is brought before us, are we at liberty to reject this amendment, and thus say to New Hampshire, in substance and by implication, that she may continue to exclude men from office on account of their faith?

In regard to nativity, if we reject this amendment we say to the States, "You cannot exclude men because of their color, but you are still left at liberty to exclude them because of their nativity." Are we prepared to say that?

James W. Patterson [N. H.] said that the religious qualification demanded of a Representative in his State was a dead letter, and that he thought the citizens would be willing to have it set aside. However, he believed in an educational qualification for voters, such as was in force in Massachusetts.

Self-government is not possible until a people have advanced somewhat in civilization; and it presupposes the maintenance of that intelligence by commerce and schools, by the press, and restrictions of law upon the influx of barbarism and arbitrary power from abroad. A restriction of that kind is no wrong done to the voter, for it simply protects the purity and integrity of the Government under which all his rights are secured. The consumer has just as much right to complain of a protective tariff which guards national industry and capital against the serf labor of Europe as an ignorant population have to complain of the restriction of intelligence which guards the political institutions under which they live. Why, sir, the voter discharging the obligation of an elector fulfills an official duty as truly as the judge exercises the functions of an office when he administers justice between man and man; and, as some knowledge of law is a prerequisite in the judge to the proper discharge of his duties, so it would seem that some intelligence, some mental discipline, some little knowledge of the laws and spirit of a country are necessary to a safe participation in its government.

Suffrage is the most sacred of all our rights; and why should we throw open this portal of political power and let into the strongholds of our Government the emissaries of arbitrary power, the minions of despotism? Why should we let barbarism come in like a flood? If you do that the period may not be far distant when you will have so degraded the intelligence of your people that they will be unequal to self-government, and then, like the early republics, you will roll down the bloody grade of revolution into the most abject and absolute despotism.

I know that, as we stand to-day, an educational test may not be necessary; but it will do no harm. If the people have the intelligence prerequisite to self-government, an educational test will not limit very much the extent of suffrage. There will be about as many votes cast with it as without it. It is simply a safeguard against a possible evil. I would have the intelligence prerequisite to the exercise of suffrage very low, so that it may be easily reached by our foreign population or by any of our native population who may lack the means of education. I desire it, among other things, as an encouragement to popular intelligence. I say simply this, that the way to suffrage should be open to all. To deny it on account of race or color or want of property is doing violence to the civilization of our age, and insults Christianity; but to protect and guard it against the incoming floods of ignorance and barbarism is simply to preserve the jewel of liberty. This is my view of this subject, both as an abstract and practical question. For this and for no other reason am I opposed to the amendment of the gentleman from Massachusetts.

Senator Wilson stated that the educational qualification in Massachusetts which had been praised by Senator Patterson was "practically of no value whatever." It did not keep five hundred men from voting. He had opposed it when it was proposed, and had refused to take advantage of it in an election where it would have been helpful to his party to do so.

"I would be ashamed to look a man in the face when I put such a test to him. I believe in manhood, and I believe the ballot is an educator."

Roscoe Conkling [N. Y.] objected to the substitute, in particular the provision regarding office holding. What, prevent a State requiring educational qualifications in a legal or medical office?
John Sherman [O.] replied that the amendment guaranteed only the right to hold office, but not a particular office nor class of offices.

The amendment applies one general, universal rule, that, whenever the laws of the United States make a man a citizen, the laws of the United States and the State must recognize his right to hold office and to vote at all elections. That is all there is to it; and we should not be safe, in my judgment, in stopping short of this general provision.
I believe that there is scarcely an example in the history of this country where these limitations upon the elective franchise

and upon the right to hold office have been enforced. In the early history of the Government all remember the case of John Randolph, where the question was made upon him that he was not old enough to hold the office of Representative in Congress. His reply was given, "ask my constituents," and he was sworn in although he was but twenty-four years of age. So Albert Gallatin by a strict party vote was excluded from the office of Senator of the United States for want of residence in this country after he became a citizen; but everybody who participated in the act was ashamed of it.[1] Now, I doubt whether in any State of the Union these provisions which make discriminations between citizens can be or would be enforced.

SENATOR SUMNER.—James Shields [Illinois] was excluded from the Senate.

SENATOR SHERMAN.—General Shields was kept out for a time; and afterward reëlected and sent back. There is no case, so far as I can now recall, in the history of this country where these exceptional exclusions and discriminations against particular citizens have been enforced, or where public sentiment would allow them to be enforced.

We ought to deny to States the right to discriminate between citizens on account of anything except age, residence, and sex. In all other respects citizens should have an equal right to vote. We ought to regard it as a fundamental principle of our Government that all persons arriving at a certain age are entitled to equal rights. We can fairly base our action upon that fundamental principle and submit that action to the people with a certainty that it will be adopted. But, sir, if I go before the people of Ohio with a constitutional amendment such as that which is sent to us by the House of Representatives, or that which is proposed by the Judiciary Committee, how shall I be met? I shall be told, "Here are white citizens excluded from voting in Massachusetts because they cannot read and write; here are people excluded from office in New Hampshire because they are not Protestants. Why do you not correct these evils at your own door, evils brought upon the country by your own friends, and why should you protect only and seek to extend only the right of suffrage to the colored race, who are just emancipated from bondage, who are ignorant, who are without the capacity, probably, for self-government unless they become enlightened?" How can you answer it? It is impossible to answer, especially when you meet a prejudiced people who have got to vote on this question.

[1] Mr. Gallatin had taken the oath of allegiance eight years before, and nine years of citizenship is required of a Senator.

The people of Ohio come from all the old States, many of them from Virginia and Maryland and other of the old slave States. They are full of prejudices. Unless you show that you are willing to adopt a universal rule which tramples down their prejudices, and the prejudices of the people of other portions of the old States where they have not adopted, probably, the more advanced rules on this subject—unless you can show that you have dealt with this question in an enlightened spirit of statesmanship, you will be borne down by popular clamor. It will be said this is a mere party expedient to accomplish party ends, and not a great fundamental proposition upon which you should base your superstructure.

Senator Wilson's amendment was carried by 31 yeas to 27 nays.

A proposition was now introduced and supported with equal zeal by Senators Morton and Charles R. Buckalew [Pa.] proposing an amendment to the pending resolution, which should in effect be a sixteenth amendment to the Constitution. Its aim was to take from the States the power now confided to them by the Constitution, to direct the manner in which electors of President and Vice-President shall be chosen. The declared motive for the change was to prevent the possibility of the electors being chosen by State legislatures as had been done in some cases, and to guarantee the certainty of a popular vote in their selection in every State of the Union. To insure this result it was proposed in the amendment that the entire power over the choice of electors should be transferred to Congress. After brief debate the amendment was agreed to, and the two proposed articles included under one resolution were adopted by the required two-thirds majority of 39 yeas and 16 nays, and sent to the House for concurrence.

The House, not being willing to accept the Senate's amendments, refused by formal vote to concur, and asked for a conference. The Senate took the unusual step of declining a conference, promptly receded from its own amendments, and sent to the House the original proposition of that body. The House, not to be outdone by the Senate in capricious change of opinion, now refused to agree to the form of amendment it had before adopted,

and returned it to the Senate with the added requirement of nativity, property, and creed, which the Senate
had originally proposed. The Senate in turn rejected all
it had before proposed. The strange controversy was
finally ended and the subject brought into intelligible
shape by a conference committee, which reported the
Fifteenth Amendment in the precise form in which it
became incorporated in the Constitution. It received
the sanction of the House by a vote far beyond the two-
thirds required to adopt it, the ayes being 145, the nays
44. In the Senate the ayes were 35, the nays were 13.
The action of Congress on the amendment was completed
on the 26th of February, six days before General Grant
was installed in the presidency.

The bill went to President Johnson on February 27.
He did not sign it, but as it had been passed by a two-
thirds majority it became effective without his signature.

When it had been ratified by three-fourths of the
States the amendment was proclaimed a part of the Constitution on March 30, 1870.

CHAPTER IV

FEDERAL POWER TO SUPPRESS ABUSES AGAINST CIVIL RIGHTS

[THE KU-KLUX OUTRAGES]

President Grant Reports Progress of Reconstruction—Admission of Hiram R. Revels [Miss.], a Negro, to the Senate—Congress Completes Reconstruction—Ku-Klux Outrages in the South—Oliver P. Morton [Ind.] Moves Appointment of Senate Committee to Investigate Them—Debate: in Favor, Willard Warner [Ala.], James W. Nye [Nev.], Zachariah Chandler [Mich.]; Opposed, Eugene Casserly [Cal.], Thomas F. Bayard [Del.], Allen G. Thurman [O.]; Committee Appointed—Majority and Minority Reports—John Sherman [O.] Moves That the Committee Bring in a Bill to Suppress the Outrages—Debate: in Favor, Sen. Sherman, John Scott [Pa.], John Pool [N. C.], Sen. Morton; Opposed, Sen. Bayard, Gen. Francis P. Blair [Mo.]; Resolution Is Passed, and Bill Is Enacted.

IN his first annual message of December 6, 1869, President Grant reported the status of reconstruction in the States which were excluded from representation in Congress.

Georgia had qualified for this representation, save that the legislature had, as subsequently decided by the Supreme Court of the State, violated its new constitution by unseating negro legislators and seating white men who were disqualified by the Fourteenth Amendment. The President recommended Congress to require the Governor of Georgia to convene the rightfully elected members and exclude those unlawfully seated, requiring all the legislators to take the oath prescribed by the reconstruction acts; when this had been done the State should be admitted to representation in Congress.

Virginia had qualified for readmission to the Union, and he recommended that she be admitted.

162

Elections to the legislature had taken place in Mississippi and Texas; the results were not yet known.

It is to be hoped that the acts of the legislatures of these States when they meet will be such as to receive your approval and thus close the work of reconstruction.

Congress followed the recommendation of the President in regard to Georgia in an act which he approved

RECONSTRUCTION, OR "A WHITE MAN'S GOVERNMENT"
From the collection of the New York Historical Society

on December 22, 1869. In accordance with this act the legislature of the State was reconvened and the lawful members reseated. It ratified the Fifteenth Amendment on February 2, 1870, this being one of the conditions of the act. On July 15, 1870, the State was admitted to representation in Congress, completing the work of reconstruction.

On January 26, 1870, the President approved an act of Congress admitting Virginia to representation in the national legislature. On February 23 Mississippi was similarly admitted to such representation. Already, in anticipation of such admission, Senators from the State had been admitted, one of them, Hiram R. Revels, being a negro. Though Senator Revels was a man of intelligence and good character, this seating in the national legislature for the first time of a person of African descent greatly embittered the South and the Democrats of the North who remained consistent in opposition to exalting the black man to the level of the white. The Republicans, on the other hand, were gratified that the admission of a negro to the highest rank in the Government save that of President and Vice-President, and, possibly, that of the Supreme Court, completed their work for his race in such a significant manner. Says Mr. Blaine of Senator Revels' admission:

"He sat in the seat which Jefferson Davis had wrathfully deserted to take up arms against the Republic and become the ruler of a hostile government. Poetic justice, historic revenge, personal retribution were all complete when Mr. Revels' name was called on the roll of the Senate."

One of the Senators from Virginia and one from Georgia were Democrats. All the other Senators from the ex-rebel States were Republicans.

As each State was reconstructed Federal military government was withdrawn from it and civil government was completely restored.

Upon the establishment of civil government in the ex-rebel States and the consequent withdrawal of Federal troops therefrom reports began to appear of outrages upon negroes, white Republicans, and Northern men and women who had gone South to educate the negroes. The chief cause of these assaults seemed to be the grant of suffrage to the negroes with the result of the elevation to office of some of their number and more white Republicans, both carpet-baggers and scalawags [see page 152]. Most of the outrages were committed by bands of midnight marauders, which were parts of a secret order called the Ku-Klux Klan. The name (derived from the Greek word *kuklos*, meaning circle) and the form of organization of this order were adapted in a spirit of burlesque from the Greek-letter fraternity system of American colleges, thereby indicating that the originators of the"Klan" were well-educated young men who in their high spirits began by masking themselves as for a fraternity initiation, and frightening negroes as a more or less innocent prank, and then, seeing the power they exercised over their superstitious victims, employed this for political purposes, in which work they were joined by less educated and, possibly, more unprincipled persons. Negroes who were leaders of their race were frightened into political inaction or else driven from the community, and the same treatment was extended to white Republicans and to Northern settlers whose friendliness to the negroes, if not, indeed, whose very presence in the South, holding as they did alien social, political, and even religious sentiments, was obnoxious to their white neighbors.

INVESTIGATION OF SOUTHERN OUTRAGES

SENATE, JANUARY 18–APRIL 5, 1871

On January 18, 1871, Oliver P. Morton [Ind.] introduced in the Senate a resolution to appoint five Senators as a committee to investigate the truth or falsity of the reports of these outrages.

Eugene Casserly [Dem.], of California, opposed the resolution, the effect of which (he would not say purpose) was to "fan into new life the embers of a great civil war, the embers of sectional conflict and hate."

It was, he charged, a desperate attempt of a perishing party to stay its doom. There is no party, and never was, "which is worth so much to the country as to compensate in the smallest degree for renewing the sectional and fratricidal animosities of the last ten years."

I care not how great any party may be in its pretensions or its power, I care not how distinguished a leader in that party a man may be, I say that party is an evil, and that man is mischievous, when he or it seeks to revive in the country the bloody memories of the past, or to fix upon a great portion of our people a brand of disgrace before the world as savages scarcely fit to exist, and to put upon them at home the badge of a galling inferiority.

I do not believe either in the accusations or in the policy that prompts them. I can well understand that there are in the South disorderly and violent men. They are the natural fruits of the war and of your own misgovernment. They are but a handful, easily dealt with by any government dealing with them in the right spirit. But what I do not believe is that the mass of the Southern people are the barbarians they have been represented to be, over and over on this floor, by prominent Senators of the majority. It would be a great deal better for the dignity of this body, for the peace of this country, for the good standing of the American people before the enlightened judgment of Christendom, to say at once what is the object of all this exaggerated outcry of outrages in the South; of all this hollow parade of investigations—far better to come directly to the point like men, and let it be understood that no one of the States lately in insurrection will be permitted to come back here until she sends to the Senate and to the House of Representatives men whose party politics shall be acceptable to the accidental party majority in each.

Let that be understood; then will there be no need any more for the periodical performances here, for the demonstrations of passion or the torrent of studied vituperation poured out against the people of the South. If I thought the tenth part of such vituperation could be true, I should mourn over the land that had nursed such children as inevitably lost. Nobody knows better than the members of this Senate who have been longest here how easy it is anywhere throughout that Southern land, upon which, from this Capitol, Congress frowns with aspect so malign—with its whole system of labor disorganized, with its social system broken up from the very foundations, filled with ruined men, with all the rankling animosities left by a great civil war, as well in the victor as in his victim—to obtain from idle, ignorant, malignant, or suborned witnesses just as much testimony as is wanted here for the purpose of blackening the character of the people of the Southern States, exasperating the dominant party, and preparing the way for fresh operations in the line of "reconstruction."

Sir, we ought to have some patience with the people of the South. The terrible evils of such a civil war as we have gone through, its disorders and its rancors, are not to be allayed in a day. For the sake of those people and of the country, I regret that the question has been turned into one of party ascendency in the Government, but especially in Congress. But for that Senators would have patience. But for that we might

safely trust to the natural goodness of men, here and elsewhere, to be a little patient with a people so sorely tried, to
give time for bitterness to depart, for disorders to subside, for
society to recover its healthful and normal action.

If the elections which have been held in the South and
which resulted unfavorably to the dominant party are to be
set aside as a party necessity, let it be done manfully and above
board; but let not the Senate, in addition, go into the business
of defaming the country. You do defame the country when
you blast the character of any considerable portion of its people
before the world. It is idle for the rest of the country to hope
to escape. The judgment of history is a judgment in general,
and justly so. When the most prominent men of the dominant
party of the United States for the last ten years announce to
the world over and over, as their deliberate judgment, that a
large portion of the territory of the United States and a large
portion of the people of the United States are in a condition
little better than barbarous by reason of the disorders there, the
want of security for life, limb, property, or rights of any kind,
they inflict a wound upon the character of the whole American
people.

Willard Warner [Rep.], of Alabama, replied to Senator Casserly.

I occupy a standpoint in regard to the Southern people that
entitles me to speak as to the condition of affairs there. I have
offered to the Southern people, in my person, from the end of
the war, from the time that I took off the uniform of a Federal
soldier, the olive branch of peace. I have said to them, again
and again, upon the rostrum in Alabama and here, that I was
willing and anxious to forgive the past; that I fought as a Federal soldier only for the union of my country and for its peace
and welfare and liberty in the future. I say that to-day. I
cherish no animosities for the past. I am as ready to-day as I
have been since the war to rise above all the passions of the
past, and in a spirit of Christian statesmanship to do that which
shall seem to me best for the welfare of my country now and in
the future.

I am to-day with the Senator from California, and will vote
with him, when the opportunity is presented, to offer amnesty
for rebellion. But, sir, I should be sorry to know that that
carried with it amnesty for murder and violence to-day. And
I shall be pained to learn that this is a question of party

ascendency; that there is any party in this country, and particularly the party to which the honorable Senator belongs,
which depends for its ascendency upon an organized band of
Ku-klux assassins, who override the will of the people in some
sections of the country, and persecute and murder men because
of their political opinions. If there be a party in this country
whose ascendency is dependent upon such work as that, then it
is time that we and the country should know it. I hope that it
is not true, and that the great Democratic party of the country
rests upon the basis of broad principles which commend themselves to the judgment and to the will of the American people,
and that it is not necessary for them, even in the lately rebellious States, to resort to violence and to a secret organization
to reverse, as the President says in his message, the will of
the people in order to maintain their ascendency.

Sir, I should suppose that we could come to the investigation of this matter with one accord, and I cannot see why party
lines should be drawn upon it. This is a motion for investigation into the actual condition of things, and I hope that there
are no parties and no partisans here who fear that they are to
suffer by the investigation. If my party shall suffer from it,
let it suffer. I am willing that all the sins that rest upon the
shoulders of my party shall be brought to light, and I, for one,
will discountenance them, and feel that my party is the stronger
for the exposure, for it will tend to purify it. If it shall appear, upon the other hand, that the success of the Democratic
party in the South has been the result of fraud and violence
and intimidation of voters, and through the agency of a secret
organization, then I hope my Democratic friends on this floor
will be willing to discountenance such things, and to join us in
applying the remedy, if there be one, under the Constitution,
in the hands of Congress.

I cannot think that this will be made a question of party
ascendency, nor do I think that the whole body of the Southern
people approve of these outrages. I am convinced that there is
a great body of men in the South—men, too, who belong to the
same party organization that my friend from California does—
who disapprove and denounce these things. They do it to me
privately; but such is the terror in certain localities there that
they dare not do it publicly. I have had men who occupied
seats in Congress before the war, men of the Democratic party,
and who now belong to it, tell me privately that the newspaper
editors and other leaders who are inflaming the passions of the
people and producing this violence throughout the State are

fools; but they lack the moral courage to say it publicly and to create a public opinion which shall crush out these organizations and give freedom of the ballot and political toleration throughout the South.

Thomas F. Bayard [Del.] opposed the motion.

Sir, this Administration commenced with words that were fair. "Let us have peace" was the incoming cry of the Administration. That sentiment gave to that party, probably more than anything else in the canvass, the success which they achieved. Since the incoming of the Administration, however, we have seen but little action in accordance with that sentiment on the part of those to whom the Government of this country has been intrusted.

The air has been filled with rumors that some such scheme was on foot of patching up this wretched system of reconstruction as should in effect again place the entire Southern people under martial law, wielded by the present Administration and its followers. How is it that after the lapse of more than five years, with unlimited power of legislation, with unlimited power to fill all the offices in the Southern States, new committees, new investigations, new laws and measures must be resorted to in order to produce good government throughout the Southern States? What a confession of incapacity and error is here made!

I anticipate as a foregone conclusion the passage of this resolution. I anticipate the collection of evidence, almost cut and dried to order, for the purpose of justifying almost any such measures as we have seen in the past, or which may be even exceeded in the future. And yet that does not prevent me from giving warning to my fellow countrymen all over this country of what I believe to be the truth of the dangerous attempts now being made.

The object of this resolution, this special committee, in my solemn belief, is nothing in the world but to obtain some pretext by which you shall place the Southern people again under martial law. There is not to-day in any Southern State a single Federal officer who has not been nominated by the President of your choice and confirmed by this Senate. There is not a district judge who is to preside at trials; there is not a district attorney who is to prosecute for offences against the laws of the United States; there is not a marshal, who has the sole discretion in selecting and summoning the jurors who are to try such cases, who is not a thick-and-thin partisan of your Administration.   And yet in the face of all that you come here, disregarding the ordinary processes of the laws—and surely they are numerous enough, surely they are severe enough—and appeal to force.

We hear speeches in this Chamber in which we are told of individual acts of violence. Extracts are read of the most intensely bitter nature from certain Southern newspapers, in which it would seem that gentlemen of both political parties on this floor are equally denounced for not following those writers in their intemperate views and bitter personal feelings.   Is it not a farce to suppose that while the Senate of the United States is trying this great indictment against a whole people senatorial minds are to be affected by these irresponsible, anonymous, unsupported statements culled from the writings of bitter and disappointed men? If that be the kind of testimony upon which you are to try, not the life or the fortune or the rights of a single man, however humble, but to try the rights of a whole people to govern themselves, free from your interference, I could go to your leading papers in the city of New York, I could take papers that are almost the political Bibles of such Senators as the Senator from Massachusetts, who spoke but just now, and I could there show you evidences of a feeling against the Southern people that would shut the gates of mercy upon them and their posterity forever. If I bring you, then, from the Northern press extracts as bitter, as unreasonable, as unjust as those which have been read to you from the South, will you send your committee to the North and reconstruct those States until no man shall print or say anything that seems offensive to the ear of a Radical majority? Is that to be your test of liberty?

There is one fact which I do not think will be disputed by any gentleman on this floor, let him come from what section he may. It is one of which I have personal knowledge by my own individual experience, and which I believe is concurred in by the entire country, and it is that in regard to the class of voters whom in fact you rely upon, and rely upon alone, in the Southern States, whom you have by your so-called constitutional amendments and laws made in pursuance thereof granted the right of suffrage, that class has exhibited in every part of this country—I make no exception—the utmost tyranny in respect of allowing any difference of opinion in themselves or to the majority of them. All over this country there has been one concurrent current of testimony to the effect that no colored man in the North or in the South can vote against the majority of his own class and his own people except at the peril of his life.

I have never believed, and I have not been disappointed, I am sorry to say, that the Southern States have any chance on God's earth before the Congress of the United States unless they completely submit themselves to the will of the dominant party. The remedy for that is where? It is in that section where that party has its strength and existence.

THE PRECARIOUS SITUATION

From the collection of the New York Public Library

There is in the common heart of humanity something that partisans cannot reach and cannot touch. There is in the abstract sense of justice, simple fair play, common good faith, something that appeals to the hearts of men in masses, and to which they do respond; and if the Northern people shall look upon the humbugs and the shams that you have called republican governments in the reconstructed States, if they shall see a people misrepresented here in Congress after Congress, men assuming to speak for them when every man in his heart knows that there is no moral right so to represent them, that no such thing as the voice of the chosen representatives of the people of the Southern States has been heard here for many a long year, and when you seek to keep alive that fraud and that sham by means of a constant resort to military power, then I say that, if there be not enough honesty, enough courage, enough intelligence in my fellow citizens of the Northern States to repudiate such schemes, I have no hope but that we shall live to see a government of laws supplanted by a government of force all over our country. The bitter cup you Senators and Representatives from the Northern country have pressed and now seek yet again to press to the lips of the people of the South may at no distant day be returned to your own.

ALLEN G. THURMAN [O.].—Mr. President, I want to ask the Senator who moved this resolution why it is, with his views of the power of Congress, that he limits his inquiry to these exceptional cases of violence. If he wishes to preserve the purity of elections in the South why is it that he can see nothing but some violence of a mysterious or mythical Ku-klux Klan? Why is it that he cannot look at the statute laws of South Carolina, of Florida, of Alabama, of Texas, of Arkansas, of Louisiana? Why is it that he does not see that in each of those States, unless Alabama is an exception, it is by the statute law enacted by Radical legislatures absolutely in the power of the Radical governors of those States to elect whom they please, and defeat whom they please for every important office within the gift of the people? Why is it that he cannot see that?

Talk about violence! What violence to the elective franchise on the part of a few men who violate the laws and are punishable for it is comparable to this wholesale wrong which enables one man in a State to dictate who shall be elected in that State to every office of any importance! Sir, when the proper time comes I shall present to the Senate the statutes of those States and make the remarks that are pertinent upon them. I will show that if you want to preserve the purity of elections, if you want the majority of the legal electors in those States to determine who shall be their officers, if you want the voice of the people to prevail, if you want such a thing as a true republican government in those States, then, if you have the power, there is the place to apply the remedy.

Why, sir, look at the election in Florida; look at eight counties thrown out that gave majorities for the conservative candidates, upon the merest technical grounds about their returns that ever a sophist imagined, while another county, giving a large Radical majority, and to whose returns the same precise objection applies, is counted in favor of the Radical candidates and they are installed in office. What is a little violence in

North Carolina or Alabama compared to that? Look at the election laws in Louisiana; look at them in Texas, where the governor appoints every officer in the State from the chief justice of the State down to the lowest bailiff. Talk of purity of election there! Talk of the voice of the majority of the people prevailing! No; if you want to go into the question of the purity of elections, if you want to protect the purity of elections, first cast out the beam that is in your own eye before you look for the mote that is in your neighbor's.

But, Mr. President, that is not all. There is something very singular about these investigations. Less than two years ago there was an election in the city of Washington, where Congress exercises exclusive jurisdiction. A colored man nearly lost his life at the hands of a mob on that election day; his life was only saved by the interference of the police, and for a time the police itself was borne down by the mob. What was that colored man's offence? Nothing but this, that he sought to vote a Democratic ticket. Where then were your denunciations? Where then, with full and exclusive power of legislation, were your remedies? Where then was your committee of investigation? Nothing of the kind happened. It was only a Democratic negro who was mobbed by Radical negroes, and the thing passed in silence!

Who does not know that for a colored man to vote the Democratic ticket in much the greater portion of the Southern country is to risk his life? Talk of intimidation, indeed! There never was such intimidation in the world, there never was such deliberate, concerted, effective intimidation in the world as the colored men of the South exercise toward any one of their brethren who seeks to vote the Democratic ticket. It is as notorious as that the sun shines above our heads.

Oh, but it is said, that is the very thing we shall investigate by means of this committee. Well, we shall see when the report comes in. We shall see whether there is a white side as well as a black side to it.

Mr. President, I have never uttered one word in defence of Ku-klux organizations. The Senate will bear me witness that no one spoke more strongly against them than I did at the last session. If I were looking at the subject simply in a partisan point of view, I am not so stupid as not to know that every outbreak of that kind only injures the party to which I belong, only furnishes the material for our opponents to excite the passions of the people and to excite the passions of Congress. I know it full well; and if my voice could reach every man who violates the law in the South, and could have potential influence with him, it would be addressed to him in three simple words, "Obey the laws." Such are my feelings; such are my natural instincts; and such is my interest and the interest of the party to which I belong. There is nothing to be gained by us by outrages, which only furnish our adversaries with pretexts for passing acts of legislation that but a few years ago would have shocked every sense of liberty, of freedom, and of constitutional law that had an abiding place in the American heart.

I have said, sir, I believe, all that I need to say; but I will say one word more about these Ku-klux. Mr. President, the darkest page in English history is that which records the bloody executions of the men whose heads fell from the block or who were swung upon the gallows by the oaths of Titus Oates and his confederates for complicity in an alleged popish plot. It was sufficient at that day, in the infuriated condition of the public mind, to assert that there was a plot to have it believed, to assert that there were conspirators to give credit to the statement, and to point the finger of the informer at any man to send him to the scaffold or to the block. That was the state of things there. It may be, but I hope it is not, that there are some men in this country who think that it is only necessary to assert that there is a Ku-Klux Klan to have it universally believed; to assert that there are conspirators and murderers in that Klan to find credit for their assertion; and to point the finger to a man to have it believed that he is of the Klan. It may be that there are persons who entertain such sentiment, and who, believing so, and thinking all fair in politics, are at all times ready to bring up this raw-head and bloody-bones and shake it in the face of an affrighted Congress and people. I am not one of them.

James W. Nye [Nev.] read an account of the Ku-Klux Klan from a message to the North Carolina legislature by Gov. W. W. Holden, November, 1870.

"These combinations were at first purely political in their character, and many good citizens were induced to join them; but gradually, under the leadership of ambitious and discontented politicians, and under the pretext that society needed to be regulated by some authority outside or above the law, their character was changed, and these secret Klans began to commit murder, to rob, whip, scourge, and mutilate unoffending citizens. This organization or these combinations were called the Ku-Klux Klan, and were revealed to the public, as the result of the measures which I adopted, as 'The Constitutional Union Guards,' 'The White Brotherhood,'' and 'The Invisible Empire.'

"Unlike other secret political associations, they authorized the use of force, with deadly weapons, to influence the elections. The members were united by oaths which ignored or repudiated the ordinary oaths or obligations resting upon all other citizens to respect the laws and to uphold the government. These oaths inculcated hatred by the white race against the colored race. The members of the Klan, as above stated, were hostile to the principles on which the government of the State had been reconstructed, and, in many respects, hostile to the government of the United States.

''They met in secret, in disguise, with arms, in a dress of a certain kind intended to conceal their persons and their horses, and to terrify those

KU-KLUX COSTUMES

From a photograph made in 1870 for **J. G. Hester**, deputy **U. S. Marshal** in North Carolina, who captured the disguises

Illustration in Green B. Raum's "The Existing Conflict"

whom they menaced or assaulted. They held their camps, and under their leaders they decreed judgment against their peaceable fellow-citizens, from mere intimidation to scourgings, mutilations, the burning of churches, schoolhouses, mills, and in many cases to murder. This organization, under different names, but cemented by a common purpose, is believed to have embraced not less than forty thousand voters in North Carolina. It was governed by rules more or less military in their character, and it struck its victims with such secrecy, swiftness, and certainty as to leave them little hope either for escape or mercy. The members were sworn to obey the orders of their camps, even to assassination and murder. They were taught to regard oaths administered before magistrates and in courts of justice as in no degree binding when they were called upon to give testimony against their confederates. They were sworn to keep the secrets of the order, to obey the commands of the chief, to go to the rescue of a member at all hazards, and to swear for him as a witness, and acquit him as a juror. Consequently, grand juries in many counties frequently refused to find bills against the members of this Klan for the gravest and most flagrant violations of law; and when bills were found, and the parties were arraigned for trial, witnesses, members of the order, would in nearly every case come forward, and, taking an oath before the court on the Holy Evangelists to tell the truth, the whole truth, and nothing but the truth, would swear falsely, and would thus defeat the ends of justice.

"In fine, gentlemen, there was no remedy for these evils through the civil law; and but for the use of the military arms, to which I was compelled to resort, the whole fabric of society in the State would have been undermined and destroyed, and a reign of lawlessness and anarchy would have been established."

SENATOR NYE.—Sir, the time has come when these truths should be told, and the Republican party as such have long enough fought on the defensive. These things have been done; and the honorable Senator from California now invokes forgetfulness of the past. Sir, how ready am I to forget; how ready is every man to forget; but they will not let us forget. The man we clothe with citizenship to-day lies stark and stiff a murdered victim to-morrow. A State Senator goes to the capital and is slain in the very door of the capitol of his State. And yet my honorable friend from California says "Let us forget it." Sir, I would be glad to forget it; but these men are citizens of the same Government as myself. I demand protection from my Government, in the name of its power, for my personal rights as I pursue my duties. What I demand for myself they are entitled to, and so far as my power goes they shall have it if the Democratic party and the Republican party die together.

Sir, never since the dawn of the morning star has there been such an exhibition of magnanimity toward offenders as the Republican party have extended to these men. Day after day Senators from the Southern States have asked that these individuals be relieved from the disabilities under which they labor by reason of having been rebels; and those relief bills have been carried by a Republican Congress, and what is the return? Consult the record and see what is the return. It is a return of vengeance more direful than we had any right to expect. Instead of one principle of gratitude welling up, we behold them staining again and afresh their hands with innocent blood.

Sir, I confess I am sick of it, and I often inquire of myself has this Government the power, and if it has will it exercise it, to protect its citizens at home? But a few years ago the American nation was made to rejoice when in a foreign port, finding that an American citizen, and he not a native but a naturalized citizen, had been improperly seized by a foreign power, one of our commanders, with a single man-of-war, opened his port-holes and demanded the surrender of that American citizen. How the American heart leaped with joy at this exhibition of its power and the willingness to use it. Now not merely are there isolated cases such as I have submitted, but they have become familiar, and so familiar that we cease to be moved by their frequent occurrence. I have often thought that it is much like the first field of battle that the soldier sees—terrible on first view, but a familiarity with it begets a feeling quite different from the first impression.

I hope the time has not yet arrived when we shall be unmindful of appeals such as come up here for the protection of our own citizens. If that time has arrived with others it has not with me. The boast of the British Government is that it protects its citizens wherever they are. The boast of the American Government should be that it protects its citizens wherever they are.

But, sir, we are told—it is suggested by the honorable Senator from Ohio—that the blacks are intolerant. If the black man has outraged the right of a citizen of the United States, bring him at once to judgment; and if the State power is inadequate, then I invoke the power of the Federal Government to do it. If our agencies will not perform their duty we must do it ourselves. Reverse the picture, and if a white man, who my friend from Ohio evidently thinks is so much the superior of the black, can so far forget his manhood as to trample on his inferior, bring him on the "double-quick" to the shambles for judgment.

But we are asked why these State governments do not do it. The answer is in the message I have submitted; they cannot do it. Here are organizations of men bound by oaths which chill the blood in the veins of an American citizen, under the penalty of their own death, to commit perjury, murder, rapine, the whole catalogue of crimes, and their brethren are sworn to swear them through.

Sir, gentlemen on the other side seem to consider this a political movement. In my judgment, in a matter like this politics sink into insignificance, and the cheek of a man who thinks of them in this connection ought to mantle with shame, while from every quarter of the lately rebellious States comes every day the repetition of the story of wrongs and outrages to which our citizens there are subjected. Sir, I think the Republican party has done more for this country and the world than any other

VIII—12

party; but I would strike out its past history, I would let its future go, before I would consent that a cry should come up here from unprotected citizens that their lives and their property are in danger and there is no source of succor for them.

Better by far that all our political recollections should be blotted out; for I tell you, Mr. President, and I say to my brethren in this Senate, that when a nation reaches that point that it does not give ample protection to its citizens that nation had better die. It is the citizens that make the nation; it is the citizens that uphold its pillars; it is to the citizens that you turn in the hour of danger; it is to the citizens that you turn in every aspect in which the Government is viewed; and when the Government in its power refuses to listen to their cries of outrage and wrong it is led in a wrong direction.

Gentlemen say it is to perpetuate the power of the Republican party. Sir, what higher claim could the Republican party or the Democratic party have to the confidence of the community than that they were willing to yield a ready ear and to make quick response to the cry of danger to the rights of the citizen?

ZACHARIAH CHANDLER [Mich.]—The Senator from California accuses the Republican party with having maligned the Democratic party, and in a spirit almost of commiseration talks of the waning strength of the Republican party. Sir, when the Republican party desire his sympathy they will make application; but, so far from maligning the Democratic party, I desire to say that the English language is incompetent to perform that task. [Laughter.] The very worst malignment that can possibly be uttered against that Democratic party is to tell the plain naked truth.

The day is far distant when that old Democratic party that attempted to overthrow this Government will again be intrusted with power by the people of this nation. The Senator from Delaware says that there is no other way to reform the abuses that he alleges to exist except by the vote of the North. Let me inform that Senator that he will live to be old and that his children will be on the stage of life long before he will see this great Republican party that has saved the nation rebuked by the people of the North.

On January 19 the appointment of the investigating committee was agreed to. On the 20th Vice-President Colfax appointed the following Senators as the committee: John Scott [Pa.], chairman; Henry Wilson

[Mass.], Zachariah Chandler [Mich.], Benjamin F. Rice [Ark.], Thomas F. Bayard [Del.]. Later Francis P. Blair, Jr. [Mo.], and James W. Nye [Nev.] were added to the committee.

The first session of the Forty-second Congress (March 18-April 20, 1871) was largely occupied with discussion of outrages in the South.

ENFORCEMENT OF THE FOURTEENTH AMENDMENT

SENATE, MARCH 18–APRIL 5, 1871

On March 10 majority and minority reports were submitted to the Senate from the Committee of Investigation.

On March 18 John Sherman [O.] brought forward for discussion in the Senate a resolution that the Committee on Judiciary be instructed to report a bill to enable the President and the courts of the United States to execute the laws, punish organized violence, and secure the constitutional rights of citizens in the ex-rebel States.

The committee on investigation of alleged outrages in these States, he said, had already secured enough evidence to justify, indeed, make imperative, such a bill.

He referred particularly to the condition of affairs in North Carolina, the State which had been especially investigated by the committee.

Sir, the witnesses show that many of the young men who were arrayed in the Confederate army joined a secret military organization, with all the benefit of the discipline they had gained while in armed hostility to the Government of the United States. They are there in violation of the very liberal terms granted them by General Grant, and in violation of the treaty of capitulation under which they surrendered themselves as prisoners of war. They are armed with the very weapons they used against our own soldiers, and arms have flowed freely into North Carolina since the war was over, arms of the best character. They are disciplined and organized, according to the testimony of these high officers, in almost every county of North

Carolina; but in most of the counties, perhaps in a large majority of the counties, they have committed no outrages; but there they lie quiet, organized, ready at a moment's notice to spring to arms. In several of the counties of that State, as I will show you by the testimony of these witnesses, they have brought about a condition of affairs that is revolting to every instinct of humanity.

Senator Sherman then read the oath of this organization. It required the initiate to swear that he was not a member of the Union League, Grand Army of the Republic, "or any other organization whose aim and intention is to destroy the rights of the South, or of the States, or of the people, or to elevate the negro to a political equality with yourself; and that you are opposed to all such principles, so help you God!"

"You further swear before Almighty God that . . . you will oppose all Radicals and negroes in all of their political designs; and that should any Radical or negro impose on, abuse, or injure any member of this brotherhood, you will assist in punishing him in any manner the camp may direct."

I have read this oath, showing that here is a political organization, with political ends, political aims; and, although the language is somewhat covert, it shows that the object and intent of that political organization is to prevent large masses of the people of the Southern States from enjoying a right which has been guaranteed to them by the Constitution of our country.

It is essentially a rebel organization, and no conscientious man who was a Union man, North or South, white or black, during the war, could become a member of it unless he entertained and was willing to fight for and defend and obey the orders of his rebel leaders. That is the spirit of this organization.

These men are not only armed, disciplined, oath-bound members of the Confederate army, but they work in disguise; and their instruments are terror and crime. Why, sir, we are already familiar, and perhaps too familiar, with the common description of these Ku-Klux Klans riding at night over a region of country, going from county to county, coming into a county town, and spreading terror all over a community; and not only that, but they endeavor to excite superstition. They pretended, I believe, in the outset to be the representative ghosts of the Confederate dead. That was the idea which they sought to give out; the ghosts of the Confederate dead were coming back to punish those who had been disloyal to the Confederate service; and they terrified men, women, and children, white and black. They excited the superstition of the ignorant negroes of the South, endeavored to frighten them first by superstition, then by intimidation, by threats, by violence, and by murder.

Mr. President, I do not know anywhere an organization similar to this Ku-Klux Klan. I have thought of the Thugs of India. They murdered, and they murdered secretly; but they did not disguise themselves while they were in the act of murder. If any Senator now, in looking over the record of crime in all ages, can tell me of an association, a conspiracy, or a band of men who combined in their acts and in their purposes more that is diabolical than this Ku-Klux Klan I should like to know where it was. They are secret, oath-bound; they murder, rob, plunder, whip, and scourge; and they commit these crimes, not upon the high and lofty, but upon the lowly, upon the poor, upon feeble men and women who are utterly defenceless. They go out at night, armed and disguised, under color of superstitious forms, and commit their work. They go over vast regions of country, carrying terror wherever they go. In all the record of human crime—and God knows it is full enough—where is there an organization against which humanity revolts more than it does against this? I know there is not a Senator here but feels that this thing ought to be put down.

Wherever there is a strong Republican majority or a strong Democratic majority this organization lies quiet; but wherever there is a close county and terror is necessary to enable them to carry the election, there they rise. Wherever the negro population preponderates, there they hold their sway, for a few determined men, disciplined as these men are, can carry terror among ignorant negroes, uneducated, full of superstition, without arms, equipment, or discipline. The testimony shows that this organization is powerful in that State; and it extends to the other States.

Senator Sherman then entered at great length into the details of the Ku-Klux and similar outrages.

On March 20 Thomas F. Bayard [Del.], a member of the investigating committee, replied to Senator Sherman. He charged that the motion was a Republican caucus measure which it was intended should be put through Congress whether justified or not. He declared that the general indictment made by the Senator against the

South was totally unwarranted, as testimony had been taken by the committee in the case of North Carolina alone. Take Virginia, for instance; by the confessions of the Senator and other Republicans law and order prevailed there. Why? It was the only State controlled by the Democrats since its readmission to the Union.

Senator Bayard then entered extensively into the testimony concerning the outrages in North Carolina, impeaching the credibility of witnesses because of their interest in securing an affirmative report from the committee, showing that they themselves were members of secret political organizations formed to prevent the free exercise of the suffrage, and affirming that the outrages proved were not different essentially from those which prevailed all over the Union.

Senators, I have served upon that committee, I trust with fidelity. I am very sure that I was there with no partisan or unfair purpose. I am very sure the suffering of no inhabitant of that State fell upon my ear without sympathy for their suffering and great regret for it, and a strong desire to punish the perpetrators of these wrongs; but I tell you to-day I believe there is more safety in the State of North Carolina, that there is less crime and less danger to human life in North Carolina, than there is in Washington city, in the District of Columbia. A comparison of the dockets of the respective criminal courts would establish this fact.

Look at the organizations now among the miners of coal. See what leagues they have formed for their protection and to keep up the prices of their labor, and see the disastrous results of all this upon the community in raising the price of coal, a necessity to all men, to a rate that almost forbids its use and entails great suffering. These things are all against law; but will you undertake to enter into those States to assume to yourselves the complete police power of each and every State in the Union? If so, pray what will you call your Government? Certainly do not so insult the intelligence of the people as to consider it any longer a Federal Union of equal States.

I am not here to apologize for or approve the creation of these secret political societies on any side. I have been opposed to them all my life. It is with me an inherited opposition in a republican form of government to creating secret political orders. The oaths of these societies, which have been read, are very much the same as the oaths I have seen published of the Know-Nothings and other secret orders of that kind, all of which, I think, are inconsistent with a republican form of government, and certainly contrary to the Constitution of the United States.

Senator Bayard charged that the negroes, the chief laboring element of the South, had been organized by their white leaders into "Union Leagues" and other secret political associations, and that these were primarily responsible for the disorders in North Carolina.

How can there be peace in a community where there has been a deliberate organization of all the laboring men in hostility to the men from whom they are to receive employment? It is race against race. It is labor against capital. How would such a party be regarded in the Northern States? Let that fact go before the people of the North, that all the workingmen of the country are to be organized and inveigled into secret societies, each intimidating the other, the object of the organization being to control politically the operations of capital throughout the country. Why, sir, is it not a complete destruction of all the sweet affiances of life? Is it not a complete destruction of all the relations between man and his fellows? Is not the employer to use the justifiable influence of affection, of instruction, of counsel, and kindly services with those whom he assists to get their bread, and who in their turn assist to make his capital available to himself and them also? What peace can be expected to society where the two great coöperative classes essential for each other's safety shall be perverted from their natural friendship into foes by organization?

I ask those who profess political friendship for the colored people in the State of North Carolina whether they really believe that class will be safer in the hands of these political adventurers who are seeking to organize them for their own party purposes than they would be in the hands of those from whom alone they can obtain employment, and who were their friends in the past as they are now? The relation of the races during the war showed that there was no hostility between them. There was love and affection borne by the colored race toward those who were their masters. The history of that war will be hereafter, I am satisfied, the very best answer to the slanders against the white people of the Southern States. Throughout that war, if the negroes had those wrongs to avenge which your novelists, lecturers, and other libelers[1] have averred them to have, they certainly would have availed themselves of the constant opportunities to avenge them; but the history of the war showed that those wrongs never could have existed, and that there were between those people, until disturbed by political adventurers, the strongest ties on each side of affection and protection.

Why not, therefore, Mr. President, let these colored people alone, that they may choose their friends as other men choose theirs? Why should they be controlled by these political adventurers? Why not leave them free to go back under the control of those who have been true and kind to them, and with whom naturally there is an affinity of feeling and interest? The answer is plain, that the welfare of the colored race is to be sacrificed for the benefit of the Radical party. That is the only reason for it. These poor people whom you profess to desire to see advanced are made nothing but cat's-paws for the purpose of gaining a political advantage.

Mr. President, the committee were charged with the examination of the security of property. The destruction of property by incendiarism was but one danger to which it was subjected. There was another and still more wholesale destruction of property, caused by the corrupt and wasteful mismanagement of the State's credit. The fact, Mr. President, is one beyond all doubt; is concurrently stated by the witnesses on both sides, that the State debt of North Carolina at the close of the war amounted to about fourteen million dollars, and that, in a little less than eighteen months after that State had been forced by the reconstruction acts under the control of Holden and his associates, that debt was increased from $14,000,000 to $35,000,000, and that without any benefit to the State, no trace where the money has been usefully expended, but the State is crushed under this fearful burden of debt. And who are to pay this? The Union Leagues of Governor Holden, the eighty thousand voters whom he has relied upon to retain political power in that State? No, sir. There would not be five per cent. of the taxation necessary to pay such a debt or the interest on it which the members of his party individually would have to pay. The result of this fearful accumulation of debt was to fill the minds of the people of that State with apprehensions of the gravest character. Bankruptcy was inevitable. They knew of Holden's complicity. It is proved abundantly by witnesses on both sides.

[1] There is particular reference here to Albion W. Tourgee, a "carpetbagger" from Ohio, who settled in North Carolina after the war, becoming a judge in a Ku-klux district. He was a popular lecturer, and wrote several novels which dealt with the Ku-klux, and had a great sale.

On March 22-23 John Scott [Pa.], chairman of the investigating committee, replied to Senator Bayard.

The charge is made that Governor Holden, as the head of a conspiracy, seeks perpetuation of his power against the wishes of the people, and that the Senate lends itself to this scheme by instituting this inquiry.

I must notice here a remarkable statement made by my friend from Delaware. I was astonished that a gentleman usually so acute as he is, and so logical, should in one part of his argument have said to the Senate that the imbecility, the inefficiency, and the corruption of Governor Holden's administration were so great in all its departments, including the judiciary, that there was no protection for life and property, and people had to resort to violence for the purpose of redressing their wrongs, and then, in his argument and in his report, saying to the country that life and property were as secure there as they were in any part of the United States. When the assault was made on the administration of Governor Holden, then there was no protection for life and property in that State; but when it was necessary to screen the Ku-Klux, then life and property could be protected in the courts there as well as any place else. That will be something for some of the Senator's colleagues to reconcile when they follow him.

And, sir, with the fact staring the world in the face that these outrages were perpetrated for the purpose of overthrowing the reconstruction policy of Congress, the Senator from Delaware tells us that reconstruction is a failure, and he points us to Virginia as the only State in which the Democratic party is in power and where reconstruction is a success. Did he reflect that he could have paid no higher compliment to the Republican party of the nation? In Virginia under the reconstruction acts the Democratic party got into power, and there is no Republican Ku-Klux organized there. They submit, and yet the Democratic party is the party of law and order! When reconstruction resulted in putting the Radical party in power in North Carolina the members of your party organized the Ku-Klux and sought to overthrow it by rapine and murder and violence.

Senator Scott then analyzed the testimony before the committee to prove his charge that the Democrats of North Carolina had organized the Ku-Klux with the above purpose, and that grievous disorders had resulted therefrom.

Now, sir, having gone over these offences and their effects, I come to the reasons that are given in excuse or justification for them; first, the reconstruction acts, of which I have already spoken, and then the establishment of Union Leagues. On the general question of the utility of secret political societies in a republic I have such decided convictions that I have no hesitation in expressing them here or elsewhere. I think they are totally at war with the spirit and genius of republican institutions. I can hardly conceive of an emergency in a republican government which will justify the establishment of a sworn, secret political organization. When the ballot ceases to be the expression of the individual conviction of the voter, and is simply cast in obedience to a former oath, or as the result of the combinations of race, color, creed, clan, or nationality, then it ceases to be the true element of republican government. Therefore, I say, there ought to be no secret political organizations.

But, sir, the Union League that is alleged as one of the provoking causes of these disorders was established in the North during the war. It had a political purpose; there is no doubt about that. That is disclosed. So we say in the report. It was established in the South in 1867 or 1868. Whatever may be said of their inexpediency, as an abstract question did these leagues ever, as an organization, decree murder, rapine, or violence? The leagues established in 1867 or 1868 did not; but two or three organizations established within the last year or so, in imitation of the Union Leagues and in retaliation for the Ku-Klux, did. The Union Leagues, as such, never did, according to any testimony that is reliable, decree the burning of property or the murder of or personal violence to any man. That individual members committed wrong there is no doubt; but there is just as clear proof that in all the cases where the members of these organizations have been indicted there has been no trouble in convicting them.

The Senator then showed that, on the other hand, the outrages committed by the Ku-Klux were of the nature of organized conspiracies, and included arson, murder, and personal violence, and yet their perpetrators had escaped punishment by the courts.

He concluded:

I have no desire to overdraw this picture. If I could, by stretching forth my hand over these Southern States, restore them all to peace and quietude, stop this disorder, no man would more willingly do it. All the feelings of my heart go out in the warmest desire for the peace and security of the South. Brothers of my own blood are there, and I would be recreant to all the dictates of duty, as well as of humanity, if I said one word that was calculated to give a wrong impression as to the true state of affairs. I do not wish to do it. I wish to see the honest men, the true men, of the Democratic party in the South stand up in the front, as ex-Governor Reid did, and stay the waves of this seething mob, lest ere long their own homes and hearthstones be buried in the general anarchy that must ensue. We want not the government of the mob in this land. We want a government in which the law will be supreme, in which (quoting the thought of another, for I have not his language) supreme justice will moderate the whole tone and tenor of public morals. Justice is the object at which all governments should aim. Justice is at once the brightest emanation of the Gospel and the greatest attribute of God. It teaches the lofty that he cannot sin with impunity. It teaches the lowly that the law is at once his protection and his right. And I trust that before this Congress rises, if we can do nothing else, we shall put some law on the statute book which shall satisfy the people of this land and of the world that we wish again, instead of disorder and strife, to inaugurate the reign of that supreme justice which introduces order and peace and love into a world which but for her would be a wild waste of passion.

On March 31 John Pool [Rep.], of North Carolina, reviewed at great length the origin and nature of the political outrages in his State. In the course of this presentation he replied to the rebuke administered by Senator Bayard to the white Republicans of North Carolina for organizing the negroes, who had proved their peaceful disposition during the war, into aggressive political societies, leading to the present disorders.

The negroes during the war did indeed behave themselves. They behaved very much better than anybody else on either side, and they ought to be entitled to consideration for it by the men who got the benefit of that good behavior. But, sir, they are now freemen; they have tasted the sweets of liberty for five or six years. No people who have once been free will be reduced to slavery, or *quasi*-slavery, without a struggle to maintain their liberties.

What was wrong, then, in aiding them to make this resistance? If they did not resist and their rights were overthrown the Federal Government would be compelled by the Constitution to enforce these rights. This meant the reëstablishment of martial law.

Did Senators realize what this meant? He did. The South did, and feared it, and the fear would have a repressing effect.

Martial law! It means the suspension of the *habeas corpus*. It means military tribunals. It means the breaking down of that great bulwark of Saxon liberty—the trial by jury. It means the substitution of military men as judges and jurors. It means the danger that men will be convicted upon insufficient testimony, and often innocent men punished. It means the quartering of soldiers upon communities, subject to all those petty outrages that must occur where soldiers are quartered among those whom they consider their enemies and the enemies of their flag. It means the subsistence of troops, whose presence has been rendered necessary by the communities where they are quartered upon the communities. It means the impoverishment of the property holder, the taking of his means to support the troops whose presence has been rendered necessary. Sir, it means all that any lover of his section of country ought to be desirous of avoiding.

Personally he believed that President Johnson's reconstruction policy should have been adopted. But it was not, and he and other Southern men accepted the policy of Congress. Did they do wrong in so accepting? So with the Fourteenth Amendment.

I stand not here to discuss its merits. In some of its features it had my hearty approval and approbation; in other features it had not. In the great liberty principles, the great principles of right, the immunities of American citizenship, it did have my approbation. I would have preferred something different, but what were we to do? It was proposed, and proposed by those who had the power, to put it on us and to execute it. I ask if it was wise policy to attempt resistance?

It was the resistance of President Johnson and his party to the reconstruction policy and the Fourteenth Amendment that caused all the trouble, for it encouraged the South to resist these.

If there has been a murder committed, if there has been a man or a woman scourged, it can be traced to that very action and to the encouragement that was given to resist by force, if necessary, the operation of the reconstruction acts.

I do not charge the Northern Democrats with intending to produce this state of things. I do not charge them with complicity in any crime, or outrage, or disorder. Men often do things the consequences of which they do not see. I wish the attention of the country called to the damage that those who here profess to be the friends of the Southern people are doing them when they encourage by word or deed acts which, when attempted, must lead to ruin and disaster.

The Southern Democratic party therefore took heart and came forward solidified upon the issue of resistance to the Fourteenth Amendment. What could be expected but that the negroes and the white men who had been Union men during the war would form a party in opposition? This party did not create sentiment among the negroes in favor of the Amendment, for this already existed. It simply organized in self-protection those who held the sentiment.

You may talk about leagues influencing votes. I do not know what is done inside the leagues; I never was in one; but there was and is human nature even under the black skin. They had liberty offered to them; they had rights offered to them; they had protection in those rights promised to them by the great and conquering nation that, with its legions, had trampled down before their eyes all opposition to its power and authority. Think you that they by any fair means could have been induced to turn their backs upon a measure that was to secure to them their rights and their liberties?

Had the negroes lost their rights Congress would certainly have intervened in their favor.

Think of the armies of the United States sent down to enforce the laws of the country and to carry out its Constitution, with all the black men on one side, and the army aiding them and supporting them in their rights, they believing that there was an effort being made by the white people to reduce them to slavery! Can any man doubt the scenes that must necessarily

follow? Why, sir, the occurrences of the rebellion would tame
down into mere insignificance in comparison to what we should
witness in every neighborhood, in every household in all that
Southern country. It was to avoid this in the future, as well
as from a sense of the innate right and justice of the reconstruction acts in their great liberty features, that a large number of the most intelligent and highly respectable white men of
North Carolina went into a movement to organize a Republican
party and to undertake to carry out in good faith the Fourteenth Amendment to the Constitution.

Reconstruction was made the national political issue.
The Democrats declared that if they were placed in
power they would use the army to disperse the "carpet-
bag" State governments. They were defeated.

The Ku-Klux organization in the South grew out of this
contest, and that is at the bottom of the whole of it. Those
men have undertaken to do with the scourge, the halter, and
the dagger what they understood their party to propose to do
with the bayonet; and they have believed that they were sustained by their party in doing so, North and South.

That is the secret of this whole affair. The question that is
now upon this nation is whether it will permit local violence to
be substituted in the place of the Constitution and laws of this
country. And if the nation does not mean to prevent it, if the
nation does not mean to have the amendment enforced, in common humanity I want the nation to say so. Do not deceive the
colored men longer. Do not longer deceive those white men
who have been standing up to the Government and standing up
to the rights of all American citizens as declared in the Fourteenth Amendment. But, sir, if the Government of the United
States means to abandon its policy, it ought to look well to the
consequences that must follow.

If the Fourteenth Amendment is not to be executed, what is
to be the condition of the colored people in the Southern States?
If they are not to have equal rights with white men, if they
are not to be secure from outrage and wrong, from scourging
and murder and assassination in the exercise of their rights,
what is to become of them? It is idle to say that a man has a
right on the statute book or in the Constitution if he dare not
exercise it. It is deception to boast that America has freed her
slaves if she denies to them the enjoyment of that freedom. It
is an empty boast that you have struck the shackles from four

millions of people if worse shackles are thereby put upon them. Do not say that you have freed them, for freedom may be a very different thing in one section from what it is in another. No, sir; it will amount to this, that you have not freed the slaves of the South; you have taken them from under the protecting hand of interested masters and made them the victims of every villain and ruffian that chooses to outrage them.

The Senator from Delaware [Mr. Bayard] said, "Why not leave these colored men free to go back under the control of their natural leaders who have been kind to them?" Is that to be the issue in 1872? If it is, let us know it. "Left free to go back." What does "go back" mean? It may have to some ears a most unpleasant ring of old slavery.

"Free to go back." Sir, they are free to go back now. Who keeps them from it? Is there any Southern man who will drive a colored man from his plantation if he proposes to go there and work for nothing, or small wages, and behave himself? He is free to go back now; but he does not choose to go back, nor will he submit to go back as long as he has a hope of preventing it.

Who are "the natural leaders," that they should have control now, not only of the persons of those who were formerly their slaves, but the votes of their former slaves? "Let them go back under the control of their natural leaders," and I imagine those "natural leaders" will not quarrel with the Fifteenth Amendment. The land owners and old slave owners of the South will not quarrel with the Fifteenth Amendment if in the place of casting one vote, as they formerly did, they can march their hundred colored men whom they have under their control to the ballot box and cast one hundred votes. But who are the "natural leaders," and I ask what have they done for the material prosperity and glory of that Southern country for the last fifty years?

These "natural leaders" had wealth; they had intelligence; they had education; they had the benefit of the labor of these very men whom it is now proposed to put back under their control; they had political power, full swing and sway; even upon the floor of the American Senate they wielded the scepter with a strong hand; and what did they do for North Carolina? Let the condition of North Carolina in 1860 tell what they had done up to that time. I will not turn to the darker picture and point to our condition now. The proposition is nothing less than to put labor under the control of capital.

Who are the laboring men of the South? Have they not an

interest in the common welfare? Have they not an interest in the country? They were born there; they were brought up there; they are attached to the soil. Whatever is to the advantage of that section is for their advantage. They are the bone and sinew of the country. It is labor upon which our institutions must rest. It is not upon capital and upon political management that we can rely for the glory or the safety of this great nation. I would not put labor under the control of capital anywhere. If disaster should come, how would it be? Those who owned wealth could fly to another place more congenial or more safe for them to live; but the laboring men of the South, white or colored, cannot flee. We have white laboring men there as well as colored; the great bulk of the population were not slave owners; the great bulk of the white men of that population are not land owners beyond just enough land to attend with their own hands or with the aid of their wives and children.

They must stand and take whatever comes. If war, if bloodshed, if murder, if Ku-Klux outrage, if lawlessness and disaster and rapine come, they with their wives and little ones must stand by their cabins and suffer all the consequences, while the "natural leaders" can flee and seek asylums elsewhere. Sir, are they to be put under the control of "natural leaders," to be bandied about as a mere football of ambition and party? If that be the proposition, I protest against it.

Francis P. Blair, Jr. [Mo.], a member of the minority of the Committee of Investigation, made a long speech consuming two days (April 3-4) in opposition to the resolution. He stated that the origin of the political situation in North Carolina was the reverse of that given by Senator Pool. The Ku-Klux was the answer to the Union League and not its provocation.

In the nature of things, a set of men go down South, naked adventurers, lusting for the spoils of a State; they make use of these ignorant and superstitious negroes; convene them in secret leagues, sworn societies, and let them loose to depredate upon the property and upon the lives of the citizens there. That this thing should naturally have given rise to measures of defence every man will admit was probable. It did; and associations were made, and the witnesses testify that this Ku-Klux organization, as it was called, was formed because, when these negroes were tried, caught, and convicted, they were pardoned by Governor Holden, and that there was no other means of restraining them from their devastations and from their crimes.

Sir, the Southern people from all time have been known as a people who were disinclined to secret societies of any kind. They were more repugnant to them than any other class of people whom I know. For a long period of time they eschewed the ballot and voted *viva voce,* such was their dislike to any secret method in their political affairs, and they were late in going into this thing, and went into it only under the pressure of proscription, of despotism. Sir, these secret leagues and these disorders are the spawn of despotism.

Oppression has in all times and in all countries been the prolific mother of disorder, and of that species of disorder which has called forth the Carbonari of Europe and all the other secret societies in Europe. These secret combinations have arisen from the pressure of despotism. These people of the South were absolutely free from them until their governments were taken away from them, until local self-government was denied to them; all the people of intelligence made incapable of holding office and incapable of voting at the first election, when this combination of carpet-baggers and scalawags and negroes was made to seize their governments and to plunder the States at large and the individuals—never until that time, and, when the governor of the State would pardon as fast as convictions were had, were these organizations made, because they were essential to the safety of the people.

Sir, you need not go back to the Democratic convention for the declarations of the Democratic party to find who instigated and who created these disturbances. They were instigated here, and created here. I do not mean that the members of Congress directly instigated these men to these crimes and disorders, but they commenced their measures of oppression; they struck down self-government at the South; they put the governments in the hands of an incapable, inefficient set of people, without character, whom nobody could respect. The magistrates were of such a character that they could not enforce obedience to the law, and inspired no respect for them or for the law.

What right had the Congress of the United States, after setting the example of violence and of lawlessness, to expect the observance of law from others? After they had trampled the Constitution under foot, robbed the people of a whole section of the country of all the rights guaranteed to them in the Constitution for their personal security and for the security of

VIII—13

their property, what right had these invaders of the law and violators of the law to expect obedience to it from other persons? Sir, I said the other day in a running debate that the Congress of the United States was the old original Ku-Klux organization, and I believed it and still believe it!

The testimony taken before the committee shows distinctly the truth of all the allegations I made in reference to the organization of this Loyal League, about its having preceded the organization of the Ku-Klux, and the purpose of the organization.

When North Carolina was reconstructed, the legislature was organized with only such persons as the negroes and carpet-baggers chose to elect to the legislature, and of those some were rejected by the military commander [Gen. Canby]. This legislature at its first meeting appropriated $25,000,000 in bonds of the State to adventurers, under the pretext of building railroads in that State, and the testimony shows that not $500,000 of that sum was ever applied to the construction of railroads or to the public works for which it was appropriated; that the presidents and others made away with it.

All the witnesses testify that this action on the part of the legislature spread consternation and terror throughout the State; that the people saw that their property was being confiscated and annihilated by this species of legislation; that the election was carried against Holden and his party mainly on this issue of their corruption, fraud, and swindling; that it was the only issue in the election until Holden attempted to save himself by using military power, by calling out the militia, and pretending that two of the counties were in insurrection, and at the same time threatening all the other counties with a similar visitation.

The President was called upon for troops. They also came, and were stationed in these so-called insurrectionary counties. But the tide could not be stayed. The illegal and unconstitutional action of the governor, instead of arresting by intimidation the aroused people of North Carolina, only added fuel to the fire. They saw that this man not only desired to plunder them, but he was willing to murder them if they would not submit quietly to be plundered. Hence the defeat and the overthrow of this party, and hence the appeal to Congress to reinstate these men in power.

North Carolina is not an isolated State in that respect. The same policy has bred the same evils everywhere in the South. Wherever reconstruction has gone it has carried with it plunder and recklessness and lawlessness and violence.

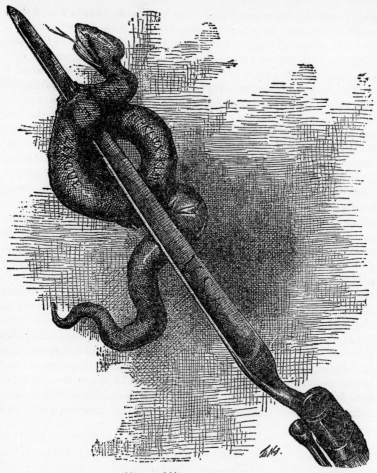

"GO ON!"—U. S. GRANT

THE CONSTITUTION OF THE UNITED STATES MUST AND SHALL BE PRESERVED AND PROTECTED

Cartoon by Thomas Nast

From the collection of the New York Public Library

Here the Senator discussed extensively the corruption of the governments of the various reconstructed States. He then presented his view of the proper remedy for the abuses and outrages in these States.

I deem it essential to the reëstablishment of anything like order or government in the South that the men of intelligence and respectability and character in the South should be allowed to take part in their government. I think there is no hope until that is done. When that is done I believe the people of the South are willing to give negro suffrage a fair trial, and if it is found to be compatible with the existence of our institutions I believe there will be no effort to take from them the ballot. I do not believe, from what I hear from eminent men of the South, that there is any disposition even now to deprive the negro of the ballot. I have seen a letter from a very distinguished man, Mr. Stephens, of Georgia, in which he uses the very words I have used, that the people of the South are willing to give negro suffrage a fair trial, and that they do not desire to take judgment upon the failure which has already occurred, because they believe that the negroes, surrounded by the influences that they are now surrounded by, banded together as they are in these loyal leagues, incited to animosity by shameless adventurers of the North and others no better, and sustained as they have been by the military power of the Government, have not had a fair trial under that system, and cannot have a fair trial, until the influence of the men of character and men of intelligence of the South, who have the welfare and interest of the South at heart, can be fairly felt and exercised.

If it shall be found in time that under the best influences that can be thrown around them, the influences of those who have everything at stake in the South, free institutions cannot be sustained but must perish or the ballot be taken from the negro, I think there will be a means, and a constitutional means, discovered by which our institutions will be preserved.

Many of the citizens of the South, those who had been eminent in a civil or military capacity during the war, were debarred by the Fourteenth Amendment from holding Federal or State offices. To some of these, elected to the State legislatures, seats had been refused by the Republican State governments. This refusal was not in accord with the Amendment, since legislators are not "officers" of government, as decided in the case of William Blount. These were the very men to be seated.

Oliver P. Morton [Ind.] replied to Senator Blair.

This society of the Ku-Klux is the result of a general purpose, of a matured plan for the subjugation of the South by a party that is in hostility to the Government of the United States, by the party which organized and conducted the rebellion. It proposes to gain the supremacy by driving Republicans into submission and silence, or by compelling them to fly from the State. It electioneers by murder, and persuades men by the lash and destruction of their property. It seeks to waste the courage of men and their devotion to principle by causing them to go to bed at night with a dread that they may be murdered and their houses destroyed by fire before morning. It works by means that sap the mental as well as the physical strength of men and lead them to sacrifice their principles and their feelings to purchase security for themselves and their families. It leaves no room for neutrality. All must take their stand upon the one side or the other—absolute submission upon the one hand, or total insecurity for life and property upon the other.

But as a party policy, it is short-sighted and wickedly foolish. Victory purchased by blood cannot be permanent or glorious. The spots which it makes upon the escutcheons of the party can never be washed out, but will deepen and redden from generation to generation. The blood which is spilled cries from the ground, and in a few years the avenger will come and punishment will fall suddenly and terribly upon the criminals.

The Democratic party may say that it has not committed these crimes; but the judgment of mankind will be that it has held the garments of those who did; that it has stood by in approving silence; that it has uttered no word of condemnation; that it has raised no hand to bring the guilty to punishment; and, while it may not have been the actual perpetrator of the deed, yet it has received the political profits that result from its perpetration. The Democratic party can relieve itself from these terrible imputations by denouncing the crimes, by admitting their existence, by uniting with others for their suppression, by showing a willingness to use all the means that may be within their power to protect life, liberty, property; but failing to do these things, it will be held responsible by the verdict of history.

The best remedy for these evils is their full and complete exposure, that they may be known, understood, and execrated by all men, so that a public opinion may be created which shall have power for their ultimate suppression. To remain silent from any cause is to approve of these crimes, is to encourage their continuance, is to give to their perpetrators security and impunity. We cannot remain silent without becoming participants, without implicating ourselves in the deed.

The persistent declarations of Northern politicians that the reconstruction acts are unconstitutional and void, that the peo-

ple of the South have a right to resist them, and that the Government of the United States has wickedly oppressed these people and wantonly inflicted upon them liabilities and degradation have largely conduced to their present unhappy condition.   The Southern mind, irritated by defeat, accepted these
declarations as evidence of sympathy and of the justness of
their cause, and the crimes and outrages that have been committed are in great part the natural and inevitable result.   Had
these politicians advised the people of the South to accept the
situation and accommodate themselves to the result, who can
doubt that peace, good-will, and prosperity would have been
restored?

When the war ended many men who had been in the Union
army remained in the South, intending to make it their home
and identify themselves with its fortunes.   Others emigrated
from the North, taking with them large capital, believing that
the South presented fine prospects for business, individual success, and general prosperity.   In the reconstruction of the
Southern States it so happened, and was, in fact, necessary, that
many of these men should be elected to office and take a leading part in the government of the States in which they settled.
This was their right and the natural result of the circumstances
by which they were surrounded; but they were denounced as
adventurers and intruders, and the odious slang of "carpet-
baggers" was reëchoed by the Democracy of the North, who
sent word to the South that these men had no rights they were
bound to respect.

Emigration is a part of the genius of the American people.
They are composed of those who came from abroad or their descendants.   To emigrate from State to State, and there to enjoy
all the privileges and immunities of citizens of the United
States, is guaranteed by the Constitution, and it is an odious and
anti-American doctrine that a man has no right to be elected to
an office in a State because he was not born in it or has not
lived in it many years.   When we consider the circumstances
under which the Territories were settled and new States formed,
the rapid transition of our population from one part of the
country to another, we shall comprehend the infamy and villainy of this slang against "carpet-baggers."

Why, sir, it is the same spirit in another form which a few
years ago attempted to deny equal political rights to men of foreign birth and insisted that the offices should be held only by
those who were born upon the soil; and it is humiliating that
any portion of the people of the North should endeavor to ex-

cite the people of the South against their own citizens who have gone there to find homes. What the South needs is emigrants with carpet bags well filled with capital to revive industry, organize labor, and develop her resources; and the howl against this class of citizens is insane and suicidal.

Those who were born in the South and remained faithful to the Government, or have since joined the Republican party, are stigmatized as the "scalawags," as low persons of the baser sort, disgraced and degraded by every opprobrious epithet, and all of this execrable Billingsgate is reëchoed, with additions, in the North.

The mass of the people in the South are honest, humane, and kindly feeling, like the people of any other section of the country, and do wrong chiefly where they think they are doing right. But, for political purposes, their passions are artfully stimulated, their prejudices against negroes excited to madness, and skillful operators constantly reopen and aggravate the wounds and hatreds of the war.

Will the people of the South never learn that for thirty years the Democratic party has been their most deadly enemy? But for its baneful influence they would never have embarked in the rebellion. They were encouraged in the belief that the right was upon their side, that the Democracy of the North were their friends and allies and would never permit them to be coerced to remain in the Union; and after the war had lasted two years were urged to protract the struggle by holding out to them the prospect that a revolution was going on in the sentiment of the North that would soon acknowledge their independence. They clung to these fatal delusions until they were overwhelmed by defeat. Their allies deserted them at the critical moment, the revolution in the North never came, their prospects faded like an evening cloud, and the sun of the Confederacy went down in blood.

The Democratic party can come into power only by carrying all the Southern States, in which case the Southern Democracy will constitute the majority of the party, and will be the controlling element. The Southern Democracy would refuse to vote taxes and appropriations for pensions, except upon condition that Confederate soldiers and their widows and orphans should be pensioned, and put upon equal terms with those of the soldiers of the Union. The Southern Democracy would never vote taxes and appropriations to pay the national debt unless they were paid for their slaves. The Northern Democracy, who are committed by endless resolutions and years of declamation to the position that slavery was wrongfully and unconstitutionally abolished, would sustain them.

The Southern question will be the great issue in 1872 that will dwarf into insignificance every other. No merely economical question can divide public attention with it. Shall reconstruction be maintained; shall the constitutional amendments be upheld; shall the colored people be protected in the enjoyment of equal rights; shall the Republicans of the South-

"IT IS ONLY A TRUCE TO REGAIN POWER"
Cartoon by Thomas Nast [1872]
From the collection of the New York Public Library

ern States be protected in life, liberty, and property? are the great issues to be settled in 1872. Questions of tariff, currency, civil service reform, will play some part, but it will be a subordinate one. In all the Southern States the Republicans will struggle for life, for the privilege of living in peace and security, while the Democratic party will struggle to regain their former power, and, as experience has shown, will not hesitate as to the means that may be used for that purpose. And in view of the solemn fact that everything is at stake for which we struggled and suffered through ten years of war and storm, let us bury all personal grievances, and forgetting past differences, banishing all selfish considerations, unite again as a band of brothers, and with unbroken front move forward resolved to conquer for the right.

The resolution of Senator Sherman was agreed to on April 5, by a vote of 38 to 12.

The bill, which the resolution instructed the Judiciary Committee to report, was superseded by one already presented in the House of Representatives.

The House had referred that portion of the President's message relating to interference in the South with the Fourteenth Amendment to a select committee. On March 28 Samuel Shellabarger [O.], chairman of this committee, reported a bill to enforce the amendment.

The debate on this bill naturally covered the same ground as that in the Senate, being based on the same testimony. The bill was passed on April 6 by a vote of 118 to 91. It was passed by the Senate, with amendments, on April 14—yeas 45, nays 19. There were several conferences over the amendments between committees of the two Chambers, which finally reported the bill as follows:

(1) Any person who, under color of a State enactment, shall deprive any person of the rights guaranteed by the amendment shall be liable for redress to the party injured, by prosecution in the Federal courts under the act of April 9, 1866;

(2) Two or more persons conspiring to break or nullify the amendment in any of its provisions or effects shall be punished by fine or imprisonment, or both, and any party injured by this conspiracy may obtain redress as above stated;

(3) Where such conspiracy became an insurrection by extending to the deprivation of a portion or class of the people of a State of their rights, and the State is unable or unwilling to suppress the insurrection, the President shall employ the army and navy, or other means, to suppress the insurrection, and to deliver the insurgents to the marshal of the proper district to be dealt with according to law;

(4) When the insurrection extends to a rebellion, by either overthrowing or setting at defiance the constituted authorities, the President shall, if he deems it necessary, suspend *habeas corpus* within the revolted district;

(5) Jurors serving in enforcement of the act shall take oath that they were or are not party to its infringement, and, if swearing falsely, shall be found guilty of perjury and punished accordingly;

(6) Persons having knowledge of the infraction of the act

202 GREAT AMERICAN DEBATES

and power to prevent it, but failing to prevent it, shall be liable for redress to a party injured thereby, or, in case of a murder, to the widow of the deceased, or, if there be no widow, to his next of kin, the damages in case of murder being not over $5,000; and,

(7) The act shall not supersede former acts except in instances of repugnancy.

The Senate agreed to the report on April 18 by a vote of 32 to 16, and the House on April 19 by a vote of 93 to 74. President Grant approved the act on April 20, 1871.

CHAPTER V

The Second Civil Rights Bill

Gen. Benjamin F. Butler [Mass.] Introduces in the House a Bill to Protect All Citizens in Their Civil Rights—Debate: in Favor, John R. Lynch [Miss.], Gen. James A. Garfield [O.], Gen. Butler [Mass.]; Opposed, Alexander H. Stephens [Ga.], Lucius Q. C. Lamar [Miss.], Charles A. Eldridge [Wis.], John Y. Brown [Ky.]; Bill Is Passed by House and Senate and Is Approved by the President.

ON February 3, 1875, Benjamin F. Butler [Mass.] reported in the House from the Committee on Judiciary a bill "to protect all citizens in their civil rights."

The bill provided that all persons within the jurisdiction of the United States should be entitled to the full and equal enjoyment of the accommodations, advantages, facilities, and privileges of inns, public conveyances, theaters, etc., subject only to conditions established by law and applicable alike to all citizens irrespective of race.

Offenders against the act were to pay the injured person $500 (recoverable, with costs, by trial at law) and to be fined not less than $500 nor more than $1,000, or imprisonment for not less than 30 days nor over a year.

No discrimination on account of color should be made in selecting jurors; offenders against this provision were to be fined not more than $5,000.

No discrimination on account of race should be made in the disposition of public educational funds. Separate schools for white and negro children were allowed.

Cases arising under the act should be reviewed by the Federal Supreme Court.

Federal officers were empowered to enforce the act.

203

CIVIL RIGHTS BILL

HOUSE OF REPRESENTATIVES, FEBRUARY 3-4, 1875

John R. Lynch [Miss.], a negro, supported the bill. He replied to the argument of its unconstitutionality, which had been made by such Representatives as Alexander H. Stephens [Ga.] and Lucius Q. C. Lamar [Miss.]. These gentlemen had stood on the decision of the Supreme Court in the "Slaughter-house" cases, which was that only the privileges and immunities of citizens of the *United States* were placed under the protection of the Tenth Amendment to the Constitution, and those of citizens of the *States* were not further protected thereby.

But, said Mr. Lynch:

So far as this decision refers to the question of civil rights— the kind of civil rights referred to in this bill—it means this and nothing more: that whatever right or power a State may have had prior to the ratification of the Fourteenth Amendment it still has, *except in certain particulars.* What are those particulars wherein the Fourteenth Amendment confers upon the Federal Government powers which it did not have before? The right to prevent distinctions and discriminations between the citizens of the United States and of the several States whenever such distinctions and discriminations are made on account of race, color, or previous condition of servitude; and that distinctions and discriminations made upon any other ground than these are not prohibited by the Fourteenth Amendment. As the discrimination referred to in the slaughter-house cases was not made upon either of these grounds, it did not come within the constitutional prohibition. As the pending bill refers only to such discriminations as are made on account of race, color, or previous condition of servitude, it necessarily follows that the bill is in harmony with the Constitution as construed by the Supreme Court.

But Mr. Stephens and other State Rights opponents of the bill, while granting that the recent Amendments to the Constitution guarantee to negroes the privileges accorded to white persons, declare that it is the province of the several States and not of the Federal Government

to enact the laws enforcing these guaranties. This is
the crux of the question. The Supreme Court had decided against this position, saying that by the fifth section of the Fourteenth Amendment the Federal Government was authorized to enforce the amendment *in case
the States did not conform their laws to its requirements.*

As the Supreme Court has decided that the above constitutional provision was intended to confer upon Congress the
power to prevent distinctions and discriminations when made
on account of race or color, I contend that the power of Congress in this respect is applicable to every office under the constitution and laws of any State. Some may think that this is
extraordinary power; but such is not the case. For any State
can, without violating the Fourteenth or Fifteenth Amendments
and the provisions of this bill, prohibit anyone from voting,
holding office, or serving on juries in their respective States,
who cannot read and write, or who does not own a certain
amount of property, or who shall not have resided in the State
for a certain number of months, days, or years. The only
thing these amendments prevents them from doing in this respect is making the color of a person or the race with which
any person may be identified a ground of disqualification from
the enjoyment of any of these privileges. The question seems
to me to be so clear that further argument is unnecessary.

I will now endeavor to answer the arguments of those who
have been contending that the passage of this bill is an effort
to bring about social equality between the races. That the
passage of this bill can in any manner affect the social status
of anyone seems to me to be absurd and ridiculous. I have
never believed for a moment that social equality could be
brought about even between persons of the same race. I have
always believed that social distinctions existed among white
people the same as among colored people. But those who contend that the passage of this bill will have a tendency to bring
about social equality between the races virtually and substantially admit that there are no social distinctions among white
people whatever, but that all white persons, regardless of their
moral character, are the social equals of each other; for if
conferring upon colored people the same rights and privileges
that are now exercised and enjoyed by whites indiscriminately
will result in bringing about social equality between the races,
then the same process of reasoning must necessarily bring us

to the conclusion that there are no social distinctions among whites, because all white persons, regardless of their social standing, are permitted to enjoy these rights. See then how unreasonable, unjust, and false is the assertion that social equality is involved in this legislation. I cannot believe that gentlemen on the other side of the House mean what they say when they admit, as they do, that the immoral, the ignorant, and the degraded of their own race are the social equals of themselves and their families. If they do, then I can only assure them that they do not put as high an estimate upon their own social standing as respectable and intelligent colored people place upon theirs; for there are hundreds and thousands of white people of both sexes whom I know to be the social inferiors of respectable and intelligent colored people. I can then assure that portion of my Democratic friends on the other side of the House whom I regard as my social inferiors that if at any time I should meet any one of you at a hotel and occupy a seat at the same table with you, or the same seat in a car with you, do not think that I have thereby accepted you as my social equal. Not at all. But, if anyone should attempt to discriminate against you for no other reason than because you are identified with a particular race or religious sect, I would regard it as an outrage; as a violation of the principles of republicanism; and I would be in favor of protecting you in the exercise and enjoyment of your rights by suitable and appropriate legislation.

No, Mr. Speaker, it is not social rights that we desire. We have enough of that already. What we ask is protection in the enjoyment of *public* rights. Rights which are or should be accorded to every citizen alike. Under our present system of race distinctions a white woman of a questionable social standing, yea, I may say, of an admitted immoral character, can go to any public place or upon any public conveyance and be the recipient of the same treatment, the same courtesy, and the same respect that are usually accorded to the most refined and virtuous; but let an intelligent, modest, refined colored lady present herself and ask that the same privileges be accorded to her that have just been accorded to her social inferior of the white race, and in nine cases out of ten, except in certain portions of the country, she will not only be refused, but insulted for making the request.

Mr. Speaker, I ask the members of this House, in all candor, is this right? I appeal to your sensitive feelings as husbands, fathers, and brothers, is this just? You who have affectionate companions, attractive daughters, and loving sisters, is this just? If you have any of the ingredients of manhood in your composition you will answer the question most emphatically, No! What a sad commentary upon our system of government, our religion, and our civilization! Think of it for a moment; here am I, a member of your honorable body, representing one of the largest and wealthiest districts in the State of Mississippi, and possibly in the South; a district composed of persons of different races, religions, and nationalities; and yet, when I leave my home to come to the capital of the nation, to take part in the deliberations of the House, and to participate with you in making laws for the government of this great Republic, in coming through the God-forsaken States of Kentucky and Tennessee, if I come by the way of Louisville or Chattanooga, I am treated, not as an American citizen, but as a brute. Forced to occupy a filthy smoking car both night and day, with drunkards, gamblers, and criminals; and for what? Not that I am unable or unwilling to pay my way; not that I am obnoxious in my personal appearance or disrespectful in my conduct; but simply because I happen to be of a darker complexion. If this treatment was confined to persons of our own sex we could possibly afford to endure it. But such is not the case. Our wives and our daughters, our sisters and our mothers, are subjected to the same insults and to the same uncivilized treatment. You may ask why we do not institute civil suits in the State courts. What a farce! Talk about instituting a civil-rights suit in the State courts of Kentucky, for instance, where the decision of the judge is virtually rendered before he enters the court-house, and the verdict of the jury substantially rendered before it is impaneled. The only moments of my life when I am necessarily compelled to question my loyalty to my Government or my devotion to the flag of my country is when I read of outrages having been committed upon innocent colored people and the perpetrators go unwhipped of justice, and when I leave my home to go traveling.

Mr. Speaker, if this unjust discrimination is to be longer tolerated by the American people, which I do not, cannot, and will not believe until I am forced to do so, then I can only say with sorrow and regret that our boasted civilization is a fraud; our republican institutions a failure; our social system a disgrace; and our religion a complete hypocrisy.

The enemies of this bill have been trying very hard to create the impression that it is the object of its advocates to bring about a compulsory system of mixed schools. It is not my intention at this time to enter into a discussion of the question as

to the propriety or impropriety of mixed schools; as to whether
or not such a system is essential to destroy race distinctions
and break down race prejudices. I will leave these questions
to be discussed by those who have given the subject a more
thorough consideration. The question that now presents itself
to our minds is what will be the effect of this legislation on the
public-school system of the country, and more especially in the
South It is to this question that I now propose to speak. I
regard this school clause as the most harmless provision in the
bill. If it were true that the passage of this bill with the
school clause in it would tolerate the existence of none but a
system of mixed free schools, then I would question very seriously the propriety of retaining such a clause; but such is not
the case. If I understand the bill correctly (and I think I do),
it simply confers upon all citizens, or rather recognizes the
right which has already been conferred upon all citizens, to
send their children to any public free school that is supported
in whole or in part by taxation, the exercise of the right to remain a matter of option as it now is—nothing compulsory about
it. That the passage of this bill can result in breaking up the
public-school system in any State is absurd. The men who
make these reckless assertions are very well aware of the fact,
or else they are guilty of unpardonable ignorance, that every
right and privilege that is enumerated in this bill has already
been conferred upon all citizens alike in at least one-half of
the States of this Union by State legislation. In every Southern
State where the Republican party is in power a civil-rights
bill is in force that is more severe in its penalties than are the
penalties in this bill. We find mixed-school clauses in some of
their State constitutions. If, then, the passage of this bill,
which does not confer upon the colored people of such States
any rights that they do not possess already, will result in breaking up the public-school system in their respective States, why
is it that State legislation has not broken them up? This proves
very conclusively, I think, that there is nothing in the argument whatever, and that the school clause is the most harmless
provision in the bill. My opinion is that the passage of this bill
just as it passed the Senate will bring about mixed schools practically only in localities where one or the other of the two races
is small in numbers, and that in localities where both races are
large in numbers separate schools and separate institutions of
learning will continue to exist, for a number of years at least.

The following editorial appeared in a Democratic paper in
my own State—the Jackson *Clarion,* the leading conservative

paper in the State, the editor of which is known to be a moderate, reasonable, and sensible man:

The question has been asked what effect will the civil-rights bill have on the public school system of our State if it should become a law? Our opinion is that it will have none at all. The provisions of the bill do not necessarily break up the separate school system unless the people interested choose that they shall do so; and there is no reason to believe that the colored people of this State are dissatisfied with the system as it is, or that they are not content to let well enough alone. As a people, they have not shown a disposition to thrust themselves where they are not wanted, or rather had no right to go. While they have been naturally tenacious of their newly acquired privileges, their general conduct will bear them witness that they have shown consideration for the feelings of the whites.

The race line in politics never would have been drawn if opposition had not been made to their enjoyment of equal privileges in the government and under the laws after they were emancipated.

The colored people in asking the passage of this bill do not thereby admit that their children can be better educated in white than in colored schools; nor that white teachers because they are white are better qualified to teach than colored ones. But they recognize the fact that the distinction when made and tolerated by law is an unjust and odious proscription; that you make their color a ground of objection, and consequently a crime. This is what we most earnestly protest against. Let us confer upon all citizens, then, the rights to which they are entitled under the Constitution; and then if they choose to have their children educated in separate schools, as they do in my own State, then both races will be satisfied, because they will know that the separation is their own voluntary act and not legislative compulsion.

The negro question ought to be removed from the politics of the country. It has been a disturbing element in the country ever since the Declaration of Independence, and it will continue to be so long as the colored man is denied any right or privilege that is enjoyed by the white man. Pass this bill, and there will be nothing more for the colored people to ask or expect in the way of civil rights. Equal rights having been made an accomplished fact, opposition to the exercise thereof will gradually pass away, and the everlasting negro question will then be removed from the politics of the country for the first time since the existence of the Government. Let us, then, be just as well as generous. Let us confer upon the colored citizens equal rights, and, my word for it, they will exercise their rights with moderation and with wise discretion.

I will now refer to some of the unfortunate remarks that

were made by some gentlemen on the other side of the House during the last session—especially those made by the gentleman from North Carolina [William M. Robbins] and those made by the gentleman from Virginia [John T. Harris]. The gentleman from North Carolina admits, ironically, that the colored people, even when in bondage and ignorance, could equal, if not excel, the whites in some things—dancing, singing, and eloquence, for instance. We will ask the question, Why is it that the colored people could equal the whites in these respects, while in bondage and ignorance, but not in others? The answer is an easy one: You could not prevent them from dancing unless you kept them continually tied; you could not prevent them from singing unless you kept them continually gagged; you could not prevent them from being eloquent unless you deprived them of the power of speech; but you could and did prevent them from becoming educated for fear that they would equal you in every other respect; for no educated people can be held in bondage. If the argument proves anything, therefore, it is only this: That, if the colored people while in bondage and ignorance could equal the whites in these respects, give them their freedom and allow them to become educated and they will equal the whites in every other respect. At any rate I cannot see how any reasonable man can object to giving them an opportunity to do so if they can. It does not become Southern white men, in my opinion, to boast about the ignorance of the colored people, when you know that their ignorance is the result of the enforcement of your unjust laws.

So far as the gentleman from Virginia is concerned, the gentleman who so far forgot himself as to be disrespectful to one of his fellow members, I have only this remark to make: Having served in the legislature of my own State several years, where I had the privilege of meeting some of the best, the ablest, and, I may add, the bitterest Democrats in the State, it gives me pleasure to be able to say that, with all of their bitterness upon political questions, they never failed to preserve and maintain that degree of dignity, self-respect, and parliamentary decorum which always characterizes intelligent legislators and well-bred gentlemen. Take, for instance, my eloquent and distinguished colleague [Mr. Lamar] on the other side of the House, and I venture to assert that he will never declare upon this floor or elsewhere that he is addressing only white men. No, sir; Mississippians do not send such men to Congress, nor even to their State legislature. For, if they did, it would not only be a sad and serious reflection upon their intelligence, but it would also be a humiliating disgrace to the State.

Such sentiments as those uttered by the gentleman from North Carolina and the gentleman from Virginia are certainly calculated to do the Southern white people a great deal more harm than it is possible for them to do the colored people. In consequence of which I can say to those two gentlemen that I know of no stronger rebuke than the language of the Saviour of the world when praying for its persecutors:

Father, forgive them; for they know not what they do.

The opposition to civil rights in the South is not so general or intense as a great many would have the country believe. It is a mistaken idea that all of the white people in the South outside of the Republican party are bitterly opposed to this bill. In my own State, and especially in my own district, the Democrats as a rule are indifferent as to its fate. It is true they would not vote for it, but they reason from this standpoint: The civil-rights bill does not confer upon the colored people of Mississippi any rights that they are not entitled to already under the constitution and laws of the State. We certainly have no objection, then, to allowing the colored people in other States to enjoy the same rights that they are entitled to in our own State. To illustrate this point more forcibly, I ask the clerk to read the following article from the ablest conservative paper in the State:

A civil rights bill is before the Senate. As we have civil rights here in Mississippi and elsewhere in the South, we do not understand why Southern Representatives should concern themselves about applying the measure to other portions of the country; or what practical interest we have in the question. On the 29th, Senator THOMAS M. NORWOOD, of Georgia, one of the mediocrities to whom expediency has assigned a place for which he is unfitted, delivered himself of a weak and driveling speech on the subject in which he did what he was able to keep alive sectional strife and the prejudices of race. We will venture to say that his colleague, General JOHN B. GORDON, who was a true soldier when the war was raging, will not be drawn into the mischievous controversy which demagogs from both sections, and especially latter-day fire-eaters who have become intensely enraged since the surrender, take delight in carrying on.

The opposition to civil rights in the South is confined almost exclusively to States under Democratic control, or States where the legislature has failed or refused to pass a civil-rights bill. I ask the Republican members of the House, then, will you refuse or fail to do justice to the colored man in obedience to the behests of three or four Democratic States in the South? If so, then the Republican party is not made of that material which I have always supposed it was.

Some well-meaning men have made the remark that the discussion of the civil rights question has produced a great deal of bad feeling in certain portions of the South, in consequence of which they regret the discussion of the question and the possibility of the passage of the pending bill. That the discussion of

THE ''CIVIL RIGHTS'' SCARE IS NEARLY OVER

THE GAME OF (COLORED) FOX AND (WHITE) GOOSE

Cartoon by Thomas Nast

From the collection of the New York Public Library

the question has produced some bad feeling I am willing to admit; but allow me to assure you, Mr. Speaker, that the opposition to the pending bill is not half so intense in the South today as was the opposition to the reconstruction acts of Congress. As long as congressional action is delayed in the passage of this bill, the more intense this feeling will be. But let the bill once pass and become a law, and you will find that in a few months reasonable men, liberal men, moderate men, sensible men, who now question the propriety of passing this bill, will arrive at the conclusion that it is not such a bad thing as they supposed it was. They will find that Democratic predictions have not and will not be realized. They will find that there is no more social equality than before. That whites and blacks do not intermarry any more than they did before the passage of the bill. In short, they will find that there is nothing in the bill but the recognition by law of the equal rights of all citizens before the law. My honest opinion is that the passage of this bill will have a tendency to harmonize the apparently conflicting interests between the two races. It will have a tendency to bring them more closely together in all matters pertaining to their public and political duties. It will cause them to know, appreciate, and respect the rights and privileges of each other more than ever before. In the language of my distinguished colleague on the other side of the House, ''They will know one another, and love one another.''

The white-man's-government, negro-hating democracy will, in my judgment, soon pass out of existence. The progressive spirit of the American people will not much longer tolerate the existence of an organization that lives upon the passions and prejudices of the hour. But, when that party shall have passed away, the Republican party of to-day will not be left in undisputed control of the Government; but a young, powerful, and more vigorous organization will rise up to take the place of the democracy of to-day. This organization may not have opposition to the negro the principal plank in its platform; it may take him by the right hand and concede him every right in good faith that is enjoyed by the whites; it may confer upon him honor and position. But if you, as leaders of the Republican party, will remain true to the principles upon which the party came into power, as I am satisfied you will, then no other party, however just, liberal, or fair it may be, will ever be able to detach any considerable number of colored voters from the national organization. Of course, in matters pertaining to their local State affairs, they will divide up to some extent, as they sometimes should, whenever they can be assured that their rights and privileges are not involved in the contest. But, in all national contests, I feel safe in predicting that they will remain true to the great party of freedom and equal rights.

I appeal to all the members of the House—Republicans and Democrats, conservatives and liberals—to join with us in the passage of this bill, which has for its object the protection of human rights. And, when every man, woman, and child can feel and know that his, her, and their rights are fully protected by the strong arm of a generous and grateful republic, then we can all truthfully say that this beautiful land of ours, over which the Star Spangled Banner so triumphantly waves, is, in truth and in fact, the ''land of the free and the home of the brave.''

On February 4 Charles A. Eldridge [Wis.] spoke against the bill.

The legislation of Congress since the close of the war upon the negro question, and the effects of that legislation upon the Southern States and even upon the Union itself, stand a perpetual reproach to the party by whom it was enforced, and an ever-present remonstrance and protest against further enactments in the same direction.

It ought to be enough to "call a halt" that entire States, once proud and majestic commonwealths, are in ruins, lying prostrate before us, in the very struggle and article of death— the work of our legislation. Look at South Carolina; that once proud and prosperous State with her three hundred thousand property holders, two hundred and ninety thousand of them white, including the intelligent, educated, refined men and women of the whole State, subjected by this kind of legislation to the control, domination, and *spoliation* of an uneducated, semi-barbarous African race just emancipated from the debasing and brutalizing bonds of slavery. Look at Mississippi, Arkansas, Alabama, and Louisiana, once the most genial and fairest portion of the Republic—grand, mighty States of the Union, marching rapidly and proudly forward in the outward and upward march of wealth and civilization, rent and torn by civil strife, ravaged, desolated, and destroyed by *actual war*—a war of races brought on and kept up by congressional legislation. This state of things is not the result of natural causes, but it is the result of the *unnatural relation* in which the two races have been placed to each other. It is the result of the conflict which may always be expected when it is attempted to subject men of culture, civilized men, men accustomed to freedom, to the domination and rule of brute force. The history of the world furnishes no instance of harmonious government brought about by the forced equality and commingling of such antagonistic forces, and certainly not by the subjugation of the intellectual to the physical. The white race, with its pride of blood, the memory of its achievements, the consciousness of its superiority and power, will never brook African equality or live under Africanized governments; and the sooner this truth is realized by American statesmen the sooner will the remedy for the evils that are upon us be devised.

Sir, this negro question is the mightiest problem of the age; none of half its magnitude, so far as the future of the Republic is concerned, confronts the statesman of this country to-day. It will not do longer to treat it as a mere partisan question or allow the passions evoked by the war to control legislation in regard to it. The excuses heretofore made for imposing African governments upon the Southern white men will not do. Higher considerations must control. You cannot turn from this sickening reality and foul work of your hands with the flippant and senseless plea so often interposed, even if it were true (which it is not), that slavery embruted and unfitted the emancipated negro for the duties devolved upon him for the government of himself and those you have placed under him, and that it is only a just retribution upon his former master who had so long oppressed him.

This retort, which has been so successful in prejudicing the ignorant and thoughtless and so effectively used in persuading your partisan followers, will not avail at the bar of statesmanship. The very statement refutes itself. It matters not now who was or was not responsible for slavery, whom it injured, or how deep the degradation and wrong it wrought. The question for the statesman is and always was, in view of the facts, what are the demands of patriotism? So far as the freedmen were concerned in introducing them into the governing force of the country, as a part thereof, it was a question of their *fitness* for the duties imposed and no other consideration should have entered into its determination. No partisan consideration should have been allowed to divert the mind from the real question involved.

Are they according to the fundamental principles that underlie our system, in the broad light of our civilization, qualified according to the requirement and experience of enlightened statesmanship to govern themselves as a race, as a people? Nay more, is it safe and wise, considering only the true interest of the Republic, to intrust them not only with the government of themselves, but with the government of their former masters, their wives and children and all the vast and varied interests of state? None but the merest partisan and demagog could *pretend* that by an act of legislation the negro race can be invested all at once with those high qualities of statesmanship, that self-control, that moderation of conduct, that consideration for individual rights, those sensibilities and refinements, that sense of reciprocal duties and obligations, and those exalted ideas of government which, whatever the white race now possesses, whatever it *now is*, have been the growth and accumulations of ages and have sprung *from* and are a part of our civilization.

In making these suggestions I would not disparage or discourage the negro race. I would not deprive them of any legal right. Nor would I throw any impediment in the way of their growth and development as men. They should have a fair field and an equal chance in the race of life—a full, free opportunity to overcome all natural or acquired prejudices against them, and to demonstrate if they can that they are capable of attaining to the high civilization of the white race. To put them in places of trust, of responsibility, and power without any qualification, without any preparation, is simply to do them the greatest possible injury and at the same time, whenever it is done, to endanger our system of republican government. This has been done already to the great detriment of both the black and white races.

No man or community of men, no race or people on the face of the earth, ever was thrust forward by any other people or race, so far as legislation can put them forward, so rapidly and so regardless of the welfare of both races as the white race has the negro of America. I do not believe there is a candid man, certainly no *statesman,* who will now deny that the investiture of the great mass of ignorant, stupid negroes with the power of government was a mistake. It would have been far better, in my judgment, for the black race, for its future as well as its present well-being, to have required some previous preparation, some educational qualification as a condition to the exercise of the right of suffrage. It would have been more in consonance with our system, the corner-stone of which we profess is the intelligence of the people, to have made intelligence the condition of the exercise of the exalted privilege and duty of governing in common with the white race. This, I believe, would have stimulated the black man to greater efforts and given him a better appreciation of the privilege itself. It would have modified his conceit and been an inducement to acquaint himself with the duties he would take upon himself; it would have moderated his demands for place and power by a better comprehension of the great responsibility imposed, and it would have made him far less offensive and obnoxious to those whose conviction and prejudice were against the equality the law conferred. In any and every view that can be taken of the subject it would have been better both for the negro and the white man, for the whole country, to have had some period of probation and preparation, some learning and knowledge of the science of government as a prerequisite to its administration, and as some assurance of his fidelity to and capability for the performance of the duties required.

Sir, I will not deny it must be admitted on all hands that the negro has not been justly and fairly dealt by. He has not been sincerely and candidly treated by those who have made the greatest professions of being his friends. His present nor his future welfare nor any of his greatest interests as a man and a citizen of the Republic in his relations with the white race have been much considered in the legislation claimed to be in his interest and for his advantage. He has been made the sport and convenience of the Republican party ever since his emancipation; he has been a sort of shuttlecock cast about for the amusement or *advantage* of those who have made him believe they were his special guardians and friends. The right or privilege of suffrage, for which so much is demanded of him by those who still for their own purposes champion his cause and claim to be *par excellence* his friends, was not conferred because of love for him or his race or any real advantage it was believed it would be to him, but because it was supposed it would add to and strengthen their political party and prolong their crime. Herein was committed the grand error, mistake, blunder, or crime, whichever it should be called, upon the negro question. Both he and the State and all the most vital interests of both have been sacrificed and made subservient to the supposed interests of a mere political party.

The black man has been literally forced into his present attitude in relation to the white race; forced, too, without knowledge or any comprehension of what is to be the result. He is little to be blamed for the condition in which he now is or the circumstances that surround him. He has been and is being "ground as between the upper and the nether millstone" by two antagonistic and opposing forces. He is no longer loved by either except for the use that can be made of him, and his welfare is at all times sacrificed to the paramount interest of party. The pretended affection of the Republican party has been his delusion and snare. It deluded him into faith in its friendship and into its support, and thereby into sharp and hostile antagonism to those among whom he was reared and must live, and with whom every interest of happiness and prosperity demands he should be friends. It deluded him into the giving up of a *real* for a *pretended* friendship, and caused him to sacrifice the toleration and encouragement of those whose interests were in common with his own for those who had nothing in common with him and who could never care for him except in so far as he strengthened them in the control of political and partisan power. It induced him to separate from and antagonize his natural ally and friend in an unnatural and partisan alliance with men who had no higher motive than to use him for their own selfish purposes, regardless of the consequences to him or his race.

Mr. Speaker, it would be interesting and instructive, if we had time, to commence at the beginning of the history of the Republican party upon the negro question and note its development and progress step by step down to the present time. I think we should be able to see and comprehend the motive by which it has been actuated and controlled. We should see how at one time or another it has disavowed with indignant denial most or all of the measures it has afterward advocated and enforced. We should see that party exigencies and party considerations alone have controlled it in the most of what it has done. We would then see how little the welfare and advantage of the colored race had entered into its consideration or controlled its action in relation thereto.

In 1868 in its national platform upon which President Grant was first elected it denied the right of the Federal Government to control the suffrage of the loyal States, and declared as a fundamental principle that the control of it belonged exclusively to the people of the several States. Before the President was inaugurated, in January, 1869, a distinguished member of this House from the State of Massachusetts, afterward Secretary of the Treasury, and now a Senator of the United States in the Senate [George S. Boutwell], reported by the direction of a majority of the Judiciary Committee of the House in favor of the enforcement of universal suffrage by the Federal Government. He enforced his views by a lengthy and impassioned speech, urging the conferring of suffrage upon the colored man almost upon party grounds alone. He assured the House and the country that it was *"the last of the series of great measures" with which the "republican party was charged"* for the pacification of the country and for the establishment of the institutions of the country upon the broadest possible basis of *"republican equality, both State and national."* And his main argument was based upon the fact that this measure would add *one hundred and fifty thousand votes to the Republican party "who are ready to battle for us at the ballot box* in favor of human rights."

This is the sordid, selfish appeal that has been made upon this negro question from the beginning. Not *his interest,* not the *interest of the Republic,* not the gerat interest of *patriotism* and *humanity,* but the interest of the Republican party.

One hundred and fifty thousand men stand ready to do battle for *us, for our party,* for the *Republican party;* and can we decline the *tempting offer?* They may be ignorant of the first principles of government—unable to read, write, or even to speak and understand *any intelligent language*—unqualified in every respect according to the requirements of our system; they may endanger the Republic, jeopardize our most cherished institutions, drag down and degrade the white race, injure and destroy the colored race by bringing the two races into fatal collision; but it will add *one hundred and fifty thousand votes to our party.* These are the considerations, *the controlling* considerations of the past upon this subject, and such are the motives for further agitation for civil and social rights and social equality of the races. In these motives and in this spirit your civil-rights bills and all like measures have their origin and growth. They are the pandering of party to the ignorance, conceits, unreasoning ambitions, untrained and selfish instincts of the least advanced and spoiled portion of the negro race. The better class, the most thoughtful, those who are really capable of understanding something of the situation and condition of affairs, are beginning to see through these schemes and machinations of their pretended friends. They see the folly and danger of these measures—of pressing the demands of the lowest portion of the race for place and position without preparation, without qualification, and against the prejudice which is more because of this ignorance and unfitness than any other repugnance which may be felt. They comprehend the situation so far, at least, as to understand that the demand for further recognition and *"the protection of their civil rights"* comes from those the least competent to understand or appreciate what has been done for them or the rights they now may enjoy. They understand that the clamor for civil rights comes from the most ignorant and dissolute, the dishonest, scheming politician of their own race, instigated by the unprincipled "carpet-bagger," "scalawag," and "pot-house" politician, who would make merchandise of all the rights of the colored race and of their bodies and souls, if thereby they could keep themselves in control of place and power. The most intelligent and worthy of the black race are grateful and contented that so much has been done for them, and that with so many favorable surroundings their destiny is in their own hands. They have sense enough to comprehend, in some degree at least, the solemnity and greatness of the work of self-government under even the most favorable circumstances, and, knowing that immunities and privileges imply obligations and duties, would not force themselves forward without preparation. The colored race in this country **have** opportunities such as no other race or people in the history of the world ever had.

The chains of slavery wherewith they were bound are broken and removed, and the whole people placed at once, by the race that held them in bondage, upon terms of perfect, *absolute equality with themselves*. They are not only in the enjoyment of all that *freedom* itself can give, but the lights of the highest civilization are shining upon them, and the examples of refinement, education, patriotism, and progress—the development of centuries—are before and around them, to guide and exalt their aspirations. If they have in them any elements of growth, civilization, and greatness; if in the economy of the Almighty they are or *are to be* capable of self-government and the comprehension and appreciation of the great principles of civil liberty and republican government—nothing on earth is now in their way. They start from vantage ground—with everything to stimulate, inspire, and guide them.

The law has done all it can accomplish for them. So far as the law is concerned, the black man is in all respects the equal of the white. He stands, and may make the race of life, upon terms of perfect equality with the most favored citizen. There is no right, privilege, or immunity secured to *any* citizen of the Republic that is not confirmed to the colored. There is no court, no tribunal, no judicial jurisdiction, no remedy, no means of any sort in the land, provided by law for the redress of wrongs or the protection of the rights of life, liberty, or property of the white man that is not equally open and available to the black man. The broad panoply of the Constitution and the whole body of laws, civil and criminal, and every means provided for their enforcement, cover and extend to every American citizen, without regard to color or previous condition. The white man may with no more legal impunity trench upon or invade the dominion of the black man's rights than the black man may the white man's. The barriers of laws surrounding and protecting them are the same. There is no distinction, no exception, no immunity in favor of the white race. And let it never be forgotten that voluntarily, in the pride and majesty of its power, the white race has thus far *done it all*. With sublime indifference and disregard of all natural and conventional differences, if not with *sublime wisdom and discretion,* the *liberator,* the white race, decreed and proclaimed to the world that his *former slave, the negro race,* whatever he may have been or may become, is henceforth and forever shall be under the law of the Republic a co-citizen and an equal.

And, sir, what would gentlemen, what would the greatest patriot, the greatest philanthropist, have more? What would the intelligent negro, the man best capable of comprehending the wants, the necessities, the highest good of his own race, ask for more? The common-law rights of both are the same. Both are equal in its protection. White and black may alike invoke its interposition for the protection of rights and the redress of wrongs. If equality, exact and impartial equality, of legal rights and legal remedies is desired, it is now enjoyed alike by both. If you would not place one race above the other; if you would make no distinction "on account of race or color or previous condition"; if you would have the recent amendments to the Constitution impartially administered; if you would have the laws of the land throughout its length and breadth, in their application to the citizen, take no note of the color of his skin or the race from which he sprang, let the "common law" remain unchanged; let there not be one law for the white man and another for the black man. No change, no distinction in favor of the one or the other can fail to injure both.

To make the colored citizen feel that he is the pet, the especial favorite of the law will only feed and pander to that conceit and self-consequence which is now his weakest and perhaps most offensive characteristic. If he be made to feel that extraordinary provisions of law are enacted in his favor because of his weakness or feebleness as a man, the very fact weakens and enfeebles him. The consciousness that there is necessity for such legislation and protection for him must necessarily humiliate and degrade him. Such laws, too, are a constant reminder to him that he is inferior to the white race. They not only remind him of his inferiority and the superiority of the white race in its not requiring these special enactments, but they naturally and necessarily awaken in him a feeling of bitterness and unfriendliness toward the white race. It is impossible that the negro race should live upon terms of mutual confidence and friendship with a race from whom it requires to be protected by a special code—against whose wrongs and oppressions he is not safe except those wrongs are denounced by extraordinary laws and penalties. There can be no peace, no harmony, no confidence, no mutual respect, no feeling of equality between two races living together and protected from the infringement of each other's rights by different laws and different penalties. It is useless to deprecate or deplore the natural or acquired prejudice of the races so long as the laws

enacted for their government in their very nature necessarily
awaken, keep alive, and foster them. And whether the prejudice be the plant of the Almighty or the growth of slavery, it
cannot be removed by legislative enactments. It may be, as in
my judgment it most certainly will be, increased and aggravated
by such legislation as this, but it cannot be lessened. If the
Southern man believes, correctly or erroneously, that the negro
race is an inferior race, this kind of legislation is certainly not
calculated to remove that belief. This bill and all such bills go
upon the ground that the colored race is inferior, feebler, and
less capable of taking care of itself than the weakest and most
inferior white man. *This* is the very predicate of this legislation. And, whether he claims the natural equality of the races
or not, it is an insult to every colored man in the Republic. It
is an unnecessary exaggeration and parading of the distinction
between them.

Sir, I have intimated already, and it has been illustrated and
demonstrated in and by the effects of previous similar legislation, that the greatest danger now to be apprehended lies in the
bringing of the two races into fatal antagonism of rights and
interests. If there be natural prejudice, if there be antipathy,
if there be antagonisms between the races, almost the entire
legislation of Congress on the negro question has been and is
calculated to increase and intensify them all. I have referred
to some of the effects upon the colored race; but the effects upon
the white race and its disposition toward the colored cannot be
less deleterious. Born and reared with the idea that they were
masters and the colored men slaves, it was not the work of a
moment, or a small thing, to reconcile themselves to the changed
condition. And yet, under all the circumstances, they may appeal with confidence to this House, the country, or the world
that they have conducted themselves with commendable patience
and forbearance. Have we not all been disappointed and surprised at their magnanimity and submission? Have they not
commended themselves to our warmest sympathy and approbation? Have they not borne themselves under the greatest trials
and the severest ordeals to which poor human nature can be
subjected with a greatness and grandeur almost sublime?

Without malice, without resentment, without reproach, they
have acquiesced in the emancipation of their slaves and their
elevation to free and equal citizenship with themselves.

If there have been some factions, dissatisfied, and turbulent
spirits, it was to have been expected. But the hostile collisions,
strifes, and conflicts, I believe on my soul, are more to be at-

tributed to the political and unwise legislation of Congress than to all other causes combined. But, because they have thus far with almost broken spirits submitted, we must not forget there is a point beyond which Congress must not go. We must not from the past presume too much. We must not for political or partisan considerations seek to degrade or dishonor them. The white people of the Southern States are a proud, honorable, intelligent people. They are the depositaries of the civilization of many centuries. The negro race, possessed of all the natural capabilities the most enthusiastic African admirer can claim for it, even with the example of the white race constantly before it, must grow and develop rapidly for many, many years before it will attain to the same civilization.

Let us beware, then, how we create the means for irritation and strife between the whites and the blacks of the South. It can be no doubtful or uncertain struggle. Let party exigencies and party necessities be whatever they may seem, it is worse than madness, it is a crime without a name, to bring the two races by our legislation into collision. The white men of the South cannot be brought to submit to the domination of the black man. The attempt will bring ruin and destruction upon the black man or it will end in the extinction of both black and white. The black man *has been* a slave, *the white man never*. The black man has with submission and patience worn the yoke of bondage and threw it not off himself; the white man never did and never will submit to be ruled by any race but his own. He may and probably will for a time submit to the sword of the Federal power, but I pray gentlemen not to presume upon that *too far*. His ancestors long ago taught the Anglo-Saxon the idea of opposition to *"intolerable burdens."* And no Anglo-Saxon can bear dishonorable burdens, or burdens imposed upon him by other hands than his own, without seeking the first opportunity to throw them off. The pride of blood and race will never brook the rule of inferior men. The gentleman from Massachusetts [Mr. Butler] well said "social equality could not be brought about by legislation." Neither can you by legislation make the white man submit to the rule and domination of the black. I beg gentlemen, as I did in speaking upon this subject in 1868, to "hesitate long before they attempt to bring it about." It will, *it must* end in the overthrow and destruction of the weaker race.

JOHN Y. BROWN [Ky.].—I had hoped that this measure would fail; but it is now manifest to all of us that it is a foregone conclusion that to-day's sun may set upon it as a law of the land. Men upon the opposite side have been dragooned into its support, and its success has been in a measure accomplished by a daring and revolutionary innovation on the time-honored rules of this House. It is the culminating, crowning iniquity of radicalism. It is born of malignity; it will be passed in defiance and in violation of the Constitution; and executed, I fear, in violence and bloodshed.

I regard it as a part of the machinery which is to be set in motion in this country for the campaign of 1876. I believe now that a deliberate conspiracy has been formed for the overthrow of our constitutional liberties. The people of the country do not favor these radical schemes; they have repudiated their originators. You men who propose to pass them have been weighed in the balance and found wanting. Judgment has been passed upon your political record, and nearly two-thirds of that side of the House retired to private life.

THE SPEAKER [James G. Blaine].—The gentleman will address the Chair.

MR. BROWN.—And your conduct now in this and other matters, Mr. Speaker, reminds me of a passage in Junius where he describes a bad tenant, having received notice to quit, breaking the furniture, putting the premises in disorder, and doing all he could to vex the landlord. Gentlemen and Mr. Speaker, the South is broken; it lies in its helplessness and despair before you; homes dilapidated, fields wasted, bankruptcy upon it. Is there nothing in its situation to touch your pity? And, if your magnanimity cannot be reached, will you not be moved by some sense of justice?

In 1872, by a conspiracy between the Attorney-General, Governor Kellogg, and a drunken Federal judge, the sovereignty of a State [Louisiana] was overthrown. That usurpation has been perpetuated since by bayonets. And but recently one of your generals [Philip H. Sheridan] entered the legislative halls of Louisiana, like General Oliver Cromwell when he invaded the English House of Commons with his Colonel Pride, and, keeping touch and time to what had gone before in the sad history of that State, ruthlessly expelled its duly qualified members.

Onward and onward you go in defiance of the sentiment of the country, without pity and without justice, remorselessly determined, it seems, to devote these distressed Southern people to complete destruction, to give their "roofs to the flames, their flesh to the eagles." Your lieutenant-general but steps upon the scene when he sends his dispatch to the world that they are banditti. We have heard it echoed elsewhere that they were thieves, murderers, night-riders. The clergy of that State, Jew and Gentile, have denied it. The business men and the Northern residents there have denied it. A committee of your own House, a majority of whom were Republicans, have given it their solemn and emphatic contradiction and nailed the slander to the counter. But still it is echoed and reëchoed. Now again that accusation has come from one—I speak not of men but of language, and within the rules of this House—that accusation against that people has come from one who is outlawed in his own home from respectable society; whose name is synonymous with falsehood; who is the champion, and has been on all occasions, of fraud; who is the apologist of thieves; who is such a prodigy of vice and meanness that to describe him would sicken imagination and exhaust invective.[1]

General James A. Garfield [O.] supported the bill.

Mr. Speaker, I concur with those gentlemen who have said that this is a solemn and an interesting occasion. It recalls to my mind a long series of steps which have been taken during the last twenty-five years in the greatest of all the great moral struggles this country has known; and the measure pending here to-day is confronted, in the last assault which has been made upon it, by the first argument that was raised against the anti-slavery movement in its first inception; I mean the charge that it is a sentimental abstraction rather than a measure of practical legislation.

The men who began this anti-slavery struggle forty years ago were denounced as dreamers, abstractionists, who were looking down to the bottom of society and attempting to see something good, something worthy the attention of American statesmen, something that the friend of human rights ought to support in the person of a negro slave. Every step since that first sentimental beginning has been assailed by precisely the same argument that we have heard to-day. I expressed the hope years ago, Mr. Speaker, that we had at last achieved a position on this great question where we could remit the black man to his own fate under the equal and exact laws of the United States. I have never asked for him one thing beyond this: that he should be placed under the equal protection of the laws, with the equal right to all the blessings which our laws confer;

[1] The reference was to Gen. Butler.

VIII—15

that, as God's sun shines with equal light and blessing upon the lofty and the humble alike, so here the light of our liberty shall shine upon all alike! and that the negro, guaranteed an equal chance in the struggle of life, may work out for himself whatever fortune his own merit will win.

THE MURDER OF LOUISIANA

From the collection of the New York Public Library

The warnings uttered to-day are not new. During the last twelve years it has often been rung in our ears that by doing justice to the negro we shall pull down the pillars of our political temple and bury ourselves in its ruins.

I remember well when it was proposed to put arms in the hands of the black man to help us in the field. I remember in the Army of the Cumberland, where there were twenty thousand Union men from Kentucky and Missouri, and we were told that those men would throw down their arms and abandon our cause if we dared to make the negro a soldier. Nevertheless, the men whose love of country was greater than their prejudice against color stood firm and fought side by side with the negro to save the Union.

When we were abolishing slavery by adopting the Thir-

teenth Amendment we were again warned that we were bringing measureless calamity upon the Republic. Did it come?
Where are the Cassandras of that day who sang their song of

LOUISIANA AND THE NATION

Louisiana.—"I have been wronged, Mr. President, bitterly wronged.
I ask for justice—shall I ask in vain?"

President.—"Down with your arms, then. The nation cannot parley
with armed citizens. Order first, and then the righting of your wrongs,
but not till then."

ruin in this hall when we passed that Thirteenth Amendment?
Again when the Fourteenth Amendment was passed the same
wail was heard, the wail of the fearful and unbelieving. Again
when it was proposed to elevate the negro to citizenship, to give
him the ballot as his weapon of self-defence, we were told the
cup of our destruction was filled to its brim. But, sir, I have
lived long enough to learn that in the long run it is safest for
a nation, a political party, or an individual man to dare to
do right, and let consequences take care of themselves, for he
that loseth his life for the truth's sake shall find it. The recent disasters of the Republican party have not sprung from
any of the brave acts done in the effort to do justice to the
negro. For these reasons I do not share in the fears we have
heard expressed to-day, that this bill will bring disaster to those
who shall make it a law. What is this bill? It is a declaration
that every citizen of the United States shall be entitled to the
equal enjoyment of all those public chartered privileges granted
under State laws to the citizens of the several States. For this
act of plain justice we are told that ruin is again staring us in
the face! If ruin comes from this, I welcome ruin.

Mr. Speaker, the kind of cowardice which shrinks from the
assertion of great principles has followed this grand anti-slavery movement from the beginning until now; but God taught
us early in this fight that the fate of our own race was indissolubly linked with that of the black man on this continent—
not socially, for none of us are linked by social ties except by
our own consent, but politically in all the rights accorded under
the law.

This truth was stated early by one of our revered poets when
he said:

> We dare not share the negro's trust.
>   Nor yet his hope deny;
> We only know that God is just,
>   And every wrong shall die.
>
> Rude seems the song; each swarthy face,
>   Flame-lighted, ruder still;
> We start to think that hapless race
>   Must shape our good or ill;
>
> That laws of changeless justice bind
>   Oppressor with oppressed;
> And close as sin and suffering joined
>   We march to Fate abreast.[1]

[1] "To a Slave Singing at Midnight," by John G. Whittier.

Their fate politically must be ours. Justice to them has always been safety for us. Let us not shrink now.

General Butler spoke in support of his bill:

I had hoped, when this bill was first brought before the House, that, in all kindness of heart, in all singleness of purpose, with all propriety of tone and thought, we should discuss one of the most momentous questions of civil liberty that can be raised; a question the solution of which, for good or for evil, will affect our country longer, much longer, than we shall remain on the earth; but I have been disappointed.

It is a question of equal civil rights to all citizens—a doctrine in which I was brought up from my earliest boyhood. I have always been taught that the foundation of all democracy was equality of right, equality of burden, equality of power in all men under the law. And when, a few years ago, a religious and partisan furore shook the land, and it was attempted to disfranchise from some of their rights in many of the States a portion of our citizens because of their foreign birth and because of their religion, when the cry went out "put no one but Americans on guard," I stood in my State in almost a hopeless minority, indeed almost alone, in saying that the privilege of American citizenship, once granted, was like the privilege of the Roman citizen—to be to him the same in Latium and at Athens. And I stood firmly to that until all that prejudice was rolled away from the foreign-born citizen by his standing shoulder to shoulder with our brothers and sons in the red track of battle.

Now comes another question of prejudice in which I was educated in my youth differently—the rights of the colored man. He has been made, by right or by wrong, but under the forms and with the force of constitutional law, a citizen of the United States. And, were he as black as the black diamond, he has an equal right to every privilege with any citizen who is white as an angel. And upon that ground alone can a democratic republic stand. Upon that ground alone is civil and constitutional liberty on this continent to be preserved. And, therefore, I wonder with amazement when I hear it here stated that this bill is intended as a stab to constitutional liberty. Why, sir, this bill is the very essence of constitutional liberty. What does it do? It simply provides that there shall be an equality of law all over the Union.

My friend from Mississippi [Mr. Lamar] says that in Mississippi the white man and the colored man have equal privileges. Be it so. Good for Mississippi. This was so made by a Republican legislature in which was a colored majority. But where is the like law in Kentucky, the "dark and bloody ground"? Where is that law in Tennessee? Where is that law —without stopping to enumerate—in a majority of the Southern States? But, if it is a good law in Mississippi, why should it not be extended over all the Southern States? If it is a good law, and my friend from Mississippi agrees it is a good law and works well there, why should it not be enforced by proper and sufficient penalties to restrain bad men from violating it? And that is all the bill does.

Now, then, what are the objections here made to this bill? The first objection stated on the other side is that this bill establishes social equality. By no means; by no means. I undertook to show, when up before, how social equality is not touched by the bill. It allows men and women of different colors only to come together in public, in theaters, in stage-coaches and cars, in public houses. I am inclined to think that the only equality the blacks ever have in the South is social equality; for I understand the highest exhibition of social equality is communication between the sexes.

Now, sir, the next question we have to encounter is that this bill is born of malignity. Sir, I have a good authority on this point. It is generally supposed and believed that this bill was originated by Charles Sumner, of Massachusetts. The gentleman from Mississippi [Mr. Lamar], speaking the honest sentiments of his heart, no doubt, in regard to that great man and this bill,[1] says:

He did not hesitate to impress most emphatically upon the Administration, not only in public, but in the confidence of private intercourse, his uncompromising resolution to oppose to the last any and every scheme which should fail to provide the surest guaranties for the personal freedom and political rights of the race which he had undertaken to protect.

. . . .

The spirit of magnanimity, therefore, which breathes in his utterances and manifests itself in all his acts affecting the South during the last two years of his life was as evidently honest as it was grateful to the feelings of those to whom it was displayed.

When Mr. Sumner came to contemplate death his great regret was that he had not time to finish this work, that of passing the civil rights bill which lies upon your table now.

But this was not the origin of the civil rights bill. When

[1] In his eulogy in the House upon Sumner, who died March 11, 1874.

we go down into the depths of the origin of civil rights it is much further down than that. There was an old man of Puritan stock, a fanatic, if you please, who undertook to carry equality of rights into the wilderness of Kansas. He was there met by the bludgeon and the dagger and the pistol as the emblems of that civilization which he sought to overthrow. Almost crazed by that, but yet with a full belief that God had ordained that slavery should no longer exist, he organized a band of men, seventeen in number, at the head of which he put himself, and into which he took his two promising sons, defying the power of the commonwealth of Virginia, defying the power even of this great Government, and made an invasion into Virginia and established himself there for the purpose of freeing the slaves; not in any purpose of malignity, but of love for the slave, but with a belief that God himself would interfere by a miracle and set right this great wrong, now acknowledged by all to be such. He was a brave, strong old man; he inaugurated that movement to which we are now about to put the finishing stroke.

He did it, you say, against the law. Pardon me; he had seen the law so outraged in support of slavery in Kansas that he had got his brain muddled on the question of legal right and wrong. The great brave act which he did there has been recognized by his countrymen in gratitude. Monuments have been erected to his memory, and it became the rallying cry to which marched the armies of liberty. He had many good qualities; he was a brave man; he never did a cowardly act; he never struck at anybody behind his back; and, more than that, he never told a lie. Even when he lay in prison, and the Governor of Virginia visited him and offered him life itself if he would but state what was not true, the old man spurned the bribe and went to the scaffold and gave his life for a poor and lowly race. And his disembodied spirit rose from thence to heaven, wafted there by the prayers and blessings of all the meek and lowly and of all the Christians in the land, and there it looks down smiling upon us from the realms of bliss, into which no *liar* shall ever go. His name was John Brown, the elder; not the younger of that name.

There was another scene in the great drama of human liberty. There was a revolt in the South against the Constitution of the United States. There was an attempt to form a new confederation, whose cornerstone was slavery. There was an effort made to carry off eleven States from the constellation of stars. There was a treasonable endeavor to overturn this

Government by force of arms in the interest of slavery. And that brought to the front another John Brown. I dare not trust myself to be a eulogist of that John Brown, the younger of that name. Therefore I pray the Clerk to read it from the report of the Committee on Elections of this House, where it is set out in language that must be parliamentary, however severe.

[From the Louisville *Courier*, May 15, 1861]

ELIZABETHTOWN, *April* 18, 1861.

Editors Louisville Courier:

My attention has been called to the following paragraph which appeared in your paper of this date:

"JOHN YOUNG BROWN'S POSITION.—This gentleman, in reply to some searching interrogatories put to him by Governor Helm, said, in reference to the call of the President for four regiments of volunteers to march against the South. '*I would not send one solitary man to aid that government, and those who volunteer should be shot down in their tracks.*'"

This ambiguous report of my remarks has, I find, been misunderstood by some who have read it, who construe my language to apply to the *government of the Confederate States*. What I did say was this:

"Not one man or one dollar will Kentucky furnish *Lincoln* to aid *him* in his *unholy war against the South*. If this *Northern army* shall attempt to cross our borders *we will resist it unto the death;* and, if one man shall be found in our commonwealth to volunteer to join them, *he ought* and I believe will be *shot down before he leaves* the State."

This was not said in reply to any question propounded by ex-Governor Helm as you have stated, and is no more than *I frequently uttered publicly and privately* prior to my debate with him.

Respectfully,

JOHN YOUNG BROWN.

ROBERT S. HALE [N. Y.].—I raise the question of order that this document read from the desk has been improperly read, and not to be allowed to go into the *Record*.

MR. BUTLER.—I think I have a right to show how what has been read is pertinent to this discussion.

THE SPEAKER.—The Chair will hear the gentleman.

MR. BUTLER.—The gentleman from Kentucky [Mr. Brown] made a speech against the civil rights bill, and I have endeavored to put his published sentiments, as reported upon by a committee of this House, before the House to show how little heed we should pay to anything he says on the subject unless he has deeply repented; and I have no knowledge of his repentance.

Again it is pertinent in this: He accused me of being the only one who charged that there were murderers in the South. I produce the solemn report of a committee of the House and his own letter to show that there were men who counseled murder in the South, and not only murder, but assassination, and that, instead of my being his accuser, he was his own accuser; and that this state of things existed, which shows how completely the negro, if we do not protect him in his rights, is at the mercy of the same men who would have shot down the gentleman from New York himself if he had ever dared to step across the line of Union bayonets during the war. [Applause on the floor and in the gallery.]

Now, sir, having vindicated my right to say what I please upon this question, and I do not please to say anything that I have not a right to say, I desire to say in all kindliness to the Southern people that I sympathize with them in their deplorable condition. It is different from what it is with us in the North. When the Northern army was disbanded hundreds and thousands of men were sent back home, some of whom, if unemployed, would have become the pests of society. But we rapidly absorbed all those, with a very few exceptions, because we had employment—mechanical, manufacturing, seafaring, and other employments—to take up all the unruly and uneasy spirits that got into the army and were demoralized by camp life.

But with the South it was different. Their system of labor had prevented the white man from laboring, even from learning to labor, and, when the Southern army disbanded, it threw upon society a class of men demoralized by war, without work, without employment, largely without education by which they might divert their minds, with nothing on earth to do except to brood upon their defeat and think how wrong it was that the result of the war had been such as to take from them the negro who had earned their living for them before the war. And that state of natural irritation has brought forward in the South a large number of unruly men, demoralized men, who make substantially all the disturbances there. Most of the "white-leaguers," that are not young men simply growing up with the teaching of the war, are men of that class.

I call upon the good men South, if they want prosperity, that they themselves check and control this class of men. They are impoverishing the South; they are impoverishing our country. And, when I spoke of the South having a large minority of murderers and night-riders, I spoke of that class of men that make the Ku-Klux and White Leagues. It never occurred to me that any man on this floor could suppose for a moment that I referred to men who are here, or to a majority of the men in the South, who, I have no doubt, honestly desire peace and quiet. I am bound in all fairness to say so much; and it is done without compulsion.

I have now an answer to make to the gentleman from Virginia [Thomas Whitehead], who told us yesterday that, if we passed this civil rights bill, the people of the South would export their cotton and tobacco directly to Europe and would not let us of the North make a profit on it. What an argument to address to men of common intelligence! Think of it a moment. If we do what is right to preserve the rights of the negro, who raises the cotton and tobacco, and without whose labor there would not be a bale of cotton or twenty pounds of tobacco raised there, we are threatened that the South will sell it all to England! Will you indeed? And you will not buy our goods, you say. Now that depends upon whether we can sell goods to you cheaper than England can. You know you would buy wooden nutmegs if we sent them down there, and they were cheaper than the real articles.

The day has gone past when the merchants of New York were kept in the slavery column by threats that the South would not trade with them. Why, sir, ten years have passed, a great war has passed; and are we to be thrown out of our propriety here by an argument of that sort?

Another argument: We are told that if we pass this bill we shall not come back to Congress, and we are reminded that this bill was the great issue in the last election. But I say in the face of the country that it is my deliberate conviction that the reason why some here have not been sent back is because we did not pass this bill a year ago. The people turned from us because we were a do-nothing party, afraid of our shadows; because we were aptly described by that portion of Scripture which relates how it was written to the angel of the church of the Laodiceans:

I know thy works, that thou art neither cold nor hot: I would thou wert cold or hot. So then because thou art lukewarm, and neither cold nor hot, I will spew thee out of my mouth.

The Republican party being neither hot nor cold, the country rightly spewed us out of its mouth. When I am met in the argument by the assertion, "You do not represent the people; you were beaten in your election," my answer is that my successor—a very estimable gentleman he is in every sense— could no more have come here than he could have been translated to heaven as Elijah was if he had not agreed to stand upon the doctrine of equality of races and of men before the law, and so declared on every stump in my district. Nor could one Democrat have been elected from Massachusetts, not even my old friend who voted with me fifty-seven times for Jeff Davis, unless it was understood that he stood with me for the equal rights of all men.

I say again, as you on the other side were compelled in your platform of 1872 to declare for equality of rights of all men before the law, so every Republican was bound to stand by that. And where we were beaten it was because we had neglected to do the thing we had promised, and it was not made an accomplished fact. When we passed the Thirteenth Amendment to the Constitution of the United States we lost Ohio the first year; but we regained it the next. So now, if the Republican party will finish their great work, pass the civil rights bill, and by bayonet or otherwise bring peace, prosperity, law, and good order in the South, and put down those that ride by night there to murder and burn, which the South ought to do for itself, you will find that we will come back here sustained by voices of the loyal Union-loving men of the country.

The bill was passed by a vote of 162 to 99. The Senate passed it on February 27 by a vote of 38 to 26. It was approved by the President on March 1.

President Grant's successor, Rutherford B. Hayes [O.], entered upon his administration with the avowed purpose of conciliating the South, and that section was permitted to settle the negro question for itself. Complaints of intimidation of the negro gradually ceased, though it was charged by Republicans that he continued to be deprived of the suffrage and of his civil rights in general by even more effective, though less forceful, means, such as State laws discriminating against him, frauds in election, etc.

At various times since Hayes's Administration Northern statesmen have proposed bills for enforcing civil rights in the South (stigmatized by their opponents as "force bills"), but these resulted in no legislation. In the presidential campaigns of 1880 and 1884 Republican speakers used the South's denial to the negro of his civil rights as an argument for keeping the Democratic party out of national control, but this "waving of the bloody shirt," as the Democrats called it, was laid aside thereafter for appeals to the reason and material interest, rather than the emotions and prejudices, of the voters.

"OF COURSE HE WANTS TO VOTE THE DEMOCRATIC TICKET!"

Democratic "Reformer."—"You're as free as air, ain't you? Say you are, or I'll blow yer black head off!"

Cartoon by A. B. Frost

CHAPTER VI

The Seminole War

Resolution of Censure in the House of Representatives against Gen. Andrew Jackson for Barbarous Treatment of the Seminoles—Debate: in Favor, Thomas W. Cobb [Ga.], James Johnson [Va.], Henry Clay [Ky.], Charles F. Mercer [Va.], Joseph Hopkinson [Pa.], John Tyler [Va.]; Opposed, John Holmes [Mass.], Richard M. Johnson [Ky.], Alexander Smyth [Va.], Lemuel Sawyer [N. C.], George Poindexter [Miss.]—Resolution Is Negatived—Later History of the War.

THE political status of the Indian in this country has been from the beginning of our Government an anomalous one. The various tribes were considered as quasi-foreign nations, with whom treaties were made by the Government, yet over whom it acted as a responsible guardian. This relation brought on at several times a conflict between the Federal Government and the government of the States within whose boundaries the tribes were located, since in their desire to possess the lands of the Indians, who were without the protection of representation in the State legislatures, the white settlers, acting through these bodies, with the purpose of driving the tribes from their borders, imposed upon them annoying restrictions and civic disabilities in violation of treaties made with them by the Federal Government.

It was during the administration of Andrew Jackson that this conflict became most critical, and it is therefore important that the attitude of this President toward the Indians be understood from the time that, as a general in the United States Army, he came into contact with them, particularly with the Seminoles and their kinsmen, the Creeks.

The Seminoles were originally a part of the Creeks

237

of Georgia. Early in the eighteenth century they split off from the main stock and occupied Florida, thus receiving the name *Simanoli,* or "Runaways," a term which was further justified by the accession to their ranks of a number of fugitive slaves. About the beginning of the eighteenth century they possessed a score of villages, the chief of which were Mikasuki and Tallahassee. The people of Mikasuki were the leaders in warlike enterprises, which (although they claimed provocation) led them into Georgia, where they committed depredations and murderous outrages on the white settlers besides inciting slaves to run away with them. They were known as "Red Sticks" from their practice of setting up a painted pole as an emblem of war.

In 1817 General Andrew Jackson was sent to the Florida frontier of Georgia to suppress the outrages committed by the "Red Sticks." Despite the fact that Florida was Spanish territory, during this and the following year he pursued them to their homes in the peninsula and destroyed their principal towns and hanged two Englishmen, Alexander Arbuthnot, a trader, and Robert C. Ambrister, an adventurer, for inciting the Indians to their outrages upon the Georgia settlers. He also seized Pensacola in spite of the remonstrance of the Spaniards. These actions created intense excitement in England, and, had it not been for Spain's weakness, would have involved us in war with that country. After considerable correspondence Great Britain was pacified, and the difficulty with Spain was settled by the purchase from her of Florida in 1819 for $5,000,000 (paid by the United States assuming claims to that amount of American citizens against Spain), and by our giving up all claims to Texas, the ownership of which had been in dispute between Spain and the United States since the Louisiana Purchase.

During the session of Congress following Jackson's high-handed actions (1818-19) a resolution of censure was presented against him, particularly for his hanging Arbuthnot and Ambrister, it being claimed that the former was clearly innocent of the charge against him, and that the latter, though he may have been guilty, had not been proved so by the proper forms of law. The debate soon developed charges of barbarities committed by General Jackson on the Indians. It continued from January 12 to February 8, 1819, when the resolution was separated into two sections, one relating to the trial of Arbuthnot and one to the trial of Ambrister; and the former was negatived by a vote of 108 to 62, and the latter by a vote of 107 to 63. The chief speakers in favor of censure were Thomas W. Cobb [Ga.], James Johnson [Va.], Henry Clay [Ky.], Charles F. Mercer [Va.], Joseph Hopkinson [Pa.], and John Tyler [Va.]. Those opposing censure were John Holmes [Mass.], Richard M. Johnson [Ky.], Alexander Smyth [Va.], Lemuel Sawyer [N. C.], and George Poindexter [Miss.].

CENSURE OF GENERAL JACKSON

HOUSE OF REPRESENTATIVES, JANUARY 12-FEBRUARY 8, 1819

The report of the military committee was read through, concluding with the following resolution:

"*Resolved*, That the House of Representatives of the United States disapproves the proceedings in the trial and execution of Alexander Arbuthnot and Robert C. Ambrister."

MR. COBB declared that illegal evidence had been accepted at the trial. The rules of evidence, in courts-martial, differ very little, in principle, from those established in the courts of common law. It was so declared by the only American authority (Macomb on Martial Law) on that subject. If we test the evidence produced in those trials by these rules, we shall blush at the shameful perversion of justice therein displayed. The evidence of papers, not produced or accounted for, the *belief* of persons whose testimony of *facts* ought to have been doubted, *hearsay*, and *that* of *Indians, negroes*, or *others* who, had they been present, could not have been sworn, were all indiscriminately admitted and acted upon. Miserable, indeed, will be the precedents established by *this* court-martial for *others* which may hereafter be formed!

I would also call the attention of the committee to the principle by which the commanding general professes to have been governed in ordering the execution of Ambrister, and which, in its extent, as contended by the report of the committee under consideration, applied with equal force to the case of Arbuthnot. It is in these words: "It is an established principle of the law of nations that any individual of a nation making war against the citizens of another nation, they being at peace, forfeits his allegiance, and becomes an outlaw and a pirate." The military committee, in their report, have very properly denied the establishment of any such principle in the law of nations. Sir, I boldly challenge any man of common sense to prove the existence of such a principle to the extent it is here laid down. Reason, propriety, justice, and humanity all cry aloud against such a principle! So far as my researches have gone, it is absolutely denied by the writers on national law; and I sincerely hope will be absolutely denied by every member of this committee. If this principle was true, then Lafayette, DeKalb, Pulaski, and a large host of foreigners who joined the standard of our fathers in the Revolution, and, by their blood and at the expense of their lives, aided in the establishment of the independence of this nation, were "outlaws and pirates"; and, had they been captured, were subject to have been tried and sentenced to an ignominious death by a court-martial. For, when they entered our service, they were "individuals of a nation at peace" with England, and they, after they joined our arms, "made war upon England and her citizens, and thereby forfeited their allegiance." Sir, is this committee prepared to brand these men with the titles of "outlaws and pirates," by their sanction to this principle? I will not yet believe it.

But, it may be said that, these Englishmen, having "joined a savage nation who observe no rules and give no quarter," we have a right to treat them precisely as we might treat the savages whom they have joined, and that we would have a right to put the savages to death, upon a principle of retaliation. Let this position for a moment be admitted, and yet it will be evident that the principle under which we should proceed would be a very different one—to wit, that of retaliation. For even savages cannot regularly be put to death until they refuse "to observe rules or give quarter."

Does the commanding general of the American army possess the power to exercise the right of retaliation? If in its exercise there is any responsibility, it is placed upon the nation. They are accountable to all other nations for the manner in which they conduct their wars. To the nation, therefore, it belongs to establish the rules of war, by which it would be governed; and the authority by which they were to be established was that in whose hands was vested the right of declaring war. In their establishment, the character of the nation for justice, for humanity, etc., was deeply involved. Who are the legitimate guardians of the character of this nation but Congress—the war-declaring power? I am not singular in this opinion. The late President of the United States, the virtuous James Madison, was of the same opinion. For when, during the late war, it was thought necessary to apply the retaliatory principle, did he believe himself clothed with power to do it, although Commander-in-Chief? No—he believed it was in Congress alone. To Congress he applied for the power, and, by a special act, they conferred it on him.

MR. HOLMES.—It is not, sir, because General Jackson has acquired so much glory in defence of his country's rights that I defend him—it is not for the splendor of his achievements or the brilliancy of his character. I would not compromit the rights and liberties of my country to screen any man, however respectable. If General Jackson has been ambitious, I would restrain him; if cruel, I would correct him; if he is proud, I would humble him; if he is tyrannical, I would disarm him. And yet, I confess, it would require pretty strong proof to produce conviction that he has intentionally done wrong. At his age of life, crowned with the honors and loaded with the gratitude of his country, what adequate motive could induce him to tarnish his glory by acts of cruelty and revenge?

I assure the gentleman from Georgia that, in endeavoring to anticipate the arguments of the friends of General Jackson and the President, he has not anticipated me. I admit, in the outset, that the President has no right to commence a war, even against Indians, without the consent of Congress. If, with these admissions, the President and General Jackson cannot be defended, they cannot, in my opinion, be defended at all.

It is, then, incumbent on me to show that the Indians commenced the war.

On the 9th of August, 1814, a treaty was signed at Fort Jackson between the United States and most of the chiefs and warriors of the Creek Nation. By this treaty certain lands were ceded to the United States, and the inhabitants of the frontiers understood that the war was ended. But it was soon found that several of the hostile Creeks and the Seminoles had, within the limits of Florida, associated for the purpose of commencing hostilities against the United States. By the instigation and aid of a certain Colonel Nicholls a fort was erected on the Appalachicola, and within the province of East Florida, to facilitate their hostile designs. At this place were assembled a motley banditti of negroes, Indians, and fugitives from all nations, and trained and instructed in the arts of robbery and murder. The people of the United States soon felt the effects of their vengeance. Several families, including women and children, were barbarously murdered. In 1816 a boat's crew were cruelly butchered, one of whom was tarred, set on fire, and burned to death. On the 30th of November last Lieutenant Scott and his party, consisting of about fifty men, women, and children, were murdered in a manner too shocking to describe.

The war having been commenced by the Seminoles and their associates, and the President of the United States having the power, by the Constitution and laws of the United States, to meet and repel the enemy, the inquiry is important on what ground he may meet them. I differ from many gentlemen in regard to the political rights of the Indians. Whatsoever may be their rights in peace, either by natural or conventional law, in war I deem them as sovereign. Their residence within the limits of the United States, limits to which they have never assented, neither brings them within our protection nor entitles us to their allegiance. The laws of the United States have no operation upon them, and, if they levy war, they are not punishable as traitors. A tribe of Indians whose territory is exclusively within our limits may wage war and make peace with us; pursue, capture, and destroy us; send and receive flags; grant and receive capitulations, and are entitled to a reciprocation of every act of civilized warfare, and subject to the same rules of severity and retaliation as other nations. To invade their territory and cross their line is, as to them, passing out of the limits of the United States. And, if General Jackson had no right in this war to cross the Florida line, neither had he a right to cross the Indian line within our limits. If there is any force in the argument so often urged on other occasions that every war of invasion is an offensive war, and one, consequently, which the President could not wage without the authority of Congress; then it follows that Congress must declare war before the President can march the militia across the Indian line, even within the limits of the United States. But such a construction of the Constitution is totally inadmissible. When war is commenced by savages it becomes the duty of the President to repel and punish them. To follow them to the line affords us no security. The invasion cannot be effectually repelled but by pursuing them into their own territory and retaliating on them there. Such has been the uniform construction of the power of the President ever since the adoption of the Constitution. In no instance that I recollect has Congress declared war against an Indian tribe. The defeat of St. Clair and subsequent victory of Wayne were on Indian territory. The battle at Tippecanoe (fought by my friend from Ohio [General William Henry Harrison] with so much honor to himself and satisfaction to his country) was within the limits of the Indian nation. In neither of these instances was a declaration of war deemed necessary by Congress.

The territory of these Indians is on both sides of the Florida line. Their possessions and residence are transient and ambulatory, without regard to this line. The nation, if such they may be called, is at war with us, and in this war they can occupy their territory in Florida in spite of Spain. Singular, indeed, would it be if we should be engaged in war with an enemy who had a perfect right to be where we had no right to meet him. Spain claims a jurisdiction to a territory occupied by our enemy; she has no power nor inclination to expel him; and yet it is gravely said this enemy cannot be pursued to this territory without an act of hostility against Spain. Unfortunate, indeed, would be the condition of the United States if a horde of unprincipled banditti, holding a residence on our borders, could prosecute a cruel and exterminating war upon our citizens, and then take refuge across an ideal line, where the laws of nations forbid us to approach them. Sir, let gentlemen tell me of another instance where your enemy has a right to perfect security against your approach. It would be a war of a peculiar character, where one side only gives the blows.

Why, then, should not General Jackson and his army cross? Will any gentleman point to me the clause in the Constitution or laws of the United States that forbids him. The Seminoles, being enemies and having a right in Florida beyond the control of Spain, the inference is irresistible that you have a right to pursue and fight them there in your own defence.

I lay Spain out of the question. Poor, miserable, degraded Spain, too weak and palsied to act or think! She has but the shadow of authority in Florida, and, so far from being able to control the Indians, or even her own subjects, the country, as to her, is a perfect derelict. I will ask this committee to go back with me to the year 1813, and from that period to the capture of Pensacola, to witness the Spanish officers exciting the Indians to vengeance, furnishing them with the arms and munitions of war, tamely acquiescing in the most flagrant violations of their pretended neutrality, and suffering the territory to be prostituted to every banditti who might be disposed to annoy or distress the people of the United States.

MR. JOHNSON [Va.].—I proceed to examine into the propriety of the course pursued on the trial and execution of Arbuthnot and Ambrister. It is laid down by Vattel, p. 416: "An enemy not to be killed after ceasing to resist." In the same page an exception is noted—except where the safety of the general, of his army, or of the prince is thereby conserved.

I can scarcely believe that it will be pretended that the safety of the general or his men required the execution of these prisoners. Did, then, the safety of the prince (that is, in this country, the people) require the execution of these men? Was it necessary to offer them up on the altar of public safety—to hold them up as a terrible example to future instigators and abettors of Indian wars? If so, their fate should have been referred to the people; that is, to their representatives—to the Congress of the United States. The commanding general had no right, no authority, to decide the question whether the safety of the people required the sacrifice of these captives. We are told—and very seriously told—that this execution of prisoners may be justified on the principles of retaliation. What, retaliate the cruelties and barbarities of savages? It is a doctrine unsupported by precedent and law, and is shocking to the principles of humanity. It may be said, as it was remarked the other day by a gentleman from Virginia (Mr. Nelson), that this is a sympathy for miscreants—a sympathy resulting from morbid sensibility—a sympathy for British subjects. It is not so, Mr. Chairman. I have no sympathy for British subjects. When I look at yon ruin (pointing to the Capitol), when I recollect the massacres at the River Raisin, Frenchtown, and many other places in the United States, during the late war, I recognize in the late British forces an enemy not less cruel and savage than the Seminole Indians—the outlawed Red Sticks. Yet did the highest officer in this Government, during the late war—the Commander-in-Chief of your army—the President of the United States—consider himself vested with authority to retaliate the acts of cruelty perpetrated by the enemy or those threatened? No.

What has been, since the period of our independence, the uniform and unvarying policy pursued by this Government toward the Indian tribes? Has it been a policy tempered by mercy, brightened by generosity, and ameliorated by Christianity? Have we been constantly engaged in the humane work of civilizing them—of sending emissaries among them to preach the gospel—to distribute the copies of the Bible collected by different societies? Is this policy to be suddenly changed under the auspices of General Jackson? Shall we, at the close of a war of extermination, go through the ceremony of appointing committees to meet members from the Society of Friends, to devise the means of civilizing this unfortunate, misguided, and deluded race of beings?

MR. CLAY [Speaker].—In noticing the painful incidents of this war it was impossible not to inquire into its origin. He feared that would be found to be the famous treaty of Fort Jackson, concluded in August, 1814; and he asked the indulgence of the Chairman that the Clerk might read certain parts of that treaty. [The Clerk of the House having accordingly read as requested, Mr. C. proceeded.] He had never perused this instrument until within a few days past, and he had read it with the deepest mortification and regret. A more dictatorial spirit he had never seen displayed in any instrument. He would challenge an examination of all the records of diplomacy, not excepting even those in the most haughty period of imperious Rome, when she was carrying her arms into the barbarian nations that surrounded her; and he did not believe a solitary instance could be found of such an inexorable spirit of domination pervading a compact purporting to be a treaty of *peace*. It consisted of the most severe and humiliating demands—of the surrender of large territory—of the privilege of making roads through even what was retained—of the right of establishing trading-houses—of the obligation of delivering into our hands their prophets. And all this of a wretched people, reduced to the last extremity of distress, whose miserable existence we had to preserve by a voluntary stipulation to furnish them with bread! When even did conquering and desolating Rome fail to respect the altars and the gods of those whom she subjugated? Let me not be told that these prophets were impostors who deceived the Indians. They were *their* prophets—the Indians believed and venerated them, and it is not for us to dictate a religious belief to them. It does not belong to the holy character of the religion which we profess to carry its precepts, by force of the bayonet, into the bosoms of other people. Mild and gentle persuasion was the great instrument employed by the meek founder of our religion. We leave to the humane and benevolent efforts of the reverend professors of

Christianity to convert from barbarism those unhappy nations yet immersed in its gloom. But, sir, spare them their prophets! Spare their delusions! Spare their prejudices and superstitions! Spare them even their religion, such as it is, from open and cruel violence. When, sir, was that treaty concluded? On the very day, after the protocol was signed, of the first conference between the American and British commissioners, treating of peace, at Ghent. In the course of that negotiation pretensions so enormous were set up by the other party that, when they were promulgated in this country, there was one general burst of indignation throughout the continent. Faction itself was silenced, and the firm and unanimous determination of all parties was to fight until the last man fell in the ditch rather than submit to such ignominious terms.

What a contrast is exhibited between the contemporaneous scenes of Ghent and Fort Jackson! What a powerful argument would the British commissioners have been furnished with if they could have got hold of that treaty! The United States demand!—the United States demand!—is repeated five or six times. And what did the preamble itself disclose? That two-thirds of the Creek nation had been hostile and one-third only friendly to us. Now, he had heard that not one hostile chief signed the treaty. If the treaty really were made by a minority of the nation, it was not obligatory upon the whole nation. It was void, considered in the light of a national compact. And, if void, the Indians were entitled to the benefit of the provision of the ninth article of the Treaty of Ghent, by which we bound ourselves to make peace with any tribes with whom we might be at war on the ratification of the treaty, and restore to them their lands as they held them in 1811. I do not know how the honorable Senate, that body for which he had so high a respect, could have given their sanction to the treaty of Fort Jackson, so utterly irreconcilable as it is with those noble principles of generosity and magnanimity which he hoped to see this country always exhibit, and particularly toward the miserable remnant of the aborigines. It would have comported better with those principles to have imitated the benevolent policy of the founder of Pennsylvania, to have given to the Creeks, conquered as they were, even if they had made an unjust war upon us, the trifling consideration, to them an adequate compensation, which he paid for their lands. That treaty, I fear, was the main cause of the recent war. And, if so, it only added another melancholy proof to those with which history already abounds that hard and unconscionable terms, extorted by the power of the sword and the right of conquest, served but to whet and stimulate revenge, and to give to old hostilities, smothered, not extinguished, by the pretended peace, greater expansion and more ferocity. A truce thus patched up with an unfortunate people, without the means of existence—without bread—is no real peace. The instant there is the slightest prospect of relief from such harsh and severe conditions the conquered party will fly to arms and spend the last drop of blood rather than live in such degraded bondage. Even if you again reduce him to submission, the expenses incurred by this second war, to say nothing of the human lives that are sacrificed, will be greater than what it would have cost you to have granted him liberal conditions in the first instance. This treaty—I repeat it—was probably the cause of the war. It led to those excesses on our Southern borders which began it. Who first commenced them it was, perhaps, difficult to ascertain. There was, however, a paper on this subject, communicated at the last session by the President, that told, in language so pathetic and feeling, an artless tale—a paper that carried such internal evidence, at least, of the belief of the authors of it that they were writing the truth that he would ask the favor of the committee to allow him to read it.

The following is a part of the letter from ten of the Seminole towns that Mr. Clay read:

To the commanding officer at Fort Hawkins.

DEAR SIR: Since the last war, after you sent me word that we must quit the war, we, the red people, have come over on this side. The white people have carried all the red people's cattle off. After the war I sent to all my people to let white people alone and stay on this side of the river; and they did so, but the white people still continue to carry off their cattle. Barnard's son was here, and I inquired of him what was to be done—and he said we must go to the head man of the white people and complain. I did so, and there was no white head man, and there was no law in this case. The whites first began, and there is nothing said about that; but great complaint made about what the Indians do. This is now three years since the white people killed three Indians; since that they have killed three other Indians and taken their horses and what they had; and this summer they killed three more, and very lately they killed one more. We sent word to the white people that these murders were done, and the answer was that they were people that were outlaws, and we ought to go and kill them. The white people killed our people first—the Indians then took satisfaction. There are yet three men that the red people have never taken satisfaction for. On that side of the river the white people have killed five Indians, but there is nothing said about that; and all that the Indians have done is brought up. All the mischief the white people have done ought to be told to their head man. When there is anything done you write to us, but never write to your head man what the white people do. When the red people send talks, or write, they always send the truth. The cattle that we were accused of taking were cattle that the white people took from us. Our young men went and brought them back, with the same marks and brands. There were some of our young men out hunting and they were killed; others went to take satisfaction, and the kettle of one of the men that was killed was found in the house where the woman and two children were killed; and they supposed it had been her husband who had killed the Indians, and took their satisfaction there.

Mr. Clay continued:

I should be very unwilling to assert, in regard to this war, that the fault was on our side—but I fear it is. I have heard that that very respectable man, now no more, who once filled the executive chair of Georgia, and who, having been agent of Indian affairs in that quarter, had the best opportunity of judging of the origin of this war, deliberately pronounced it as his opinion that the Indians were not in fault.

The first circumstance which, in the course of General Jackson's conduct, fixes our attention is the execution of the Indian chiefs. How did they come into our possession? Was it in the course of fair and open and honorable war? No; but by means of deception—by hoisting foreign colors on the staff from which the stars and stripes should alone have floated. Thus ensnared, the Indians were taken on shore, and, without ceremony and without delay, were hung. It was the first instance that I know of, in the annals of our country, in which retaliation, by executing Indian captives, had ever been deliberately practiced. The gentleman from Massachusetts may tell me, if he pleases, what he pleases about the tomahawk and scalping-knife; about Indian enormities, and foreign miscreants and incendiaries. I, too, hate them; from my very soul I abominate them. But I love my country and its Constitution;

I love liberty and safety, and fear military despotism more even than I hate these monsters. I deny your right thus to retaliate on the aboriginal proprietors of the country; and, unless I am utterly deceived, it may be shown that it does not exist. But, before I attempt this, allow me to make the gentleman from Massachusetts a little better acquainted with those people to whose feelings and sympathies he has appealed through their Representative. During the late war with Great Britain Colonel Campbell, under the command of my honorable friend from Ohio [General Harrison], was placed at the head of a detachment consisting chiefly of Kentucky volunteers, in order to destroy the Mississinaway towns. They proceeded and performed the duty and took some prisoners. And here is evidence of the manner in which they treated them. [Here Mr. C. read the general orders issued on the return of the detachment.[1]] I hope, sir, the honorable gentleman will be now able better to appreciate the character and conduct of my gallant countrymen than he appears hitherto to have done.

But, sir, I have said that you have no right to practice, under color of retaliation, enormities on the Indians. I will advance, in support of this position, as applicable to the origin of all law, the principle that, whatever has been the uniform usage coeval and coexistent with the subject to which it relates becomes its fixed law. Such was the foundation of all common law; and such, he believed, was the principal foundation of all public or international law. If, then, it could be shown that, from the first settlement of the colonies on this part of the American continent to the present time, we have constantly abstained from retaliating upon the Indians the excesses practiced by them toward us, we were morally bound by this invariable usage, and could not lawfully change it without the most cogent reasons. From the first settlement at Plymouth or at Jamestown it has not been our practice to destroy Indian captives, combatants, or noncombatants.

---

[1] The following is the extract which Mr. Clay read:

"It is with the sincerest pleasure that the general has heard that the most punctual obedience was paid to his orders, in not only saving all the women and children, but in sparing all the warriors who ceased to resist; and that, even when vigorously attacked by the enemy, the claims of mercy prevailed over every sense of their danger, and this heroic band respected the lives of their prisoners. Let an account of murdered innocence be opened in the records of Heaven against our enemies alone. The American soldier will follow the example of his government, and the sword of the one will not be raised against the fallen and the helpless, nor the gold of the other be paid for scalps of a massacred enemy."

When did this humane custom, by which, in consideration of their ignorance and our enlightened condition, the rigors of war were mitigated, begin? At a time when we were weak and they were comparatively strong; when they were the lords of the soil, and we were seeking, from the vices, from the corruptions, from the religious intolerance, and from the oppressions of Europe, to gain an asylum among them. And when is it proposed to change this custom, to substitute for it the bloody maxims of barbarous ages, and to interpolate the Indian public law with revolting cruelties? At a time when the situation of the two parties is totally changed—when we are powerful and they are weak: at a time when, to use a figure drawn from their own sublime eloquence, the poor children of the forest have been driven by the great wave which has flowed in from the Atlantic Ocean to almost the base of the Rocky Mountains, and, overwhelming them in its terrible progress, has left no other remains of hundreds of tribes now extinct than those which indicate the remote existence of their former companion, the mammoth of the New World! Yes, sir, it is at this auspicious period of our country, when we hold a proud and lofty station among the first nations of the world, that we are called upon to sanction a departure from the established laws and usages which have regulated our Indian hostilities. And does the honorable gentleman from Massachusetts expect, in this august body, this enlightened assembly of Christians and Americans, by glowing appeals to our passions, to make us forget our principles, our religion, our clemency, and our humanity?

Why is it we have not practiced toward the Indian tribes the right of retaliation, now for the first time asserted in regard to them? It was because it is a principle, proclaimed by reason and enforced by every respectable writer on the law of nations, that retaliation is justifiable only as calculated to produce effect in the war. Vengeance was a new motive for resorting to it. If retaliation will produce no effect on the enemy, we are bound to abstain from it by every consideration of humanity and of justice. Will it, then, produce effect on the Indian tribes? No; they care not about the execution of those of their warriors who are taken captive. They are considered as disgraced by the very circumstance of their captivity, and it is often mercy to the unhappy captive to deprive him of his existence. The poet evinced a profound knowledge of the Indian character when he put into the mouth of the son of a distinguished chief, about to be led to the stake and tortured by his victorious enemy, the words—

"Begin, ye tormentors! your threats are in vain:
 The son of Alknomok will never complain."

THOMAS MOORE.

We are fighting a great moral battle for the benefit not only of our country but of all mankind. The eyes of the whole world are in fixed attention upon us. One, and the largest portion of it, is gazing with contempt, with jealousy, and with envy; the other portion with hope, with confidence, and with affection. Everywhere the black cloud of legitimacy is suspended over the world, save only one bright spot which breaks out from the political hemisphere of the West, to brighten, and animate, and gladden the human heart. Obscure that by the downfall of liberty here, and all mankind are enshrouded in one universal darkness. To you, Mr. Chairman, belongs the high privilege of transmitting unimpaired to posterity the fair character and the liberty of our country. Do you expect to execute this high trust by trampling, or suffering to be trampled down, law, justice, the Constitution, and the rights of other people? By exhibiting examples of inhumanity, and cruelty, and ambition? When the minions of despotism heard in Europe of the seizure of Pensacola, how did they chuckle and chide the admirers of our institutions, tauntingly pointing to the demonstration of a spirit of injustice and aggrandizement made by our country in the midst of amicable negotiation. Behold, said they, the conduct of those who are constantly reproaching kings. You saw how those admirers were astounded and hung their heads. You saw, too, when that illustrious man who presides over us adopted his pacific, moderate, and just course, how they once more lifted up their heads, with exultation and delight beaming in their countenances. And you saw how those minions themselves were finally compelled to unite in the general praises bestowed upon our Government. Beware how you forfeit this exalted character. Beware how you give a fatal sanction, in this infant period of our Republic, scarcely yet two score years old, to military insubordination. Remember that Greece had her Alexander, Rome had her Cæsar, England her Cromwell, France her Bonaparte, and that, if we would escape the rock on which they split, we must avoid their errors.

MR. JOHNSON [Ky.].—With regard to the treaty of Fort Jackson I shall enter into no long argument, but I differ exceedingly from my honorable colleague. Have we not a right to dictate terms to a conquered enemy? Was not the war which was terminated by that treaty an unprovoked war? Was it not instigated against us, and without cause, on the part of the Indians? On whose head should the blood fall if you cannot control the Indians with the Bible? I wish to God you could, and toward that object I will do, and have done, as much in my sphere as anyone. There is at this moment, in the heart of my country, a school for the education of the Indians in the arts of civil life. But when you come into contact with them— when they flourish their tomahawk over your head—are you to meet them with the Bible in your hands, and invoke their obedience to that holy religion of which the Speaker tells us? I should be the last to raise the sword against them if the employment of such means would appease their fury. Experience had shown it would not; and it became necessary to meet and chastise them.

I now come to the consideration of the right of the President to make war on the savages; and on that point I contend that we have on the statute book a perpetual declaration of war against them. I hope gentlemen will take down the expression and attend to my explanation—I say we have a permanent and everlasting declaration of war—and why? The reason is very obvious. I shall not differ from gentlemen as to the policy and justice of observing the duties of humanity toward that unfortunate people. God forbid that a drop of Indian blood should be spilled except on the principles of civilized man. But the President would be wanting in his duty to his country and to his God if he did not use the strong arm of power in putting down the savages by the force he is authorized to employ, if they cannot be put down by the precepts of our holy religion; and Congress, had they not passed such a statute, would be wanting in duty to their country. Do the Indians ever declare war against their enemy? Do they embody themselves and engage in open conflict with their adversary, or do they come, like a thief in the night, and carry death to the unfortunate women, to the aged and infirm men, and the children whom they meet in their incursions? Is or is not that the universal practice? Let history answer the question. Should we, under these circumstances, have acted rightly to take no precaution, but fold our arms in listless apathy until roused by the Indian yell? Our predecessors too well knew their duty to do that. As early as 1787, and farther back if it were necessary to trace, provisions of the same nature as those now existing were enacted by the venerable Congress of the Confederation. By various statutes the same provisions had been continued to the present day. The statute gave to the

President a discretionary power to employ the forces of the United States, and to call forth the militia to repress Indian hostility; and gave it to him properly, on the principles of the Constitution.

MR. SMYTH.—I lay down, with regard to the savages, this rule of warfare. Whatever degree of force, whatever destruction, whatever punishment for violating the usages of war or by way of retaliation are found necessary to deter them from robbing our citizens and massacring our women and children; that force, destruction, and punishment they should be made to feel, and no more. So much we have an undoubted right to inflict on the principle of self-preservation. And, if we do not inflict so much, we fail in our sacred duty to preserve the people.

I find this opinion fully supported by the authority and example of the greatest man that this or any other country has produced. General Washington, who knew when to silence pity, if its exercise was injurious to his country, did not consider the usages of war or the principles of humanity as applicable to a war carried on for the punishment of the unprovoked and atrocious hostilities of savages.[1] In his order to General Sullivan, directing his operations in the Indian country, I find the following clauses:

"The expedition you are appointed to command is to be directed against the hostile tribes of the Six Nations of Indians, with their associates and adherents. The immediate objects are the total destruction and devastation of their settlements, and the capture of as many prisoners of every age and sex as possible."

"Our future security will be in their inability to injure us—the distance to which they are driven, and the terror with which the severity of the chastisement they receive will inspire them—peace without this would be fallacious and temporary."

"When we have effectually chastised them, we may then listen to peace; and endeavor to draw further advantage from their fears."

These orders were executed by General Sullivan, and Congress passed a vote of approbation of his conduct.

Had Brandt and Butler fallen into the hands of General Washington, they would, no doubt, have met the fate of Arbuthnot and Ambrister. So resolved was General Washington that a severe example should be made that he would not even listen to proposals of peace until it had been done. In the present case, also, the punishment was inflicted for example; to preserve the peace of the frontier; to preserve from the hatchet and scalping-knife women and children. Many will be

[1] Vattel, 340.

saved by the example; but, should only one be saved, Arbuthnot and Ambrister have not died in vain.

MR. MERCER.—Who, sir, were the Indian captives condemned to death? It has been said of one of the Suwanee chiefs that he was the author of the massacre of Scott's detachment, destroyed in that Indian territory which our army was not only preparing to invade, but had, in fact, invaded; and the participation of this chief in the bloody massacre which closed this scene is unsustained by any proof whatever.

As to his unfortunate comrade, the Indian prophet, what are his imputed crimes? That he was himself the victim of superstition; that he deluded his wretched followers. Such was the guilt, sir, of all the augurs and soothsayers of the ancient republics, sometimes prætors, consuls, and dictators, not to Rome alone, but to a conquered world. A guilt in which lies still involved three-fourths of the human race; many of whom yet groan, in cities, in palaces and temples, beneath a superstition compared with which the religion of the wandering inhabitants of our Western wilds is simple, peaceful, and consolatory. Or did his guilt consist in returning home with a foreign commission, after having crossed the Atlantic in quest of aid to sustain the sinking fortune of his tribe? Has it, then, become a crime in our day to love our country; to plead her wrongs; to maintain her rights; or to die in her defence? Sir, had not the God I worship, a God of mercy as well as truth, taught me to forgive mine enemies, did he, as the Great Spirit whom the Seminole adores, allow me to indulge revenge; were I an Indian, I would swear eternal hatred to your race. What crimes have they committed against us that we have not, with superior skill, practiced upon them? Whither are they gone? How many of them have been sent to untimely graves? How many driven from their lawful possessions? Their tribes and their very names are almost extinct. My honorable colleague [Mr. Barbour] will not condemn in a poor Seminole Indian that love of country of which, if it be indeed a crime, no man is more guilty than himself. But it seems he was an Indian. The Suwanee chief, his comrade, was so too. Arbuthnot and Ambrister, who inspired their counsels and led them to combat, are to be regarded as themselves, and, under the law of retaliation, they were all liable to suffer death at the pleasure of General Jackson. And thus, Mr. Chairman, the clemency which has been observed for two centuries in all our conflicts with the aborigines of America is at length discovered to have been an impolitic abandonment of the rights which we derive from the laws and usages of war. Nay, sir, the victories of all our former commanders, in all other Indian wars, are cast into the shade, in order to magnify the effect of this new policy. In the hard-fought battle of Point Pleasant, in which I have heard that three hundred Virginians fell, my colleague [Mr. Smyth] tells us that only eighteen Indian warriors were found dead on the field. Before the impetuous charge of the gallant Wayne but twenty fell. At Tippecanoe but thirty. On the banks of the Tallapoosa, General Jackson left eight hundred Indians dead. Sir, it is consolatory to humanity to look beyond these fields of slaughter to the peace which followed them, the only object of a just war. From the battle of Point Pleasant to the present day, Indian hostilities have ceased in Virginia. The victories of Wayne led to the treaty of Greenville, which was followed by a peace of eighteen years. The treaties of Hopewell, of New York, and of Colerain, of Georgia, preceded by no battles, were succeeded by a peace which, with the Creeks and Seminoles, it required, after the lapse of nineteen years, another British war to disturb; and which, with the Choctaw and Chickasaw Indians, endures to this moment. While the splendid victory of Tallapoosa and the treaty of Fort Jackson have not yet, it is said, secured to us peace, although aided by our new code of retaliation and its practical commentary, the execution, in cold blood, of four Indian captives.

MR. SAWYER.—I beg leave to quote General Jackson's own words, for, as ably as he has been defended on this floor, I believe his own defence, considering all circumstances, is nearly as good as any that can be made for him. I will take the liberty of reading an extract from his letter of the 5th of May last, dated at Fort Gadsden, to the Secretary of War. This letter affords another proof that he had the heart to conceive, the hand to execute, and the talents to defend the best measures which the urgency of the occasion required.

"I hope the execution of these two unprincipled villains will prove an awful example to the world, and convince the government of Great Britain, as well as her subjects, that certain, if slow, retribution awaits those unchristian wretches, who, by false promises, delude and excite an Indian tribe to all the horrid deeds of savage war. It has been stated that the Indians at war with the United States have free access into Pensacola, that they are kept advised, from that quarter, of all our movements; that they are supplied from thence with ammunition and munitions of war; and that they are now collecting in a body, to the amount of four or five hundred warriors, in that town; that inroads from thence have been lately made on the Alabama, in one of which eighteen settlers fell by the tomahawk. These statements compel me to make a movement to the west of the Appalachicola, and, should they prove correct, Pensacola must be occupied with an American force, the governor treated according to his deserts, or as policy may dictate. I shall leave strong garrisons in Forts St. Marks, Gadsden, and Scott, and in Pensacola, should it be necessary to possess it. It becomes my duty to state it as my confirmed opinion that, so long as Spain has not the power or will to enforce the treaties by which she is solemnly bound to preserve the Indians within her territory at peace with the United States, no security can be given to our Southern frontier without occupying a cordon of posts along the shore. The moment the American army retires from Florida the war hatchet will be again raised, and the same scenes of indiscriminate massacre, with which our frontier settlers have been visited, will be repeated, so long as the Indians within the territory of Spain are exposed to the delusion of false prophets and poison of foreign intrigue; so long as they can receive ammunition, munitions of war, from pretended traders and Spanish commandants, it will be impossible to restrain their outrages. The burning their towns, destroying their stock and provisions, will produce but temporary embarrassments. Resupplied by Spanish authorities, they may concentrate and disperse at will, and keep up a lasting and predatory warfare against the United States, as expensive to our Government as harassing to our troops. The savages, therefore, must be made dependent on us, and cannot be kept at peace without being persuaded of the certainty of chastisement being inflicted on the commission of the first offence. I trust, therefore, that the measures which have been pursued will meet with the approbation of the President of the United States; they have been adopted in pursuance of your instructions, and under a firm conviction that they alone were calculated to insure peace and security to the Georgian frontier.''

MR. HOPKINSON.—The United States are at war with certain tribes of Indians inhabiting the Spanish territory. The real origin of this war is the same with all our Indian wars. It lies deep beyond the power of eradication, in the mighty wrongs we have heaped upon the miserable nations of these lands. I cannot refuse them my heartfelt sympathy. Reflect upon what they were, and look at them as they are. Great nations dwindled down into wandering tribes and powerful kings degraded to beggarly chiefs. Once the sole possessors of immeasurable wilds, it could not have entered into their imagination that there was a force on earth to disturb their possessions and overthrow their power. It entered not into their imagination that, from beyond that great water which to them was an impassable limit, there would come a race of beings to despoil them of their inheritance and sweep them from the earth. Three hundred years have rolled into the bosom of eternity since the white man put his foot on these silent shores; and every day, every hour, and every moment has been marked with some act of cruelty and oppression. Imposing on the credulity or the ignorance of the aborigines, and overawing their fears by the use of instruments of death of inconceivable terror, the strangers gradually established themselves, increasing the work of destruction with the increase of their strength. The tide of civilization, for so we call it, fed from its inexhaustible sources in Europe, as well as by its own means of augmentation, swells rapidly and presses on the savage. He retreats from forest to forest, from mountain to mountain, hoping, at every remove, he has left enough for his invaders and may enjoy in peace his new abode, But in vain; it is only in the grave, the last retreat of man, that he will find repose. He recedes before the swelling waters; the cry of his complaint becomes more distant and feeble, and soon will be heard no more. I hear, sir, of beneficent plans for civilizing the Indians and securing their possessions to them. The great men who make these efforts will have the approbation of God and their own conscience; but this will be all their success. I consider the fate of the Indian as inevitably fixed. He must perish. The decree of extermination has long since gone forth; and the execution of it is in rapid progress. Avarice, sir, has counted their acres and power their force; and avarice and power march on together to their destruction. You talk of the scalping-knife; what is it to the liquid poison you pour down the throats of these wretched beings? You declaim against the murderous tomahawk; what is it, in comparison with your arms, your discipline, your numbers? The contest is in vain; and equally vain are the efforts of a handful of benevolent men against such a combination of force, stimulated by avarice and the temptations of wealth. When, in the documents on your table, I see that, in this triumphant march of General Jackson, he meets, from time to time (the only enemy he saw) groups of old men and women and children, gathering on the edge of a morass, their villages destroyed, their corn and provisions carried off, houseless in the depth of winter, looking for death alternately to famine and the sword, my heart sickens at a scene so charged with wretchedness. To rouse us from a sympathy so deep, so irresistible, we are told of the scalping-knife and the tomahawk; of our slaughtered women and children. We speak of these things as if women and children were unknown to the Indians—as if they have no such beings among them; no such near and dear relations; as if they belong only to us. It is not so. The poor Indian mother, crouching in her miserable wigwam or resting under the broad canopy of heaven, presses her naked infant to her bosom with as true and fond emotion as the fairest in our land; and her heart is torn with as keen anguish if it perish in her sight.

VIII—17

The war at an end; the enemy dispersed, exterminated, and broken down; having no longer the power, if he should have the will, to annoy us; the commanding general returning home because his presence can no longer be necessary; the position taken being fully adequate to put down the war should the foe have the temerity to renew it; and yet, with all this mass of facts testified to by the general himself, and this confidence of opinion expressed by himself, we are to be told of necessities; of dangers; of inroads and murders which shall justify us in one of the most high-handed measures that one nation can take against another. No, sir, these were not the motives; it was not because a few miserable, defeated, starving Red Sticks were fed by the Governor of Pensacola; it could not be because the enemy was kept advised from them of the movements of our army, after the war was over and all movement but toward their homes had ceased; it was not because the Indians had, as they always had, a free access into Pensacola that our general chose to wrest by military force this place from the hands of its owner, in violation of the laws of civilized nations; and, being an act of war, in violation of the Constitution of his country. It is not because Spain is not in a condition to insist upon her rights or resent the violation of them that the act is the more justified. The general did that which, in other circumstances, would have rightfully, on the part of the offended nation, involved us in a war; and it will hardly be said such a power, under our Constitution, is vested in any military commander. But, sir, the true motive of this bold step is exposed. The general has a confirmed opinion that, unless Spain performs her treaty with the United States, a cordon of posts along the seashore will be necessary; and he accordingly proceeds, without further consultation with his own Government, to occupy these posts. Here, then, we have a military officer undertaking to judge whether a treaty with a foreign power has been broken, and without inquiring what reason or excuse that power may have in explanation; without inquiring whether his own government has been reasonably satisfied on the subject; without examining what course the policy and interests of his own country may dictate in such a case, he proceeds to apply, of his own will and authority, the remedy he deems most proper; that is to wage immediate war on the other party; he takes into his hands the highest power the people can exercise themselves or grant to others—the power of putting the nation in jeopardy; of expending its blood and treasure and involving it in the countless calamities of war. The people of the United States have intrusted this power only to their immediate representatives, and General Jackson has walked over our heads, and the heads of the people, in assuming it himself. This must not be.

MR. TYLER.—However great may have been the services of General Jackson, I cannot consent to weigh those services against the Constitution of the land. Other gentlemen will, no doubt, yield me the correctness of this position. Your liberties cannot be preserved by the fame of any man. The triumph of the hero may swell the pride of your country—elevate you in the estimation of foreign nations—give to you a character for chivalry and valor; but recollect, I beseech you, that the sheet anchor of our safety is to be found in the Constitution of our country. Say that you ornament these walls with the trophies of victory—that the flags of conquered nations wave over your head, what avails these symbols of your glory if your Constitution be destroyed? To this pillar, then, will I cling. *Measures not men*—and I beg gentlemen to recollect it—has ever been our favorite motto. Shall we abandon it now? Why do gentlemen point to the services of the hero in former wars? For his conduct there he has received a nation's plaudits and won our gratitude. We come to other acts. If our motto be just, we must look alone to the *act* not the *actor*. It is only then that we shall judge correctly. A republic, sir, should imitate the Roman Manlius, and disapprove the conduct of her dearest son if that son has erred. From what quarter do you expect your liberties to be successfully invaded? Not from the man whom you despise; against him you are always prepared to act—his example will not be dangerous. But, sir, you have more to fear from a nation's favorite; from him whose path has been a path of glory; who has won your gratitude and confidence—against his errors you have to guard, lest they should grow into precedents and become in the end the law of the land. It is the precedent growing out of the proceding in this case that I wish to guard against. It is this consideration, and this only, which will induce me to disapprove the conduct of General Jackson.

The execution of Ambrister and the two Indian chiefs I consider indefensible. The law of nations recognizes but one reason cogent enough to authorize a general to put to death his prisoners. And that is "where the safety of his men requires it." Was that safety implicated by suffering a wretch to live? Or did the continuance of the lives of his Indian captives threaten discomfiture and overthrow? It cannot be pretended.

The first was too insignificant to have excited such fears—the power of the last was broken and all their efforts defeated. The rifle and tomahawk had been struck from their hands, and they were prisoners, defenceless and disarmed. Sir, would it not have better comported with your national character if, instead of executing these captives, the General had said to them, "Go, I give you your liberty: go to your few surviving warriors and tell them that that nation against whose defenceless frontiers you have raised the murderous scalping-knife, with whom you have ever been at war, whose blood you have delighted to drink—that nation, so abused, so insulted, has no law to punish you; it restores you to your native forests, and has only to ask that you will abandon your enmities and instruct your warriors how to respect her rights." I cannot but think that this would better have accorded with the principles of humanity and the laws of nations.

MR. POINDEXTER.—The honorable Speaker has said that we have no right to practice retaliation on the Indians; that we have foreborne to do so from the earliest settlement of the country, and that it has become the common law of the land, which we are bound not to violate. Sir, from what source does the gentleman derive the principle that a right, inherent in the nature of man, which he inhales with his first breath— which "grows with his growth and strengthens with his strength"—which has the fiat of God for its sanction and is incorporated in the code of all the nations of the earth, becomes extinct with regard to those who may forbear to exercise it, from motives of policy or humanity, for any number of years? That a common law is thereby entailed on the American people to the latest generations, by which they are required to bend beneath the tomahawk and scalping-knife of the savage, and submit to every cruelty and enormity, without the privilege of retaliating on the enemy the wrongs and injuries we have suffered by this wanton transgression of the rules of civilized warfare? We have, it is true, tolerated much of the inhuman conduct of the aborigines toward our frontier inhabitants. We have endeavored to teach them, by examples of humanity and magnanimity, the blessings and advantages of civilization; but instances are not wanting of the most severe retaliation on these monsters for their deeds of barbarity. If, however, there was not a solitary case on record of the exercise of the right, it remains inviolate and inviolable. No community has the power to relinquish it and bind posterity in the chains of slavish non-resistance. The gentleman's common law will not do for the free men of the United States; it is unique and absurd. Sir, if the committee will pardon the digression, this novel idea of common law reminds me of an occurrence which is said to have happened in the early period of the settlement of the present polite and flourishing State of Kentucky: A man, in personal combat, deprived his antagonist of the sight of an eye by a practice familiar at that day, called *gouging;* the offender was prosecuted and indicted for the outrage; he employed counsel to defend him, to whom he confessed the fact. Well, sir, said the lawyer, what shall I say in your defence? Why, sir, said he, tell them it is the custom of the country! And I presume, if the honorable Speaker had presided on the trial, he would have said, "Gentlemen of the jury, it is the common law of Kentucky, and you will find a verdict for the defendant." But, sir, to be serious, let me bring the case home to the honorable Speaker himself. Suppose a band of these barbarians, stimulated and excited by some British incendiary, should, at the hour of midnight, when all nature is wrapt in darkness and repose, sound the infernal yell and enter the dwelling of that honorable gentleman, and in his presence pierce to the heart the wife of his bosom and the beloved and tender infant in her arms—objects so dear to a husband and a father—would he calmly fold his arms and say, well, 'tis hard! but it is the common law of the country, and I must submit! No, sir; his manly spirit would burn with indignant rage, and never slumber till the hand of retributive justice had avenged his wrongs.

I have no compassion for such monsters as Arbuthnot and Ambrister; their own country is ashamed to complain of their fate; the British minister here has disavowed their conduct; and we, sir, are the residuary legatees of all the grief and sorrow felt on the face of the globe for these two fallen murderers and robbers! For I call him a murderer who incites to murder.

I shall not attempt the panegyric of General Jackson; but if a grateful country might be allowed to speak of his merits—

Louisiana would say: "You have defended our capital against the veteran troops of the enemy, by whom it would have been sacked, and our dwellings enveloped in flames over the heads of our beloved families."

Georgia: "You have given peace to our defenceless frontier, and chastised our ferocious savage foe and the perfidious incendiaries and felons by whom they were excited and counseled to the perpetration of their cruel deeds. You have opened additional territory to our rich and growing population which they may now enjoy in peace and tranquillity."

The whole Western country: "You have preserved the great emporium of our vast commerce from the grasp of a powerful enemy; you have maintained for our use free navigation of the Mississippi, at the hazard of your life, health, and fortune."

The nation at large: "You have given glory and renown to the arms of your country throughout the civilized world, and have taught the tyrants of the earth the salutary lesson that, in the defence of their soil and independence, free men are invincible."

History will transmit these truths to generations yet unborn, and, should the propositions on your table be adopted, we, the Representatives of the people, subjoin: "Yes, most noble and valorous captain, you have achieved all this for your country; we bow down under the weight of the obligations which we owe you, and, as some small testimonial of your claim to the confidence and consideration of your fellow citizens, we, in their name, present you the following resolutions:

"*Resolved,* That you, Major-General Andrew Jackson, have violated the Constitution which you have sworn to support, and disobeyed the orders of your superior, the Commander-in-Chief of the Army and Navy of the United States.

"*Resolved,* That you, Major-General Andrew Jackson, have violated the laws of your country and the sacred principles of humanity, and thereby prostrated the national character, in the trial and execution of Alexander Arbuthnot and Robert C. Ambrister, for the trifling and unimportant crime of exciting the savages to murder the defenceless citizens of the United States.

"Accept, we pray you, sir, of these resolves; go down to your grave in sorrow, and congratulate yourself that you have not served this great Republic in vain!"

Greece had her Miltiades, Rome her Belisarius, Carthage her Hannibal, and "may we, Mr. Chairman, profit by the example!"

By the treaty of Payne's Landing in 1832 the Seminoles agreed to move west of the Mississippi, but the treaty was repudiated by a considerable portion of the tribe (which in all numbered about 4,000 inclusive of 800 negroes) under the leadership of Osceola, who, on December 28, 1835, surprised and massacred the entire command (100 men) of Major Dade. The war continued until 1842, resulting in the loss of thousands of lives and the expenditure of $10,000,000. All but a few hundreds of the Seminoles were deported to the Indian Territory.

CHAPTER VII

Indian Rights

[REMOVAL OF SOUTHERN TRIBES TO THE WEST]

President Jackson on the Removal of the Southern Indians to the West—Bill for This Purpose Introduced in Congress—Debate on It in the Senate between Theodore Frelinghuysen [N. J.] (opposed), and John Forsyth [Ga.] (in favor)—Appeal of the Cherokees to the Supreme Court against Oppressive Acts of Georgia (William Wirt, Attorney); Decision in Their Favor (Opinion of Chief Justice John Marshall); Defiance of the Decision by Georgia, with the Sympathy of President Jackson.

ANDREW JACKSON in his peaceful capacity as President showed a somewhat milder visage toward the Indians than that which he had presented as a general. Very clearly he recognized that the fundamental cause of the constantly recurring difficulties with the aborigines was the conflict of a primitive stage of social organization with an advanced stage, and that the latter was compelled by the very law of its organization to be judge in its own cause and so violate the principle of equity. He therefore advised in his first message to Congress (December, 1829) that the States which included in their borders Indian tribes (who were separate sovereignties by nature as well as by treaties with the Federal Government) should temper with mercy the unavoidable injustice of subjecting them to State control. At the same time he refused to recognize the title to land claimed by the hunter upon it as equal to that of its cultivator, although he did not offer any reasons for the difference.[1]

---

[1] Herbert Spencer, in his "Social Statics," Chapter IX, edition of 1850, argued that both titles were equally bad in ethics.

263

INDIAN POLICY

PRESIDENT JACKSON IN HIS FIRST MESSAGE

The condition and ulterior destiny of the Indian tribes within the limits of some of our States have become objects of much interest and importance. It has long been the policy of Government to introduce among them the arts of civilization, in the hope of gradually reclaiming them from a wandering life. This policy has, however, been coupled with another, wholly incompatible with its success. Professing a desire to civilize and settle them, we have, at the same time, lost no opportunity to purchase their lands and thrust them farther into the wilderness. By this means they have not only been kept in a wandering state, but been led to look upon us as unjust and indifferent to their fate. Thus, though lavish in its expenditure upon the subject, Government has constantly defeated its own policy, and the Indians, in general, receding further and further to the West, have retained their savage habits. A portion, however, of the Southern tribes, having mingled much with the whites and made some progress in the arts of civilized life, have lately attempted to erect an independent government within the limits of Georgia and Alabama. These States, claiming to be the only sovereigns within their territories, extended their laws over the Indians, which induced the latter to call upon the United States for protection.

Under these circumstances the question presented was whether the general Government had a right to sustain those people in their pretensions. The Constitution declares that "no new States shall be formed or erected within the jurisdiction of any other State "without the consent of its legislature." If the general Government is not permitted to tolerate the erection of a confederate State within the territory of one of the members of this Union, against her consent, much less could it allow a foreign and independent government to establish itself there.

Actuated by this view of the subject, I informed the Indians inhabiting parts of Georgia and Alabama that their attempt to establish an independent government would not be countenanced by the Executive of the United States, and advised them to emigrate beyond the Mississippi or submit to the laws of those States.

Our conduct toward these people is deeply interesting to

our national character. Their present condition, contrasted
with what they once were, makes a most powerful appeal to our
sympathies. Our ancestors found them the uncontrolled possessors of these vast regions. By persuasion and force they
have been made to retire from river to river, and from mountain to mountain, until some of the tribes have become extinct
and others have left but remnants to preserve, for a while, their
once terrible names. Surrounded by the whites, with their arts
of civilization, which, by destroying the resources of the savage, doom him to weakness and decay, the fate of the Mohegan,
the Narragansett, and the Delaware is fast overtaking the Choctaw, the Cherokee, and the Creek. That this fate surely awaits
them if they remain within the limits of the States does not
admit of a doubt. Humanity and national honor demand that
every effort should be made to avert so great a calamity. It is
too late to inquire whether it was just in the United States to
include them and their territory within the bounds of the new
States whose limits they could control. That step cannot be
retraced. A State cannot be dismembered by Congress, or restricted in the exercise of her constitutional power. But the
people of those States, and of every State, actuated by feelings
of justice and regard for our national honor, submit to you
the interesting question whether something cannot be done, consistently with the rights of the States, to preserve this much-
injured race?

As a means of effecting this end, I suggest, for your consideration, the propriety for setting apart an ample district
west of the Mississippi, and without the limits of any State or
Territory now formed, to be guaranteed to the Indian tribes as
long as they shall occupy it: each tribe having a distinct control over the portion designated for its use. There they may
be secured in the enjoyment of governments of their own choice,
subject to no other control from the United States than such
as may be necessary to preserve peace on the frontier and between the several tribes. There the benevolent may endeavor to
teach them the arts of civilization; and, by promoting union
and harmony among them, to raise up an interesting commonwealth, destined to perpetuate the race and to attest the humanity and justice of this Government.

This emigration should be voluntary, for it would be as
cruel as unjust to compel the aborigines to abandon the graves
of their fathers and seek a home in a distant land. But they
should be distinctly informed that, if they remain within the
limits of the States, they must be subject to their laws. In

return for their obedience, as individuals, they will, without
doubt, be protected in the enjoyment of those possessions which
they have improved by their industry. But it seems to me
visionary to suppose that, in this state of things, claims can be
allowed on tracts of country on which they have neither dwelt
nor made improvements, merely because they have seen them
from the mountain or passed them in the chase. Submitting to
the laws of the States, and receiving, like other citizens, protection in their persons and property, they will, ere long, become merged in the mass of our population.

The President merely *advised* the Indians to exchange
their lands for Western territory and to remove thither,
but the facts that a bill was introduced in Congress early
in the session to appropriate money for the removal of
the Indians to what is now called the Indian Territory,
and that he signed the bill when passed, caused the opponents of the measure to charge him with responsibility
for the "inhuman policy" and even with instigating it.

The bill came before the Senate for discussion on
April 9, 1830. Theodore Frelinghuysen [N. J.] vehemently opposed the measure as a contravention of the
natural rights of the Indians, and John Forsyth [Ga.]
upheld it on the ground of the sovereignty of the Government over the tribes and the maintenance of the supremacy of the white race. The bill was passed on May 26,
1830

"NOMINATED IN THE BOND"

DEBATE ON INDIAN RIGHTS, SENATE, APRIL 9-15, 1830

SENATOR FRELINGHUYSEN said: I proceed to the discussion
of those principles which, in my humble judgment, fully and
clearly sustain the claims of the Indians to all their political
and civil rights, as by them asserted. And here I insist that,
by immemorial possession, as the original tenants of the soil,
they hold a title beyond and superior to the British Crown and
her colonies and to all adverse pretensions of our confederation
and subsequent Union. God, in his providence, planted these
tribes on this Western continent, so far as we know, before
Great Britain herself had a political existence. I believe, sir,
it is not now seriously denied that the Indians are men endowed with kindred faculties and powers with ourselves; that

they have a place in human sympathy, and are justly entitled
to a share in the common bounties of a benignant Providence.
And, with this conceded, I ask in what code of the law of nations, or by what process of abstract deduction, their rights
have been extinguished?

Where is the decree or ordinance that has stripped these
early and first lords of the soil? Sir, no record of such measure can be found. And I might triumphantly rest the hopes of
these feeble fragments of once great nations upon this impreg-
nable foundation. However mere human policy, or the law
of power, or the tyrant's plea of expediency may have found it
convenient at any or in all times to recede from the unchangeable principles of eternal justice, no argument can shake the
political maxim that, where the Indian always has been, he
enjoys an absolute right still to be, in the free exercise of his
own modes of thought, government, and conduct.

In the light of natural law can a reason for a distinction
exist in the mode of enjoying that which is my own? If I use
it for hunting, may another take it because he needs it for
agriculture? I am aware that some writers have, by a system
of artificial reasoning, endeavored to justify, or rather excuse,
the encroachments made upon Indian territory; and they de-
nominate these abstractions the law of nations, and in this
ready way the question is despatched. Sir, as we trace the
sources of this law we find its authority to depend either upon
the conventions or common consent of nations. And when,
permit me to inquire, were the Indian tribes ever consulted on
the establishment of such a law? Who ever represented them or
their interests in any congress of nations, to confer upon the
public rules of intercourse, and the proper foundations of dominion and property? The plain matter of fact is that all
these partial doctrines have resulted from the selfish plans and
pursuits of more enlightened nations; and it is not matter for
any great wonder that they should so largely partake of a
mercenary and exclusive spirit toward the claims of the Indians.

The confiding Indian listened to our professions of friendship; we called him brother, and he believed us. Millions after
millions he has yielded to our importunity, until we have acquired more than can be cultivated in centuries—and yet we
crave more. We have crowded the tribes upon a few miserable
acres on our Southern frontier: it is all that is left to them
of their once boundless forests; and still, like the horse-leech,
our insatiated cupidity cries, give! give!

Our ancestors found these people, far removed from the commotions of Europe, exercising all the rights and enjoying the privileges of free and independent sovereigns of this new world. They were not a wild and lawless horde of banditti, but lived under the restraints of government, patriarchal in its character, and energetic in its influence. They had chiefs, head men, and councils. The white men, the authors of all their wrongs, approached them as friends—they extended the olive branch; and, being then a feeble colony and at the mercy of the native tenants of the soil, by presents and professions propitiated their good will. The Indian yielded a slow but substantial confidence; granted to the colonists an abiding place; and suffered them to grow up to man's estate beside him. He never raised the claim of elder title: as the white man's wants increased he opened the hand of his bounty wider and wider. By and by conditions are changed. His people melt away; his lands are constantly coveted; millions after millions are ceded. The Indian bears it all meekly; he complains, indeed, as well he may; but suffers on; and now he finds that this neighbor, whom his kindness had nourished, has spread an adverse title over the last remains of his patrimony, barely adequate to his wants, and turns upon him and says, "Away! we cannot endure you so near us! These forests and rivers, these groves of your fathers, these firesides and hunting grounds are ours by the right of power and the force of numbers." Sir, let every treaty be blotted from our records, and in the judgment of natural and unchangeable truth and justice I ask who is the injured and who is the aggressor? Let conscience answer, and I fear not the result. Sir, let those who please denounce the public feeling on this subject as the morbid excitement of a false humanity; but I return with the inquiry whether I have not presented the case truly, with no feature of it overcharged or distorted? And, in view of it, who can help feeling, sir? Do the obligations of justice change with the color of the skin? Is it one of the prerogatives of the white man that he may disregard the dictates of moral principles when an Indian shall be concerned? No, sir. In that severe and impartial scrutiny which futurity will cast over this subject the righteous reward will be that those very causes which are now pleaded for the relaxed enforcement of the rules of equity urged upon us not only a rigid execution of the highest justice, to the very letter, but claimed at our hands a generous and magnanimous policy.

Standing here, then, on this unshaken basis, how is it possible that even a shadow of claim to soil or jurisdiction can be derived by forming a collateral issue between the State of Georgia and the general Government? Her complaint is made against the United States, for encroachments on her sovereignty. Sir, the Cherokees are no parties to this issue; they have no part in this controversy. They hold by better title than either Georgia or the Union. They have nothing to do with State sovereignty or United States sovereignty. They are above and beyond both. True, sir, they have made treaties with both, but not to acquire title or jurisdiction; these they had before— ages before the evil hour to them when their white brothers fled to them for an asylum. They treated to secure protection and guarantee for subsisting powers and privileges; and, so far as these conventions raise obligations, they are willing to meet, and always have met, and faithfully performed them; and now expect from a great people the like fidelity to plighted covenants.

Sir, if the contending parties were to exchange positions; place the white man where the Indian stands; load him with all these wrongs, and what path would his outraged feelings strike out for his career? A few pence of duty on tea, that invaded no fireside, excited no fears, disturbed no substantial interest whatever, awakened in the American colonies a spirit of firm resistance; and how was the tea tax met, sir? Just as it should be. There was lurking beneath this trifling imposition of duty a covert assumption of authority that led directly to oppressive exactions. "No taxation without representation" became our motto. We would neither pay the tax nor drink the tea. Our fathers buckled on their armor and, from the water's edge, repelled the encroachments of a misguided cabinet. We successfully and triumphantly contended for the very rights and privileges that our Indian neighbors now implore us to protect and to preserve to them. Sir, this thought invests the subject under debate with most singular and momentous interest. We, whom God has exalted to the very summit of prosperity—whose brief career forms the brightest page in history; the wonder and praise of the world; freedom's hope and her consolation; we, about to turn traitors to our principles and our fame—about to become the oppressors of the feeble and to cast away our birthright! Sir, I hope for better feelings.

It is a subject full of grateful satisfaction that, in our public intercourse with the Indians, ever since the first colonies of white men found an abode on these Western shores, we have distinctly recognized their title; treated with them as owners, and, in all our acquisitions of territory, applied ourselves to these ancient proprietors, by purchase and cession alone, to obtain the right of soil. Sir, I challenge the record of any other or different pretension. When or where did any assembly or convention meet which proclaimed, or even suggested to these tribes, that the right of discovery contained a superior efficacy over all prior titles?

And our recognition was not confined to the soil merely. We regarded them as nations—far behind us, indeed, in civilization, but still we respected their forms of government—we conformed our conduct to their notions of civil policy. We were aware of the potency of any edict that sprang from the deliberations of the council fire; and when we desired lands, or peace, or alliances, to this source of power and energy, to this great lever of Indian government we addressed our proposals—to this alone did we look; and from this did we expect aid or relief.

Who can retain a single doubt as to the unquestioned political sovereignty of these tribes? It is very true that they were not absolutely independent. As they had become comparatively feeble, and as they were, in the mass, an uncivilized race, they chose to depend upon us for protection; but this did not destroy or affect their sovereignty. The rule of public law is clearly stated by Vattel—''one community may be bound to another by a very unequal alliance and still be a sovereign state. Though a weak state, in order to provide for its safety, should place itself under the protection of a more powerful one, yet, if it reserves to itself the right of governing its own body, it ought to be considered as an independent state.'' If the right of self-government is retained, the State preserves its political existence; and, permit me to ask, when did the Southern Indians relinquish this right? Sir, they have always exercised it, and were never disturbed in the enjoyment of it, until the late legislation of Georgia and the States of Alabama and Mississippi.

To shut up every avenue of escape—to compel us to be faithful—''treaties'' are declared, by the charter of our Government, ''to be the supreme law of the land, anything in the constitution or laws of any State to the contrary notwithstanding.'' How could the inviolate character of a treaty be more effectually preserved? Let convulsions agitate the commonwealth— let the strifes of party shake the pillars of the political edifice— around the nation's faith barriers are raised, that may smile at the storm. And, sir, if these guards fail, if these defences can be assailed and broken down, then may we indeed despair. Truth and honor have no citadel on earth—their sanctions are despised and forgotten, and the law of the strongest prevails.

With all the Southwestern tribes of Indians we have similar treaties; not only the Cherokees, but the Creeks, Choctaws, and Chickasaws, in the neighborhood of Georgia, Tennessee, Alabama, and Mississippi, hold our faith, repeatedly pledged to them, that we would respect their boundaries, repel aggressions, and protect and nourish them as our neighbors and friends; and to all these public and sacred compacts Georgia was a constant party. I will now refer the Senate to the law of that State, passed on the 19th December, 1829, as evidence of the faithlessness of Georgia to her plighted word. The title of the law would suffice for my charge without looking further into its sections. After stating its object of adding the territory in the occupancy of the Cherokee nation of Indians to the adjacent counties of Georgia, another distinct office of this oppressive edict of arbitrary power is avowed to be "to annul all laws and ordinances made by the Cherokee nation of Indians." And, sir, the act does annul them effectually. For the seventh section enacts, "that, after the first day of June next, all laws, ordinances, orders, and regulations of any kind whatever made, passed, or enacted by the Cherokee Indians, either in general council, or in any other way whatever, or by any authority whatever, of said tribe, be, and the same are hereby, declared to be null and void and of no effect, as if the same had never existed." Sir, here we find a whole people outlawed—laws, customs, rules, government, all, by one short clause, abrogated and declared to be void as if they never had been. History furnishes no example of such high-handed usurpation—the dismemberment and partition of Poland was a deed of humane legislation compared with this. The succeeding clauses are no less offensive; they provide that "if any person shall prevent by threats, menaces, or other means, or endeavor to prevent any Indian of said nation from emigrating, or enrolling as an emigrant, he shall be liable to indictment and confinement in the common jail, or at hard labor in the penitentiary, not exceeding four years, at the discretion of the court; and if any person shall deter, or offer to deter, any Indian, head man, chief, or warrior of said nation, from selling or ceding to the United States, for the use of Georgia, the whole or any part of said territory, or prevent, or offer to prevent, any such persons from meeting in council or treaty any commissioner or commissioners on the part of the United States, for any purpose whatever, he shall be guilty of a high misdemeanor, and liable, on conviction, to confinement at hard labor in the penitentiary, for not less than four, nor longer than six years, at the discretion of the court." It is a crime in Georgia for a man to prevent the sale of his country, a crime to warn a chief or head man that the agents of the United States are instructed "to move upon him in the line of his prejudices," that they are coming to bribe him to meet in treaty with the commissioner. By the way, sir, it seems these treaties are very lawful, when made for the use of Georgia.

It is not surprising that our agents advertised the War Department that, if the general Government refused to interfere, and the Indians were left to the law of the States, they would soon exchange their lands and remove. To compel, by harsh and cruel penalties, such exchange is the broad purpose of this act of Georgia. But the law of Georgia is not yet satisfied. The last section declares "that no Indian, or descendant of any Indian, residing within the Creek or Cherokee nation of Indians, shall be deemed a competent witness in any court of this State, to which a white person may be a party, except such white person resides within the said nation." It did not suffice to rob these people of the last vestige of their own political rights and liberties; the work was not complete until they were shut out of the protection of Georgia laws. For, sir, after the first day of June next, a gang of lawless white men may break into the Cherokee country, plunder their habitations, murder the mother with the children, and all in the sight of the wretched husband and father, and no law of Georgia will reach the atrocity. It is vain to tell us, sir, that murder may be traced by circumstantial probabilities. The charge against this State is, you have, by force and violence, stripped these people of the protection of their government, and now refuse to cast over them the shield of your own. The outrage of the deed is that you leave the poor Indian helpless and defenceless, and in this cruel way hope to banish him from his home. Sir, if this law be enforced, I do religiously believe that it will awaken tones of feeling that will go up to God, and call down the thunders of his wrath.

The end, however, is to justify the means. "The removal of the Indian tribes to the west of the Mississippi is demanded by the dictates of humanity." This is a word of conciliating import. But it often makes its way to the heart under very doubtful titles, and its present claims deserve to be rigidly questioned. Who urges this plea? They who covet the Indian lands —who wish to rid themselves of a neighbor that they despise, and whose State pride is enlisted in rounding off their territories.

SENATOR FORSYTH.—The Senator from New Jersey no doubt hopes that his zeal and industry in the Indian cause will be crowned with success; that he will be able to persuade the Senate, and his friends in the House of Representatives, to interfere, and compel the President to take new views of the relative power of the State and general governments, and that under these new views the physical force of the country will be used, if necessary, to arrest the progress of Georgia. The expectation the gentleman has expressed, that Georgia will yield, in the event of this desirable change in the executive course, is entirely vain. The gentleman must not indulge it; with a full and fair examination of what is right and proper, Georgia has taken her course and will pursue it. The alternative to which the Senator looks, of coercion, must be the result. While I entertain no fears that the gentleman's hopes will be realized, I consider it a matter of conscience, before entering upon the discussion of the general subject of the bill, to relieve the Senator from any apprehension that it may become necessary to cut white throats in Georgia to preserve inviolate the national faith, and to perform our treaty engagements to the Indians.

I propose, sir, for his relief, to show that, considering this as a treaty question, arising under a fair exercise of the treaty-making power with a foreign government, entirely unconnected with any disputes about the relative power of the State government, and the Government of the United States, Georgia stands perfectly justified, upon his own principles, in the steps she has chosen to take with regard to those Cherokees who reside within her territorial limits. The gentleman asserts that the Creeks and Cherokees are acknowledged to be independent nations, by treaties made, first with Georgia, and lastly with the United States; that the independence of those tribes is guaranteed by the United States; that treaties with the United States are the supreme laws of the land, and must be executed, although in collision with State constitutions and State laws. The independence of the tribes rests on this argument—that the formation of a treaty is, between the parties, an acknowledgment of mutual independence. I will not stop to show the numerous exceptions to this rule; insisting, however, that the gentleman shall admit, what I presume nobody will deny, that the two parties to a treaty, independent when it was made, may, by the terms of that instrument, change their characters, and assume those of sovereign and dependent.

VIII—18

Every professional man who remembers his Blackstone knows that legislation is the highest act of sovereignty. Now, sir, by the ninth article of the treaty of Hopewell, of the 28th November, 1785, a treaty which begins with these words: "The United States give peace to all the Cherokees, and receive them into their favor and protection"—strange words to be used to an unconquered and independent nation!—the Cherokees surrender to Congress the power of legislating for them at discretion.

So much for the independence of the Cherokee nation. It may be asked, however, what has this treaty to do with the question between Georgia and the Cherokee Government? It does not follow that, because the United States have sovereignty over the Cherokees, that the State has it. The compact made by the United States with Georgia, in 1802, furnishes the satisfactory answer to this inquiry. The United States, having acquired, by the ninth article of the treaty of Hopewell, the power of legislation over the Cherokees, had the goodness to transfer it to the State. Gentlemen may amuse themselves with finding fault with this transfer by the United States of a power granted to them, and intended to be used by the United States only. They may prove it, if they choose, an act of injustice to the Cherokees—a violation of faith. We will not take the trouble to interfere with such questions. The United States obtained, by treaty, the power to legislate over the Cherokees, and transferred it to Georgia. The justice and propriety of this transfer must be settled by the United States and the Cherokees. In this settlement Georgia has her burden to bear, as one of the members of the Union; but no more than her fair proportion. If any pecuniary sacrifices are required to do justice to the injured, let them be made: if a sacrifice of blood is demanded as a propitiation for this sin, to avert the judgment of Heaven, let the victim be selected. Justice demands that it be furnished by the whole country, and not by Georgia; and if the honorable Senator from New Jersey will fix upon one between the Delaware and the Hudson, he will escape all imputations of being actuated by any motive but the love of justice—pure justice. For us it is enough to have shown that what we claim is in our bond, and, until the gentleman can rail off the seal, our claim must be allowed, though it should extend to the penalty of a pound of flesh.

The Cherokees appealed to the Supreme Court against the oppressive acts of Georgia and the support of the State's position by the act of Congress. Their advocate was the able and brilliant William Wirt, ex-Attorney-General. The complaint was not accepted by the Court on the ground of non-jurisdiction, since it described the Cherokees as a "foreign state." However Chief Justice John Marshall declared that, in the opinion of the majority of the court, the Cherokees were "a distinct political society, separated from others, and capable of managing its own affairs and governing itself," and that the courts were bound by those acts which recognized this character of the tribe.

To this opinion of the Supreme Court, as well as to a "writ of error" served by the Court in the case of a Cherokee murderer who had been condemned to death by the Superior Court of the State, Georgia paid no attention. She hanged the accused Cherokee and began a system of harassing the tribe by imprisonments on trumped-up charges, forcible expulsion on various legal pretexts from certain of their lands, and by harsh treatment of Northern missionaries to the Indians. One of these who had failed to leave the Territory within the time set for him to do so was condemned to four years' imprisonment at hard labor. His case (*Worcester* vs. *State of Georgia*, Peters vi, pp. 521 *et seq.;* Curtis x, pp. 215 *et seq.*) came before the Supreme Court, which declared all the claims made by Georgia on the ground of her "sovereignty" to be unconstitutional and the sentence of Worcester to be null and void.

The State court of Georgia refused to accept the decision of the Federal court, or to grant a writ of *habeas corpus* which was served upon it, and kept Worcester and a fellow missionary in prison for a year, when they were pardoned by Governor Lumpkin.

During this contention between Georgia and the Federal judiciary President Jackson gave no indication of his later determination to enforce Federal authority when it came into conflict with State. Indeed, it is related that he said: "John Marshall has made his decision; now let him enforce it!" Had a "Jackson man" been in the place of the Chief Justice, instead of one

who was firmly opposed to the President personally and
to his policy of increasing the executive powers at the
expense of the judicial, Jackson would probably have
not been so indifferent. As it was, his inaction in this
case was brought up against him in the debate on the
so-called "Force Bill" [see Vol. V, page 92 ss.], with the
insinuation that he was at the earlier period secretly encouraging the State.

CHAPTER VIII

REFORM OF OUR INDIAN POLICY

[GRANTING LAND IN SEVERALTY, ETC.]

Outbreak of Minnesota Indians [1863]—Representative Ignatius Donnelly [Minn.] on "Reform of the Indian System"—Philanthropic Indian Policy of President Ulysses S. Grant—Message of President Rutherford B. Hayes Recommending Grants to Indians of Land in Severalty—Debate in the Senate on Bill of Richard Coke [Tex.] to Purchase Lands of the Disaffected Colorado Utes, and to Remove These Indians Elsewhere; Discussion Develops into a General Debate on Indian Policy: Sen. Coke Supports Grants of Land in Severalty; Henry M. Teller [Col.] Opposes Such Grants, and Attacks the Mistaken Philanthropy of the Proposed Policy; N. P. Hill [Col.] Supports the Bill; John T. Morgan [Ala.] Advises Subjecting Indians to the Common Laws of the Land; Henry L. Dawes [Mass.] Advocates an Entirely New Policy, with Education as a Basis; Preston B. Plumb [Kan.] Opposes Education; James G. Blaine [Me.] Replies to Plumb; Bill Is Enacted.

DURING the Civil War there occurred an uprising of Minnesota Indians (1863), which was suppressed by the United States Army. This brought forward the questions of whether our general system of treating the Indians was not radically wrong, and whether an entirely new policy should not be adopted.

On February 7, 1865, Ignatius Donnelly [Minn.] delivered the following speech in the House of Representatives:

REFORM OF THE INDIAN SYSTEM

IGNATIUS DONNELLY, M. C.

Since the 4th of March, 1789, the Government has appropriated, directly for the benefit of the Indians, the enormous sum of $89,155,098.32.

Where now is all this wealth? Has it reached the Indians? Have its accumulations descended from father to son? Do we find it represented to-day among the tribes by comfortable homes and overflowing granaries? No. Upon our Western prairies are scattered this miserable, degraded, impoverished people, an everlasting reproach to our Christian nation and a disgrace to humanity. Where, then, are these great sums? They have gone to fill the coffers of those who stood between the Government and the Indian, and deceived the one while they robbed the other.

Mr. Chairman, I feel that it is my duty to speak of these things. The evil results of this pernicious system have descended upon my own State in fire and blood. An innocent and an unoffending population of white settlers have paid the penalty for years of misgovernment with their lives; and, although the scenes of devastation and ruin and horror have passed away from my State, I trust forever, the system still lives, and is already preparing new stores of suffering and calamity for other communities. When I have looked upon the humble homestead of the frontiersman in ashes, and beheld the corpse of its owner lying gashed and bloody beside it, I could not but trace home the terrible responsibility for all this evil to this Capitol, and to that system which, taking charge of a savage race, retained them in barbarism, made no proper efforts for their civilization, and, at last, turned them loose like wild beasts to glut their brutal passions and infuriated rage upon an unsuspecting people.

I assert, unhesitatingly and upon mature reflection, that not even our white race could rise from barbarism to civilization against the pressure of such a system as that under and by means of which it is proposed to civilize the Indians.

Let us look at some of its details.

One of the Red Lake Chippewa chiefs of Minnesota said but two years since, when solicited to part with the lands of his tribe: "When we sell our lands we dig our graves."

The savage had summed up the question in a sentence. The Indian is a hunter, and requires large areas of land in which to find his support. Deprive him of these lands, fill them with a white population, which drives out the wild game, and at the same time give him no instruction to enable him to compete in the arts of agriculture with the white man, and he becomes, perforce, a vagabond, a thief, and, it may be, even an assassin.

The civilization of the Indian becomes, therefore, a matter

of the first necessity to the comfort and safety of his white neighbor. Injustice to him is injury to ourselves.

> "This sword's hilt is the sharpest, and cuts through
> The hand that wields it."

But what is the course of the Government? It concentrates upon a small strip of land the population for whose sustenance the whole of the ceded territory was before necessary. It surrounds this fragment this island of barbarism, with a dense civilized white population. The savage must either remain upon his reservation and starve or invade the precincts of the white man and beg and steal. The strain is too great for human nature. Collisions follow, and both white and red are speedily involved in common suffering and ruin, equally victims of a pernicious system.

But it may be said that the Indian can become an agriculturist on his reservation.

Civilization is a tender plant. Centuries of contact with the Roman power left our own ancestors still savages. When, at last, the spark of civilization was warmed into a little flame, how many slow and weary ages did it take to light up the horizon with its blaze? The lapse of thousands of years extends between the nomad of eastern Europe, who carried the scalp of his enemy at his saddle-bow, and the highly refined citizen of England or America. Shall we, then, hope that, by the mere power of the human will and the force of a few legislative enactments, we shall, in a fortnight, turn a band of savages, collected on their reservation like cattle in an inclosure, into civilized men?

The Government seems to have possessed some faint conception of what was required of it. It employs a farmer for the tribe, it hires a blacksmith, and it furnishes some agricultural implements. These are, it is true, glimpses of the truth: but there it stops. What is the result? The Indian who has industry and energy enough to cultivate a field and raise a crop lies at the mercy of every roaming vagabond of the tribe, who, returning bootless from his hunting excursion, descends upon his store of maize and potatoes, and reënacts

> "The good old rule, the simple plan,
> That they shall take who have the power,
> And they shall keep who can."

There is no military or police force to protect industry against robbery. What white man would overcome all the prejudices of education, all the habits of years, all the teachings of superstition, and endure the cold of winter and the heat of summer to find, at last, the results of his labor swept away from him by some idle and savage neighbor?

Nor is this all. This insecurity extends to the very fields the Indian cultivates. It has been the policy of the Government to withhold from him that encouragement to labor which accompanies possession of the soil. If it is true, as believed by some, that a system of periodical redistribution of the land among all the members of the clan arrested the growth of civilization in the British islands for centuries, what shall we say of this system which deprives the Indian of his field, not periodically, but at the bidding of a distant and unseen power, or which leaves him a mere occupant and squatter, open at any moment to invasion by his more powerful white neighbors? Again, I ask, what white man could be induced to labor to enhance the value of his fields if the very increase of their value tended only to hurry him more rapidly from them? Who is he that toils willingly for the advantage of another?

But even this is not all. It was said by some one of old: "If vice were on the whole profitable, then the wise man would be the villain." The essence of virtue is that it meets with its reward. Hence, any system of government that rewards equally vice and virtue, indolence and industry, is corrupt and rotten, and can breed only the most disastrous consequences. And yet this is the system adopted by us in our treatment of the Indians! The annuities are distributed among the members of the tribe without any regard whatever to the conduct of the recipients. The ruffian who robs his industrious neighbor draws an equal share with the poor wretch he has despoiled. Nay, more, he may go outside of the reservation and prey upon the adjacent white population, and the claims of the white man for the damages he inflicts are paid by the agent out of the total fund of the tribe; so that the many who are innocent suffer for the one who is guilty. In such a state of society the highest premiums are offered for crime and disorder; and it may well be believed that the most sagacious would find it to their interest to become the most vicious.

I need not here enlarge upon that other evil, and parent of many evils, the unjust treatment of the Indians by their agents. I do not assert that all those who occupy or have occupied such positions have proved themselves dishonest; but I do believe that, under the present system, the temptations are too strong for ordinary human virtue. The agent finds himself far away from white society, in the midst of a barbarous population, sunk in ignorance and debauchery and regardless of their own interests; while through his hands pass large sums of money intended for their benefit. He is asked to protect those who cannot protect themselves; to deal honestly by those who are unable to bring him to account; and to feel his responsibility to morality and justice in an almost irresponsible position. Until we can find among the followers of the great parties of the day a sufficient number of pure-minded and disinterested philanthropists to fill all these agencies, and to endure exile, discomfort, and small salaries for honesty and righteousness' sake we must expect this evil to continue. The evil is in the system, not in the men who represent it. If the reproach can be addressed to our Government which was made to Tiberius: "It is you that are to blame for these things, that have committed your flocks, not to shepherds, but to wolves"; the deeper reproach can also be uttered against us, that we have for years permitted a system which, by its own force, has created those wolves even out of the most trusted of our shepherds.

What should be the course adopted by the Government toward the Indians?

In the first place, the whole system of treaties should be abrogated. We have filled a thousand octavo pages of our statutes with such useless compacts. We need no such plea to justify us in taking the lands of the Indians. If one hundred human beings can support themselves on a tract of land where one savage finds a precarious subsistence, the one hundred have a right to go there and take possession of and cultivate it. The right of man to life and to the earth as a means of life is paramount to all else. But, in seizing the Indian's territory, the new-comers must not consign him to starvation; they must share the land with him, and teach him those arts by which a small portion of it will sustain him as fully as the whole did formerly.

In the next place, whatever land is given to the Indian should be given him by irrevocable patent; so that he can never be disturbed in his possession by the pressure of an advancing population. It should also be guarded in such manner that he cannot, for many years, sell or incumber it. The Government must treat him in this respect as its helpless and dependent ward.

In the next place, it would be well that each reservation should be located near to or surrounding a military post, so as to secure at all times a perfect administration of justice through the military authorities, and full protection to the industrious and deserving from the vicious and depraved.

In the next place, there should be erected for each family a comfortable log house; and a field should be broken sufficient for their support upon the land patented to them by the Government. They should be furnished with sufficient tools, seed, and working cattle for its cultivation. The aid of the Government should then be given liberally to the most deserving, leaving the worthless to work or starve. A few successful farmers would civilize a whole community, even as among ourselves a few cultivated persons will refine an entire neighborhood.

In the next place, while it is recollected that the knowledge of a civilized language does not constitute civilization, nevertheless the English language should be introduced among them; and the education of their children should at the same time be made compulsory.

It should be recollected that civilization consists of certain habits of life, productive of comfort and ease; upon these may repose a higher structure of generous thoughts and ennobling religious impulses. Christianity does not consist in the holding of certain points of doctrinal belief, nor in the employment of any particular routine of expression, but in that adaptation of the whole inner nature of the man to the purity and elevation of its great principles. Hence it can never be the religion of savages. To leave the Indian in his barbarian state and, at the same time, seek to force into his mind the sublime doctrines of the Sermon on the Mount is to attempt nature in an inverted order. *The religious influence of the nation should, therefore, first lend itself to a reformation of the general system.* Having prepared the soil it can then proceed with some hope of success to the process of the cultivation of the individual.

But how, it may be asked, are we to avoid the corruption so generally admitted?

I answer, by some such system of checks as is used in all other departments to insure honesty. Why cannot the law provide that the various goods distributed among the Indians shall be dealt out by the military officer of the post, or by the quartermaster of the post, taking their receipts, witnessed by the agent? The report of the military officer could thus be compared with the report of the agent, and fraud could only follow by collusion between them. The military officer, holding his place for life, would have much less inducement to fraud than the agent who anticipates removal in a short period of time.

It might also be well to locate the reservations of the Indians outside of the organized States, and as far as possible from the white settlements. In this way their new customs and usages will have attained some solidity before they are brought into contact with the whites. When the wave of population rolls around the reservation, the white pioneer will find the red man a farmer like himself, occupying land held like his own by irrevocable patent, and possessing some share of intelligence and education with which to understand and defend his rights. No longer vicious and thieving, he will recognize in him a quiet and peaceable neighbor, and will feel no desire and be under no necessity to drive him from his home.

I would further suggest that, while a tract of one or two hundred acres of land should be given to each family, the tribe should be gathered together in villages, with a house for each family surrounded by five or ten acres of cultivated land. An Indian family will not ordinarily use more than that amount. When the energy of any individual oversteps this limit he can cultivate his separate farm. It requires the highest types of the highest races to encounter a life of isolation and solitude upon large farms on the frontier. The weaker races are gregarious. Moreover, thus assembled they are more susceptible of control and instruction.

In fact, this system of concentration could, in course of time, be applied to all the Indians within the limits of the United States. Their total number is but 314,622. They could be concentrated, if civilized, upon an area no larger than two or three of our counties; they could be speedily made self-sustaining; and, instead of inflicting injuries on our frontiers to a degree vastly disproportionate to their numbers, they could be converted into harmless agriculturists and peaceful citizens.

But the question may be asked: Is the Indian capable of civilization? I answer unhesitatingly, yes.

Here the speaker quoted extensively from "The Conquest of Mexico," by William H. Prescott, to show the high state of civilization attained by the Mexican Indians.

It may be urged that the Aztecs and the ordinary Indians of our Western prairies are two distinct races. This is not so. They are but different tribes of the same race. The construction of their languages, as well as their physical conformation, evidences that all the varieties of the red man on both the continents are ethnologically members of the same race. The Aztecs were a wild tribe who descended upon the more civilized Toltecs, and in a few centuries passed from a condition analogous to that of our Western Indians to the one in which Cortes found them. If, then, it was possible for the red man to create, of his own force, a civilization, can it be doubted that it is in the power of a superior race, under just and wise laws, to communicate civilization to him?

We of the northern races of Europe expelled the Indian as we colonized the country; but in the regions of the continent settled by the Latin races this has not been the case. In Mexico, in Central America, and in South America, the aboriginal population continued in the occupancy of the land, and, from the time of their conquest, they have been steadily absorbing by intermarriage the European blood among them, so that at this day those countries possess less of white blood than they did a century since. As the native population awakens from the torpidity of subjugation and begins to feel the power of superior numbers, it is seeking to regain political ascendency. The Creole population does not increase in numbers; the Indian, on the contrary, is advancing with rapid strides. To-day, in Peru proper, the Indians are more than three times the entire population of every other kind. From a condition of slavery they have risen into freedom. Formerly excluded from the schools, even as our own slaves were excluded in the South, all the institutions of learning are now thrown open to them, and they are entering in large numbers the colleges of the country.

While we find Mexico electing, in the person of Juarez, an Indian to its presidency, we are at the same time informed that secret movements are on foot to reëstablish the sovereignty of the ancient race in Peru, Bolivia, Ecuador, and Chili.

Let us not be blind to these great movements; they are God's solution of the vexed questions of race which now agitate the world. Who shall say that the Indian shall not, through the instrumentality of our institutions and under the protection of our Government, establish once more upon this continent the civilization of the Montezumas and the Incas, kindled into new splendor by the genius of universal liberty, and softened into refined beauty by the touch of Christianity? The custodians of a civilization which we did not originate, we have no right to withhold it from those races, whatever may be their color, with whom we may come in contact; nor can the nation find a nobler task than that of so bending its energies that this entire New World, from one extremity to the other, shall exult, through all its diversities of climate and all its zone of color, in one continuous and unending display of human industry and happiness. In that not distant day, when vast communities of black men along the Gulf, and still larger communities of red men in Mexico and South America, shall be united to us by all the affiliations of commerce and all the sympathy of kindred institutions, let us not have to reproach ourselves with having destroyed or permitted the destruction of any portion of the people of this continent. Let it not be said of us that, while we were reflecting civilization and liberty upon the world, we, at the same time, exterminated the aboriginal population of our own country.

President Ulysses S. Grant inaugurated a philanthropic policy toward the Indians, the direction of which he placed largely in the hands of humanitarians.

In his first annual message to Congress, in December, 1869, he said:

A System to Preserve and Not Extinguish the Race

President Grant on Indian Policy

From the foundation of the Government to the present the management of the original inhabitants of this continent, the Indians, has been a subject of embarrassment and expense, and has been attended with continuous robberies, murders, and wars. From my own experience upon the frontiers and in Indian countries I do not hold either legislation or the conduct of the whites who come most in contact with the Indians blameless for these hostilities. The past, however, cannot be undone, and the question must be met as we now find it.

I have attempted a new policy toward these wards of the nation—they cannot be regarded in any other light than as wards—with fair results so far as tried, and which, I hope, will be attended ultimately with great success. The Society of Friends is well known as having succeeded in living in peace with the Indians in the early settlement of Pennsylvania, while their white neighbors of other sects in other sections were constantly embroiled. They are also known for their opposition to all strife, violence, and war, and are generally noted for their strict integrity and fair dealings. These considerations induced me to give the management of a few reservations of Indians to them, and to throw the burden of selection of agents upon the society itself. The result has proven most satisfactory.

For superintendents and Indian agents not on the reservations officers of the army were selected. The reasons for this are numerous. Where Indian agents are sent there or near there troops must be sent also. The agent and the commander of troops are independent of each other, and are subject to orders from different departments of the Government. The army officer holds a position for life; the agent one at the will of the President. The former is personally interested in living in harmony with the Indian, and in establishing a permanent peace to the end that some portion of his life may be spent within the limits of civilized society. The latter has no such personal interest. Another reason is an economic one; and still another, the hold which the Government has upon a life officer to secure a faithful discharge of duties in carrying out a given policy.

The building of railroads, and the access thereby given to all the agricultural and mineral regions of the country, is rapidly bringing civilized settlements into contact with all the tribes of Indians. No matter what ought to be the relations between such settlements and the aborigines, the fact is they do not harmonize well, and one or the other has to give way in the end. A system which looks to the extinction of a race is too horrible for a nation to adopt without entailing upon itself the wrath of all Christendom, and engendering in the citizen a disregard for human life and the rights of others dangerous to society. I see no substitute for such a system except in placing all the Indians on large reservations as rapidly as it can be done, and giving them absolute protection there. As soon as they are fitted for it they should be induced to take their lands in severalty and to set up territorial governments for their own protection.

The results of this policy were set forth by his successor, Rutherford B. Hayes, with recommendations for its extension, in his third annual message of December 1, 1879.

LAND IN SEVERALTY FOR THE INDIANS

PRESIDENT HAYES

After reporting outbreaks of the White River Utes in Colorado and of the Apaches of New Mexico under

Chief Victoria, resulting in bloodshed and destruction of property, the President said:

While these occurrences, in which a comparatively small number of Indians were engaged, are most deplorable, a vast majority of our Indian population have fully justified the expectations of those who believe that by humane and peaceful influences the Indian can be led to abandon the habits of savage life and to develop a capacity for useful and civilized occupations. What they have already accomplished in the pursuit of agricultural and mechanical work, the remarkable success which has attended the experiment of employing as freighters a class of Indians hitherto counted among the wildest and most intractable, and the general and urgent desire expressed by them for the education of their children, may be taken as sufficient proof that they will be found capable of accomplishing much more if they continue to be wisely and fairly guided. The "Indian policy" sketched in the report of the Secretary of the Interior [Carl Schurz], the object of which is to make liberal provision for the education of Indian youth, to settle the Indians upon farm-lots in severalty, to give them title in fee to their farms inalienable for a certain number of years, and, when their wants are thus provided for, to dispose by sale of the lands on their reservations not occupied and used by them, a fund to be formed out of the proceeds for the benefit of the Indians, which will gradually relieve the Government of the expenses now provided for by annual appropriations, must commend itself as just and beneficial to the Indians, and as also calculated to remove those obstructions which the existence of large reservations presents to the settlement and development of the country. I therefore earnestly recommend the enactment of a law enabling the Government to give Indians a title in fee, inalienable for twenty-five years, to the farm lands assigned to them by allotment. I also repeat the recommendation made in my first annual message, that a law be passed admitting Indians who can give satisfactory proof of having, by their own labor, supported their families for a number of years, and who are willing to detach themselves from their tribal relations, to the benefit of the homestead act, and to grant them patents containing the same provision of inalienability for a certain period.

The experiment of sending a number of Indian children, of both sexes, to the Hampton Normal and Agricultural Institute, in Virginia, to receive an elementary English education and practical instruction in farming and other useful industries, has led to results so promising that it was thought expedient to turn over the cavalry barracks at Carlisle, in Pennsylvania, to the Interior Department for the establishment of an Indian school on a larger scale. This school has now one hundred and fifty-eight pupils, selected from various tribes, and is in full operation. Arrangements are also made for the education of a number of Indian boys and girls belonging to tribes on the Pacific slope in a similar manner, at Forest Grove, in Oregon. These institutions will commend themselves to the liberality of Congress and to the philanthropic munificence of the American people.

Last spring information was received of the organization of an extensive movement in the Western States, the object of which was the occupation by unauthorized persons of certain lands in the Indian Territory ceded by the Cherokees to the Government for the purpose of settlement by other Indian tribes.

On the 29th of April I issued a proclamation warning all persons against participation in such an attempt, and by the co-operation of a military force the invasion was promptly checked. It is my purpose to protect the rights of the Indian inhabitants of that Territory to the full extent of the executive power. But it would be unwise to ignore the fact that a Territory so large and so fertile, with a population so sparse and with so great a wealth of unused resources, will be found more exposed to the repetition of such attempts as happened this year, when the surrounding States are more densely settled and the westward movement of our population looks still more eagerly for fresh lands to occupy. Under such circumstances the difficulty of maintaining the Indian Territory in its present state will greatly increase, and the Indian tribes inhabiting it would do well to prepare for such a contingency. I therefore fully approve of the advice given to them by the Secretary of the Interior on a recent occasion, to divide among themselves in severalty as large a quantity of their lands as they can cultivate; to acquire individual title in fee, instead of their present tribal ownership in common, and to consider in what manner the balance of their lands may be disposed of by the Government for their benefit. By adopting such a policy they would more certainly secure for themselves the value of their possessions, and at the same time promote their progress in civilization and prosperity, than by endeavoring to perpetuate the present state of things in the Territory.

The question whether a change in the control of the Indian

service from the Interior to the War Department should be made, was in the Forty-fifth Congress referred to a joint committee of both Houses for inquiry and report. Since then, the committee having reported, the question has been decided in the negative by a vote in the House of Representatives.

In view of the fact that further uncertainty on this point will be calculated to obstruct other much needed legislation, to weaken the discipline of the service, and to unsettle salutary measures now in progress for the government and improvement of the Indians, I respectfully recommend that the decision arrived at by Congress at its last session be permitted to stand.

On March 22, 1880, Richard Coke [Tex.], chairman of the Committee on Indian Affairs, introduced in the Senate a bill to purchase the lands offered by the disaffected Ute Indians of Colorado, the Indians agreeing to move to unoccupied lands elsewhere. It came up for discussion on April 2. The discussion at once took on the form of a general debate on Indian policy.

OUR INDIAN POLICY

SENATE, APRIL 2-12, 1880

Said Senator Coke:

The policy of the bill is to break up this large reservation, to individualize the Indians upon allotments of land; to break up their tribal relations and pass them under the jurisdiction of the Constitution and laws of the United States and the laws of the States and Territories in which the lands are situated, to aid them with stock and with agricultural implements, and by building houses upon their allotments of lands, to become self-supporting, to be cultivators of the soil; in a word, to place them on the highway to American citizenship, and to aid them in arriving at that conclusion as rapidly as can be done.

The bill is in many respects a departure from the ancient and established policy of the Government with reference to the Indian tribes. The advance of settlements in the West has been so rapid that it has been found inexpedient and impolitic, as leading to collisions between the whites and Indians, to continue the system of locking or attempting to lock up large tracts of land within their exclusive occupancy. The whites cannot be restrained from intrusion upon these large reservations. The

VIII—19

Indians will not use them except for hunting purposes and the whites will not permit them to remain unused.

This bill simply recognizes the logic of events, which shows that it is impossible to preserve peace between the Indians and the whites with these immense bodies of land attempted to be locked up as Indian reservations.

I will state that this bill is regarded by the Secretary of the Interior as of the very first importance, and it is hoped that it will be acted on at once by the Senate and passed. It is necessary in view of the approach of spring, the time for farming operations, if we intend that these Indians shall do anything during the ensuing agricultural season, that they shall go on at once.

It is necessary for an additional reason that the reservation which is ceded by this agreement is being invaded at all points or intruded upon by whites who are locating ranches and staking off mining claims, and, unless the cession is completed, under existing treaties with the Ute Indians it is protected against this intrusion, and this must necessarily lead to collisions with the Indians.

Henry M. Teller [Col.] opposed the bill.

Mr. President, we have now arrived at a stage in the public mind when the question is asked in every portion of the country, what shall we do with the Indians? The people are dissatisfied with the conduct of Indian affairs and demand a radical change. It is demanded alike in the interest of the whites and of the Indians. The continued Indian wars, terminating in disaster to both races, treaties and agreements made to be broken on both sides, have convinced the people that there is a defect in the present system. The men who have studied this problem the most are the most outspoken in their condemnation of the system and its management. Is it possible to adopt a system that shall do justice to the Indian and white man alike, that shall put the Indian on the road toward civilization and Christianity? If this can be done, all will admit that it is the duty of the dominant race to take all necessary steps to accomplish so desirable an end. That it is a difficult task, the almost unbroken line of failures for nearly three hundred years sufficiently demonstrates.

The early settlers of this country attempted this task, devoting much time and money to the education of this people, and not less than four of our principal schools were organized for the education of Indians, and Indians alone. I need not say that the attempts to civilize Indians by first educating them failed, and that the efforts of the worthy men to make Christians of these pagans not only failed, but brought destruction on the objects of their solicitude. The powerful tribes with which they fought and treated and fought and treated again have in many instances no living representative left.

The early history of the country is full of the conflicts between the whites and Indians, and as the lines of settlement swept westward toward the setting sun the conflict increased in intensity. The history of the country may be said to be one continued history of Indian wars, for not a year passed but in some part of the land the conflict was carried on; burned houses, wasted fields, murdered settlers, indignities on the dead, and worse ones on the living are recorded in every chapter of our history.

Is it strange that the men who have carried the lines of settlement westward and have come in contact daily with the Indians, feeding them one day and fighting them the next, studying their character in the school of experience, knowing their many vices and few virtues, and who of all men are interested in a peaceful solution of this problem, should demand of the men to whom this solution is intrusted more than a passing acquaintance with the subject?

Mr. President, would it not be thought essential that the men to whom this great work was intrusted should be learned in the history of the Indian race, should have a knowledge of their character, laws, customs, or religion; should even have studied the history of the past efforts at civilization? Yet we have relied and still rely on agents ignorant of all these things to accomplish the greatest work ever given to man to do for his fellow, that is, to bring a savage into a civilized state.

Theories worn out and disproved, systems tried and abandoned long ago, are at once adopted by these neophytes and we are promised an immediate solution of this problem. Flouring mills are to be built in the wilderness hundreds of miles from grain fields; reapers and mowers are to be sent by the car load for the use of Indians whose very religion it is to despise manual labor and who will choose death in preference to the degradation of work; houses are to be built for dwellers in tents whose religion makes it a crime to remain in a house where there has been a death, and when the first death occurs the house must be burned or abandoned.

I am told, although I do not know how true it is, that the

honorable Secretary of the Interior has discovered a system which once adopted on the part of the Government will work wonders with the savage Indian. I do not know the title of the bill prepared, but I do understand the principle on which it is based. This system will be presented to us in a few days, and for the lack of other title it might be entitled: An easy solution of the Indian problem in one lesson. What is this system that is to work such wonders? Land in severalty. Give, says the honorable Secretary, to each Indian. great and small, from one hundred and sixty to three hundred and twenty acres of land, mark it on a map, fix its boundaries in a book, build a house on it, tell the Indian it is his, and the great work is accomplished! It is the lack of land in severalty that has kept the Indian a savage for centuries! The problem that has disturbed the people of Europe and America for three hundred years is solved in a day, and how simple it is!

Mr. President, this is called by the honorable Secretary the "new system." This system is not without merit, but it is not a new system and not original with the honorable Secretary of the Interior. In 1646, John Eliot, the apostle to the Indians, procured the allotment of land in severalty to certain Massachusetts Indians, but they remained savages still. It has been a feature in every administration of Indian affairs since this Government was founded, and within the last thirty-six years we have provided in not less than sixty treaties and agreements that land should be allotted to the Indians in severalty. In all of these the Indians might have taken lands, and in nearly all of them they pledged themselves to take the lands in severalty; but the record shows that very few did so take land, and those who did make selections did not as a general thing remain on the land. Land in severalty as a means of civilization has proved a failure.

Since 1868 the Ute Indians might have taken land in severalty; their treaty so provided; but not one application was made. If Indians can be induced to take lands in severalty and reside on the same, one step at least has been taken toward civilization. But it is not the first nor the second step and will not be taken by the Indian until he has made some progress in civilization.

The social organization of all the Indians is by clans or families, each clan consisting of a body of relatives. Two or more clans compose a band, and several bands a tribe; several tribes a confederation. The only permanent and stable organization is that of the clan. The tribes and confederacies may dissolve and fall apart, but the clan never. The only dissolution of a clan is by the death of its members.

The right of property as recognized by an Indian is the right in his clan. Property in severalty is unknown to the wild Indian. If a hunter kills a deer or a buffalo, it belongs to the clan and not to the hunter. His rights are no greater in it than those of any other member of the clan. All right to the soil and the productions thereof inheres in the clan, and he who takes land in severalty or cultivates the common soil, claiming the productions thereof for himself alone, is guilty of a crime against Indian society and one not likely to be forgiven. It has been well said that Indian virtues consist chiefly in the recognition of clan rights, and crimes in Indian society consist chiefly in a violation of those rights.

In dealing with Indians it should never be forgotten that the institutions of civilized society are crimes in Indian society, and the moral sentiment of the Indian against such recognized crimes is not less severe than the moral sentiment of civilized people against recognized crimes. The murder of an enemy or the robbery of a foe is not a crime in Indian society, but the violation of a clanship right is. The destruction of the clan is to the Indian mind the destruction of the Indian himself, and he therefore instinctively rebels against any movement that tends to weaken his clan. To adopt the habits, customs, and laws of the white man is, in his judgment, to cease to be an Indian, and the meanest Indian in the land would not exchange his place with that of the most favored white.

Thus, when we compel an Indian to take land in severalty, we compel him to commit a crime against Indian society, and, as he believes, to aid in his own destruction.

We have not been able (save in a limited way) to induce the most civilized Indians to take land in severalty. The Indians of the Indian Territory resist with great energy all attempts to induce them to take land in severalty, and the Indians in the State of New York, with surrounding civilization, refused to take land in severalty until after 1842. Many of them refuse to take it to this day.

The ideas entertained by Indians for centuries will not be abandoned in a day by the adoption of a new system on the part of the Government, or an old one labeled a new one.

A few years since [early in Grant's administration] the attention of the whole country was directed toward this Indian question. The system then pursued was with one voice pronounced defective. We then adopted an addition to the already cumbersome machinery of the Indian Bureau, by creating a board of Indian commissioners, composed of men noted for their philanthropy and intelligence; and, that their motives might not be suspected, we required them to give their time and attention to the Government without price. In the main they have been good men; but they have been inefficient, failing to discover some of the most glaring outrages of the Indian Bureau in time to save the credit of the nation.

It was thought by many at the time that with the appointment of this board the Indian trouble would cease. It promised as much good as the present new system. Every new system will have its advocates, and the less a man knows of the difficulties of dealing with the Indians the more ambitious he is to introduce a new system and the more confident he is of its success.

Mr. President, the great trouble in our dealing with the Indian is our ignorance of his laws, customs, character, and religion. We insist on treating him as if he was a civilized man, when he ought to be treated as a savage, full of the superstitions and weaknesses that belong to savage life. This error is shown in this agreement and bill before us. The Secretary tells us it is a fair and intelligent settlement between the whites and Indians, or, in other words, between civilization and savage society. And he would fain make us believe that he has discovered a way to destroy a prejudice, the growth of centuries, in a day, and force the savage mind to adopt the ideas, customs, and laws of civilized life at one step. It cannot be done either by the new system or the old.

What has called forth this effort on the part of the Secretary of the Interior? Why does he appear before the committees of the House and Senate and urge this bill?

He says to avert a war, to save money and blood. In my judgment it is to save the reputation of his department; it is to cover up, under the plea of keeping the peace, the stupidity and ignorance that have signalized the conduct of the Indian Office during the last three years. The honorable Secretary of the Interior cannot be unmindful of the fact that from all parts of the country where Indians are located complaints are made by both whites and Indians of mismanagement. Rose-colored reports, depicting the astonishing rapidity with which the Indians are progressing in civilization, will not cover up or disguise the fact that within the last three years the most disgraceful chapter of Indian history has been written.

The removal and treatment of the Poncas in the Indian Territory; of the Nez Percés in Idaho and subsequently in the Indian Territory; the murdered settlers in Kansas whose death is charged to lie close to the door of the Indian Bureau; the conflict with the Northern Cheyennes; the killing of Thornburgh and his brave troops in Colorado; the murder of the philanthropic Meeker and his associates; the treatment of the captive women whose husbands and fathers were victims of savage hate; murdered citizens in Colorado, Wyoming, and New Mexico—these are incidents in the history of Indian affairs as administered by the present officials that have attracted the attention of the whole country. Both whites and Indians have suffered by this mismanagement.

Mr. President, peace will not come with this bill. There can be no peace with the Indians until the Government shall do justice to both whites and Indians alike.

When the officials to whose charge the administration of Indian affairs is intrusted shall become acquainted with the character, customs, laws, and religion of the Indians, and shall be moved to do justice to the Indians and whites alike, then this problem will be solved. Injustice to the whites will as surely end in the destruction of the Indians as if that injustice was practiced on the Indians themselves.

This bill is just neither to the Indians nor the whites; and, if it becomes a law, the Indians will be the greatest sufferers in the end.

It is unjust to the Indians because it provides no punishment for those guilty of crimes, makes no distinction between those who kept peace with us and those who fought us; because it gives them a false and exaggerated idea of their powers and rights. We treat with them without either punishment or rebuke. It is a reward for their crimes, and they will so understand it. They are the wards of the Government, it is said, but we fail to exercise the full powers of guardian over a ward when such exercise is clearly demanded in the interest of the ward.

It is unjust to the people of Colorado, because it leaves these Indians who fought Thornburgh and killed Meeker and his associates unpunished; and, flushed with victory on the battlefield and in diplomacy, they will be incited by the very mercy of the Government to commit other and greater crimes against our people.

We ought not to forget that we are dealing with savages—brutal, bloody savages—and we never should deal with savages as we deal with civilized people. Precautions against savages should be taken that are not required in dealing with civilized people.

It is unjust to the people of Colorado and the Indian alike in that it proposes to settle the Indians in Colorado under circumstances of great hardship to both whites and Indians. No wisdom is shown in the selection of the place where it is proposed to make savages learn to labor; and it is safe to say that no class of white men, situated as these Indians will be, would succeed.

If we propose to make a pastoral people of them, we do not give them enough land. If we propose to make farmers of them, we give them too much, and have selected a most unsuitable place to try the experiment. If it is intended that the Government shall support these Indians, we ought to put them where the supplies can be procured at less cost than in their present location, and where they will not be, as they now are, a continual menace to the peace of the people of Colorado.

The people of Colorado are interested in this experiment. If it succeeds they will be safe from savage hate and ferocity; but, if it fails, who can depict the disasters that may follow such failure? It will fail. All the circumstances connected with and surrounding this experiment make it morally certain to fail. Under the most favorable circumstances it would be likely to fail. What shall we say of the probability of failure with the temper of the Indians unfavorable, with all the natural obstacles it must encounter? If it fails, what will become of the Indian? Let the friends of this bill answer.

The people of Colorado are neither bloodthirsty nor cruel. That they are bitter against these Indians I do not deny; but it is because of the wrongs they have suffered at their hands, and they believe there will be no permanent peace while the Indians remain in the State. And no man in Colorado is firmer in that conviction than I am. It is forced on us by our knowledge of the character of these Indians and our lack of confidence in the administration of Indian affairs. The want of information on the part of the Indian Bureau exhibited in this bill is sufficient to warrant the people in distrusting the ability of the Indian Bureau to deal with this subject.

The fundamental idea in dealing with the Indian should be that he is a savage. This bill ignores that fact and treats him as having made some progress in civilization when in fact he has made none. The natural order in which men rise from a savage state to a civilized one is, first, pastoral and then agricultural. This bill proposes to make them agriculturists first, and that, too, with natural obstacles to contend with that might well deter the most energetic Anglo-Saxon.

This bill appropriates over $400,000, and yet not a dollar of this is for hoes, plows, or harrows, and not one dollar for an irrigating ditch, when every man who has the slightest information on the subject understands that not a pound of farm produce can be raised in that section of the country until there is an expenditure of from fifty to one hundred thousand dollars for irrigating purposes. And yet the honorable chairman of the committee says, acting under the advice, as I know, of the Secretary of the Interior, that it is important that these men should be put upon this land at once, that they may commence their spring farming. If there ever was a fair specimen of stupidity on the part of public officials, this comes fairly within the rule as exhibited by the Interior Department when they urge the consideration of this bill on that ground.

The people of Colorado believe that these Indians have by their misconduct forfeited all treaty rights, and the warrant for that belief they find in the treaty itself. The Indians who fought Thornburgh, murdered Meeker and his associates, outraged the female captives, were shielded and protected by the other Indians, who to this hour have refused to make known the name of a single one of the culprits. They believe, therefore, it was the duty of the Government to have declared the treaty at an end, and with a firm hand to have punished the offenders, if they could have been identified, and to have taken the Indians and put them on land suitable for pastoral and agricultural pursuits, where they would not necessarily come in contact with the whites; that they should be made to feel the restraints of law, disarmed of their firearms, and should, with the firm but fostering hand of the Government, be made to become first a pastoral and then an agricultural people.

The people of Colorado believe that this cannot be done where they are to be located under this bill. These Indians, unable longer to support themselves by the chase, will depend on the Government for support, will in the end become worse than they are now. They will occupy all the agricultural land in the vicinity of their location, and will not have the advantages of the example of industrious farmers, from whom they might learn valuable lessons, as they might in some other parts of the country. They will be surrounded by mining camps, and amid the temptations that are inseparable from such camps. They are not adapted to that kind of labor, and could not, if they would, work in the mines. If they raise cattle, they must be kept on their own land, which is insufficient to support them as a pastoral people. Their future, therefore, is not promising.

Must the State of Colorado be cursed, then, by the presence of these people whose future promises no improvement? If there was no other place for them, the people of Colorado would not complain. If the proposed location was better than any other, the hardship of having them left there would not appear so great; but there are fairer and better fields in the almost immediate neighborhood of the proposed location that are out of the State of Colorado and better adapted to their wants and use, whether they remain savages or follow the pursuits of civilized life. Why not consult the interests of Indians and whites alike, and send them to the Uintah reservation, not more than seventy-five miles distant? It is an Indian reservation belonging to the Government and not to the Indians, and there are no treaties with other Indians to interfere. It is sufficient in size for five times as many Indians as can ever be congregated on the land. It is inhabited only by four hundred Indians, speaking the same language and belonging to the same tribe. It is well watered, well timbered, easily irrigated, away from mines and mining camps. Why not send them there?

It is said by the Interior Department that they would not go to Uintah. Has it come to this, that a few hundred Indians, having murdered their agent and other employees, mutilated the dead, outraged the living, defeated our troops in battle, holding them in check for five long days, shall now dictate to us the terms of this agreement?

It is said this is cheaper than to have punished them. Is it cheaper in the end? In my judgment we should have demanded submission to our terms, and, if we had shown that we intended to compel submission, we could have avoided a war. The exhibition of firmness on the part of the Government would have commanded the respect of the savages. What must be the effect on the savage minds of the course pursued by the Government, making demands accompanied by threats of punishment if not complied with, and, on the refusal of the Indians to comply with our demands, allowing them to dictate the terms to us?

We are told that it is a great triumph of negotiations. Let us see what we demanded and what we got. To understand what we got we must know the condition of the title of the Indians as well as the obligation of the Government toward these Indians.

Mr. President, the region of country occupied by the Ute

Indians came to the United States by the treaty with Mexico. It was occupied at that time in part by these Indians and in part by other Indians. We made our first treaty with these Indians in 1849, at Santa Fé. They were then not living in the region now known as Colorado at all. It is doubtful whether they had ever been in the region that they now inhabit.

So then, Mr. President, these Indians had no title to this land at all. They stand on a very different footing from the Indians of Nebraska and the Indians of Iowa and Minnesota; and, but for the ignorance of the department that has control and management of this affair, we never should be met by this complication at all.

The honorable Secretary says we get a large amount of mining land and of valuable mining property, and that we should take that into consideration; that in a mile square there is money enough, perhaps, to pay the whole of the fund which is to be set apart to pay the annuity. To whom does this mineral land belong? Will any Senator say that it belongs to the Indians? It belongs to the Government of the United States. Under the decision of the Supreme Court, repeated again and again, with particular emphasis in 19 Wallace, they have no right to mine a single pound of ore in that mineral land. It is not theirs, it is ours, and, under the rule there laid down, the United States has the right, without the violation of any treaty, to provide that any prospector or settler may go upon it and extract the ore.

It is proposed to give them eight hundred thousand acres of land, and to give them that in the mountain regions of Colorado, surrounded on every side by mines, to be surrounded on every side by mining camps in the next six months; and, when you shall have destroyed the tribal relations, as the Senator from Texas says you will, when you shall have taken them out from underneath the protecting clauses of the national statute with regard to the sale of liquor and other things, it is expected that they will immediately move on to civilization! It is preposterous; it is hopeless; it is useless; it is an insane effort that no man who has the good of the Indians at heart and a thorough knowledge of the facts would ever be guilty of making.

Not only is the country where these Indians are to go to be surrounded by mining camps and miners, but the very land upon which they are expected to farm is mining land, rich in placer diggings, the coveted land now, not of the people of

Colorado, but the coveted land of the people of Iowa and of Illinois, and the people clear back to the Atlantic Coast. It is the men who are going to Colorado who are to go upon these lands, and not the men there now who are so much concerned. It is coveted, I say, by the people who are going in there, as they have a right to covet it. It ought not to be locked up from the honest hand of toil. It ought to be open to every man to go there and unearth and bring forth its hidden treasures. It is an outrage upon the whole people of the country to put these wild Indians, who are the purest type to-day of the native savage existing on the continent, upon this land and surround them with all the temptations that there must be, and expect us to live in peace and harmony with them, especially after the Government has admitted its doubt whether it could cope with them in battle, and has shown its inability to cope with them in diplomacy.

N. P. Hill [Col.] supported the bill because it would avert a costly and bloody war with Indians in mountain fastnesses and hasten the settlement and development of their lands by the whites.

I am in favor of the bill because it inaugurates a new line of policy in dealing with the Indians. It breaks up the tribal relation, which has always been a curse to the Indians of the United States. It gives to each Indian property which will be owned and held by him separately and individually. It holds out inducements for a civilized mode of life. It abolishes all Indian reservations in the State and subjects all Indians residing in the State to the jurisdiction of the courts. It is true the Indians give up eleven million acres of land which it is claimed they own under the stipulations of a treaty. But this land has always been useless to them, and always will be useless. It has always stood in the way of their progress in the pursuits of civilized life. They will remain savages and barbarians so long as they can roam at will over a tract of seventeen thousand square miles of mountainous country. Their settlement in severalty upon agricultural lands would contribute more to their welfare than any donation of money or land, however liberal, which the Government could make. I am in favor of the bill because its defeat would confront us with the following plain alternative: either to keep the Utes in possession of the whole reservation, instead of about one-twentieth part of it, or to drive them out by war after they have offered to give it up peaceably.

I am not overcharged with sympathy for the Ute Indians. They are a worthless set of vagabonds as a whole. But the policy of exterminating them could not be entertained by an enlightened nation. As between a war with them, with all its attendant evils, and the peaceable methods which will be reached by the operations of this bill, there seems to be but one choice.

The lands, he said, are cheap at the price proposed. There may be single acres of this tract which in the next few years will produce more in minerals than the cost of the entire reservation. If the Indians owned the land it could not be said to be a dear purchase. If they did not own it, it would still be difficult to convince Congress of that fact.

On April 5 John T. Morgan [Ala.] opposed the bill. He would pass a law stating that, whereas the Utes had not taken advantage of the privilege offered in the treaty of 1868 to take lands in severalty, and whereas that they do so was the essential purpose of the treaty, they must now make their selections and become subject to all the laws affecting citizens of the United States.

Let us say to these Indians: We will place ourselves in the stead of the government that we have destroyed by this act of Congress. We will assume its trusts and exercise its powers with reference to you. We will enact laws by which you are to be governed. We will, if you choose, employ your tribal traditions and laws and customs and agencies to administer what you call or consider justice between yourselves until we choose to supplant them with some better system.

It seems to me that the door now stands wide open for the pursuit of a policy like this. It would be far better to let the Indians understand that we have dethroned these rulers, that men like Ouray and many others among them, who have ruled these Indians against their will and with an arbitrary and a cruel hand, have no longer this power to wreck and destroy them in reference to their property rights; for there are not in this whole world more absolute despotisms than exist between the rulers of the Indian tribes and the Indians themselves. There are thousands and tens of thousands of the Indians who, if they had dared to break loose from their rulers, would have become free thinkers and independent, honest laboring men. The act of Congress of March 3, 1871, destroys and dethrones these tyrants and will allow the Indian people to come forward and exercise their right of individual manhood under the laws and Constitution of the United States and under the protection of our Government.

Henry L. Dawes [Mass.] opposed the entire Indian policy of the Government.

We have always treated with the Indians, up to the statute which the Senator from Alabama has alluded to, as independent tribes, capable of negotiating with us and having some sort of right in the soil we found them in the occupation of, that we would purchase of them, and not extinguish by violence, as we perhaps might have done. But when we purchased it of them we purchased it of a savage race, having no knowledge of our language, without ability to treat or to understand what they were treating about, and neither the tribes themselves nor the people of the United States, till within a few years, ever stopped to consider the future of the Indian. We, on our side, have always treated with him, up to within these few years, on the idea that we would make the best possible bargain with him; and the Indian, on the other hand, having no thought for his morrow, considered only the color of the trinkets which we put off on him for vast tracts of country, out of which great and independent States have sprung up in this Union. It is only when the question has forced itself upon us so that it was impossible for us to ignore it that we have stopped to consider in our treatment with the Indian what shall be done with him in the future; whether it is not incumbent upon us, who have taken away his possessions and his means of support, to make some provision for him if he makes none for himself in the future. And not a little has that question been pressed upon us in the form that he whom we have thus treated, multiplying daily upon our hands, is a savage who knows no law or restraint but a chain; and the Indian himself has come to have some faint glimmering of what is before him, as the very walls of the continent have approached him on the one side and on the other, with apparent certain destruction awaiting him.

But we come to this question after long years of such treatment of the Indian that he has lost faith in us. He no longer, if he ever did, believes that we intend to keep our promises with him; he has been too often deceived, he has too often trusted

"MOVE ON!"

HAS THE NATIVE AMERICAN NO RIGHTS THAT THE NATURALIZED AMERICAN IS BOUND TO RESPECT?

Cartoon by Thomas Nast

From the collection of the New York Public Library

only to find that engagements with him are kept while they are of advantage to us, and no longer; and when we approach him he suspects that some lurking advantage is to be gained over him in the future, which he cannot quite understand, least of all can he protect himself against.

The Senator from Colorado [Mr. Teller] talked of the Indian's character, of his faithlessness, of the outrages he has committed upon the white people on the borders. I am not disposed to criticize the Senator. I do not know that the Senator or his State particulariy is to be held accountable in any way for any infraction of good faith on our part toward these Indians.

SENATOR TELLER.—There has never been a Ute Indian killed by any citizen of Colorado since the country was settled. We have invariably respected their rights; we have respected the obligations of the Government as made with them; and I believe that I may say here that pretty nearly the only white man in the United States who has attempted to enforce the treaties of the United States with them is my humble self. I followed this Secretary of the Interior from the time he came into office until the outbreak last summer, to have the money paid that the Senator has said was unjustly withheld, and I repeated over and over again to him that it was a cause of complaint, and that it put our people in jeopardy that it was not paid.

SENATOR DAWES.—Why, Mr. President, I had it not in my mind to intimate that either the people of Colorado or the State itself or the Senator was to blame——

SENATOR TELLER.—I know; but I want to add one other statement that, since the country was settled, at least fifty white men have been killed by these Indians; innumerable houses have been burned; innumerable farms on the edge of the reservation and off it have been destroyed; and yet the people of Colorado have never retaliated.

SENATOR DAWES.—The Senator cannot but know that such is the character of this savage that he visits the wrongs he receives from the strong upon the weak; such is his nature and such is the limit of his knowledge of men and of government that he only knows that it was white men who broke faith with him, and it is white men upon whom he visits his revenge. But the very State in which the outrage upon the peaceable agent at White River and his family and employees was inflicted by these savages, the very existence of the State itself, is a gross and palpable violation of the plighted faith of this Government, which in a solemn treaty with the Cherokee

Nation pledged itself sacredly never to permit any territorial or State government to be erected upon their Western border, but that the free, unobstructed passage and control and jurisdiction westward, as far as the jurisdiction of the United States should extend, should be forever kept for the Cherokees. And yet, in violation of that treaty obligation, the State of Colorado is erected right across that western boundary of the Cherokee Nation, in obedience to that law of growth and progress in civilization in this land, stronger than all human laws and human treaties; but the Indian does not understand that.

SENATOR TELLER.—I should like to ask the Senator whether he thinks that the Ute Indians ever heard of that treaty, and if he does not know that when the treaty was made this very ground in controversy, every acre of it, was a part and parcel of the Republic of Mexico.

SENATOR DAWES.—I know this last statement and I think it likely the other is true; but I know that the treaties stipulated that the territory as far as the jurisdiction of the United States should thereafter extend should be kept open. And, as to the Utes ever knowing about that treaty, it is not necessary for the argument that I am making here that they should understand that treaty. They understand, and every Indian understands, that, when the white man approaches him with treaties in his hand, something is to be gained on the one side and something is surely to be lost on the other. No tribe of Indians ever entered into a treaty with the United States that did not result in putting fetters upon them. They have been lassoed into imprisonment and confinement within limits that the necessities of growth in this Government required, and no sooner have we made treaties than we have gone to work deliberately to violate them.

But it is not treaty obligations alone of which the Indian has to complain. Why, sir, the treatment of Indian agents, and the army, and the whole department with the Indian for long back, is covered with blots and stains, and bad faith, and aggravations to the Indian and provocation to violence on his part. While we have been deliberating over this very measure in our Committee on Indian Affairs, a peaceable Indian chief, who never raised his hand in violence upon a white man, whose home had been ceded to him by words of grant on the part of the United States as solemn and effective as a warranty deed, in consideration of his good behavior and peaceable deportment toward the United States—this is the language of the grant— who had been driven at the point of the bayonet from that home into the malaria of the Indian Territory, has there been enticed by false pretences into the Indian agent's own house, an agent of this modern civilization, and there shot down upon the floor in cold and cowardly murder by the soldiers of the United States under the direction of an Indian agent!

Sir, the Northern Cheyennes, taken by the army from their home and the graves of their fathers, among the cool mountain streams of the Northwest, down to the torrid jungles and malaria of the Indian Territory, there to fall before the ravages of disease, when they broke away and wandered through the wilds of western Kansas, seeking their old home, were taken by the armed soldiers of the United States and shut up in mid-winter, in January, in a guardhouse, when the thermometer was ten degrees below zero, without clothing to protect them from the inclemency of the weather. They were told by the officer whose official report I have here, "You shall have neither food nor drink nor fuel till you consent to go back to your doom in the Indian Territory," and there they were kept without either food or fuel or drink four or five days—the officer reports four, the Indians say it was seven—in what an officer calls "the freezing-out process"; and then, when the chief was called out of the guardroom under pretence of a conference, armed soldiers were placed in side rooms, out of sight, and when he and his fellows came into a room for a peaceable conference they were seized and put in irons, and those in the guard-house, breaking out, with the resolution to die in flight for their homes rather than to die in the Indian Territory, the victims of disease, were fired upon with shot and shell, and every male member of the band but those in irons and two others, with thirty women and children, were laid corpses in the process.

Sir, I have before me the process pursued toward men supposed to be guilty of the murder of a young man from Massachusetts upon a stage route in Arizona. When an officer of the army called the Indians into council, having previously arranged with a halfbreed that, like Judas, he should go among his brethren and betray the men he was willing to say were guilty, and when that process was gone through with, under the pretence of a council with friendly Indians, soldiers, at a given signal, shot them all dead.

Does anybody wonder, when these instances multiply around us every day, when flags of truce, like that under which General Canby fell at the hands of the Modocs, are violated by our own soldiers when they treat with the Indians; when the whole history of the dispensing of the Indian annuities and of the Indian appropriations is one long history of plunder; when we make our promises with no apparent intention of keeping them, is it to be wondered at that the Indian question has come upon us with difficulties almost passing solution?

Sir, before we can do anything toward making something out of the Indian we must do justice to him. The process of extermination, I think, is substantially abandoned by our people. It has proved a failure at least, with all the advantages under which it has been tried and the fidelity with which it has been pursued, sparing no expense of Indian warfare or cruel treatment, transferring the Indian from place to place, taking him from the cold regions of the North to the almost inhospitable and uninhabitable regions of the Indian Territory, there to die by hundreds; still the truth stares us in the face that there are more of them to-day than there were yesterday.

Sir, it seems to be agreed that this policy which we have pursued so faithfully has got to be abandoned, and I thank God that it has.

Then we have to deal with the Indians by some other process. One process is like that shadowed forth in the argument of the Senator from Alabama [John T. Morgan], that we shall violently break up their tribal relations and scatter them, wild and savage and uneducated, abroad in the community, subject to the laws and enjoying all the rights and privileges of citizens of the United States, having no other restraint upon them than the feeble and ineffectual restraint that comes from bringing them into a court of justice to plead to an indictment they cannot understand for the violation of a law they do not know the meaning of.

Sir, the Senator from Colorado [Mr. Teller] well described the strength of the cords which bind the Indians in their bands. I venture to say there is not power enough in the United States to violently and against their will rend those cords. If there were no question of humanity in it, it is an impossibility. You cannot, with an army larger in number than all the bands themselves, rend asunder by violence those cords and attachments which bind them one to another in families, any more than you could invade the homes of the civilized, scatter them, and think vainly that thereby you had broken asunder all the ties that bind man to his family and to his kindred.

You might just as well turn loose the inmates of an insane asylum and impose upon them the restraints of law, and require at their hands obedience to the obligations of citizenship, as to undertake by this process to make of these Indians self-supporting citizens, obedient to the law of the land.

Then, sir, if you can neither exterminate them nor, by the puny, ineffectual attempt at an enactment here at your desk, disintegrate and scatter them around through the forty-five millions of people we have here in this land, what next? Sir, you ought to improve them, make something of them, under- take to relieve yourselves of this burden which comes upon you as a just retribution for the long line of treatment in the past which finds no justification in any standard of justice or of right between the powerful and the weak. No one expects that you can make much out of the adult Indians. You cannot teach them much how to work and support themselves. Indus- trious habits do not come by the force of enactments. Indus- trious habits are the result of long years of training, beginning with early life. You have them, too, without the ability to speak our language, to understand those with whom they are obliged to treat daily in order to obtain the merest necessities of life. Take one of them, allot him in severalty, which seems now to be the panacea for all evils, one hundred and sixty acres of land, and surround him, as this bill and the other propose, with the enterprising Western pioneers who purchase the real estate, the one hundred and sixty acres on each side of him, and what then? He goes out to support himself. He cannot understand his white neighbors. He only knows from sad ex- perience, because he cannot forget that he never treats with that color without having the worst of it. How long would he live and support himself?

I had an interesting conversation a few days since with a chief of one of these tribes, as intellectual a man, as clear- headed, and as honest and truthful a man, according to the department and everybody else, as anyone could be, a man who realized the condition of the Indians, a man who made a study, as well as he could, of what, so far as his tribe was con- cerned, was the best solution of this question. I asked him if he could have for each male member of his tribe one hundred and sixty acres of land allotted in severalty, with the condition that it could not be alienated for twenty-five years, what he would say to that. It was a great while before he could be made to comprehend what I meant, with an earnest desire to understand the full meaning of these words; and when at last he seemed fully to comprehend them, shaking his head, he said: "It would not do us any good; it might our children; but we do not understand your language; we do not know how to treat

with white men; they always get the better of us; they would
pluck us as you do a bird." Then I put the question in another form: "Suppose you were allotted, and a good, honest
Indian agent"—my friend from Illinois [David Davis] almost
laughs when I say that—"a good, honest Indian agent were put
over you to keep off the white people and let you develop yourselves?" "We don't know how to work very well; we were
never taught to work; if our children could be brought up to
understand your language and to understand what comes of
work, to understand that what they earned to-day is theirs,
and they can hold it against the world, they could take these
lands and they could take care of themselves and of us, but we
cannot do it."

There is more philosophy in that Indian's statement of the
question than all that has been developed in the Indian policy
of the Government for the last quarter of a century. Take
their children; above all, take their girls into schools in which
they may be taught the English language and English ways
and English habits and ideas. They bring up the families;
they take care of the children; from them the children learn
to talk and learn to think and learn to act; and yet, in all the
schools established in Indian agencies for the education of the
Indian, the Indian girl is hardly thought of. Take the boy
and make something of him; not keep him till he forgets his race
and his parentage, but keep him until there shall be inspired
in him a missionary spirit to go forth among those of his blood
and attempt to make something of them. Appropriate this
$125,000 which in this bill you pledge yourselves to distribute
every year *per capita* around among these people to the education each year of these four thousand Ute Indians, and, by
the time this experiment shall have failed and the Indian question, so far as Colorado is concerned, shall have come back
upon us with increased force, you will have raised up among
those Indians a restraining and at the same time an elevating
influence that shall quicken in the whole tribe a desire to acquire, and with it shall come also the desire to protect and
keep their daily earnings, and with that come the necessity
and the desire for peace, and with peace comes respect for law,
and that is the simple, natural process and the only one, it
seems to me, Mr. President, which opens up to us with any hope
of success.

It is a long and tedious process out of this difficulty; it is
beset with embarrassments and discouragements on every side;
but those who understand best and appreciate more fully than

I do all these difficulties have themselves the strongest confidence in its ultimate success. Certainly, sir, these puny efforts on the part of the Government to deal with the Indian question, these homeopathic doses, are idle and are folly in the extreme. If I could see any good to come from this bill, recognizing as I do the imperative necessity of action in respect to these Utes, recognizing, as I am free to do, the earnest desire on the part of the Indian Department to do the best possible thing, I should like to support it. I know that with great propriety and with necessity the department turns to Congress; for it is Congress, and Congress alone, that can solve this question; but I fear that by no such processes as those we are considering to-day, involving, as they do (and which I do not think the Senate quite realize), an enormous expenditure of public moneys with so little return, can the great result I desire be accomplished.

On April 9 Preston B. Plumb [Kan.] replied to Senator Dawes.

I object to any anticipations that may be derived from the bill of the kind spoken of by the Senator from Massachusetts in the way of education under the direction of the President at Carlisle Barracks, or Hampton Roads, or the Uintah Valley, or anywhere else on the supposition that that can ever be of any perceptible service to the Indian race in making the Indians better qualified, by making them useful and self-supporting citizens of the United States. That result never will be reached. They may go out on the plains, they may take charge of a herd of cattle, they may in some degree adapt themselves to agriculture of an inferior kind; but, when it comes to the competition for which we seek to prepare them by education, and without which education will be of no use to them, they will inevitably go to the wall. They can only stand anywhere on the face of the earth by the protection of government, and not at all in competition with the white man.

Mr. President, an eminent citizen of the Senator's own State —I think it was Oliver Wendell Holmes—characterizes and settles definitely the status of the Indian when he speaks of him as simply a member of a provisional race. He is simply here to get out of the way at the proper time; he was not expected to be here in the way of the white race. In no way did he ever become a factor of civilization; in no way did he ever become enduring either by amalgamation or otherwise.

Within fifty years there will not be probably one single full-blooded Indian on the American continent; and within a hundred years there will not be a single person living who, in his features or in his blood, will bear the impress of a single characteristic of the Indian character. He will be entirely gone. The only question to be considered is what shall we do as a matter of humanity to take hold of these people whose lot has thus been provisionally cast among us?

James G. Blaine [Me.] replied to Senator Plumb.

I think the Senator felicitates himself quite too freely when he says that in fifty years from this time we shall not see within the area of the United States the face of an Indian, nor one that has Indian blood in his veins. If the statistics of the Indian Department are correct, there are to-day nearly or quite as many Indians within the area of the United States as there were when Columbus discovered America. I believe there never has been a census of the Indians made upon any assignable basis of fact that gave a number beyond one hundred thousand greater than that which is now known to exist.

I believe the Indian question is one that is going to exist very many years beyond the time when the Senator from Kansas, in his sanguine feeling, thinks it will cease to trouble us. It will not depart. Three hundred thousand men, living in a healthy climate, expanding all the time under the area that is given to them, do not die out very soon. I remember a distinguished Senator of the United States, who went South in what we call the "Andy Johnson" days, when we were troubled a good deal about the matter of reconstruction, and he came back and said: "You are troubling yourselves a great deal about this question of the negro; freedom is going to destroy him; you will not have any negroes in twenty years." When asked why we were not going to have any, his reply was, "Why, the smallpox, every form of disease, is coming in to ravage them and destroy them," and he was certain the negro was not to be known on the face of the earth within a very short time. I think the census of 1880 will show a pretty large and healthy increase of that troublesome member of society, as some gentlemen regard him. And when we attempt to deal with the Indian question on the theory that they are going to disappear we are proceeding upon a foundation that is not true. We shall have to deal with them as an ever-present question, which our descendants will confront as we have been confronting it for nearly four centuries in this country; and it will be here for four centuries more, I venture to prophesy to the honorable Senator from Kansas, and with all the more confidence, as neither of us will ever be able to contradict the other on the ultimate solution of it.

The Senate passed the bill on April 12, 1880, by a vote of 37 to 16. The House passed it on June 7 by a vote of 174 to 15. President Hayes signed it on June 16.

CHAPTER IX

WOMAN SUFFRAGE

[DEBATES CONNECTED WITH THE FIFTEENTH AMENDMENT]

Memorial to the Senate in Behalf of Woman Suffrage by Mrs. Gerrit
Smith [N. Y.] *et al.* Debate: John B. Henderson [Mo.], Willard
Saulsbury [Del.], Charles Sumner [Mass.], Richard Yates [Ill.]; Memorial Is Tabled—Thomas E. Noell [Mo.] Offers Resolutions in Favor
of Woman Suffrage—Charles A. Eldridge [Wis.] Presents Memorial
from the American Equal Rights Association in Favor of Woman Suffrage—Debate: Mr. Eldridge, Rufus P. Spalding [O.], Mr. Noell—
Petition of Victoria C. Woodhull [N. Y.] for Supplementary Legislation Making Operative Her Right to Vote under the Constitution and
the Fifteenth Amendment; Tabled—Henry Wilson [Mass.] Introduces
Bill for Woman Suffrage in the Territories; Referred—Petition from
the American Woman Suffrage Association for Woman Suffrage in the
District of Columbia and a Constitutional Amendment Removing Sex
as a Political Disability—Speech of Stevenson Archer [Md.] in the
House on "The Reaction from Woman Suffrage"—Petition of Dr.
Mary E. Walker [D. C.] on Woman Suffrage.

IN the great contest to secure equal manhood suffrage,
culminating in the passage of the Fifteenth Amendment, we have seen that the question of extending
the elective franchise to women played an important
part. Many advocates of votes for women, however,
were not sincere, being, indeed, opponents of any extension of the suffrage, and presenting the proposition
merely to convict the advocates of negro suffrage of inconsistency.

So determined were some of the friends of the negro
to secure to him his vote that they refused to increase the
opposition to the measure by considering the case of the
woman. Of these Senator Charles Sumner [Mass.] was
the most eminent. During the debates of 1865-66 on

negro suffrage in the District of Columbia [see Chapter
I] Senator Sumner presented, with an apology, a memorial from a number of ladies of various States praying
that suffrage be granted to women. To rebuke him for
the apology the wife of Gerrit Smith [N. Y.], the Abolitionist, and twenty-seven other ladies, most of them from
the same State, sent another memorial to the Senate.
This was presented on February 21, 1866, by John B.
Henderson [Mo.]. He read the letter of Mrs. Smith
which accompanied the petition.

"I send you a petition, signed by twenty-eight intelligent women of
this State, who are native-born Americans—read, write, and pay taxes,
and now claim representation! I was surprised to-day to find Mr. Sumner presenting a petition, with an apology, from the women of the Republic. After his definition of a true republic, and his lofty peans to
'equal rights' and the ballot, one would hardly expect him to ignore the
claims of fifteen million educated taxpayers, now taking their places by
the side of man in art, science, literature, and government. I trust, sir,
you will present this petition in a manner more creditable to yourself and
respectful to those who desire to speak through you.

"Remember, the right of petition is our only right in the government;
and, when three joint resolutions are before the House to introduce the
word 'male' into the Federal Constitution, 'it is the proper time' for the
women of the nation to be heard, Mr. Sumner to the contrary notwithstanding."

Senator Henderson remarked:

The right of petition is a sacred right, and, whatever may
be thought of giving the ballot to women, the right to ask it of
the Government cannot be denied them. I present this petition without any apology. Indeed, I present it with pleasure.
It is respectful in its terms, and is signed by ladies occupying
so high a place in the moral, social, and intellectual world that
it challenges at our hands at least a respectful consideration.
The distinguished Senators from Massachusetts and from Illinois must make their own defense against the assumed inconsistency of their position. They are abundantly able to give
reasons for their faith in all things; whether they can give
reasons satisfactory to the ladies in this case I do not know.
The Senators may possibly argue that, if women vote at all,
the right should not be exercised before the age of twenty-one;
that they are generally married at or before that age, and that,
when married, they become, or ought to become, merged in their
husbands; that the act of one must be regarded as the act of

the other; that the good of society demands this unity for purposes of social order; that political differences should not be
permitted to disturb the peace of a relation so sacred. The
honorable Senators will be able to find authority for this position not only in the common law, approved as it is by the
wisdom and experience of ages, but in the declaration of the
first man, on the occasion of the first marriage, when he said,
"This is now bone of my bone and flesh of my flesh."

It may be answered, however, that the wife, though one with
her husband, at least constitutes his better half, and, if the
married man be entitled to but one vote, the unmarried man
should be satisfied with less than half a vote. [Laughter.]
Having some doubts myself whether, beyond a certain age, to
which I have not yet arrived, such a man should be entitled to
a vote, or even half a vote, I leave the difficulty to be settled
by my friend from Massachusetts and the fair petitioners. The
petitioners claim that, as we are proposing to enfranchise four
million emancipated slaves, equal and impartial justice alike
demands the suffrage for fifteen million women. At first view
the proposition can scarcely be met with denial, yet reasons
"thick as blackberries" and strong as truth itself may be
urged in favor of the ballot in the one case which cannot be
urged in the other.

Willard Saulsbury [Del.].—I rise to a point of order.
My point of order is that a man who has lived an old bachelor
as long as the Senator from Missouri has no right to talk
about women's rights. [Laughter.]

Senator Henderson.—I had no idea that that was a point
of order, sir. Whatever may be said theoretically about the
elective franchise as a natural right, in practice, at least, it
has always been denied in the most liberal States to more than
half the population. It is withheld from those whose crimes
prove them devoid of respect for social order, and generally
from those whose ignorance or imbecility unfits them for an
intelligent appreciation of the duties of citizens and the blessings of good government. To women the suffrage has been
denied in almost all governments, not for the reasons just
stated but because it is wholly unnecessary as a means of their
protection. In the government of nature the weaker animals
and insects, dependent on themselves for safety and life, are
provided with means of defense. The bee has its sting and the
despised serpent its deadly poison. So, in the governments of
men, the weak must be provided with power to inspire fear,
at least, in the strong, if not to command their respect.

Political power was claimed originally by the people as a means of protecting themselves against the usurpations of those in power, whose interests or caprices might lead to their oppression. Hence came the republican system. But it was never thought the interests or caprices of men could lead to a denial of the civil rights or social supremacy of woman. All races of men are unjust to other races. They are unjust because of pride. That very pride makes them just to the women of their own race. There may be men who have prejudice against race; they are less than men who have prejudice against sex. The social position of woman in the United States is such that no civil right can be denied her. The women here have entire charge of the social and moral world. Hence woman must be educated. First impressions are those which bend the mind to noble or ignoble action, and these impressions are made by mothers.

To have intelligent voters we must have intelligent mothers. To have free men we must have free women. The voter from this source receives his moral and intellectual training. Woman makes the voter, and should not descend from her lofty sphere to engage in the angry contests of her creatures. She makes statesmen, and her gentle influence, like the finger of the angel pointing the path of duty, would be lost in the controversies of political strife. She makes the soldier, infuses courage and patriotism in his youthful heart, and hovers like an invisible spirit over the field of battle, urging him on to victory or death in defense of the right. Hence woman takes no musket to the battlefield. Here, as in politics, her personal presence would detract from her power. Galileo, Newton, and Laplace could not fitly discuss the laws of planetary motion with ignorant rustics at a country inn. The learned divine who descends from the theological seminary to wrangle upon doctrinal points with the illiterate, stubborn teacher of a small country flock must lose half his influence for good. Our Government is built as our Capitol is built. The strong and brawny arms of men, like granite blocks, support its arches; but woman, lovely woman, the true goddess of Liberty, crowns its dome.

SENATOR SUMNER.—Before this petition passes out of sight I wish to make one observation, and only one. The Senator from Missouri began by an allusion to myself and to a remark which fell from me when I presented the other day a petition from women of the United States praying for the ballot. I took occasion then to remark that, in my opinion, the petition at that time was not judicious. That was all that I said. I did not undertake to express any opinion on the great question whether women should vote or should not vote. I did venture to say that, in my opinion, it was not judicious for them at this moment to bring forward their claims so as to compromise in any way the great question of equal rights for an enfranchised race now before Congress.

The Senator has quoted a letter suggesting that I did not present the petition in a creditable way. I have now to felicitate my excellent friend on the creditable way in which he has perfomed his duty. [Laughter.]

RICHARD YATES [Ill.].—Allow me to say that I think the two gentlemen, one of whom has arrived at the age of forty-nine and the other sixty-three, have no right to discuss the question of women's rights in the Senate. [Laughter.]

At the suggestion of Senator Henderson the petition was laid on the table without demur. During the next session, however woman suffrage was to find earnest advocates—indeed, it formed a chief part of the debate on the question of suffrage in the District of Columbia.

EQUALITY OF SUFFRAGE

HOUSE OF REPRESENTATIVES, FEBRUARY 4-18, 1867

On February 4, 1867, Thomas E. Noell [Mo.], an administration Republican, offered in the House of Representatives resolutions in favor of equality of suffrage. They were partly in earnest and partly ironical, the final resolution being intended as a hit to the "progressive" State of Massachusetts. In this Representative Noell was probably imitating the attitude of Edgar Cowan [Pa.], the eminent administration Republican of the Senate [see page 26]. Omitting a proposition to abolish disfranchisement on account of sex in the District of Columbia the resolutions read:

Resolved, That governments were made for the people, and not the people for the government; that every adult citizen of sound mind in any State or Territory has the right to a voice in the formation of the constitution of said State, and in the representation and laws of said State, and that any State which disfranchises any class of its citizens on account of sex is not republican in form and should be overturned by Congress.

Resolved, That the Committee on the Judiciary are instructed to report a bill calling a convention and authorizing every adult citizen of sound mind in the State of Massachusetts to vote for delegates to said convention for the purpose of making a constitution for said State republican in form.

On Friday the 11th, the resolutions came before the House for discussion. Mr. Noell not being present, Charles A. Eldridge [Wis.] presented a memorial from the American Equal Rights Association, signed by Lucretia Mott, president; Theodore Tilton, Frederick Douglass, Elizabeth Cady Stanton, vice-presidents, and Susan B. Anthony, secretary. The clerk read the petition:

The undersigned respectfully but earnestly protest against any change in the Constitution of the United States, or legislation by Congress which shall longer violate the principle of republican government by proscriptive distinctions in rights of suffrage and citizenship on account of color or sex.

Your memorialists would respectfully represent that neither the colored man's loyalty, bravery on the battlefield, and general good conduct, nor woman's heroic devotion to liberty and her country, in peace and war, have yet availed to admit them to equal citizenship, even in this enlightened and republican nation.

We believe that humanity is one in all those intellectual, moral, and spiritual attributes out of which grow human responsibilities. The Scripture declaration is: "So God created man in his own image; male and female created he them." And all divine legislation throughout the realm of nature recognizes the perfect equality of the two conditions. For male and female are but different conditions.

Neither color nor sex is ever discharged from obedience to law, natural or moral, written or unwritten. The commands, thou shalt not steal, nor kill, nor commit adultery, know nothing of sex in their demands; nothing in their penalty. And hence we believe that all human legislation which is at variance with the divine code is essentially unrighteous and unjust.

Woman and the colored man are taxed to support many literary and humane institutions, into which they never come, except in the poorly paid capacity of menial servants. Woman has been fined, whipped, branded with red-hot irons, imprisoned, and hung; but when was woman ever tried by a jury of her peers?

Though the nation declared from the beginning that "all just governments derive their powers from the consent of the governed," the consent of woman was never asked to a single statute, however nearly it affected her dearest womanly interests or happiness. In the despotisms of the Old World, of ancient and modern times, woman, profligate, prostitute, weak, cruel, tyrannical, or otherwise, from Semiramis and Messalina to Catharine of Russia and Margaret of Anjou, have swayed, unchallenged, imperial scepters; while in this republican and Christian land, in the nineteenth century, woman, intelligent, refined in every ennobling gift and grace, may not even vote on the appropriation of her own property or the disposal and destiny of her own children. Literally she has no rights which man is bound to respect; and her civil privileges she holds only by sufferance. For the power that gave can take away, and of that power she is no part. In most of the States these unjust distinctions apply to woman and to the colored man alike.

Your memorialists fully believe that the time has come when such injustice should cease.

Woman and the colored man are loyal, patriotic, property-holding, tax-paying, liberty-loving citizens, and we cannot believe that sex or complexion should be any ground for civil or political degradation.

In our Government one-half the citizens are disfranchised by their sex, and about one-eighth by the color of their skin; and thus a large majority have no voice in enacting or executing the laws they are taxed to support and compelled to obey with the same fidelity as the more favored class, whose usurped prerogative it is to rule.

Against such outrages on the very name of republican freedom your memorialists do and must ever protest. And is not our protest preëminently as just against the tyranny of "taxation without representation" as was that thundered from Bunker Hill when our revolutionary fathers fired the shot that shook the world?

And your memorialists especially remember, at this time, that our country is still reeling under the shock of a terrible civil war, the legitimate result and righteous retribution of the vilest slave system ever suffered among men. And in restoring the foundations of our nationality your memorialists most respectfully and earnestly pray that all discriminations on account of sex or race may be removed, and that our Government may be republican in fact as well as form; a government by the people, and the whole people; for the people, and the whole people.

During the reading of the long memorial Rufus P. Spalding [O.] moved, amid the laughter of the House, that Mr. Eldridge have leave to print the remainder. On this being ruled out of order because Mr. Eldridge had the floor for an hour, Mr. Spalding, amid renewed laughter, insisted that Mr. Eldridge, evidently as a punishment for boring the House, be made to read the petition himself. Mr. Eldridge explained that gallantry to the ladies was alone prompting him in the matter, for he was no upholder of their cause and, now that Mr. Noell had returned, he would yield the floor to him as one "who will advocate their cause, as he has always done by his acts and words." [Laughter.]

Mr. Noell then occupied the rest of the day with his speech, which he completed on February 18.

THE ENFRANCHISEMENT OF WOMEN

THOMAS E. NOELL, M.C.

Mr. Speaker, I have been asked frequently if I were sincere in advocating woman suffrage. If my principles are sound, why inquire my motive? People must believe that politicians are sincere, for they look to them for earnest advice. But politics is a farce. The actors in the play smile at each other behind the scenes and congratulate themselves that they have "knocked" the people. We discuss interminably the difference between tweedle-dum and tweedle-dee. The *Congressional Globe* of last session had more wind in it than Ulysses' bags. A little seriousness of purpose would act as a great carminative to that journal.

Mr. Noell began his serio-comic dissertation with a discussion of the origin of civilization.

Who civilized the world? Neither Guizot nor Buckle nor Hallam can answer this question. We must glean along the waste stubble fields, whence history has garnered her stores, for facts to aid us in solving this question. We derived our civilization from Rome; the latter derived her civilization from Greece; and this last country derived her civilization from Egypt. Who civilized Egypt? The women!

It was shortly after the great flood, when the world was hung out in the universe to dry, that Egypt, which was to civilize the world, civilized herself, and the women civilized Egypt. The periodical overflowings of the Nile caused the people to meet together in the high places. The men and women mingled together, everyone bending his or her energy to minister to the general welfare during the overflow. Here the native genius of the women displayed itself in devising conveniences and comforts and in the various ways in which genius must assert itself when the conventionalities of society are broken down. The dull, plodding, thick-headed men of Egypt —the most talented men in the world—found that they knew nothing compared to the knowledge of the women. For their own interest they constituted the women the controlling class. We have no Nile to overflow and break down the conventionalities of society; but we are threatened by a destructive overflow of the *Niger,* and I think it is time to bring the women into the high places.

The women of Egypt were the traders and merchants. They enriched that country and gave a start to the arts and sciences. They were the heads of families. When the parents grew old the daughters and not the sons were bound by law to support them. In the marriage contract the woman promised to support her husband, and the husband in turn promised to obey his wife. The Egyptian women traded in Tyre and Sidon; the Arabian merchants carried on traffic between the Hindoos and the Egyptian women.

When the little corporal of Lodi crossed into Egypt to build by conquest the fabric of an oriental dream, well might his soul expand as he said: "Soldiers of France, from yonder pyramids forty centuries look down upon you!" Napoleon did not say anything of the mummies of illustrious females, through whose eyes, now empty, gluey sockets, once beamed the civilization of the world. Napoleon, like all warriors, held that only one function belonged to women—to bred men for the ranks. Some one asked him who was the greatest woman in France; he replied, "She who has borne the most children."

The women taught mankind to wear fine clothes. Adam was not made with breeches on. As a symbol of power, Eve was

VIII—21

entitled to them.   She was the controlling genius in Eden.   The devil knew which one to tempt.   Fine dressing was the first impulse to commerce.   Babylon, with her fifty miles of wall and her hundred gates of brass, her stately palaces and hanging gardens, was built by a woman.   Its fabrics of scarlet and fine linen, rich vestments and embroidery, were the handiwork of women.   Carthage was founded by a Phœnician woman, and the traders of that city used to transport the jewels and fabrics of the East to the barbarians of the West.

Sumptuary laws were passed against women.   In the time of Romulus women were forbidden to taste wine, and several husbands killed their wives for violating this custom.   The women, to be above suspicion, used to kiss every man who called on them.   If the Congressional Temperance Society will inaugurate that custom we will all join it.

The speaker proceeded to discuss the position of women in the Dark Ages, and the rise of chivalry.

Defenseless women were liable to be ravished by any robber ruffian who captured one.   To prevent this they were shut up in strong castles, where they were guarded from the spoiler. Afterward it was sufficient for any valiant chieftain to declare a woman under his protection, and that he would avenge any insult to her.   This gave rise to orders of chivalry and knighthood, and a woman might demand protection from any knight, and he was bound in honor to extend it to her.   The pride of the men being flattered by this tribute to their power, the sentiment of chivalry became enthusiastic.   The women cultivated their charms assiduously to make themselves objects of devotion.   They decorated their persons with costly ornaments and gave fresh encouragement to the hitherto persecuted peddlers.

The women had always been the chief patrons of the peddlers.   It makes a man aguish to see a peddler come to his house.   He always tries to send him off before his wife gets a glimpse of him.   If the biographies of all these strolling peddlers were written, I do not think a single example could be found where one had unpacked his bundle and showed his wares and fabrics in the presence of a woman without finding a purchaser.   The courage displayed by those strollers in those barbarous days appealed to woman's nobler feelings and excited her sympathy.   Women are never commonplace.   Most women, when they read the lives of old Jack Sheppard, Dare-Devil Dick, or John A. Murrell, wish that their husbands were just like these heroes. Every girl of sixteen, poetically inclined, wishes she was a bandit's bride. Desdemona married a negro because of the dangers he had incurred. The Sabine women so admired the pluck of their Roman ravishers that they pleaded for and remained with them. This heroic instinct caused the ladies to take the peddlers under the wings of their protection.

Costly fabrics and jewels from the farthest ends of the world were eagerly sought for, and every lord desired his lady to appear more beautiful than any other woman in the world, and was ready to run his sword through any man who doubted that she was the most beautiful: a kind of demonstration entirely satisfactory in those days and at this time. These ornaments were costly and could not be had unless paid for at great expense. Household expenditures increased fearfully. The barons could not afford to consume all their crude produce in supporting retainers; so the retainers were dismissed and the armies disbanded, and peace necessarily ensued. Thus the women of the middle ages instilled refinement and love of virtue and true valor into the men, built up society on a solid foundation, scattered the standing armies that filled every castle, gave an impetus to commerce, and established the arts of peace; for women, since the days of Delilah, have been averse to men's belligerent propensities.

Notwithstanding woman has been the lovely instrument through which civilization has been imparted to the world, she has received but little benefit from that civilization. From what is our system of housing and hampering women derived but the barbarous customs of duennas and eunuchs?

It is said that women do not ask to vote. Is that any reason why we should withhold from them a right which is a prime necessity with her? The Scripture teaches us to sit modestly down toward the foot of the table and wait to be invited up to a more honorable position.

Did the negroes ask to be emancipated? Take away the Freedman's Bureau to-day and leave to a vote of the people, white and black, and they would almost unanimously vote to reëstablish slavery. Social power and physical power control sentiments and expressions. The gentleman from Massachusetts [Nathaniel P. Banks] said wisely that universal suffrage would not make the South loyal, because the negroes would vote as the whites wished. Women do not ask to vote, because they know that they would be cried down as strong-minded. It is supposed that none but long-haired men and strong-minded women are in favor of this measure of justice. Therefore

women say they do not wish to vote.   They are afraid to kick
against the goads.

They are taught from childhood that they must be deceitful.
The whole system of their education leads them to suppression
of truth.   A woman's no proverbially means yes.   The first
deceit which a girl learns is the concealment of her age, preparing for future contingencies.   They know that men and owls
like spring chickens; and to cater to men's craving for tender
meat, girls never get older than sixteen.   If a well-bred girl is
asked to marry she invariably says, "No"; but her sweetheart
knows by her drooping eyes and heaving bosom that she means
yes.

There is a deep tragedy underlying most marriages, and that
is that prudent mothers bargain off their daughters for so many
shekels.   Women are an expensive and useless commodity which
must be disposed of to the best advantage.   Like oysters, they
cannot be kept fresh.   They must be sold in reasonable time
or pickled in vinegar.   This bartering of intelligent human
beings to the highest bidder is the case of bickerings and heart-
burnings, and unhappy homes.   This causes *ennui*, dissipation,
extravagance, and crime.

Women are repressed in every way.   They must follow certain fashions or they become the subjects of animadversion.
Their high aspirations are subdued by careful teaching.   The
mind of a woman is regarded as a secondary consideration.
The study of cosmetics engages her whole attention.   She learns
geography only at the watering places.   She learns French in
order to perplex the male sex by throwing gibberish in their
teeth.   She learns to soak lithographs in turpentine and daub
them over with variegated colors, not so brilliant as those of
the rainbow but much more solid, and then she asks you how
you like her painting.   She learns to make wax flowers, making
a wonderful improvement on nature, there being no withered
petals nor worm-eaten leaves in wax flowers.   She learns from
her botany that charming dialect known as the language of
flowers.   If you give a young lady a flower she invariably
blushes and asks you "Do you mean it?"

If in a pleasant walk through the woods on a May morning a
sweet nymph, over whose head thirty summers have shed their
brightness, should hand you a violet, she means that she is
too young to leave her mother.

If a buxom maid hands you a "touch-me-not" she intimates
that she is a frail thing, and mutely beseeches you not to crush
her.   If a laughing girl, with a rosy, pouting mouth, gives

you a tulip, she means "kiss me if you can"; and I would not give much for a man that could not.

The art of divination has always been appropriated by the women. The sibylline books were written by a woman. The oracle of Delphi was a woman. No astonishing occurrence was ever related to a woman that she did not invariably reply, "I told you so." Among the gypsies the women tell the fortunes. In the New England States a century ago nearly every door had a horseshoe nailed over it to guard it from the spells and enchantments of the old women who were regarded as witches. If a woman were old and ugly, this was *prima facie* evidence that she was a witch, and it required but an idiot's tale to send her to the gallows. Our Puritan forefathers were as merciless in exterminating old women as their descendants are in exterminating rebels.

I have enumerated some of the accomplishments of girls who are expected to move in good society. Their education teaches them deceit, seductiveness, and vanity. The idea of her being a helpmeet is long discarded by society. This idea must be generated by a higher civilization than we now enjoy. Women are, as a class, burdens on society. Their lives are devoted, not to high purposes or useful pursuits, but to creating a comeliness of person in themselves which will entice men of inflammatory feelings from the freedom of single blessedness. We are amazed at the harems of the East. We do not reflect that there may be harems with only one woman in them. When Artemus Ward was in Utah one of the elders died, and all his wives flocked around the waxworks man and besought him to marry them. He replied that they were pretty enough, and individually he would not object to marrying any of them, but that it was the muchness of the thing that he objected to. That is the difference between our system and that of the East. What baser prostitution than for a woman to marry a man for his money, when she had as lief take a toad in her bosom as to enfold her arms about him?

What spectacle more humiliating than to see, at a ball, young ladies sitting like "the four and twenty tailors, all in a row," decked in costly jewels and rich laces, eager as so many roaring lions seeking whom they may devour? Their dressing makes them caricatures on humanity. Fashion! What folly and misery does not that word invoke. Paris leads the fashion in dress and Eugénie leads the fashion in Paris. She is *passé*, therefore shall all Christendom wear large hoops; she has a bald spot on the crown of her head, therefore shall all

shave tonsures on their heads.   In the time of the elder Bonaparte there was great lack of population owing to the wars,
and all the energies of society were devoted to supplying the
deficiency.   It was the fashion for women to appear matronly,
so they stuffed their waists to attain fashionable proportions
and look as interesting as possible.   Now the women have a pro-
pensity for being squeezed in that locality—hence small waists.
What if our great grandmothers could walk out from their
pictures on the walls and appear in fashionable circles, would
not all the young ladies snicker and say, ''Grandmother, what
makes your waist so big; grandmother, what makes your hair so
prim; grandmother, what makes your back so straight?''   But
would not the old ladies be surprised in turn at the dress of
their great-granddaughters?   When they saw the long trails, the
tilting hoops, the embroidered petticoats, the laced waists, the
cotton busts, the red-topped boots, the sawdust legs, the rats and
mice and braids and crimps, the jet chains and frizzles; but,
above all, when the old ladies saw the wonderful waterfalls of
our girls they would go back into their pictures and giggle
forever.

I have briefly alluded to the position and aspirations of
women who are above want.   It is this class of well-bred fools
who do not wish to take upon themselves the burden of thinking.   Their first business is to catch husbands, or, if they have
succeeded, their lives are devoted to playing the part of namby-
pambies.   The mind demands some excitement, and, for want
of something sensible to entertain themselves, women fly to dissipation.   Some put in their time reading novels, others gad
around among their neighbors, and the majority, like Mrs.
Toodles, go to auction.   The subordinate position occupied by
old women is not a matter of surprise to me when I consider
how they are reared.

We laugh at women concealing their ages.   How heroically
they struggle to retain the only source of power left to them!
Gray hairs on a man's head are only the spring flowers of a
green old age, but on a woman's head they are the waifs of a
desert island, toward which she is irresistibly drifting; an island
bleak and barren and lonely.   Not for her the social converse,
not for her the power of intellect, not for her the pleasures of
literature; not for her the teachings of philosophy; she is a
dethroned queen, who must forever weep in the darkness of a
mental dungeon for the kingdom she has lost.

Our Puritan ancestors did practical charity to their grandmothers when they hung them as witches.

What shall we say of the condition of the lower million? While the upper ten need the ballot to teach them that they are mortal and are to be the helpmeets of men in politics as well as household affairs, the lower million need it to give them an equal chance with their fellow mortals in their life struggle, their labor for bread. All over the North we sing the plaintive strains of suffering negrodom, but the Song of the Shirt is not fashionable.

As population increases, some get rich, but the pauper class increases tenfold. In London live the merchant princes of the world in costly palaces; but in the dark alleys and squalid hovels, the garrets and cellars of that great human anthill, dwell a class of wretches who are walking illustrations of poverty, misery, and vice. We, too, have a pauper class growing up in the United States, which has been fearfully increased of late years by the calamities of war and the fluctuation of money values. Our pauper class must for two hundred years consist exclusively of women and invalids. The extent and cheapness of land are such that every able-bodied man can get good wages. The invalid can be supported by public charities. But who shall provide for poor women?

> "Old King Cole was a merry old soul,
>   A merry old soul was he,
>   He had a little girl and he kicked her out of doors
>   Because she was a *she!*"

What shall be done with the women? The world has been asking that question more than three thousand years. The answer might readily suggest itself. Let the women have an equal chance to take care of themselves. If they fail, then let us devise a means. Women have been bartered as merchandise, housed up in harems, made to perform such drudgery as men would not do, until men have an abiding faith in their own superiority in all lucrative employments. God made woman free and gave her the gift of understanding, and gave her hands to work. Let us not, out of an excess of love, tie her hands and let her starve.

An Irish farrier once sent a bill to Lord Donahue: "For doctoring your honor's mare to death, £3 5s." Are we not guarding the women to death? Ordinarily a woman has but one means of livelihood—that is her needle. Oh, the pains of stifled breasts and aching eyes and dizzy heads that daily ascend, a voiceless prayer of millions of sewing-women, to the throne of Him who created woman for some purpose. Think not that the dumb prayer of myriad aches is unheeded. A tree grows up in strength and beauty; a poisonous worm is gnawing at its roots; slowly will the tree wither, its leaves fall off, its fruit turn bitter, until at last it is dead as if blasted by the shivering stroke of a thunderbolt. We cannot violate the laws of nature with impunity. If women are raised higher or dragged lower than nature intended, evil must befall. Let one of my radical friends who is voting against women's franchise go out on Pennsylvania Avenue, and before he walks five squares he will see a Babylonian woman, dressed in scarlet and fine linen, and burned with fire more scorching than the blazing faggots of a Hindoo widow's pyre; a fire which corrodes the body and sears the soul; a fire which raged in Sodom and Gomorrah long before the skies rained brimstone, and before Lot's wife had crystallized into a salty monument of woman's curiosity.

These scarlet women are the holocausts of society. They are mostly uneducated. They have all been pretty girls, and have been innocent babes. Take one of the most depraved of these wretches and trace back her life, and you will probably find that it was not want of virtue but want of bread which dragged her down the fatal abyss of crime. The child has grown up and is left in the world with no capital but her beauty. Brainless and breadless she must henceforth do battle for herself. Bread alone does not satisfy; she must dress, for her business is to catch a man. Before she is aware of it she is in debt. Then the struggle and humiliation commence. There is no honest labor for her to do, but hard drudgery, poorly paid. The seducer comes to her with an offer of bread and clothes and undying love. In a fatal moment of weakness her virtue is conquered, and she submits to his embrace. She is henceforth to be banished from society, and rushes down to lower sinks of infamy, until the last step, where all good Christians consign her, to hell! Her seducer moves in good society, attends church, and marries and is an exemplary man in every way. Does it not strike you that there is something wrong somewhere?

If women were allowed to clerk in stores and perform any labor which they have the capacity to perform, there would be more independence among them, and they would be less subject to the temptations of evil. Virtue is instinctive with woman. When she falls, the blame, in nine cases out of ten, does not rest with herself. The question of the education and employment of women is one of the gravest in the world. On this question we are in the same condition which the barbarous ages left us.

I have shown you that the Radical party was a "whited sepulcher." That it had no republicanism in it; that it sought to enfranchise the negro for commercial and financial schemes. This will not satisfy the people. Woman suffrage is a grand principle pervading society in all its ramifications, and will increase in importance till the millennial day, when "seven women shall lay hold of one man."

What harm will it do to allow women to vote? Those who do not choose to vote may remain at home. I have been told that this would corrupt society and make women rude. Is there anything corrupting in a man's going to the polls with his wife and his daughters, and all of them putting their ballots into a box? The very fact that women were to be at the polls would close every drinking saloon and keep every community orderly on that day. Women attend Fourth of July orations and public speaking in every decent community, and if there is any person who forgets the proprieties that are due to their presence there are twenty stalwart arms to put him out or take him to jail.

Can Charles Sumner consistently ask for the enfranchisement of the negroes when a majority of the adult citizens of Massachusetts of sound mind and good character are disfranchised? The election of two negroes to the legislature of Massachusetts does not wipe out the stain from her escutcheon. And who are the disfranchised? The gamblers? No. The drinkers of whiskey? No. The smokers and chewers of tobacco? No. The criminals and convicts? No. The politicians and other vagrant non-producers? No. It is the frugal, industrious, and virtuous class which is disfranchised.

We are asked to disfranchise the white rebel because he is an aristocrat, and to enfranchise the negro to break down this aristocracy. But the aristocratic manufacturer of Massachusetts, who sports a gold-headed cane and wears a broadcloth coat with a tail much resembling a codfish, shall vote, while the poor factory girl who wears her life away with dreary, unpromoted toil has no voice in the Government.

The husband and wife are one in law, and he is that one, her lord and master. He may give her a thrashing every morning, and, if arrested and tried for beating her, he pleads *molliter manus imposuit*,[1] and comes clear, for she is his slave in law. She may be intelligent and thrifty, striving hard to earn a

[1] "He has laid his hand on lightly."

livelihood for her children, whom, under no circumstances, can a mother abandon. But her drunken sot of a husband can drive her about from pillar to post and prevent anyone from even giving her shelter. How often do we see the advertisements in the newspapers, "I warn all persons not to harbor my wife"? If she works hard to accumulate property or earn a support for herself and her children, he must take the proceeds, for he is entitled to her wages, and money paid to her without his authority is no payment in law. She cannot dispose of her separate property, make a will, nor even a dying donation without his written consent. These barbarous statute laws are being modified in some States, but are not the social laws against women still more oppressive?

In no State are the statute laws as liberal toward women as they should be. Why? Look at the materials of which elections are composed! The saloon influence is the acknowledged strongest power in every community. Look at the workings of that influence (always hating and hated by women) in the last election. The Radicals had the money. They held the public offices and were supported by all the moneyed powers in the North. A Radical canvasser buys half a gallon of radical whiskey (which has paid a radical tax for the distillery of two dollars per gallon for the whiskey, and is, notwithstanding this tax, sold at $1.75 per gallon, radical poison); with this bottled lightning he drenches the voter, and this sovereign and lord of creation goes reeling up to the polls as drunk as a fiddler's dog, to vote "according to the spirit that is in him." Do you not think his poor starving wife could vote as wisely?

You shut woman out from all the easy and honorable ways of earning a livelihood. If a woman is highly educated she may teach school; if not, she must be a sewing-woman, a beer-jerker, or a harlot! If she clerks in a store she is an exception, and must meet the scornful criticism of the world. Nice young men, counter-jumpers, the tulips and daisies of society, who labor under the heavy responsibility of supporting small mustaches, are the proper persons to measure ribbon, sell hose, and corsets, and vote! How many sunny-haired girls grow up to find that their freedom of labor is curtailed, their ambition hopeless? They find it necessary to cultivate the baser and more artful part of their natures in order to catch a man. She must have a man to protect her from that beast of prey called society. Whence arises this dread among women of becoming old maids? They are willing to mate themselves with men far inferior to them in every way. Many a woman of genius, whose heart beat high with ambition, has examined, in the agony of her slavery, "Oh, that I were a man!"

If a poor man has a family of daughters, his life is a misery to him, and his heart aches when he asks himself, "What will become of my children when I die?" The wealthiest men in the land have commenced life as poor boys. Every young man has a fair prospect for a fortune; but what woman ever made a fortune, or ever rose by her own exertion from poverty, except by the wages of sin?

But we are told to wait. This will complicate questions. What more simple than to follow a principle to its corollaries? It is said that woman suffrage will bring odium on negro suffrage! Have the women got so low down in the scale of humanity that their privileges would bring odium upon the enjoyment of the same privileges by the untutored African? If so, shame upon this barbarous people who have reduced them! Why should we wait? There are thousands of women, widows and orphans of men who have fallen in battle, starving and freezing for want of the ballot. There are thousands of virtuous women who are on the brink of crime for want of bread. There are thousands who are now in the meshes of Satan and cry loudly for help; for bread! Why wait and refuse to discuss measures when such grave results hang upon the issue?

It would be superfluous to discuss woman's capacity to vote. She is the natural superior of man in every way. A poet says of nature:

> "Her 'prentice han' she tried on man,
> And then she made the lasses O."

I grant that she is not now as intellectual as man. She has not the education. She has never been taught to think. The women know as much about law as the majority of doctors; and much more about medicine than lawyers. What lawyer could have ever invented catnip tea?

Let us allow women the chance to use their learning and they will soon become educated. Let us allow women to be useful to themselves and to society and they will cease to be so helpless and will be more courted. Why is it that a barbarian woman is a subject of purchase, the man being willing to trade his cattle or his other goods for a wife? It is because they are useful. Why is it that, when society has become civilized, every inducement and penalty is needed to force men to marry, and women are willing and anxious to marry without?

Why is it that with the increase and wealth of a country woman only becomes more burdensome on society? The new demands for labor springing out of the diversification and division of labor find no place and offer no wages to woman. Men's wages increase, but women are still helpless burdens on the community. In my district this is not the case. We have not only the prettiest girls in the world but the most useful women. The men find great difficulty in getting married, for the girls are independent and can earn a livelihood without marrying.

But look around in your cities and you will see a great contrast. There the women are like ravenous wolves or cunning man-traps. A man has to "bevare of the vidders!" A poor man is in continual trepidation lest he should fascinate one of them. If he is married he brings his nose to the grindstone. She can be of no earthly use to him in business, her ideas run in a different current from his, and she can have no social relations to him except to ask him the news and detail to him the gossip and slander of the day.

I know that success in my undertaking to enfranchise the women is not likely. The gentleman from Pennsylvania [Thaddeus Stevens]—the modern sea-green incorruptible—is an old bachelor. He knows that if women were in power the scepter would pass from Israel. When the great archangel of radicalism is hostile to the female cause, what may we expect of his imps?

Then the clerks in cities who compose the voting class will be hostile to this measure. If women were allowed to clerk in stores these counter-jumpers would lose their places. They fear the competition. The saloon influence, the strongest power in the land, is hostile to woman suffrage. A woman whose husband and sons have been poisoned would not show much quarter to the dealer of poisons. As long as the men vote right the women would be slow to obtrude themselves upon the public. But in great public emergencies they would step forward and save the nation.

When France was beleaguered by foes and was about to fall under the dominion of a foreign scepter, the dark-eyed Maid of Orleans buckled on her armor and headed her nation's hosts and saved her country. And at a later day, when terror reigned in the republic, and a radical party, drunk with blood, had struck down religion and law, when every fireside was invaded, and the busy guillotine chopped off the heads of conservatives all day and all night, day after day, until men were struck dumb with fear, the blue-eyed Maid of Caen came down to

Paris, and Charlotte Corday struck her dagger to the heart of the chief of the infernal triumvirate and turned back the red waves of the surging revolution. Women are timid and averse to destroying anything; but when danger is so great that the stoutest hearts of men are appalled a woman's courage rises to the full height of her divine nature, and she is always ready to sacrifice herself for the good of others.

Let me say generally that men are fast losing sight of the great principles of patriotism and justice. They are generally controlled by implacable hatred and prejudice or by sectional selfishness and greed. Women could not do half so badly as the men.

Though I have no hope of practical results from this Congress, I confidently expect that the Forty-first Congress will come here pledged to give the women their rights. If the prominent women of the United States withdraw their support from the Radical party, it will fall, to rise no more. If you provoke opposition from such women as Mrs. Mott, Mrs. Stanton, Anna Dickinson, Lucy Stone, and Fannie Gage, they will drive your radical orators from every stump in the North. Who get up your organizations and societies; who raise your funds; who get up your sanitary fairs? The women! It was through them that millions of dollars have been raised for the men of the Radical party to spend. I tell you, gentlemen, that every woman of talent throughout the North is impressed with the conviction that she is injured by this forced repression and social ostracism. These ladies say truthfully that genius and talent have no sex.

Intelligence is gradually restoring to women the rights that are withheld from her by force. The world is fast learning that war costs more than peace. The gentleman from Minnesota [William Windom] demonstrated to us that it cost this Government over two million dollars to kill an Indian, and with that amount we could support the whole Indian race for a longer time than it takes to make the longest campaign. Killing is the most costly amusement which mankind enjoys. Let the women vote and we will have no more war. A woman would bear a great deal before she would plunge the country into war, for she is more injured by war than any other portion of society. Among the Romans the women were not taxed for war debts. On one occasion, in a great distress for money, a tax was laid upon the property of women. Hortensia and four thousand Roman matrons appealed to the prætor. She made a speech against war, and against the injustice of taxing women for war, that has come down in history as a remarkable piece of eloquence. The prætor struck women's names from the tax list.

The women are oppressed because they have submitted without a murmur. But that time is now past, and from this time on this question will be agitated. Our forefathers submitted to the imposition of unjust taxation without representation until the burdens became so onerous that they passed non-intercourse resolutions and threw off the yoke of Great Britain. Let the women imitate our forefathers and have nothing to do with men who deny them their rights, and these self-constituted lords of creation will soon be humbled as the British lion was.

CONSTITUTIONAL RIGHT OF WOMEN TO VOTE

Upon the passage of the Fifteenth Amendment it was claimed by many woman suffragists that under the Constitution, fortified by this amendment, women could claim the right to vote.

On December 19, 1870, Mrs. Victoria C. Woodhull, of New York City, presented a petition to Congress claiming her right to vote under the Constitution in general and this amendment in particular, and asking that proper legislation be enacted to enable women to exercise this right.

The memorial . . . showeth . . . that she is a citizen of New York and the United States, over 21 years of age; that since the adoption of the fifteenth article of amendments to the Constitution neither the State of New York, nor any other State, nor any Territory has passed any law to deny or abridge the right of any citizen of the United States to vote, as established by the said article, neither on account of sex or otherwise; that nevertheless the right to vote is denied to women citizens of the United States by the operation of election laws in the several States and Territories which were enacted prior to the adoption of the said fourteenth and fifteenth articles, and which are inconsistent with the Constitution, as amended by them, and therefore the said laws are void and of no effect, but which, being still enforced by the said States and Territories, render the Constitution inoperative as regards the right of women citizens to vote; and whereas article six, section two, declares "that the Constitution and the laws of the United States which shall be made in pursuance thereof, and all treaties made

and which shall be made under the authority of the United
States, shall be the supreme law of the land; and the judges in
every State shall be bound thereby, anything in the constitution or laws of any State to the contrary notwithstanding";
and whereas no distinction between citizens is made in the Constitution of the United States on account of sex, but as the fourteenth article of amendments to it provides that "no State shall
make or enforce any law which shall abridge the privileges or
immunities of citizens of the United States"; "nor deny to any
person within its jurisdiction the equal protection of the laws";
and whereas Congress has power "to make laws which shall be
necessary and proper for carrying into execution all powers
vested by the Constitution in the Government of the United
States," and to make or alter all regulations in regard to the
times and manner of holding elections for Senators and Representatives, and especially to enforce by appropriate legislation
the provisions of the said fourteenth article; and whereas the
continuance of the enforcement of said local election laws denying and abridging the right of citizens to vote on account of
sex is a grievance to your memorialist and to various other citizens of the United States being women; therefore, your memorialist would respectfully petition your honorable bodies to make
such law as in the wisdom of Congress shall be necessary and
proper for carrying into execution the right vested by the Constitution in the citizens of the United States to vote without
regard to sex.

The memorial was tabled. Mrs. Woodhull became a
candidate for President in 1872.

On January 18, 1872, Henry Wilson [Mass.] introduced in the Senate a bill to give women the right to
vote and to hold office in the Territories. It was referred
to the Committee on Territories.

On February 17 George F. Hoar [Mass.] presented
in the House a memorial from Lucy Stone, president of
the American Woman Suffrage Association; Julia Ward
Howe, chairman of the executive committee, and other
officers, praying that the right to vote and hold office
be granted to women in the District of Columbia, and
that an amendment to the Constitution be made to prohibit political distinctions on account of sex throughout
the Union. Among the officers of the association may be
mentioned Thomas Wentworth Higginson, Mary A. Liv-

ermore, George William Curtis, George W. Julian, William Lloyd Garrison, James Freeman Clarke, and Moses Coit Tyler.

On May 20, 1872, Stevenson Archer [Md.] made an extended speech in the House against woman suffrage, which is notable in that it recommends and, to a certain extent, records, an organized movement among women against the grant of suffrage to their sex.

The Reaction from Woman Suffrage

Stevenson Archer, M.C.

The advocates of woman suffrage say that woman will go forth from her home panoplied in purity, and after correcting the political evils of the day will bring back with her all the domestic virtues unsullied. A most preposterous proposition, carrying absurdity on its face, even if history did not give it, a thousand times, the lie direct. The political corruptions that defile our fair land cannot be exorcised by the enchantment of woman's smile or by the magic of her touch. It might as well be affirmed that Proserpine was not polluted by being carried off to the infernal regions; that not a smirch befouled her snowy robe or her damask cheek during all the long time she abode in that smoky prison house of dismal horrors. This rape was a grievous blow to her mother Ceres, who dearly loved her daughter. She sought her in vain all over Sicily, and when night came she relighted Mount Etna, which had become extinct, and by its glare continued her search throughout the world. So shall disconsolate Virtue in our land grieve for the loss of her daughters; and she, too, shall search in vain to find them as they were. She, too, will relight the great mountain torch of Christianity, which shall by that time be quite extinguished; and it may be that by its light she will be able to find what Ceres found, her daughter's veil (that is, her modesty) torn and rent; and she may also meet with a Hecate, as Ceres did, to tell her the dreadful secret that the devil had her daughter in his keeping. Ceres, who had the earth in her special care, smote it with barrenness and desolation, so that it should yield no more until her child should be restored to her arms. And just so, as long as our women shall remain groping in the tainted atmosphere of politics and unrestored to weeping virtue, the delicious fruits of domestic peace and happiness will be denied us;

the homes of America will, indeed, be as barren places, and so must remain, for there will be no redemption; that of the cross will have failed, and there is no other. As the great Maro sang:

"Facilis descensus Averni;
Sed revocare gradum, superasque evadere ad auras,
Hoc opus, hic labor est;"

which, freely translated, means, "It is easy enough to go down into hell; but to get back—there's the rub!"

But there is still a class of women who are as much more worthy as they are now more numerous than the other two classes, and who will make a noble struggle against the ruinous innovation; such a struggle as shall deserve a better fate than failure; yet fail it will in spite of all that can be done. A time will come when there will be but one thing remaining to be done to save the country; no, not to save it, but to prolong for a little while its wretched existence. That one thing will be that these women who have so long kept away from the pollution of the hustings shall march up at last and deposit their votes, and counteract the pernicious effects produced by the votes of a million women, who by this time, wholly unchristianized themselves, will be doing all they can to unchristianize the entire people. And when this noble class are once forced from the cradle and hearth into publicity and kept there, their career from that time forth must inevitably be down, down. These descending steps are as easy to imagine from what has gone before as they would be sad to trace.

It is impossible to read the vile talk of the present advocates of woman suffrage in their conventions, or to pursue the vile writing in any one of their numerous ably conducted journals, and not conclude—and that without the least hesitation—that the constant tendency of their teachings is to undermine Christianity. The *Women's Journal* says that the Young Women's Christian Association of Massachusetts are the right wing of the woman suffrage army. When Wendell Phillips wound up one of his peace-making speeches with the gentle expression, "God damn the Commonwealth of Massachusetts!" because that State for once would not chime in with some of his lovely schemes, that well-known woman's rights advocate, Lydia M. Child, clapped him so vehemently that she broke her wedding ring. And Mrs. Elizabeth Cady Stanton, who relates the delicate incident in *The Revolution*, says that such an oath is not one iota more objectionable than to say, "By George!" and that even her own sweet and gentle nature is often so deeply stirred by the wrongs of her sex that to think "damn it!" is no unusual thing with her.

Hear also the language of yet another of their leading organs, and while you tremble for your country and for Christianity shudder at the shocking sentiment: "When all the women are Victoria Woodhulls, and all the men Theodore Tiltons, then, and not till then, will the millennium have arrived." Why, if we knew nothing of the precedents of this precious pair, the single fact that the she-male's biography of the he-male was lately suppressed in Germany for its unendurable nastiness should be enough to damn them both with all decent people. That biography was such a mass of moral putrefaction, from cover to cover, that it was feared it might contaminate the whole German Empire. And this same Victoria Woodhull is the woman's candidate for the presidency of the United States!

The dissolution of the marriage relations at the pleasure or caprice of either party is openly advocated by these revolutionists, and this alone would wipe out the Christian religion from the face of the earth. Just such looseness of the marriage tie did more to destroy Rome than all the Goths and Huns that ever swooped down upon her with fire and sword.

This laxity of the marriage bond is a necessary result of the woman's rights movement, and would soon evolve itself out of that movement without any special advocacy of it in the revolutionary journals and speeches. For what man would bind himself to dwell for life beneath the same roof with a masculine woman?

But perhaps the most melancholy effect of such a state of things is yet to be told. The children—Heaven pity the children when "free love" shall hold high carnival over this land! —boys and girls alike will then have no kind hand to guide them. The father will care not for them, for he cannot know which are his, and which are some other man's. The mother will be mostly from home, at the hustings, drinking, swearing, and brawling. The children will give full head to their instincts and do whatever sin they please, whatever their natural depravity, let loose and spurred on by passion, shall prompt them. The family will have become, in fact, a family of mere animals. That institution which is the foundation of society and of the State—the only foundation on which either can ever rest secure—will be uprooted, and the whole social and political superstructure must fall in hideous ruin. The family is to civilization and Christianity what the Coliseum, according to the old prediction, was to Rome:

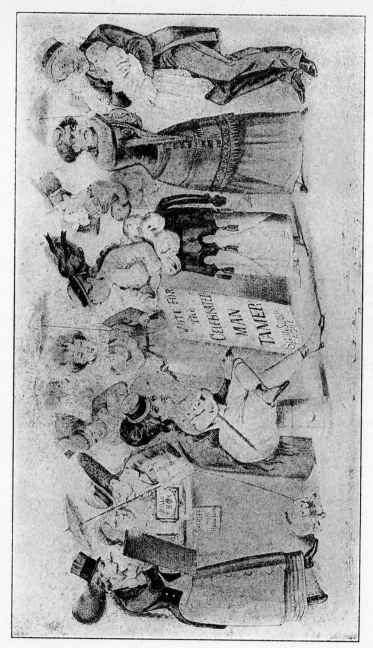

THE AGE OF BRASS

From the collection of the New York Historical Society

"While stands the Coliseum, Rome shall stand;
When falls the Coliseum, Rome shall fall;
And when Rome falls—the world."

These deluded women are exceedingly fond of quoting Plato's "Commonwealth" to prove their position. Well, let them accept the conditions he prescribes. Let woman go forth to the bloody field conquering and to conquer. Let us have modern Semiramises and Zenobias. Let her, if she so elect, imitate that Amazon queen Penthesilea, who, with more valor than discretion, essayed to cope in mortal strife with the terrible Achilles under the walls of Troy, and paid the forfeit of her life.

But these women have no notion of going to war. Not they! They say over and over again that the good Lord has in his infinite wisdom (and mercy they might well add) so constituted them that they are wholly unfit for the hardships and perils of horrid war. Oh, no, not that; anything but that. They will send forth (and will do it cheerfully) their fathers and husbands and sons, when danger threatens the dear country, but themselves will stay at home and vote, and manage the entire governmental machinery. And here would, indeed, be presented an anomaly in government. Not only would those who had charge of the affairs of the nation be wholly unrepresented in the army sent forth to defend that nation, but it would otherwise be to the eternal interest of those governing, since they would have no dangers to encounter, to bring on a war whenever they wished to get into power; and, worse still, it would be to their interest to keep that war up until enough men were killed to enable them to carry all the elections, and so continue in power.

Moreover, it is a well-known fact that even now when a nation becomes involved in war the women are the last to give up, although it rends their very heart-strings to lose those dear to them. The nation which should go to war with women swaying the councils and men alone in the field, where would be the end of bloodshed? It would be the Kilkenny cats tragedy acted over again. Now, although I have never heard the sex of those famous cats explicitly and authoritatively stated in any official report of the battle, yet the universal opinion has gone abroad that they were male cats; and it is my firm conviction that they would never have fought that terrible battle—ending, as we all know, in two pitiful tails—had not the female cats been inciting them on.

There is an instance in our own history to which these

women often point with a triumphant air as a precedent for extending suffrage to their sex. The instance is the extension of suffrage to the women in New Jersey in the year 1790. This privilege remained with them from that time until 1807. The newly enfranchised, however, voted on but three occasions during that period. How many on the first two of these occasions availed themselves of the hitherto masculine prerogative does not, so far as I can learn, appear outside the unpublished records. The last occasion, however, was too memorable a one not to be transmitted to us in all its novel particulars; and it is as instructive as memorable. In the last-named year a vote of the people of Essex County was taken on the question of erecting a new courthouse and jail. Whether or not all the women turned out may be judged of by the fact that the female vote cast exceeded alone the whole lawful vote of both sexes in the county. The men, if we may judge by the sequel, were very much alarmed as well as disgusted; for the cowardly and ungracious monsters enacted a bill at the very next session of the legislature restricting the right of suffrage forever thereafter to "free white male citizens," and the New Jersey women kept mum on the sore subject of politics thenceforth for half a century. While the strong-minded of the present day frequently cite the above instance of the enfranchisement of their sex, with the view of influencing public opinion in their favor, they always fail to add that the right was abrogated by reason of the disgraceful conduct of those on whom it had been conferred.

Now, if women could virtually stuff ballot boxes in deciding such a trivial question as the building of a jail or courthouse, and that, too, right at the beginning of the movement, when it is fairly presumable they were on their best behavior, as everyone promoted to a new and untried situation is, or ought to be, the question arises, what infamous practices would they not be capable of when momentous issues were at stake, and when after a little while their modesty should have been entirely and hopelessly deflowered by being jostled throughout long and bitter campaigns, by the hard-fisted "roughs," and the unscrupulous and veteran tricksters whom they must needs encounter at every turn, and from whom they would soon take lessons in the exquisite art of low intrigues and barefaced bribery?

Let deluded woman beware how she comes down from that lofty pedestal which she now occupies, how she casts off the almost celestial garments in which her weakness and her virtue, the only sure guaranties of his love and protection, have clothed her in the eyes of man. Let her beware how she comes down from that proud position, and, standing on the same level with man in all things, challenges him to a contest for supremacy. As a mere animal he is the stronger, and in such a struggle as that she must go to the wall. She can rule him now and do with him even as she will, always with the proviso that she keep within that sphere to which revelation and her own nature assign her. Let her reflect that man when in that primitive state to which her rebellion from this sphere will bring them both again becomes not only an animal but a savage animal. Let her contemplate the indescribably wretched condition of the Comanche squaw.

Let each true woman of the nation exert herself and avert the impending danger. Nor, in order to do so, need she leave for a single moment her proud throne—for proud it is, though seemingly so humble—beside the hearthstone, from which, knowingly or not, she rules her little world. And inasmuch as the great world is made up of such little worlds, the true women already rule that great world, and this, too, while they keep politics afar. May it ever be so! But, that it may, let them not be idle; let them make known throughout the length and breadth of the land, not only the vast majority of their numbers over the innovators, but let them, in the modest way that they know so well, put forth their sentiments in language so plain that he who runs may read, and particularly the demagogue who "runs" for an office, and is perhaps at this very moment currying favor with the strong-minded sisterhood, telling them how he will favor them now if they will but do the same for him when they shall have been enfranchised by his aid. Let them write, and scatter abroad in the land, words of such burning eloquence as shall make him—yes, hardened demagogue though he is—tremble in his shoes and think again before he sells his influence to the devil. Let them write such words, too, as shall make the soft-shell wing of the woman suffrage party (those who sympathize with the movement but remain decently at home —there is no penetrable point in the hard-shell portion) blush that they should ever have favored their erring sisters, even in thought.

That there are true women among us who can write thus effectively is proved by the following memorial presented about a year ago to the legislature of Ohio, as an antidote to one of the opposite stamp:

"We acknowledge no inferiority to men. We claim to have no less ability to perform the duties which God has imposed upon us than they have to perform those imposed upon them.

"We believe that God has wisely and well adapted each sex to the proper performance of the duties of each.

"We believe our trusts to be as important and as sacred as any that exist on earth.

"We feel that our present duties fill up the whole measure of our time and ability, and that they are such as none but ourselves can perform.

"Their importance requires us to protest against all efforts to compel us to assume the obligations which cannot be separated from suffrage, but which cannot be performed by us without the sacrifice of the highest interests of our families and of society.

"It is our fathers, brothers, husbands, and sons who represent us at the ballot box. Our fathers and brothers love us. Our husbands are our choice, and one with us. Our sons are what we make them.

"We are content that they represent us in the cornfield, the battle-field, and at the ballot box; and we represent them in the schoolroom, at the fireside, and at the cradle, believing our representation even at the ballot box to be thus more full and impartial than it could possibly be were all women allowed to vote.

"We do, therefore, respectfully protest against any legislation to establish 'woman suffrage' in our land or in any part of it."

So long as our women shall stand upon such a platform as that there is hope for the country. Demagogues may agitate, traitors may plot, usurpers triumph for a little season; corruptions may eat up much of her substance; but her million homes linked together in the triple bonds of purity, virtue, and a common Christianity are a million imperishable points whence shall go forth, at all times and in all seasons, an influence that shall preserve the whole social, political, and religious fabric from destruction.

Apropos of the allusion of Mr. Archer to the voting of the women of New Jersey, it is in place here to cite a later petition to Congress by Mary E. Walker, M.D.

Petition of Dr. Walker

Whereas the women of New Jersey exercised the rights, duties, and privileges of the elective franchise before the Constitution of the United States was adopted, and continued to exercise the same until 1844, long after the framers of the Constitution as well as the adopters were all dead, clearly proving that the fathers intended to make this country a *perfect* republic instead of a *limited* one: Therefore,

Your memorialist, in behalf of the women citizens of the United States, asks your honorable body to pass the following bill to protect women citizens from State laws that are clearly in conflict with the Constitution of the United States of America.

BILL TO PROTECT WOMAN IN HER FRANCHISE

Be it enacted by the Senate and House of Representatives of the United States in Congress assembled. That the penalties made and provided for the hindering or preventing men citizens from the free exercise of the elective franchise on election days shall be in full force in regard to women citizens in all the States and Territories of the United States.

MARY E. WALKER, M.D.

WASHINGTON, D. C., *January* 15, 1877.

CHAPTER X

WOMAN SUFFRAGE

[RECENT DEBATES]

Status of Woman Suffrage in the Various States—Resolutions for Woman Suffrage Amendment to the Constitution Submitted in the House by John E. Raker [Cal.], A. W. Lafferty [Ore.], Edward T. Taylor [Col.], Victor L. Berger [Wis.], *et al.;* Referred to Committee on Judiciary, Consisting of Henry D. Clayton [Ala.], Chairman, Martin W. Littleton [N. Y.], Edwin W. Higgins [Conn.], John W. Davis [W. Va.], *et al.*— Debate in the Committee Hearing: in Favor of the Resolution, Miss Jane Addams [Ill.], Miss Leonora Reilly [N. Y.], Mr. Raker, Mrs. Jean Nelson Penfield [N. Y.], Mr. Taylor, Mr. Lafferty, Mrs. William Kent [Cal.], Mrs. Ida Husted Harper [N. Y.], Mr. Berger, Miss Mary E. McDowell [Ill.], Miss Caroline A. Lowe [Mo.], James L. Laidlaw [N. Y.], Mrs. Elsie Cole Phillips [Wis.]; Opposed, Mrs. Grace Duffield Goodwin [D. C.], Miss Ella C. Bréhaut [D. C.], Mrs. Francis W. Goddard [Col.], Judge Moses Hallett [Col.].

IN many States of the Union a limited suffrage has been exercised for some time by women. As far back as 1838 Kentucky gave school suffrage to widows with children of school age. In 1861 Kansas gave it to all women, and her example was followed: in 1875, by Michigan and Minnesota; in 1876, by Colorado; in 1878, by New Hampshire and Oregon; in 1879, by Massachusetts; in 1880, by New York, Mississippi, and Vermont; in 1883, by Nebraska, and in 1887 by North Dakota, South Dakota, Montana, Arizona and New Jersey. In 1891 school suffrage was given to women by Illinois; in 1893, by Connecticut; in 1894, by Ohio. In 1894 Iowa gave bond suffrage to women. In 1897 Kansas granted municipal suffrage to women. In 1898 Delaware gave school suffrage to tax-paying women; Louisiana gave to the same class the right to vote upon all questions submitted

345

to taxpayers, and Minnesota gave women the right to vote for library trustees. In 1900 Wisconsin gave women school suffrage. In 1901 New York gave tax-paying women in all towns and villages the right to vote on questions of local taxation. Kansas gave bond suffrage to women in 1903. In 1907 the new State of Oklahoma continued school suffrage to women, already granted in the Territory. In 1908 Michigan gave all women who pay taxes the right to vote upon questions of local taxation and the granting of franchises. In 1910 New Mexico gave school suffrage to women. On July 1, 1913, an act of the legislature of Illinois went into effect giving women the right to vote for Presidential electors and statutory officers.

Women are equal guardians with the fathers over their children in Colorado, Connecticut, District of Columbia, Illinois, Iowa, Kansas, Kentucky, Maine, Massachusetts, Minnesota, Nebraska, New Hampshire, New York, Oregon, Pennsylvania, and Washington. The guardianship laws of Utah and Idaho, although not equal by express definition, are practically so interpreted.

Full Suffrage to Women

In nine States women have full suffrage: Wyoming, Colorado, Idaho, Utah, Washington, California, Arizona, Kansas, and Oregon. In token of this fact the flag of the woman suffrage movement in the United States bears nine stars, each of which has been added upon a new State granting the suffrage.

Wyoming is the pioneer equal suffrage State in America, full political equality having been the basis of its government as long as it has had a government at all. The words "equal rights" form the motto on its State seal. The very first legislative council, after its organization as a Territory, passed, in 1869, a bill providing that women should have the same rights as men to vote and hold office, and when it was admitted as a State in 1890, before any other State had given women the vote, equal suffrage was made a part of its constitution.

During the early days of woman's enfranchisement in Wyoming several attempts were made at securing a repeal, but they all failed. At the time statehood was applied for a determined opposition was made in Congress to the admission of a Territory with a woman

THE WOMAN TRUMPETER

By courtesy of the " Woman's Political Union," New York City

suffrage clause in its constitution. So violent was the feeling that the territorial delegate in Congress, Joseph M. Carey, afterward governor of the State, telegraphed the legislature that he feared statehood would not be granted if the suffrage clause were not abandoned. The legislature, which was then in session, telegraphed back: "We will remain out of the Union a hundred years rather than come in without woman suffrage."

During the forty-three years that the measure has been in effect every governor has testified to its good effects, including the territorial governors, who are appointed by the President and are not, therefore, dependent upon votes.

In 1893, and again in 1899, the House of Representatives adopted resolutions declaring that woman suffrage had been an unmixed advantage to the State. In 1901 the legislature as a whole unanimously adopted similar resolutions and added an appeal to other States to adopt the measure as one tending toward the amelioration of all evil social conditions.

It has been repeatedly stated by various officials that from 80 per cent. to 90 per cent. of the women eligible cast their ballots.

Though eligible to all offices few women in Wyoming have held the higher positions. One woman has served as a member of the House of Representatives in the legislature, and numbers as state superintendent of schools, county clerk, recorder, treasurer, etc., and as justices of the peace. In territorial days women served very generally on juries—to the satisfaction of the judges, who expressed their opinions on such service. Later the practice fell into disuse through the desire of a chief justice that women be not interfered with in the performance of domestic duties. However, women are still summoned in special cases.

It is claimed that women have exerted considerable influence upon legislation in Wyoming. They have helped to secure measures making gambling illegal; giving women absolute rights over their own property; providing that men and women teachers shall receive equal pay for equal work; raising the age of protection of young girls to 18; providing penalties for child neglect, abuse, or cruelty; forbidding the employment of children in certain industries; making it unlawful to give or sell liquor or tobacco to children; establishing kindergartens and a State industrial school; providing for the care of dependent children and infirm, indigent, or incompetent persons; making State pure food regulations conform with the national law; and providing for the initiative and referendum, the commission form of government, direct primaries, accounting for campaign expenses on the part of candidates for political offices, and the headless ballot.

COLORADO conferred suffrage upon women in 1893 by

enactment of a law which was submitted to the voters and carried by a majority of only a little over 6,000. In 1890, after women had been exercising the privilege for seven years, the measure carried as a constitutional amendment by a majority of 17,000. From 75 to 85 per cent. of the women eligible to vote exercise the franchise.

In 1899 the Colorado legislature passed, by a vote of 45 to 3 in the House and 30 to 1 in the Senate, a resolution declaring that during the time that equal suffrage had been in operation women had used the vote as generally as men, with the result that better candidates had been selected for office, election methods had been purified, and the character of legislation improved, civic intelligence increased, and womanhood developed; and recommending the adoption of the measure by all the States and Territories of the Union.

Women have held office more extensively in Colorado than in any of the other suffrage States. From 1900 to 1912 from one to four women have served in each legislature, and on one occasion a woman Representative distinguished herself by acting as Speaker of the House during a stormy session that would have confused any but the most expert parliamentarian. The report of the investigation into the workings of equal suffrage in Colorado by Dr. Helen Sumner states that the women members have averaged above the men members in intelligence, although there has never been a woman member who equaled the most brilliant man, and that the character of the legislation which they have introduced has averaged higher than that introduced by the men. Most of them have been married women or widows with grown or half-grown children.

From the first year of their eligibility women have held the office of State superintendent of schools. Dr. Sumner says: "The women who have held the office of State superintendent of public instruction in Colorado have made better records than the men who formerly held the office."

The offices of county superintendent of schools usually go to women, and women are frequently elected

county clerks, treasurers, coroners, assessors, clerks of
district and county court, auditors, etc. They also hold
several city offices. They are eligible to sit on juries, but
it has never become customary to impanel them except
in special cases.

Women have been able to influence legislation extensively, despite, it is alleged, the opposition to the
measures proposed by them on the part of certain powerful commercial interests that dominate the political
life of the State. Their most notable achievement was
the retention in office of Judge Ben B. Lindsey, of the
Denver Juvenile Court, when both political parties were
arrayed against him.

Their influence as voters has been largely instrumental in securing measures making mothers joint guardians with the fathers over their children; raising the
age of protection of young girls to 18; establishing a
juvenile court; making parents responsible for the of-
fenses of delinquent children when they have by neglect
or any other cause contributed to such delinquency;
forbidding the employment of children in certain industries; making the wife the head of the family in cases
where she provides the principal support; providing for
supervision of lying-in hospitals and maternity homes
conducted by private individuals; compelling men to
support their families and making wife-desertion a felony; providing penalties for the punishment of male and
female procurers; making it a felony for any person
under 18 to work as a servant or employee in any house
of ill-fame; making immoral solicitation a felony; imposing heavy penalties upon men for living upon the earnings of immoral women; forbidding the insuring of the
lives of children under ten years; establishing State
parental schools; establishing a State home for dependent children, two of the five members of the board to
be women; requiring that at least three of the six members of the board of county visitors shall be women;
establishing a State industrial home for girls, three of
the five members of the board to be women; requiring
one woman physician on the board of the insane asylum;

providing for the care of the feeble-minded; making' father and mother joint heirs of a deceased child; establishing a State traveling library commission to consist of five women from the Colorado Federation of Women's Clubs, to be appointed by the governor; prohibiting the gift or sale of cigarettes to children; prohibiting the sale of opium; making employers liable for industrial accidents; removing the emblems from the Australian ballot (an approach to an educational qualification for voting); establishing the indeterminate sentence for prisoners; making the Colorado Humane Society a State bureau of child and animal protection, and providing for the teaching of humanity to animals in the public schools. Before the franchise was granted, women's property rights had already been fairly well secured, and since that time the last discriminations have been removed, so that, with respect to property, women are on a basis of perfect equality with men.

In 1870, before UTAH was admitted as a State, the territorial legislature passed a measure adopting equal suffrage, and for seventeen years women voted at all elections and acted as delegates to political conventions and members of territorial and county committees, but they were not eligible to office. In 1887 Congress passed a bill taking away the rights granted by the territorial legislature [see page 471], and during the remaining nine years of the territorial period Utah women were without the vote. In 1896, however, when statehood was conferred, equal suffrage was included in the constitution. Since then women have been accepted on an equal political footing with men in all respects.

From 85 per cent. to 90 per cent. of women eligible to vote cast their ballots.

Several women have been elected to the State legislature, one to the Senate—so far the first and only woman to sit in the upper chamber of a legislature in any State. Women also serve in considerable numbers as county clerks, treasurers, recorders, auditors, assessors, and county superintendents of schools. Although eligible they do not customarily do jury service.

Women have aided in securing measures providing for equal pay for equal work for teachers; raising the age of protection for young girls to 18; establishing free public libraries in cities and towns; requiring in all schools and educational institutions supported wholly or partly by public funds systematic instruction in physiology and hygiene, including the effects of stimulants and narcotics; providing for a course of free lectures every year at the capital on sanitary science, hygiene, and nursing; providing for a curfew bell at 9 p. m. to keep children off the streets at night; making it a misdemeanor for any minor to buy, accept, or have in his possession cigarettes, tobacco, opium, or any other narcotic; providing for the protection of dependent, neglected, or ill-treated children, and for the punishment of the persons responsible; requiring the establishment of kindergartens in towns of a specified size; prohibiting traffic in women; prohibiting the employment of children in certain industries; prohibiting the employment of women more than nine hours a day or fifty-four hours a week; providing for medical examination of school children; authorizing boards of health to take certain steps to protect the public against venereal disease; providing for sanitary inspection for slaughter-houses and other places where foodstuffs are prepared; forcing wife-deserters to pay a certain sum for the support of their families; giving local option on the liquor question. Women have practically the same rights over their independent property as men.

In 1895 the IDAHO legislature voted, unanimously in the Senate and 33 to 2 in the House, to submit a woman suffrage amendment to the State constitution, and in 1896 the measure carried by a majority of 5,844.

The percentage of eligible women who vote ranges from 75 per cent. to 85 per cent.

A number of women have been elected to the House of Representatives of the legislature, and have filled satisfactorily a number of county and city offices. In 1900 the legislature passed a bill exempting women from jury service, but this was vetoed by the governor in response to a protest from the women themselves. It is not customary for women to serve, however, except in special cases.

In the first session of the legislature after they got the vote women aided materially in getting through a measure of the utmost importance to the young State, namely, an anti-gambling law. In the six sessions since then they have helped to secure measures raising the age of protection for young girls to 18; prohibiting the employment of children in certain industries; creating a juvenile court; creating a State humane society; increasing the control of married women over their independent property; establishing libraries and reading rooms and a State library commission, consisting of the president of the State University, the State superintendent of public instruction, the secretary of State, and the attorney-general; providing for a department of domestic science in the State university, and for a course of lectures on the subject in the Academy of Idaho; establishing an industrial school; providing for the inspection and regulation of places where foods and drugs are prepared; providing for the commission form of government; providing anti-trust regulations; establishing measures for the control of the sale of liquor; and prohibiting persons of lewd lives, both men and women, from voting.

The Idaho State Federation of Women's Clubs has prepared, for introduction into the next legislature, bills providing for equal guardianship of children; medical inspection of school children; instruction in sex hygiene in the public schools; the closing of houses of prostitution, and making venereal diseases reportable.

In 1883 the territorial legislature passed a bill adopting equal suffrage and for four years the women of WASHINGTON voted in as large, or larger, numbers than the men. In 1886 some question of constitutionality having arisen, the legislature strengthened the act. Nevertheless, in 1887, on the motion of what it was charged were vicious elements that had suffered by legislation enacted with the help of women's votes, the Supreme

Court declared the bill unconstitutional on the ground that it was improperly titled. The following year the legislature reënacted it—this time perfect in every respect. In 1889 the Supreme Court disfranchised women on the grounds that territorial legislatures had no power to extend suffrage.

When statehood was applied for a referendum was held and woman suffrage was defeated by a majority of 19,000. In 1898 a constitutional amendment granting it was submitted to the people, and it was defeated by a majority of 10,000. In 1910 the amendment was submitted for the third time and won by a majority of 20,000 —two to one in every election district.

In the local elections since 1910 from 85 to 95 per cent. of the women eligible to vote have cast their ballots. Women have been elected to local offices, and have served rather extensively on juries, resisting all attempts to relieve them of this duty.

In 1896 a woman suffrage amendment to the State constitution was submitted to the voters by the CALIFORNIA legislature and defeated by a vote of 26,744. In 1911 the amendment was submitted for the second time and carried by a majority of 4,000.

In the local elections since 1911 from 90 to 99 per cent. of the women eligible to vote have cast their ballots. Women have willingly served on juries.

In 1912 the full suffrage was granted to women in ARIZONA, KANSAS, and OREGON.[1]

During the congressional session of 1911-12 six joint resolutions were offered in the House, each proposing to submit to the States an amendment to the Constitution granting to women throughout the nation the right to vote. The Representatives offering these resolutions were John E. Raker [Cal.], A. W. Lafferty [Ore.], Edward T. Taylor [Col.], Victor L. Berger [Wis.], Frank W. Mondell [Wyo.], and Atterson W. Rucker [Col.].

The resolutions were referred to the Committee on Judiciary, Henry D. Clayton [Ala.] chairman.

The committee gave a hearing on March 13, at which

[1] Condensed from "Where Women Vote," by Frances Maule Björkman.

prominent advocates and opponents of the resolution appeared and spoke.

THE RIGHT OF WOMEN TO VOTE

HEARING BEFORE THE HOUSE COMMITTEE ON JUDICIARY, MARCH 13, 1912

The advocates of the resolution spoke first.

Representative Taylor introduced Jane Addams, of Chicago, as the leader of the advocates, calling attention of her prominence as a worker for social reform.

Miss Addams first drew attention to the fact that more than a million women would vote for President in November, 1912, and over a half-million more had the municipal franchise.

In fact, the remaining women of America are almost the only English-speaking women in the world who are deprived of the municipal franchise. In England women vote upon all civic matters, and all of the women in the English colonies also vote upon municipal affairs. The women in the north, particularly Finland, Sweden, and Norway, have the full franchise; and America, so far from being in the lead in the universal application of the principle that every adult is entitled to the ballot, is fast falling behind the rest of the world. A hundred years ago we occupied an advanced position in regard to the extension of the franchise; at the present moment we are quite behind in this belief that every adult is entitled to representation in his own governmental affairs.

Miss Addams then spoke of the admirable work that had been done by the women of Chicago in reforming social abuses, which was recently checked by the city government taking over the enterprises begun by these women and conducting them inefficiently. The fact that the women were thus excluded she ascribed to the sex's lack of the ballot.

She then touched upon the question of taxation of women to whom representation is denied in laying the tax.

The franchise is only a little bit of mechanism which enables the voter to say how much money shall be appropriated from the taxes, of which women pay so large a part. When a woman votes, she votes in an Australian ballot box, very carefully guarded from roughness, and it seems to us only fair to the State activities which are so largely humanitarian that women should have this opportunity.

Miss Addams then introduced Leonora O'Reilly, a social worker of New York City. Miss O'Reilly declared that working women were asking the ballot for protection of their interests.

Gentlemen, you may tell us that our place is in the home. Do not make fun of us, please. There are 8,000,000 of us in these United States who must earn our daily bread. Now, in all seriousness, because we must earn that bread, we come to tell you that, while we are working in the mills, the mines, the factories, and the mercantile houses, we have not the protection that we should have. Gentlemen, you have been making laws for us; now, we want to make laws for ourselves, because the laws you have made have not been good for us. Year after year working women have gone to the legislature in every State; they have tried to tell their story of need in the same old way. They have gone to you, believing, as they do believe, in the strength of the big brother; believing that the big brother could do for them what they should, as citizens, do for themselves.

They have seen, time after time, the power of the big interests come behind the big brother and say to him: "If you grant the request of these working women you die, politically." It is because the working women have seen this that they now demand the ballot. In New York, and in every other State, we plead for shorter hours. When the legislators learn that women to-day in every industry are being overspeeded and overworked most of them will, if they dare, vote protective legislation for the women. Why do they neglect the women? We answer, because those who have the votes have the power to take the legislators' political ladder away from them, a power that we, who have no votes, do not have. The getting of the vote and the use of the vote for self-protection as a class is another thing we working women are going to do; we are going to do it as well as we have done our work in the factory, mill, office, and shop. The world to-day knows that the women in industry are making good. But we working women maintain that the rest of the world are not keeping faith with us, in that they are driving us like mad, burning us alive, or working us to death for profits. We, of New York, remember the Triangle fire [1] cases; we saw our women burned alive, and then when our people appealed to the courts and tried to get justice we got instead the same old verdict from the courts, "Nobody to blame." The ballot is a matter of necessity with working women. We want you to put behind you all your prejudice against votes for women; we ask you for fair play. When the workingmen come to you with the power of the ballot they make you listen. We want the power of the ballot for the same reason. If there is a man who will not be just, we mean to put him out of politics. If there is a man in office who is serving humanity fairly, we will keep him in office to help make our land what it ought to be.

Gentlemen, that is my message to you from working women in general, and from all organized working women and working-men in particular. Working women want the power to protect themselves. Working women want the opportunity to work effectively for decent factory laws, sane labor laws. Working women know that we will never have a universal child-labor law until we have the heart of all the women of the land behind the framing and the enforcing of such a law.

While the doors of the colleges have been opened to the fortunate women of our country, only one woman in a thousand goes into our colleges, while one woman in five must go into industry to earn her living. And it is for the protection of this one woman in every five that I speak.

You may say the vote was never given as a right, but rather as an expedient, to any group of people. Then we demand it as an expedient. It is time that to these women who work in the factories, or wherever they work, contracting the diseases known as occupational diseases, an opportunity be given to clean our political house of its disease germs.

It is in a wretchedly unhealthy condition to-day. Men, let the women come in and help you in this political house cleaning. You have got it into an awful mess; we only ask you to do the thing you have done since Adam, namely, turn the burden of responsibility over to woman when it gets too big for you or you fear the consequences. Let us help you now, or if you will not it will look as if you are afraid of the kind of house cleaning we will give you. Well, we will give it to you, as

[1] A fire in a shirtwaist factory in which the operatives were women, mostly girls, many of whom lost their lives. It was claimed that the owners had not complied with the State laws for fire protection.

sure as fate, because we are on this job to win. [Applause.]
We see that there is not a thing in the way of this right which
we are asking but prejudice or fear; we are pleading for the
right to use our intelligence, as you use yours at the ballot box.
You believe you protect us. You say you want to take care of
the women. I can tell you as a working woman we know you
have made a very bad job of the protection and caretaking.
[Laughter and applause.] A working woman has to deal with
the facts of life; she knows when she is overtired, when her finger is taken off by a machine just because she was too tired to
take it out. That is what one of my girls calls a "fac'." Now,
men, we working women deal in "fac's." We want the ballot
in order that we may straighten out all of this economic and
political mess that your superior intelligence has gotten us into.
Is that straight? Well, that is what the working woman wants.
[Applause.]

Representative Raker was next introduced. He declared that primarily the question was one of absolute
right, and secondarily of expediency.

We are depriving one-half of the intelligence, one-half of
the ability of this Republic from participating in public affairs.
Women are just as much interested, and have the same rights
under the law to exist and to live and to work for what is right
as we have, and I believe, from the economic standpoint, from
the standpoint of better laws, better existence, better homes,
better government in the county, in the city, in the State, and
in the nation, that we need our wives', our sisters', and our
mothers' votes and assistance in elections.

There can be no doubt but that there is a special work for
women in every walk of life. They are entitled to the ballot
because of the greater influence it will give them in the affairs
of life, dear to the hearts of all femininity.

Miss Addams.—The next speaker, Mr. Chairman, is from
New York, Jean Nelson Penfield, who will address you upon her
experience in finding much of the city work taken out of their
hands when it is taken over by the city. The door of the House
of State, so to speak, is shut in their faces, when their precious
little enterprise is toddling across the threshold.

Mrs. Penfield said:

Because women have been able to accomplish many things
for civic betterment without the ballot, a great many people

think that we do not need the ballot. I ask you to remember at the beginning, however, that the important fact is not that women finally accomplish things, but that when they do succeed in their civic work without the franchise—and, by the way, the failures are not recorded—they accomplish what they do at the greatest and most needless expenditure of time and vital strength, and at the cost to the individual, and, therefore, of course, in the end, to the social world, of self-respect and dignity.

Now, these things are important, because the dominant thought in the world to-day is conservation. Women seem to represent the only great body of energy and talent that is unconserved, unutilized, and recklessly wasted along the byways of life. When men have a public wrong they want rectified they go armed with their votes to the ballot box, just as they also use the influence of the franchise with legislators after they are in office, but when women would seek redress or remedy for public wrong they must accomplish their desire by the long, hard, and indirect process, a questionable process at best, and one wasteful of vital energy and time. What an indictment of our political system it is that in the twentieth century, in a progressive, democratic government, when the very air teems with the words "efficiency" and "conservation," and even the poorest mechanic knows the economic necessity of using the best, most up-to-date tools, nearly one-half the citizens of the country should by statutes be condemned to do what patriotic service they may wish to do with the implements of a day that is dead and gone.

Mrs. Penfield then recounted the reforms which had been wrought by women in New York City and elsewhere.

Everybody in New York now demands pure milk, but I assure you it has taken a long time to secure the present splendid system of inspection, after a few women discovered and made public a number of years ago the facts about the filthy city stables, with their diseased cows. The ordinance for the protection of meats and vegetables in New York represents a labor of years by this same body of women. When women went into our public schools and reported epidemics of disease which were preventable by the observance of ordinary sanitary conditions action finally came. The now well-established institutions of manual training and domestic-science schools, playgrounds, and school gardens were all once "women's notions."

As Miss Addams has said, these things have been done, but they have been done unscientifically, because not economically, from the social standpoint. In almost nine cases out of ten, gentlemen, women have been made to finance these institutions and investigations personally. They have had to finance the institutions and demonstrate the success in each case before the city would acknowledge a public need and adopt them.

Besides this, let me call your attention to another notable feature in connection with women's successful civil work—one overlooked by many, but not to be overlooked much longer by wise statesmen. After women have made a success of these institutions, have managed them and directed them, when they are taken over by the city or State, men alone control them. I ask you to realize that more and more thinking men all over the country are beginning to be more conscious of the way we are excluded from civic interests in which we have as great a stake as have men.

Mrs. Penfield then discussed the work of women on the school boards of the country, pointing to the acknowledged superior efficiency there of women over men. Yet, she said, men held almost all the salaried positions on these boards. This was because of their political influence.

Representative Taylor said that all men who lived in an equal suffrage State agreed that there was only one side to the question—the affirmative.

The men of our mountain homes have added justice to chivalry, and have long since learned, and have the candor and manhood to acknowledge, that our women's influence in the civic housekeeping of our cities, our counties, and the State itself is as beneficial and necessary as it is in every well-regulated home.

On coming East he had found an astounding amount of misinformation about the practical operation of equal suffrage, and had become indignant as well as amazed at the brazen assertions of its opponents.

When I hear men and women who have never spent an hour in an equal suffrage State attempt to discuss the subject from the standpoint of their own preconceived prejudices and idle impressions, I feel like saying, "May the Lord forgive

them, for they know not what they say." Let me say to them
and to my colleagues in the House that it will not be ten years
before the women of this country, from the Pacific to the Atlantic, will gain the just and equal rights of American citizenship.

Mr. Taylor then recounted the beneficial legislation
which had been passed in Colorado largely because of the
influence of the women in its favor [see page 350].

The women members of our legislature have all been excep-
tionally conscientious, industrious, and capable legislators.
They devote their energies mostly to moral questions and matters affecting the home and the children, and the betterment of
health and social conditions, including humane measures for the
unfortunate of all classes.

The delegates of the Inter-Parliamentary Union, who some
time ago visited the different parts of the United States for the
purpose of studying American institutions, declared, concerning
our group of laws relating to child life in its various aspects of
education, home and labor, that "they are the sanest, most humane, most progressive, most scientific laws relating to the child
to be found on any statute books in the world."

Whenever women have a chance to express their sentiments
there is never any doubt as to the result. Every politician
knows in advance what it will be, and that is the reason some
of them loudly proclaim that woman suffrage is a failure. A
married woman's heart is always in her children and her home
—the foundation of the Republic—and any measure affecting
either is not a political question with her for a minute. There is
only one side to it, and that is the right side. A woman's vote
is always a patriotic vote.

Mr. Chairman, one of the best traits of human nature is the
desire to advise others of the benefits we enjoy in this world and
urge them to acquire the same valuable possessions. Scores of
patriotic Coloradans, both men and women, have at various
times for years traveled over this country from ocean to ocean
and from the Lakes to the Gulf, at their own expense, without
the slightest hope of reward, telling the people the value of political equality. Colorado, being the most prominent and representative equal-suffrage State, has for nineteen years been called
the principal experimental station for woman suffrage, and the
storm center of attack on the part of advocates and opponents.

All the shafts of the anti-suffragists on earth have been constantly hurled with fiendish desperation at our State.

While all the old stereotyped stock of objections and obsolete arguments that have been doing valiant service for three generations have long since been exploded and ridiculed out of existence by the women themselves and by the actual experiences of every one of our six equal-suffrage States and by every country in the world where it has been tried, nevertheless, as the subject at this time is being more generally discussed throughout the United States than ever before in our history; and as active campaigns for the adoption of equal-rights constitutional amendments are now in progress in the States of Oregon, Kansas, Wisconsin, Ohio, Michigan, and possibly some other States, I will, even at the risk of merely reiterating some of the conclusive answers that have been more eloquently given many a time before, give some of my personal observations and judgment upon a number of phases of the question. One of the first questions most often asked of me is: Do the women of Colorado vote?

Anyone can answer that question by simply loking at the election records and the census. The increased votes in the suffrage States is exactly in proportion to the total women population in those States.

It is an undisputed fact that in every State in the country where the franchise has been extended to women the vote of the men has steadily risen. The vote of the men is much larger in all the equal-suffrage States of the Union than in most of those in which women are unenfranchised.

I am often asked if the *best* women in Colorado vote. As a matter of fact, it is the good women who vote in the largest numbers, proportionately. That is, in the better residence sections of every city and town and throughout the country the women vote is much larger, in proportion to the female population, than it is in the less prosperous and less desirable localities. There is no class of women in Colorado, no matter what their station in life may be, who do not vote. In the little city of Glenwood Springs, where I live, I do not know of a woman in the city or surrounding country who does not vote. I represent in the House of Representatives nearly five times as many voters as the other members do,[1] and I ought to be, and I am, the proudest man in Congress of my constituency, especially the women in it.

[1] Mr. Taylor was Representative at large.

DO THE BAD WOMEN OF COLORADO VOTE?

It has been repeatedly stated by numerous governors of our State that there was only from one-third to one-half of 1 per cent. of the women of the State who are immoral or disreputable. Therefore, the utterly thoughtless, and in some cases willful, assertion about disreputable women outweighing the number of good women is not only a ridiculous bugaboo, but is a slander upon the women of the country.

Moreover, the women of the half world do not willingly vote at all. They are constantly changing their names and residences. They are a migratory class. They are very largely under the power of the police and sheriff's office, and unless they compel them to vote they generally stay away. And, even where they are forced to vote, not over one-fifth of them are qualified voters. So that their influence is negligible; in fact, it is actually infinitesimal. They are no menace whatever. Their numbers are not sufficient to amount to anything, and no one pays any attention to them. In fact, if it was known that they were voting for any particular ticket or candidate it would do that ticket or candidate ten times more harm than good.

Some people seem to have the queer impression that everybody in a city or town votes in the same place, and that the men and women have a general scramble to vote, and all kinds of unseemly conduct on election day. We of the West cannot comprehend how any sensible people can get such ideas. No large crowds of people vote in one place. Every city and town and the country is divided into small election precincts, usually not over 300 voters in a precinct. Everyone must vote in his or her own precinct. There are no lewd women in the country or in the small towns, and in the large towns and all cities they are strictly confined to certain districts, not in the residence portions.

In the State of Idaho prostitutes are disfranchised entirely, and, if they at any time should become a disturbing element or in the slightest affect the result of elections, that action would undoubtedly be promptly taken in the other States. One reason it has not, I apprehend, is because a great many bad men vote, and many so-called good men do not. Moreover, there is a kind of a humane sentiment that, so long as these women never take any part in elections and so few of them vote, no one should deny this most unfortunate class of human beings whatever protection a vote can give them; at least, so long as men of the same class are voters.

ARE WOMEN PARTISANS?

Among the various far-fetched and utterly groundless grounds of opposition to woman suffrage is the assertion that women would become as partisan or more so than men, and thereby merely double the party vote and accomplish no real good. Nothing could be further from the actual facts. Women, when they are enfranchised, in every State are, practically speaking, nonpartisan. They have not, like the men, inherited their politics from their fathers; and, in States where the people are nearly evenly divided between the parties, practically half of the girls marry men of different politics from that of their fathers. So that in reality they start in comparatively nonpartisan, or, at least, very independent, and the great majority of them remain so. While possibly from 75 to 90 per cent. of the married women vote mainly the general party ticket the same way that their husbands do, because their interests are the same, nevertheless, a small per cent. of them always vote independently; and all of them are perfectly free to scratch their ticket, and a very, very large per cent. of them do so. It is very seldom that either party elects a straight ticket. We nearly always have a mixture of officeholders. In other words, the women are nothing like as partisan as the men. They are very intelligent voters. They know the art of scratching thoroughly; they are exceedingly proficient in throwing out fellows who are no good.

And this freedom of action never causes any friction whatever in the home. I have never in my life heard of a Colorado man having a quarrel or even assuming to complain or criticize his wife for exercising her choice and best judgment. In fact, some strong party men, who feel that for party regularity they should not vote against anyone on their own ticket, at the same time haven't the slightest objection to their wives exercising an intelligent independence which they know is for the general good, and which they feel it is not policy for them to exercise.

Women are not natural-born politicians like men are. They are not as crafty or ambitious politically as the men are. The natural result is that the men practically control politics, i. e., the party machinery of the State. At the same time the women read the papers. They talk among themselves. They learn quite fully about all the candidates and what they stand for. They discuss political issues and the candidates with the male members of the family, and they are thoroughly advised as to who's who. Women's interests cannot, generally speaking, be roused very much by mere partisan strife. Women never become hysterical, and very seldom show much enthusiasm over a mere party nominee. Men look after the business interests and financial questions, while the moral and humane questions appeal more to the women. In other words, men and women are different in their character and thoughts, and the influence and judgment of both are beneficial in civic and governmental affairs just the same as they are in well-regulated and orderly family relations.

ARE WOMEN OFFICE-SEEKERS?

There has never been any rush of women for offices in Colorado. Giving a woman the right to vote does not change her feminine characteristics or her womanly nature in the slightest. The women as a class are not chronic nor inveterate office seekers. In fact, there is not one out of five hundred who ever thinks of being a candidate for any office. They are not avaricious for power and influence like men are. Men are shrewder politicians and much more unscrupulous than women. In nine cases out of ten when a woman does seek the nomination for an office she is earnestly solicited to do so by many of her friends and acquaintances who recognize her exceptional qualifications for the position. Moreover, women scarcely ever strive for or want the more important positions that the men want. The men want the positions that pay the large salaries and require executive ability and other responsibilities, and that involve control of party machinery, patronage, and large affairs. Women do not care to be political bosses. They are contented with the educational and charitable positions and minor places that require energy and much painstaking diligence and conscientious work, and which are compensated by smaller salaries.

DOES EQUAL SUFFRAGE CAUSE DIVORCES?

There is not a single instance on record anywhere in any court in the State, and there never in twenty years has been a case in Colorado, where a divorce has been granted on account of political differences, or arose from them. Differences in religion between husbands and wives produce a thousand times more quarrels than differences in politics do, and yet no one would nowadays ever think of trying to compel a woman to choose her religion to suit her husband.

DO WOMEN LOSE ANY OF THEIR INFLUENCE OR CEASE TO BE AS
MUCH RESPECTED?

The brazen claim that women will become unsexed or lose
any of the respect of men is utterly absurd. In the olden times
men had the right to chastise their wives. Have the men nowadays got any less respect for their wives because they cannot
lick them any more? Respect for woman is based upon her
moral character, her intelligence, and her own self-respect.
Women are not becoming less respected because they have been
admitted to colleges and universities. Women are just as feminine in Colorado as any place on earth, and they are better
wives because they are better informed and more companionable
to their husbands. The enfranchisement of the wife has given
another common interest to the household. It has had no tendency to create discord in the home. On the contrary, it has
brought a comradeship in politics, something similar to that of
religion, that used to be found in many families in the East.

There is nothing whatever degrading to a woman to quietly
go down to the polls on election day once or twice a year and
cast her vote along with her husband or brother or with women
friends. There is not the slightest tendency whatever in Colorado among the men to omit the ordinary politeness due the
women. In fact, I believe our women, by their superior general intelligence and companionable charms, command and receive more courteous attention than in any other State. Under
equal suffrage there is a much more chivalrous devotion and respect on the part of men, who look upon their sisters not as
playthings nor as property, but as equal and full citizens. We
are proud of our Colorado women. I have little regard for a
son who swells up and says that he is better than his mother.
To-day a boy in his teens in a country or a State where women
have the right to vote does not look upon his mother or his
sister as belonging to the sex that must be kept within a prescribed sphere, but as a human being, clothed with the dignity
of all those rights and powers which he hopes to enjoy within
a few years.

The differences between men and women are natural; they
are not the result of disfranchisement. The fact that all men
have equal rights before the law does not wipe out the natural
differences of character and temperament between man and
man. Why should it wipe out the natural differences between
men and women?

To us people of the West it is utterly stupid for anyone to assume that the vote will lessen the present influence of women. The influence of any class of men, or any individual man, has never in the world been lessened because he had the power to vote.

The objection that "it is unwomanly" has been made to every change in the status of woman from the time she ceased to be a beast of burden and we men decided to give her a soul and a seat at our dinner table to the present time. The days when ridicule and contempt were the reception accorded any attempt of the woman to enlarge her activities or broaden and enrich her life belong to another century. We have to-day urgent need for better fathers and wiser mothers. The feminist leaders of Europe and the United States are changing the attitude of the race toward one-half of its members.

To-day girls form 56 per cent. of the pupils enrolled in our secondary schools and a large majority of those in all our high schools. The old days when women were compelled to keep silent are past. To-day in every field of human endeavor her voice is heard. By the legal establishment and recognizing of woman citizenship, the intellect and character and reciprocal estimation of both sexes have been raised. The possession of the ballot has given women an interest in general as well as political affairs, and this has naturally stimulated the men.

There is no real ground of fear for American marriages and the home. Nothing can break the bond between the sexes. Our own higher development will bring better conditions. We will have higher and happier marriages than ever before.

DO WOMEN NEGLECT THEIR HOMES AND CHILDREN?

We have from childhood constantly heard the solemn assertion that the place for women is the home. I have never heard of anyone denying that platitude, and certainly the women of Colorado do not deny it. If there is anything in this world that a woman naturally wants it is a home. That is her natural place, and her main task in this world is home making. In fact, every married woman in this country is a self-appointed and *ex-officio* member of the Mothers' Home Protective League. But nowadays home is not contained within the four walls of an individual house. Home is merely the center of her sphere from which her influence should radiate. The home is largely the community, and the city or town full of people is the larger family of womankind. All government to-day is in a certain sense merely housekeeping on a large scale. For some parts of this housekeeping the men may always remain better qualified than women. In other parts of it women will always be better qualified than men. But it takes both men and women to make a home.

But there is another serious and important consideration. There are upward of 7,000,000 women in the United States to-day who in reality have no home. Economic conditions have driven them into the factory, the mill, the shop, and the store. They have not left their homes of their own volition; they are not earning a livelihood in competition with the men of their own election. No one will ever assert that women voluntarily leave their homes to become wage earners. If some of them think the ballot would help them to better their conditions and enable them to have homes, are they to be blamed and ridiculed for entertaining that hope?

Ninety-nine per cent. of the women of Colorado take no more time in politics than to attend probably two or three political meetings every two years and go to the polls on election day to cast their vote. The women of Colorado, generally speaking, do not spend 1 per cent. of their time in political matters that they spend in social duties. It only takes a Colorado woman ten or fifteen minutes away from her home to cast a vote. But during those few minutes she is wielding the most tremendous power any woman ever had on this earth for the protection of her home and the homes of all others.

DOES IT INCREASE OR DIMINISH CORRUPTION IN POLITICS?

There is no man worthy of the name who will deny the statement that the influence of his mother and his wife and his sister and his daughter is good. When you grant equal suffrage to women, it is our mothers and wives and sisters and daughters who are going to vote.

I have never heard of a woman being prosecuted, or even seriously charged with the commission of a crime in regard to an election. I have heard it repeatedly stated, and I believe it is true, that the men are guilty of 99 per cent. of all political corruption in Colorado.

There may possibly be a few very rare cases where a woman has been implicated in some political crookedness, but if there are any such cases that I have never heard of you will find that she was put up to it by some men who were trying to shield

THE ANTI-SUFFRAGIST AND THE PRO-VICE DELEGATION

Spokesman.—''We have called to express our extreme gratichude fer the bee-utiful fight you are making in our behalf.''

Reprinted from the Saturday Evening Post of Philadelphia. Copyright, 1913, by the Curtis Publishing Company themselves behind her, and there will be 99 men more guilty than she.

One sure way of answering the question as to whether or not equal suffrage increases corruption in politics is to inquire as to who are the opponents of equal suffrage. Everyone who knows anything about woman suffrage, or about human nature, knows that the vicious and criminal vote is always cast solidly against equal rights for women. All those who thrive upon the violation of the law in any way, or upon corruption in politics, are the bitterest enemies of woman suffrage. Every gambler, every ballot-box stuffer, every political thug, every professional debaucher of the public morals, and every conceivable variety of crook will never cease exhausting his vocabulary cursing woman suffrage.

DOES IT DOUBLE THE IGNORANT, OR FOREIGN, OR CRIMINAL VOTE?

As there are one-third more girls than boys attending the high schools of this country, the women are very rapidly becoming the more educated class. According to the last census, the illiterate men of this country very greatly outnumber the illiterate women. Therefore, extending the franchise to women will actually increase the proportion of intelligent voters. Moreover, extending the franchise to women will very largely increase the number of native-born voters, because there are in the United States over twelve times as many native-born women as foreign born. It is also a matter of record that a less proportion of the foreign born than the native born vote, and, as there are much fewer women than men immigrants, the enfranchisement of women will therefore doubly tend to minimize the influence of the foreign vote.

Another important feature is that the foreign women are usually much better in morals and intelligence than the foreign men to whom the ballot is already given. Then, too, very few of them vote until they become quite thoroughly Americanized. While on ordinary questions the foreign-woman vote would be very much like the native-woman vote, and would to quite a large degree duplicate the men's vote, that would not be true of special questions affecting women and children or the home, or matters of morality, or questions of decency. This is one of the main points of the equal-suffrage question. And if women take the moral and humane side on questions affecting the welfare of the home and the good of society, it is of comparatively little importance whether or not on other questions their votes are duplicates. The taxes paid by women will very much more than meet the cost of printing and counting the extra ballots. Moreover, in a democracy like ours it is of the greatest importance and benefit to the whole people, both men and women, that all of the population interest themselves in all public questions. It has been repeatedly stated that a republic is sound at heart only when all of its adult members take an ardent interest in its affairs. Too many votes cannot possibly be cast in a right cause in a democracy which lives and breathes by the public opinion of the men and women who compose it.

There is in this country no lack in our politics of business ability, executive talent, or shrewdness of any kind. But there is much danger of lack of conscience, character, and humanity.

DO WOMEN READILY UNDERSTAND POLITICS?

Women learn how to vote mighty quickly. They do not have to serve any apprenticeship to know the difference between decency and corruption, or between an honest man and a crook. A woman always knows the difference between good and bad government, and everything pertaining to educational matters or matters affecting the home; and all politicians will very soon learn that she is exceedingly alert and well informed upon all moral questions and questions affecting society and good government and clean candidates. She comprehends intuitively and instinctively. In fact, on questions of that kind she is much more interested than men, and the advice of every married woman is of great assistance to her husband. In reality, on all questions of that kind, instead of a husband voting his wife, there is a great deal more likelihood of the wife voting the husband.

THE DEVELOPING POWER OF RESPONSIBILITY

Responsibility is one of the greatest instruments of education, both moral and intellectual, and woman never will become thoroughly versed in matters of politics until the opportunity of studying them under the stimulus and check of responsibility is given her.

When we consider her handicaps, not merely her natural handicaps, but the unnatural handicaps imposed upon her by civilization and sentiment; when we consider that for ages she has been discouraged from trying to do anything outside of the home, it is no wonder that she cannot do all things as well as men. The wonder is that she does so many things as well as she does. Every class that has been enfranchised in the history of the world required education in its new civil rights. The American woman requires it, too, but least of all.

The great economic questions of to-day affect the women just as much as they do the men. Their interests are mutual and equal, and her enfranchisement has conclusively proven in the six Western States that the result is a more enlightened and better balanced citizenship and a truer democracy. It has been said that the more civilization advances the more the interests of men and women coincide.

One-fifth of all the women of this country have been compelled to go into the field of business and take positions formerly held by men and are actively earning their own support. The ballot is just as imperatively necessary to them as it is to the men. It is not only contrary to the principles of fair dealing to deny the women the right to vote, but this country needs the influence of her ballot, as will be conclusively shown by the result of her vote wherever it has been given to her. It seems to me infamous that women should be longer classed as political nonentities, the same as lunatics, Chinamen, criminals, and children. While there is a good reason for excluding all of those political nonentities excepting women, there is no good reason under heaven for excluding an intelligent woman from trying to better the conditions which affect her by the use of the ballot.

A woman who is self-centered and satisfied with the gratification of her appetite and vanities is not the highest ideal of our race and is not performing her highest duty to society or to humanity.

There were in our State a number of women who, before they were enfranchised, did not want to vote. Since then nearly all of them have been faithfully performing their duty.

The greatest school of life is the ballot box. The present world movement for the enfranchisement of women shows that under the influence of advanced civilization the nations of the earth are becoming ready for universal suffrage and the conception of society which it implies. Feminism is a world movement. It is a part of the eternal forward march of the human race toward a genuine democracy. The whole history of the development of civilization is merely the story of broadening the channel of human liberty and opportunity. All over the world woman is doing and thinking more effectively than ever before.

Women's clubs are a wonderfully educational movement. It is within the memory of most of us when the American women first began to form themselves into clubs. At first they were merely little local literary organizations. Afterward the matters affecting the welfare of the community were taken up for consideration; and then the women commenced forming State federations and afterward national federations; and to-day the General Federation of Women's Clubs, working in conjunction with the International Council of Women, are doing a wonderfully beneficial and humane work for the amelioration of the conditions of women all over the world.

The women's organizations thoroughly realize that their cause for the betterment of humanity can be best advanced by giving the women the ballot.

The women of Colorado are quite largely members of various clubs, and they wield an influence that is hardly conceivable by people who do not live in the State. They have not only all the clubs there are in other States, but they also have political clubs; and there is a great deal of family discussion of public questions, which all has an unquestionable tendency to educate and broaden the mind not only of the wife, but of the members of the family. Increased responsibility causes increased development and improvement, and increased development means intelligent action and patriotism.

I have often heard it said that one of the largest book stores in Denver sold more books on political economy, sociology, and kindred subjects within six months after women were enfranchised than during the entire previous twenty years.

WOMAN IN THE SCHOOLS

Colorado spends more money per capita on her schools than any other State in the Union. There is no difference made in the salaries of teachers on account of sex. There is not a child in Colorado but has a seat in a school and is guarded by law compelling its parents to allow it to go to school. Does anyone believe for a moment that if the women had the power to make themselves felt in the administration of public affairs that there would be to-day 100,000 children on half time in the schools of New York City and 25,000 without seats in schools in the city of Philadelphia, and an equal proportion in Chicago and many other large cities in this country? Does any sane person believe that if the women of this country had a vote that it would have taken fifty years to have passed the bill that just passed Congress creating a Federal Bureau for the protection of children?

Women have equal suffrage in school elections, I believe, in thirty States of the Union. Has anyone ever had the effrontery to assert that their influence has contaminated or had any evil effect upon school elections or made less effective the teaching of moral instruction in those States? It is said that in many States where women have a right to vote upon school elections the women pay comparatively little attention to them. That may be true where there is no special interest or moral question involved and where the candidates are equally worthy. But where one candidate represents the moral and another the immoral side of questions affecting the welfare of children the women invariably take an active interest, and it is needless to say that they are always on the side of decency.

Women are sanely and conservatively progressive. They are wisely discriminating and shrewd in their public actions. They chiefly interest themselves in movements that are more social than political—above all, in everything relating to children.

RESULT OF EQUAL SUFFRAGE IN COLORADO

I believe I could prepare a list of at least a thousand beneficial results of equal suffrage in Colorado and an equal number of reasons why women should vote. I will not at all attempt to enumerate them, but, in addition to those I have already mentioned, will merely give in a very general and possibly somewhat disconnected way some of the results as I see them.

Equal suffrage has unquestionably compelled a very great improvement in the standing and moral character of the candidates nominated for office by all political parties.

It has equally improved the political conventions, assemblies, and public meetings and the management of all the different political campaigns previous to elections.

It has made much more orderly and better polling places and election-day customs have wonderfully improved.

It has greatly improved the interest of both men and women in the public affairs of the State and the municipalities.

It educates and broadens a woman's sphere of information, and makes her take a more intelligent interest in public affairs. It makes her more companionable, and consequently increases her intellectual standing, dignity, and influence.

It is a family bond and tie that binds the husband and wife together. In 99 cases out of 100 the best and often the only political adviser a Colorado politician has is his wife. In Colorado there is much greater weight given to women's opinions and judgment than in any State denying them the power that equal suffrage gives.

Some one has said that in our political conventions a few women are as good as a whole squad of police. It is true that more or less political chicanery always has, and probably always will exist among some politicians in the State, not because of, but in spite of woman suffrage. Just the same as crime exists, not because of criminal laws, but in spite of them.

Equal suffrage has almost entirely taken our schools out of politics. One of our prominent educators recently said that there is more politics in school matters in any one block of any large city in this country than there is in the entire 104,000 square miles of Colorado soil.

Mr. Taylor said in conclusion:

The greatest intellects of the human race have from the beginning of civilization to the present time acknowledged that naturally women are intellectually our equal and morally our superior and that they are entitled to all the rights that men enjoy. It has been the partisan, the prejudiced, the biased, and smaller minds that have always desperately opposed any advance of womanhood. I cannot resist having a lingering suspicion that the actions of some men are a tacit confession of fear of the risk to which equal suffrage would subject their imagined superiority. Practically every broad-gaged statesman of the world has denied that any portion of the human species has a right to prescribe to any other portion its sphere, its education, or its rights. The sphere of every man and woman is that sphere which he or she can properly fill. No opportunity should ever in this country be closed to any human being who has the capacity to work therein. It is a disgrace to this country and to this enlightened century longer to disfranchise the patriotic and intelligent womanhood of this Republic. The world has never enfranchised as patriotic a class of people as the American women are to-day. Patriotism is not confined to the male sex. Let us be big enough, broad-minded enough, humane enough, and honest enough to treat the women of our country as fairly as they are being treated in China.[1] Let us show to the world that we believe in the Declaration of Independence. Let us evolve our male oligarchy into a twentieth century democracy.

[1] The new Republic of China had just declared for woman suffrage.

Representative Lafferty then spoke.

I do not think that we could make a mistake, as a republic, in placing the ballot in the hand that rocks the cradle. I believe it would be a good thing if fifty of the best mothers of this country were in the House of Representatives and twenty-five were in the Senate to-day. [Applause.]

You should consider, as statesmen, that in the history of monarchies the women have participated in the Government; it is a shame that in a republic like ours, the best form of government that has ever yet been established, women cannot, under the present law, actively participate in our government.

MISS ADDAMS.—The next speaker is not a member of the House, although she is eligible. Mrs. William Kent, of Kentfield, California, will speak to us of the educational advantages of the campaign for the ballot. She has recently borne a valiant part in such a campaign.

MRS. KENT.—Mr. Chairman, the United States is committed to a democratic form of government, government by the people. Those who do not believe in the ideals of democracy are the only ones who can consistently oppose woman's suffrage.

I heard a man arguing against woman's suffrage by saying he believed in a division of labor, the men to vote and decide political questions as part of their work, and women to have other duties, equally useful. You cannot make such a division of labor if you believe in a democracy, if you believe in self-government, any more than you can give all the eating and sleeping to half the community while the other half does something else equally useful.

In the California campaign we had an effective poster with the incontrovertible, yet suggestive statement, "Lincoln believed in government by the people. Women are people." We want to be recognized as people; we want our share of responsibility in the government under which we live.

In a democracy the only hope of good government lies in an enlightened, responsible citizenship. The hope of democracy is in education. There is food for thought in the fact that the early education of all the citizens is now administered by a class who have no vote.

In the New York suffrage parade last year the mothers marched under a banner which read, "We prepare the child for the State. Let us help prepare the State for the child." What education have women received to fit them for this complement to the first office?

I have heard a man say in the same speech that women should not descend into the dirty mire of politics, and that mothers should teach their sons their sacred duties as citizens. Can we reconcile these statements? Can we really bring up our sons with a clear sense of civic responsibility when we have done?

The evidence goes to show that we have not done it. We believe that our children need what we shall learn in becoming citizens, and that the State needs what we have learned in being mothers and home makers.

Take the example of our prisons, public institutions for which the voter is responsible. These institutions do not redound to the credit of the voter, the man who has not been taught his social responsibility. We see in the prisons the result of the commercial and the military way of conducting affairs, the traditional way of the man. One's ideal of a mother and teacher is not that of a strict disciplinarian, of one bent on punishing, but an integral part of the work of most women is that of dealing with the unruly. Her problems have always been to keep her children in the path of virtue, so far as her love and her wisdom and her wits will help her, and to bring them back if they stray from that path. Prevention and correction are problems which she has lived with and studied. These are the real problems in dealing with those who have gone wrong.

And, as with the prisons, so with the other questions of our social life—which is but the family life enlarged—is not the woman's point of view needed? Can you not see that she has something to offer, and that it is a desire to serve that actuates her in asking for the ballot?

Miss Addams.—I present next, Mr. Chairman, Mrs. Ida Husted Harper, of New York City. She has been before other congressional committees with Miss Susan B. Anthony, who for so many years appeared to present this cause. Mrs. Harper has written a history of the equal-suffrage movement, and also a very fine biography of Miss Anthony. She will make the constitutional argument, and perhaps answer the questions which a member of the committee put to Mr. Lafferty.

Mrs. Harper.—Mr. Chairman, this argument presented today shall be based entirely on the Federal Constitution, and the only authorities cited will be the utterances of two Presidents of the United States within the past month.

In the Columbus, Ohio, speech of Theodore Roosevelt, opening his present campaign, he said:

I hold with Lincoln that "this country, with its institutions, belongs to the people who inhabit it. Whenever they grow weary of existing government they can exercise their constitutional right of amending it."

We appear before you representing a class of citizens who are exceedingly "weary of the existing government," but are wholly deprived by its Constitution of any right or power to change it. We ask you, therefore, what or where is our redress? But one other class could come to you as helpless—the Orientals within our boundaries—but they have not the mockery of citizenship.

I emphatically protest—

Said Mr. Roosevelt—

against any theory that would make of the Constitution a means of thwarting instead of securing the absolute right of the people to rule themselves.

Except by physical force there is but one way in which people can rule themselves and that is through choosing their own representatives in the Government by means of a vote. This is practically forbidden to women in the Fourteenth and Fifteenth Amendments to the national Constitution which authorize the State constitutions to prohibit it directly.

To quote Mr. Roosevelt once more:

The object of every American constitution must be what is set forth in the preamble to the national—to "establish justice" by means of popular self-government. If the Constitution is successfully invoked to nullify the effort to remedy injustice, it is proof positive either that the Constitution needs immediate amendment or else that it is being wrongfully and improperly construed.

When women citizens have invoked the national Constitution in their efforts to establish the justice of a voice in their own government, the Supreme Court of the United States has repeatedly construed it as not conferring this right. As women had no appeal from its being "wrongfully and improperly construed," they accepted the alternative that "it needed immediate amendment."

For this purpose they began making their pilgrimages to Washington in 1869, and they have brought their case before the committees of every Congress since that time. Some of those who address you to-day belong to the third generation who have come to this Capitol seeking "to establish justice."

Turn for a moment to the opinions of another President of the United States, the one who now occupies this exalted position. In the speech of William H. Taft at Toledo, Ohio, inaugurating his present campaign,[1] he said:

From our body politic we have excised the cancer of slavery, the only thing protected by the Constitution inconsistent with that liberty, the preservation of which was the main purpose of establishing the Union.

In the first establishment of our Union its main purpose was not to preserve physical but political liberty; and when the second struggle came, if it had been only to guarantee personal freedom, the Thirteenth Amendment to the national Constitution would have alone been sufficient, but the fourteenth and then the fifteenth were added in order to secure political freedom. And while this is still denied to half the citizens the roots of the cancer yet strike deep in the body politic.

Then, defending the courts, President Taft said:

The great body of the law . . . is founded on the eternal principles of right and morality. . . . As between the individual and the State, the majority and the minority, the powerful and the weak, financially, socially, and politically, the courts must hold an even hand and give judgment without fear or favor.

The man filling the highest elective legal position in New York City said to me a short time ago:

After many years of practice at the bar and many years of service on the bench, I am firmly convinced that women can never receive exact justice in the courts until they become voters. While judges may be absolutely impervious to every other influence, they can not wholly ignore political power.

This fact must be universally recognized that disfranchisement is not only a great handicap to women legally but also economically, and socially in the large sense of the word, while politically it puts them out of the race.

In this Toledo speech President Taft earned the profound regard of women by casting aside the flimsy pretence of universal suffrage and saying:

The best government, in the sense of the one most certain to provide for and protect the rights and governmental needs of every class, is that one in which every class has a voice. In recognition of this, the tendency from earliest time has been the enlargement of the electorate to include as many as possible of those governed; but even to-day the government is

[1] See the introduction to Volume IX.

by a majority of one-fourth. This is the nearest to a government of the whole people that we have ever had. But woman suffrage will change this, and it is doubtless coming as soon as the electorate can be certain that most women desire it and will assume its burdens and responsibilities.

Gentlemen of the committee, in the nearly a century and a half of our Government this is the only expression in favor of woman suffrage ever publicly made by a President of the United States! We appreciate it and welcome it, but we regret that Mr. Taft should impose upon women a requirement never imposed upon men in our own Government or any other in the world's history—to prove that a majority want the suffrage and would use it. No class of people in any country has ever been enfranchised at a request or with any pledges from the majority, but always because of the efforts of a few strong, patriotic leaders, and ostensibly, at least, as an act of justice by the government. If, in the words of Mr. Taft, "the best government and the one most certain to protect the rights of every class is that one in which every class has a voice," then the United States Government should no longer quibble over the exact number who desire to have their rights thus protected.

Since, however, the excuse for withholding the franchise from women has now practically narrowed down to this one point, they will accept the issue. A few days ago United States Senator Henry Cabot Lodge [Mass.] made a speech at Princeton University in which he used this sentence:

It is quite true that the voters are the means by which we necessarily obtain an expression of the popular will.

There is indeed but one sure way to learn whether women want the ballot and will use it, and that is to make them voters and watch the result. By this test the advocates of women's suffrage are willing to have the question judged.

The women of California were enfranchised in October, 1911. In Los Angeles, one month later, 85,546 registered— nearly all in the city who were eligible—and the following month 95 per cent. of these voted—a record never made by men. Within three months after the women of Washington became electors—in 1910—over 22,000 went to the polls and deposed a corrupt mayor, and last week they defeated him for reëlection. In the six States where women are permitted to vote they have satisfactorily met the supreme test of whether the majority of women want the suffrage and would use it. Basing their claim on this unimpeachable record, the women of other States demand the franchise.

I will close this argument with one more very recent quotation from President Taft. In speaking of the capacity for self-government, he said:

It is the question of self-imposed restraint that determines whether a people is fit to govern itself.

We can offer no stronger evidence of the self-restraint of women than the fact that, although they have come before these committees of Senate and House with their petitions and arguments forty-three years, only to be treated with contemptuous indifference and neglect, they have never departed from the strictest rules of dignity and self-control. Forty-three years in asking for this amendment they have followed an entirely legal and constitutional method of procedure, which has been so absolutely barren of results that in the past nineteen years these committees have made no report whatever, either favorable or unfavorable. How much longer do you expect women to treat with respect national and State constitutions and legislative bodies that stand thus an impenetrable barrier between them and their rights as citizens of the United States?

THE CHAIRMAN [MR. CLAYTON].—This committee, during my service on it, has always met with this proposition when this amendment was proposed, that the States already have the authority to confer suffrage upon women, and, therefore, why is it necessary for women to wait for an amendment to the Federal Constitution when they can go now to the States and obtain this right to vote?

MRS. HARPER.—Mr. Chairman, the women are not waiting; they are keeping right on with their efforts to get the suffrage from the States. They began in 1867 with their State campaigns and have continued them ever since. But, in sending the women to the States, you require them to make forty-eight campaigns and to go to the individual electors to get the permission to vote.

After the Civil War, the leaders of the Republican party went to State after State, and every one turned down the proposition to give the negroes suffrage. Then they passed the Fifteenth Amendment to the Constitution. You impose upon us an intolerable condition when you send us to the individual voters. What man on this committee would like to submit his electoral rights to the voters of New York City, for instance, representing as they do every nationality in the world and every class interest? If we could secure this amendment to the Federal Constitution, then we could deal with the legislatures, with the selected men in each State, instead of the great conglomerate of voters.

THE CHAIRMAN.—But if one of these suffrage resolutions should be favorably reported, and both Houses of Congress should pass it, of course it would be referred to the States, and then before it became a law it would have to have their approval.

MRS. HARPER.—Only of the legislatures, not the individual voters.

THE CHAIRMAN.—Of the States acting through their legislatures?

MRS. HARPER.—Yes.

THE CHAIRMAN.—That is the States, you know.

MRS. HARPER.—I think you would fully preserve the idea of States' rights by letting the legislatures of each State decide it. We ask for the easiest way to secure our enfranchisement.

MARTIN W. LITTLETON, of the Committee.—Assuming there is no objection to woman suffrage at all, I ask whether you would make any headway by the adoption of this amendment, and thereby make the only exception on the question of suffrage, except in the case of the negro vote. The States control suffrage absolutely. In this particular case it would be the national Government forbidding the States to deny women the right to vote. You would have to convince every legislator of the fact that this amendment to the national Constitution ought to be adopted. If you could convince the legislatures of three-fourths of the States, you could get three-fourths of them to grant the suffrage itself.

MRS. HARPER.—They could grant it only to the extent of sending us to the individual voters, while if this amendment were submitted by Congress, and the legislatures indorsed it we would never have to deal with the individual voters.

EDWIN W. HIGGINS [Conn.], of the Committee.—In other words, as I understand you, you have more confidence in the legislatures than in the composite citizenship.

MRS. HARPER.—The composite male citizenship, you mean. We suppose, of course, that the legislatures represent the picked men of the community, its intelligence, its judgment, the best that the community has. That is the supposition! [Laughter.]

THE CHAIRMAN.—That supposition applies to Congress also, does it? [Laughter.]

Mrs. Harper.—In a larger degree.

The Chairman.—The committee is very much obliged to you, Madam.

Miss Addams then asked that a statement be read from Representative Victor L. Berger [Wis.], the one Socialist in Congress. It was in part as follows:

Economics plays an increasingly important part in all our lives, and political power is absolutely necessary to obtain for women the possibility of decent conditions of living. The low pay and the hard conditions of working women are largely due to their disfranchisement. Skilled women who do the same work as men for lower pay could enforce, with the ballot, an equal wage rate.

The ideal woman of the men of past generations was the housewife, the woman who could wash, cook, scrub, knit stockings, make dresses for herself and her children, and take good care of the house. That ideal has become impossible. Those good old days, if ever they were good, are gone forever.

The housewife used to wash. Now the laundry has taken away her washtub and does the work better and cheaper. She used to knit stockings. Now the knitting factory does her knitting. The frugal housewife can buy two pair of stockings for a quarter. She can buy dresses cheaper and better than she can make them.

Even the scrubbing, ironing, and house-cleaning are now done by electricity. In many of the large apartment houses of New York and Washington no cooking in apartments is permitted. Instead there is one restaurant, where usually they have a man cook. And the workingman, as a rule, eats only one meal a day—or, at best, two meals a day—at home. The kitchen is slipping away from the woman.

In the good old days, moreover, the woman was supported by her father first and later by her husband. The situation is entirely different now. The woman has to go to work, often when she is no more than fourteen years old. She surely has to go to work some time, if she belongs to the working class. She must make her own living in the factory, the store, the office, or in the schoolroom. She must work to support herself, and often must also support her family.

The economic basis of the life of a woman has changed in America as well as in England and Germany. And therefore the argument that a woman should not vote because she ought to stay at home and take care of her family is an argument the basis for which has been destroyed. She cannot stay at home, whether she wants to or not. She must go to work to take care of the family. She has acquired the economic functions of the man, and she ought also to acquire the franchise. Without that franchise she cannot protect her interests as a wage earner.

It is often maintained that women are, as a rule, ignorant of politics and that they would make a mess of it if the franchise were given them. It cannot, however, be asserted that men have made so brilliant a success of politics as to warrant them in doubting the political capacity of women. Women, no doubt, are, as a rule, untrained in politics. Their ignorance, however, is due to a lack of training. When the vote is first given them they blunder with it, of course. So, often, do the young men of twenty-one. With more experience, with the consciousness of having the ballot and of its power for good and evil, women soon learn to use it as men use it—for the protection of their political and economic interests. That is the history of woman suffrage in the Western States.

The Socialist Party ever since its origin has stood steadfastly for woman suffrage. It has made this demand of prime importance in all of its platforms everywhere. It recognizes that one-half of the race cannot free itself while leaving the other half unfree. It demands woman suffrage for the same reason that it insists upon manhood suffrage—that the race may become politically free, as a preparation for economic freedom.

Miss Addams.—I will introduce, now, one of my fellow-townswomen, Mary E. McDowell, of the University of Chicago Settlement, who has had what I may call a distressing life in the stockyards district for many years, and she will tell you of the conditions there and what she thinks the franchise will do toward cleaning it up.

Miss McDowell.—I am not one of those who believe that if we get the suffrage we are going to have a millennium or that we can clean up the stockyards entirely and vouchsafe that all of the sausages will be exactly right. But I do believe, with Mrs. Podger, in "Adam Bede." She said, "I am not denying that women are foolish; God Almighty made them to match the men." So we are all, together, very human, both men and women; and it is because this is a human proposition, and not a woman proposition, that I am glad to speak for it. Giving the vote to women is not simply a woman's question. It is a human question. It has to do with the man, the child, the home. Women have always worked, but within less than a century millions of women and girls have been thrust out of the home into a man-made world of industry and commerce.

Acording to the census of 1900, over five and a half million women and girls in America are breadwinners; and the latest census states that 59 per cent. of the girls in America are earning some kind of a living not only for themselves, but for others as well.

Whether we like it or not, this great movement of women out from the home is too tremendous to be put aside by that old-fashioned notion, even though it be a chivalrous one, held by one of our great statesmen, who, when asked if he believed women should have the vote, answered, looking at his wife and daughters: "Oh, no; I think women should be protected." Is it not a large undertaking for the men of the old school of chivalry to protect those millions of young working girls and women? Can anyone give to women any real protection except they themselves?

Do we not see that to the working women must be given every safeguard that workingmen have, for now as they stand side by side with men in the factory and shop they must stand with them politically. The ballot may be, to be sure, but a small bit of the machinery that is to lift the mass of wage-earning women up to a higher plane of self-respect and self-protection, but will it not add the balance of power so much needed by the workingmen in their struggle for protective legislation, which will in the end be shared by the women? To-day women are cheap, unskilled labor and will be until organization and technical training and the responsibility of the ballot in their hands will develop a consciousness of their social value.

As man gave strength to developing the institution of the home, to woman must be given the opportunity to help man humanize the State. She can do this only when she has the ballot and shares the responsibility.

Miss Ella C. Bréhaut, Washington, D. C., of the executive committee of the National Association Opposed to Woman Suffrage, then presented a paper from Grace Duffield Goodwin, chairman of the District of Columbia auxiliary of the anti-suffrage association. The points made by Mrs. Goodwin were as follows:

1. The advocates of the resolution, before submitting it to Congress, should have first ascertained whether it would be adopted by the State legislatures. As such an amendment could not be ratified for many years to come, if ever, its adoption at this time would be an absolute waste of time and energy.

2. The majority of the women of this country do not favor woman suffrage, and are either indifferent or actively opposed. Miss Jessie Ashley, treasurer of the National Woman Suffrage Association, says that, according to a rough estimate, the women favoring suffrage number 3,000,000. This is a high estimate, in view of the fact that only 75,000 are organized. The last information from the Bureau of the Census gives the estimated female population of the continental United States as approximately 46,000,000. The suffrage party thus represents but a small proportion of the whole number of women.

3. American conditions in no way resemble those of the countries in which suffrage is granted to women. If it were given to all the women of this country, the large and ignorant element among negroes and naturalized foreigners, corruptible

because ignorant, would be doubled, and the difficulty of handling an already cumbersome and unwieldy electorate would be greatly increased, and the attendant expense enhanced, while the intelligent element which ought to be a source of strength would be overwhelmed by numbers and lose its direct nonpartisan power of influencing legislation, which it now possesses because unsuspected of interested or selfish motives.

4. There has been formed this year a National Association Opposed to Woman Suffrage, and State associations allied therewith are being organized with rapidity, to express the active opposition of women who have recently been aroused to aggressive effort against woman suffrage. Among the members will be found very many of the sanest, most useful, and best-known women of America, who desire their wishes in this matter to be presented to the governing bodies of our country, feeling sure that every consideration of fairness will be given them, and that their wishes and convictions will be duly weighed.

5. It is manifestly unfair that a question involving so many women should be settled at the behest of a few, and that the majority should have thrust upon them duties and burdens which they are unwilling to assume.

Miss Bréhaut, speaking for herself as a working woman, said she did not believe the majority of her class wanted the suffrage.

Miss Addams replied to Mrs. Goodwin's arguments:

The fact that the amendment must be submitted to the States, and three-fourths of the States pass upon it, will be of great educational value to each State having before its legislature an amendment to the State constitution to give the full franchise for women. Such an amendment is pending in Illinois. We cannot get the suffrage there without it.

Mr. Higgins asked Miss Addams if she was in accord with Mrs. Harper's view that the matter had better be submitted to the legislatures rather than to the citizenship of the States.

Miss Addams.—No; I should like to do it in both ways. In Illinois we would have to have a constitutional convention before we could have the State and Federal franchise. It is a long and difficult process to call a constitutional convention; it is tied up with many checks and counterchecks. We shall be glad ultimately to submit the question to the people, but in the meantime to submit the Federal amendment to the legislatures gives us an educational opportunity. We do not in the least distrust the people.

MR. HIGGINS.—Mrs. Harper's statement seems to me the worst indictment of the referendum that I have ever heard.

MISS ADDAMS.—I do not agree with Mrs. Harper altogether. If you gave the franchise to every adult woman in the United States you would approximately double the native vote, but you would not double the immigrant vote. In my neighborhood we have 20,000 Greek men and less than 1,000 Greek women. There are many more foreign men than women in this country, particularly among the Slavs. If you gave the franchise to every adult woman in the United States, you would cut your immigrant vote while you would double your American vote. I am, however, not one of the people who believe that the immigrant vote is a vote to be feared.

MR. HIGGINS.—I hold the same view expressed by Dr. Lyman Abbott on this subject. I am in favor of the suffrage if the matter is submitted to women and the majority vote for it.

MISS ADDAMS.—That has never before been required from any other class desiring the franchise. You did not wait for every negro to vote for it; they might not have had it yet. That was not done in the Chartist movement in England. The franchise was extended to the workingmen in England in that long agitation starting in 1832, not because every workingman wanted it, but because the leading statesmen saw the advantage of the ballot to the workingman himself and to the political life of the nation.

John W. Davis [W. Va.], of the committee, suggested that the disproportion of the sexes among immigrants was only temporary. To this Miss Addams agreed, saying that young unmarried men came first; later, families.

MR. HIGGINS.—If you did not think the majority of women wanted full suffrage, you would not favor it, would you?

MISS ADDAMS.—Yes, sir. It is not a question of forcing it upon the women who do not want it. It is a question of giving it to the minority who do want it.

MR. HIGGINS.—You do not take the view, then, which has been advanced by a good many, that the failure to exercise suffrage should work as a deprivation of the franchise?

Miss Addams.—No; I do not. I think if a man is not interested he ought not to vote. He does no good voting blindly.

Mr. Higgins.—So you assume an interest, always.

Miss Addams.—He should be interested, but if he is not, the man who does not want to vote ought to stay at home.

Mr. Littleton.—Do you think failure to exercise suffrage ought, as sometimes, to cause a forfeiture of it or a suspension of it?

Miss Addams.—No.

Mr. Littleton.—Do you not think the person who has suffrage and does not pretend to use it ought to have it suspended for a while?

Miss Addams.—No; I should not penalize him. The point is, that those of us who do want to vote, cannot; those who do not want to are not being forced to.

Mr. Littleton.—In election frauds that have come up in some States they punished them for the misuse of the suffrage.

Miss Addams.—I think for grafting

Mr. Littleton.—You think there ought to be some law depriving persons of the right to vote because they have misused it?

Miss Addams.—There is a difference between misusing it and merely not using it.

Mr. Littleton.—It has occurred to me there ought to be some sort of penalty or a suspension of the franchise to non-users, until they come to a realization of the use of it.

Miss Addams.—Women would be pleased to take up such questions later, after we have the vote.

Mr. Littleton.—Yes; I was anxious to have your view. Can not the constitution of Illinois be amended in any fashion without a constitutional convention?

Miss Addams.—Yes; but our constitution is very difficult to amend. The legislature can propose only one amendment at the same session, and that article cannot be again amended for four years. There are proposed amendments pending covering many years to come.

I should like to say one more thing in regard to working women. I know a great many working women, and certainly I know of no class of women who so clearly see the necessity for the vote or so sorely need the power of protecting themselves as working women do. They are becoming increasingly conscious of it. We have a ten-hour law in Illinois, and hope to soon have a law to protect the women in dangerous trades. At every session of the legislature there is more and more legislation for the protection of working women. It is the trade-union girls themselves who always appear before the legislature and make arguments. It is not a philanthropic undertaking at all. It is being pushed by the working women of Illinois.

I should like to call upon Caroline A. Lowe, of Kansas City, Mo., as the next speaker.

Miss Lowe spoke as a wage-earner and on behalf of the 7,000,000 wage-earning women in the United States. She emphasized the arguments already made on the necessity of her class being protected by the ballot. Women workers needed to be relieved of long hours of labor, to be protected from injuries by machinery, to secure better wages, etc. She related instances of great abuses arising from present non-protection in these regards. One was of a working girl during the great garment workers' strike in Chicago.

Katie Malloy had worked at Hart-Schaffner & Marx for five years and had saved $30. It was soon gone. She hunted for work, applied at the Young Woman's Christian Association and was told that so many hundreds of girls were out of work that they could not possibly do anything for her. She walked the streets day after day without success. For three days she had almost nothing to eat. "Oh," she said, with the tears streaming down her cheeks, "there is always some place where a man can crowd in and keep decent, but for us girls there is no place, no place but one, and it is thrown open to us day and night. Hundreds of girls—girls that worked by me in the shop—have gone into houses of—houses of—impurity."

Has Katie Malloy and the 5,000 working girls who are forced into lives of shame each month no need of a voice in a government that should protect them from this worse than death?

Women, said Miss Lowe, as an almost universal rule, received only about half the wages of men doing the same work.

We have equal need of food, clothing, and shelter. But at 21 years of age a powerful weapon is given our brothers for self-defense, a larger means for growth and self-expression.

We working women, because we are women and find our sex not a source of strength, but a source of weakness and offering a greater opportunity for exploitation, have even greater need of this weapon than our brothers.

For the same reason the working girl needed the ballot more than her employer.

Why is it given to him while it is denied to us? Is it for the protection of his property that he may have a voice in the governing of his wealth, of his stocks and bonds and merchandise?

The wealth of the working woman is far more precious to the welfare of the State. From nature's raw products the working class can readily replace all of the material wealth owned by the employing class, but the wealth of the working woman is the wealth of flesh and blood, of all her physical, mental, and spiritual powers. It is the wealth not only of to-day, but that of future generations that is being bartered away so cheaply. Have we no right to a voice in the disposal of our wealth, the greatest wealth that the world possesses, the priceless wealth of its womanhood?

Is it not the cruelest injustice that to the man whose material wealth is a source of strength and protection to him, and of power over us, should be given the additional advantage of an even greater weapon which he can use to perpetuate our condition of helpless subjection?

Miss Lowe declared that in public employment men were favored over women.

The Chicago teachers, firemen, and policemen had had their salaries cut because of the poverty of the city. The teachers' salaries were cut the third time. They organized to investigate the reason for the reduction. Margaret Haley was selected to carry on the investigation. As a result she unearthed the fact that large corporations were not paying the legal amount of taxes. The teachers forced the issue, and through their efforts in July, 1902, $597,033 in back taxes on the franchises of five public utility corporations was turned into the public treasury, and a few months later an additional $600,000 taxes on these franchises was paid. What was done with it? The policemen and firemen had the cut in their salaries restored, while the teachers did not. Instead, the finance committee recommended and the board of education appropriated the teachers' share to pay coal bills, repairs, etc.

Why was this? It was a clear case of the usual treatment accorded to a disfranchised class.

Miss Lowe declared that the ballot had never yet been granted by a ruling class to a serving class because of the latter's need.

Almost without exception, the extension of the franchise has taken place only when the needs of the industrial development have demanded a larger degree of freedom upon the part of the serving class; so that the serving class, driven by the very pressure of economic need, has organized as a class, and after a struggle has wrested from the grasp of the ruling class a larger share in the powers of government.

At the breaking up of the feudal system, the peasants in large numbers left the estates of their masters and entered upon the new form of industry made possible through manufacturing. To escape the robbery of the nobility, they organized in guilds. As a result of the struggle the members of the guilds forced the nobility to relinquish their exorbitant demands, and free towns came into existence.

When the industrial basis of any society, or any large portion of society, changes, the superstructure must change in accordance with it. This was again proved when the transition from the hand tool to machine production took place. Again it resulted in an extension of the franchise to a still larger portion of the working class.

Miss Lowe then declared that we were in the midst of another change of the industrial system, that from home manufacture of food, clothing, etc., to factory manufacture.

Even the education of our children is placed in the hands of the kindergarten and the public schools. There has been nothing for us to do but to follow our jobs into the great industrial centers. The political superstructure must be adjusted to conform to this change. This industrial change has given to woman a larger horizon, a greater freedom of action in the industrial world. Greater freedom and larger expression are at hand for her in the political life.

Mr. Chairman, and gentlemen of the committee, the time is ripe for the extension of the franchise to women. We do not come before you to beg of you the granting of any favor. We present to you a glorious opportunity to place yourselves abreast of the current of this great evolutionary movement. You can refuse to accept this opportunity, and you may for a moment delay its advance. But in effect it will be only as that of the old woman who, with her tiny broom, endeavored to sweep back the incoming tide from the sea. If you desire to take the broad, progressive attitude, you will support the suffrage amendment now before your committee.

MISS ADDAMS.—There are being organized all over the country leagues of men who devote themselves to the advancement of equal suffrage. It is a very great pleasure for us to have them associated with us. We have a representative here to-day of one of the leagues, James L. Laidlaw, of New York City.

Mr. Laidlaw spoke of the Men's League for Woman's Suffrage; its spread from New York to other large cities of the Union.

We believe this is the leading political question of the day, and that the time is now ripe for taking it in hand.

It has been said that women do not want the suffrage. We men of the league believe that, if only one woman in the country wants it, she should have it, and not have to wait for a majority of her sex to express a desire for it.

If then, said Mr. Laidlaw, the suffrage is a matter of right, Congress should not delay granting it in the speediest fashion. This is by constitutional amendment.

Why should we give women the right to hold property, why should we give them the right to an education, and refuse them the right to protect their interests or the right to express themselves politically? That question is being asked to-day all over the world. This is a women's era; the women in Europe and in Asia are working for the ballot just as they are in this country, and, believe me, the women of China—think of China showing us the way—appear to be nearer gaining the franchise than the women of this country. It seems a disgrace that we, the people of the United States, who vauntingly use the terms liberty, equality, democracy, should permit one country after another, oriental and European, to show us the way to a true civilization.

Mrs. Elsie Cole Phillips, a Socialist of Milwaukee, Wis., was then introduced. She replied to the anti-suffrage argument of "increasing the ignorant vote" by saying that many members of the so-called educated classes were lamentably ignorant of fundamental things in our political, social, and industrial organization, in which members of our so-called non-educated classes took great concern. To illustrate this she told an experience of Mrs. Frederick Nathan, president of the Consumers' League, of New York City. Mrs. Nathan, said Mrs. Phillips, being naturally a woman suffragist, asked a young woman clerking in a department store if she took an interest in women voting.

The girl replied indifferently, "Oh, not very much." And Mrs. Nathan said, "That is very strange to me. You ought to realize what it would mean to you to have a political expression for your needs, needs that no one but yourself can understand." The girl said, "Oh, yes; of course, that is true. All of us girls know what we need. The working girls would vote all right, but it just appalls me to think of letting in that ignorant Fifth Avenue vote." [Laughter.]

Mr. Littleton asked Mrs. Phillips what proportion of woman suffragists were Socialists. Mrs. Phillips was sorry to say that, in her opinion, it was only a very small percentage. She implied in her answer that almost all Socialists were in favor of woman suffrage.

On this point Miss Bréhaut remarked that the New York *Call,* a Socialist organ, had declared that in a recent election in Los Angeles, Cal., three Socialist votes out of five were cast by women.

Changing the subject she denied the claim that the equal suffrage States had been more friendly to humane legislation than the other States.

The model child labor law proposed by the National Child Labor Committee contains 49 sections, and the following figures show the number of these provisions already enacted in the woman suffrage States and those of similar conditions and location: Of the 49 provisions we find the law of Wyoming contains none; Idaho contains none; Colorado contains 7; Utah, 8; California, 12; Oregon, 14; Oklahoma, 15; North Dakota, 15; Minnesota, 20; Nebraska, 25; Wisconsin, 27. It is obvious that the man-suffrage States have the best child-labor laws and that the education of public opinion has more to do with the passage of good laws than women's votes.

Because of the value of woman's particular function to society and because of her physical limitations public opinion demands a limit to the hours of labor for women in industry. In 31 States laws have been passed limiting the number of hours of labor in which wage-earning women may be employed. Does any suffragist claim that these laws materialized through women's votes?

It has been claimed here to-day that low wages, speeding, etc., would be cured by votes, though it has been proved over and over again that the vote does not control economic conditions. The law of supply and demand, modified by the demands of organized labor, controls wages. Men everywhere improve their condition by unions and collective bargaining, and if they demand and obtain an uneconomic wage the industry is soon impaired and wages again adjust themselves.

Many women receive equal pay for equal work, and when they receive lower wages than men it is not because they are without votes, but because they are women, with physical and mental limitations which cannot be legislated out of existence.

Women's limitations are natural and not to her discredit. According to the Pittsburgh *Survey* she is often prevented by inferior strength from competing for the best positions. This publication gives the following facts: Of the 22,185 women employed in Pittsburgh, only 3 per cent. possess a handicraft or are engaged in skilled work. Most of the occupations of women in that city require neither training nor stability nor intelligence. Skill and judgment and the relation of one machine to another cannot be learned in three or six months, and there is no apparent utility in training a woman to a knowledge of several processes when she hopes to end her factory or shop employment in six or eight years and has a consequent lack of ambition. Together these facts produce an unbusinesslike attitude, a conscious instability. For this reason women are undesirable apprentices. They can be employed profitably only at such occupations as are quickly learned. Their opportunities for employment are, with one exception, still further circumscribed by the opposition of men's unions, and the unions that bar women are those of skilled workers; and this is true in spite of the fact that the American Federation of Labor stands for woman suffrage. Her lack of physical strength, the opposition of men's unions, and her industrial instability combine to leave women the subsidiary processes and the mechanical operations which demand little intelligence. Expectation of marriage lessens her ambition, and this lack of ambition can have no other effect than to limit efficiency.

Naturally, the subsidiary processes are stultifying, slipping a hinge into place, filling pickle bottles, packing crackers, fruit and candy, stitching seams in ready-made garments, etc. Women's trade-unions and trade training are now considered the remedy for these undesirable conditions; but, even when they become general, they will not alter the natural limitations of women, both mental and physical. With trade training her neuromuscular exhaustibility will be less apparent, and the result may be a lengthening of her trade life, but she will still desire and expect to marry. It is hoped by a number of intelligent men and women that trade training will materialize long before votes for women, and that this trade training will be a part of the public-school system or given in coöperation with boards of education. Public education, gentlemen, is not a function of the National Government, and we do not look to you to solve these economic problems.

A better distribution of immigrants in small groups to those localities where they are needed and can be Americanized would also seem to be a function of the National Government, and would certainly do more to prevent an oversupply of labor in the great centers of population than women's votes.

The implication by Mrs. Phillips that connection with the Consumers' League connotes a belief in woman suffrage has no foundation in fact. I am myself a member of the Consumers' League and point to its effective work as a proof of the power of women's organizations unhampered by partisan politics.

The most emphasized reason given to-day is that woman suffrage is right. No measure of government is right unless it be for the greatest good of the greatest number. As a political unit, would the average woman do better than the average man? If not, there can be no possible reason for compelling her to assume the responsibilities that the ballot imposes. If she failed to do much better the added vote would be only an extra expense without corresponding gain.

Would a taxpayer's wife be sufficiently interested in the welfare of women teachers to vote for men pledged to raise their pay at a greatly increased cost to the community? Would a working woman consider anything but her own convenience and comfort in voting on a subway bond issue? Would a Congressman's wife be overcritical of her husband's legislative acts or of his party? Would women generally be interested in the good of the greatest number, and, if so, would this interest lead to a large attendance at primary elections and an intelligent consideration of the relative merits of candidates for nomination? We claim that this would not result. Average women, on attaining the ballot, might for several years be on their mettle, but their interest in politics would very naturally be spasmodic and not to be counted on. Prof. Jensen says of Utah women that "their interest in politics is passive rather than active." There are thousands of women who are interested in politics, but millions who are not.

This mental attitude toward politics is perfectly natural. Should the majority of women appreciate the privilege of voting, and gain the familiarity with affairs that would make it intelligent, they would certainly be deprived of time that is necessary for recreation and physical upbuilding. Even without the burden of politics the woman of the majority (the married woman without a servant) does not generally devote enough time to this purpose. Overtired nervous women do not make for the betterment of the race, and manifold functions, except where circumstances are very favorable, do not result in well-balanced natures.

And the women who demand this full life for all women are not sincere. The full life, supposed to be consequent on entrance into politics, is only desired by a small minority of middle-class women, mostly college and professional women, who see in political position a release from the strain of competitive life. One leader, the Rev. Anna Shaw, has expressed a desire to be United States Senator. This desire for office has been expressed to-day before your honorable committee. We submit, gentlemen, that one can hardly pick up a newspaper without reading of the appointment or election of some specially qualified woman to office in States where only men vote. We do not desire that women should be appointed or elected because they are women, but only when they can demonstrate peculiar fitness. These college and professional women are making good from year to year, and new avenues of usefulness are being opened up to them. Practically all industries and professions and many elective and appointive places in municipal and State government are open to women. The greatest good to the greatest number makes it inexpedient that the whole realm of politics should be theirs.

Miss Addams states that the foreign vote of Chicago would not be doubled by woman suffrage, and refers to the large number of Greeks and Slavs in that city who have no women folk. But I would say that the birth rate among the foreign born in this country is three times as large as that among native-born Americans. The foreign born people and their children constituted, in 1900, 48 per cent. of the total population of the country, and much more than half the white population of the Northern States, reaching 79 per cent. in New York and Chicago.

According to Dr. Sidney D. Wilgus, chairman of the committee on immigration of the New York State Lunacy Commission, one out of every four immigrants is found to be an undesirable.

I don't agree with Miss Addams that education is not a necessary qualification in voters. The men and women of high ideals who have accomplished much for children would be hampered rather than helped by the votes of ignorant mothers. The tenement-house mother is so ignorant of the rights of childhood that she will hide her young daughter from the inspector that the child may continue to ruin her eyes and health by knotting willow plumes.

With reference to the alliance of the suffragists with the socialists "for convenience," and not on principle, I submit that socialistic principles are now taught by the woman-suffrage leaders, particularly the economic independence of all married women, and the State nurseries that would in such case be necessary, involving the general loosening of marriage and family ties that naturally follows with the shifting of responsibility from the individual to the State.

Miss Ashley, the treasurer of the National Woman Suffrage Association, has frequently written the weekly headquarters letters in the *Woman's Journal* (their national organ). She states that "our cities swarm with outraged, degraded, unfree women," and advises her readers to study the facts of social conditions "with an open mind," and to this end she especially recommends August Bebel's book on "Woman." This book is a translation from the German; and, besides describing and arraigning conditions that have never obtained in this country, it preaches the most radical socialist doctrines, such as free love.

Conservative women, gentlemen, see nothing but danger in woman suffrage. If the ballot is given them, patriotism would compel all right-minded women to vote. Men are nowhere excused from taking up the responsibility laid upon them by the State.

Mrs. Harper explained the apparent preponderance of Socialists among the woman suffragists by saying the Socialist party openly advocated equal suffrage.

The Democratic and Republican parties do not stand for woman suffrage, and that is why there seems to be more Socialist women than Republican or Democratic women. If the two old parties will come out for woman suffrage then the women will show their colors.

Miss Addams suggested to the committee that a commission be appointed by the House "to look into the question of woman suffrage, the possible demand for it in the various States, and the success it has gained in other States."

She closed the hearing by relating a story to illustrate the help women could give to men in public affairs. It was of a patriotic play written by a small boy in a city social "settlement."

The first act showed two Revolutionary soldiers on watch; one soldier said to the other, "Say, ain't it fierce, we ain't got no flag for this Revolution!" and the other soldier said, "Ain't it fierce!" and that was the sum of the act. The dramatic personnel of the second act were George Washington and a Revolutionary officer, and the officer said, "Ain't it fierce we ain't got no flag for this Revolution!" and Gen. Washington said, "Ain't it fierce!" and that was the sum of the second act.

The third act showed George Washington calling upon Betsy Ross, the latter in a domestic setting, rocking a baby. George said, "Betsy, ain't it fierce we ain't got no flag for this Revolution!" and Betsy Ross said, "Yes; ain't it fierce. Hold the baby and I will make one." [Laughter.]

The anti-suffragists submitted a number of papers opposed to the amendment, of which two had a special bearing on the question of the success of woman suffrage in Colorado.

WOMAN SUFFRAGE IN COLORADO

I have voted since 1893. I have been a delegate to the city and State conventions, and a member of the Republican State committee from my county. I have been a deputy sheriff and a

watcher at the polls. For 23 years I have been in the midst of
the woman suffrage movement in Colorado. For years I believed
in woman suffrage and have worked day in and day out for it.
I now see my mistake and would abolish it to-morrow if I could.

No law has been put on the statute books of Colorado for the
benefit of women and children that has been put there by the
women. The child-labor law went through independently of the
women's vote. The hours of the working women have not been
shortened; the wages of school-teachers have not been raised;
the type of men that get into office has not improved a bit.

Frankly, the experiment is a failure. It has done Colorado
no good. It has done woman no good. The best thing for both
would be if to-morrow the ballot for women could be abolished.

MRS. FRANCIS W. GODDARD,
President of the Colonial Dames of Colorado.

December, 1910.

Our State has tried the female suffrage plan a sufficiently
long time to form a fair idea of its workings. I am not prejudiced in any way, but honestly do not see where the experiment
has proved of benefit. . . . It has produced no special reforms, and it has had no particular purifying effect upon politics. There is a growing tendency on the part of most of the
better and more intelligent of the female voters of Colorado to
cease exercising the ballot. . . . If it were to be done over
again the people of Colorado would defeat woman suffrage by
an overwhelming majority.

MOSES HALLETT,
United States District Judge for Colorado.

The anti-suffragists also submitted a pamphlet containing the arguments and opinions of eminent opponents
of woman suffrage.[1]

In the presidential campaign of 1912 woman suffrage
was for the first time advocated by a major party, the
Progressive platform declaring that this party, "believ-

[1] The reader who desires to study the subject further is advised to
write for this pamphlet, as well as other anti-suffrage literature, to the
New York State Association Opposed to Woman Suffrage, 29 West 39th
St., New York City. A pamphlet and various leaflets containing opinions
and arguments of eminent advocates of woman suffrage, as well as other
literature on the subject, may be procured from the National American
Woman Suffrage Association, 505 Fifth Avenue, New York City.

ing that no people can justly claim to be a true democracy which denies political rights on account of sex, pledges itself to the task of securing equal suffrage to men and women alike.'' The Prohibition and the Socialist parties, as they had done in the past, declared for equal suffrage. The Republican and Democratic parties were silent on the question, their candidates declaring it was a State and not a national issue.

For the first time in American politics a woman took official part in a presidential convention, Miss Jane Addams of Chicago seconding the nomination of Theodore Roosevelt, the Progressive candidate for President.

CHAPTER XI

FEDERAL RECOGNITION OF POLYGAMY

[POLYGAMY AND SLAVERY]

Sketch of the Rise of Mormonism, Its Settlement of Utah, and Its Doctrine of Polygamy—Bill Is Introduced in the House of Representatives
to Grant Lands in Utah to White Settlers, Excluding Polygamists—Debate on the Exclusion as Implying Recognition of Polygamy: John M.
Bernhisel [Utah], Solomon G. Haven [N. Y.], John Letcher [Va.],
Thomas Davis [R. I.], William Smith [Va.], Williamson R. W. Cobb
[Ala.], Joshua R. Giddings [O.], Philip Phillips [Ala.], Lewis D. Campbell [O.], Alexander H. Stephens [Ga.], Gerrit Smith [N. Y.], David
T. Disney [O.], John S. Millson [Va.], George A. Simmons [N. Y.],
Samuel Parker [Ind.], Samuel P. Benson [Me.], Joseph Lane [Ore.],
Mike Walsh [N. Y.], John Kerr [N. C.], John Z. Goodrich [Mass.],
Nathaniel G. Taylor [Tenn.], Charles Ready [Tenn.], Lawrence M.
Keitt [S. C.], James L. Seward [Ga.], Hiram Walbridge [N. Y.], Caleb
Lyon [N. Y.], Charles Hughes [N. Y.], Bishop Perkins [N. Y.], William W. Boyce [S. C.], John L. Taylor [O.]—Declaration of Republican
Platform [1856] against Polygamy—Speech of Representative Justin
S. Morrill: ''Polygamy a National Reproach''—The Mormon War of
1857-8—The Morrill Anti-Polygamy Act of 1860.

JOSEPH SMITH (born Sharon, Vt., December 23,
1805; assassinated in jail at Carthage, Ill., by a
mob, June 27, 1844) was a gold-seeker near
Palmyra, N. Y., who claimed to have discovered in 1823
gold plates engraved with strange characters. Deciphering the writing by means of a divining crystal,
which he called the ''Urim and Thummin,'' he found it
to be the ''Book of Mormon,'' the ''Sacred History of
Ancient America from the Earliest Ages after the Flood
to the Beginning of the Christian Era,'' telling of the
settlement of the country by early colonies of Israelites,
and the mission to them of Jesus Christ after his resurrection, and containing references to the religious and

401

critical movements of Smith's time, with religious rules, exhortations, etc. This book he published at Palmyra in 1830; in the same year and place the "Church of Jesus Christ of Latter-Day Saints" was founded on the revelation. It is generally known by outsiders (called "Gentiles" by the believers) as the Mormon Church, and its followers are called Mormons.

Sidney Rigdon, a minister of the Disciples' Church, organized at Kirtland, O., a congregation of Mormons, and thither in February, 1831, Smith betook himself. Rigdon had imbibed communistic ideas, and these Smith incorporated in his religion, founding a city of "Zion" near Kirtland, and starting various coöperative industries in Kirtland and neighboring towns, all of which projects languished and expired, the final crash coming with the complete failure in 1838 of the Kirtland Society Anti-Banking Company, which had uttered $200,000 in notes.

In 1835, while at Kirtland, Smith chose twelve Apostles, one of whom was Brigham Young. It is charged that Smith sanctioned polygamy, and that it was practiced to some extent by his followers. In 1836 he expelled one of his first converts, David Whitmer, for opposition to the doctrine, it is said. A later sect, the "Reorganized Church of Latter-Day Saints," which was organized under the leadership of the prophet's son, Joseph Smith, claims that the doctrine of "spiritual wifery" as it is called, was introduced, not by the prophet, but by the older men, such as Rigdon.

Upon the failure of the "Anti-Banking Company" Treasurer Smith and Secretary Rigdon went to Far West, Mo., where a Mormon colony had been established, to set up there a new "Zion." Smith deposed the officers of the colony for misappropriation of funds, etc., and, a defection of Mormon officials, including two Apostles, ensuing, established, it is said, a band of "Avenging Angels" or "Danites," to terrorize his followers into remaining in the church. He also established a tithing system, the revenues of which were applied to church purposes.

On July 4, 1838, Rigdon preached a sermon in which he predicted a war of extermination between "Saints" and "Gentiles." There ensued a partisan warfare between the Mormons and their rough, pioneer neighbors, in which Governor Dunklin of Missouri, on October 27, took a hand by ordering the Mormons to be driven from the State. The leaders of the sect, including Smith, were arrested. Smith was liberated after a trial in which testimony was presented as to the fell purpose of the Danites, and the orders of the Mormon leaders to spoil the Gentiles.

Smith purchased the city of Commerce in Illinois, upon the Mississippi, changing its name to Nauvoo, said to be a Hebrew word meaning "Beautiful," and thither led his people. The place flourished because of great accessions to the church from all over the country, and from England, whither missionaries had been sent. A military company, the "Nauvoo Legion," and a "university" were organized, with the countenance of State officials, for Smith was welcomed into politics because of the solid vote which was at his complete disposal. Indeed, he became so bold that he presented to President Van Buren a claim for Mormon losses amounting to $1,381,044.55½. On obtaining no action upon his claim, he ran for President himself.

On July 12, 1843, Smith gave out his famous "Revelation on the Eternity of the Marriage Covenant, including Plurality of Wives." In this the authority for polygamy was derived from the Old Testament. Smith had twenty wives, some of whom were taken over after his death by Brigham Young.

This practice, as well as the destruction of an anti-Mormon newspaper press by the Nauvoo Legion, caused the Gentile population of the neighborhood to rise in arms against the Mormons in June, 1844. Smith and his brother Hyrum were arrested and incarcerated at Carthage. On June 27 a mob broke into the jail and brutally murdered both prisoners.

Brigham Young succeeded Smith in leadership. He sent investigators into the Far West to find a proper place for colonization, removed from a chance of disturbance for years to come. Upon their report, he selected the Great Salt Lake Valley, and thither led the Mormons, completing the emigration in 1848. With marvelous energy Young set about building a city, even contemplating the establishment of factories of all sorts, in order to render the colony independent.

But despite Young's indomitable courage and the implicit faith he inspired in his followers, undoubtedly the colony would have proved a failure had it not been for the discovery of gold in California at this juncture, bringing an almost continuous train of gold-seekers through Salt Lake City, all in need of supplies in the midst of their journey through the "Great American Desert." This event, and the subsequent building of the Union Pacific Railroad, established the prosperity of the colony and the credit and power of its leader.

Utah was a part of the cession of the United States at the close of the Mexican War, and was organized as a Territory September 9, 1850. Brigham Young was appointed governor. He took the high hand toward Federal officials sent out from the East; thus when one of them, Judge Brocehus, criticized polygamy, Young publicly called him a coward, and demanded that he "apologize to the satisfaction of the ladies." When President Pierce offered the governorship to an army officer, Lieutenant-Colonel Steptoe, stationed in Utah, Young threatened vengeance against the Federal Government for the "infringement upon his rights."

The subject of polygamy came first before Congress in connection with a bill in the House introduced from the Committee on Territories "to establish the office of surveyor-general of Utah to grant donations (of land) to actual white settlers therein, and for other purposes."

A condition of the land grant was that its benefits should "not extend to any person who shall now, or at any time hereafter, be the husband of more than one wife." This proviso created an animated discussion in which almost every Representative desired to take part. The debate was therefore conducted under the five-minute rule. Among the speakers were: John M. Bernhisel [delegate from Utah, and a Mormon], Solomon G. Haven [N. Y.], John Letcher [Va.], Thomas Davis [R. I.], William Smith [Va.], Williamson R. W. Cobb [Ala.], Joshua R. Giddings [O.], Philip Phillips [Ala.], Lewis D. Campbell [O.], Alexander H. Stephens [Ga.], Gerrit Smith ([N. Y.], David T. Disney [O.], John S. Millson [Va.], George A. Simmons [N. Y.], Samuel Parker [Ind.], Samuel P. Benson [Me.], Joseph Lane [delegate from Oregon], Mike Walsh [N. Y.], John Kerr [N. C.], John Z. Goodrich [Mass.], Nathaniel G. Taylor [Tenn.], Charles Ready [Tenn.], Lawrence M. Keitt [S. C.], James L. Seward [Ga.], Hiram Walbridge [N. Y.], Caleb Lyon [N. Y.], Charles Hughes [N. Y.], Bishop Perkins [N. Y.], William W. Boyce [S. C.], and John L. Taylor [O.].

GOVERNMENT RECOGNITION OF POLYGAMY

HOUSE OF REPRESENTATIVES, MAY 4, 1854

Mr. Bernhisél, the delegate from Utah, a Mormon, moved to strike out the proviso. Mr. Haven seconded the motion, for the reason, as he said, that he did not desire by any legislation to recognize any such institution as polygamy.

Mr. Letcher rose to ask the reason for the discrimination in the bill whereby "the settler was to be punished for having more wives than one, while office-holders" (the surveyor-general and his assistants) "who are in receipt of large salaries, not only have the benefit of money, but of the women to boot."

Mr. Davis did not see that the discrimination was worse than inserting the word "white" in all the territorial bills. Worse than polygamy existed among the Southern slaves, and that by the compulsion of law which did not recognize slave marriages. Slavery was now to be introduced in the Territories, bringing there a system of promiscuous concubinage, worse than polygamy, for the Mormons had made some regulation at least of that practice. He was opposed, however, to the introduction of either system, because of their common opposition to moral laws, as understood by every reasonable man.

Mr. Smith [Va.] denied that promiscuous concubinage existed among the Southern negroes, and affirmed that, on the contrary, the marriage tie was as sacredly observed by them as among white people in the North. Incontinence was as rare in the South as in "the great State of Rhode Island."

Mr. Cobb asked the delegate from Utah whether the proviso would work hardship to any considerable number of the inhabitants of the Territory.

Mr. Bernhisel replied yes: "The more wives a man has the more farms he needs to support them." [Laughter.]

Mr. Giddings charged the Southern Representatives with inconsistency. They had repudiated all attempts *to interfere with the domestic institutions of our Territories,* and now were in favor of interfering with the domestic institution of marriage among the Utah Mormons.

Although he was opposed to polygamy, nevertheless, while we legislated for slavery, he would deal out to the Mormons the same measure of justice that he would to the citizens of Nebraska with their hundreds of [negro] concubines.

When the Mormon marries, he does it openly before the public. The act is lawfully registered; and, when it has taken place, the woman assumes and takes the same standing in society and in the community as her husband. He recognizes her as his lawful partner. His children are legitimate. They are educated; they are taught to understand the laws of the country, and its Constitution. They become enlightened and intelligent, and may become useful members of the community.

Sir, the Mormon does not sell his wife, nor does he sell his children. No, sir. God forbid. The Mormon recognizes his child as entitled to his care, to his attention, to his protection, to the privileges of education. He does not sell his own offspring to a slave dealer. No, sir; no, sir. The gentleman over the way, from Virginia [Mr. Smith] says that negroes in the South are entitled to marriage. Why, sir, am I to stand here at this day and proclaim that there is no such institution as legal marriage among three millions of slaves in the United States? A fact of which we all are conscious. Is it not true that the gentleman who has made the declarations would sell the wife of his slave to-morrow if he could get his price for her? Or, that he would do worse, perhaps?

Mr. Phillips would not trust himself to reply to such language as had fallen from the gentleman from Ohio, but left him to his own conscience and the reprobation of his constituents. He wished to strike out the proviso, as tending to the centralization of the Government.

We are not only now undertaking to regulate the industry of the country, to regulate the education of the country, to become the general almoner for all its charities; but we are now undertaking to regulate its morality. Sir, where, in the legislation of Congress, will any gentleman point me to a precedent where such a provision as this has ever been annexed to any legislation of Congress? Why, sir, in the homestead bill which this House has passed, was there any provision that no man shall become a settler who had been an adulterer; that no man should be entitled to the benefit of a homestead who had taken the life of his brother, or who had committed a larceny, or any crime whatever? Why is it that in this bill, in reference to the only Territory where this is regarded as a legal institution, this provision is inserted. Why, sir, if, in Utah, which is an organized Territory governing itself, the marriage of more than one wife is illegal, it is punishable there as a crime; and, if legal, it is a most extraordinary thing that, having permitted the organization of a Territory where this is a known legal institution, when we pass bills for that Territory we exclude from its benefits all the person who are living in said Territory.

Why, sir, I say that there is no principle whatever on which this is founded; and the remark of the gentleman from Virginia [Mr. Letcher] to the inquiry was perfectly legitimate. For if we exclude these men from the benefit of settlements on the land, on the ground that they are in the commission of a crime, why, I ask, do you not annex the same condition to the salaries of the important officers in the same country? You have given salaries to the governor and judicial officers of that Territory. Why, then, has not this condition been annexed to those salaries?

I say that Congress has nothing to do whatever with this

transaction. We are disposing of the public land. It is not necessary or proper for this Government to make this condition. How is it to be worked out? Who is to investigate the fact? If you are making a provision it ought to be a provision with some sanction; there should be some mode of enforcing it. What provision is there here for ascertaining the fact whether the party is entitled to make the entry?

To what tribunal have you delegated the inquiry to know whether the person applying for this benefit is subject to the condition? Sir, there is nothing of all this; and it looks to me to be most out of place, and most inopportune. It is certainly without the slightest precedent in the past history of the country; and I trust, therefore, that this motion to strike out will prevail.

Mr. Campbell believed Congress had complete power over the Territories, including the morals of its people. He was as much opposed to centralization as the member from Alabama.

I am in favor of State rights and of popular rights, and am for resisting all attempts that may be made to overwhelm in the halls of legislation that which is known to be the sentiment of the people of this land. Sir, it sounds strangely to me to hear a gentleman condemning that which may seem to be, in this instance, centralization and consolidation, who is in favor of hurrying through in hot haste a measure that is to affect a vast empire in the future, when no voice has been raised from any State or from any portion of the people of this land in favor of it.

Mr. Stephens said that the member from Ohio was mistaken; that the legislatures of Georgia, Louisiana, and other States had spoken in favor of the proviso.

The chairman declared that the speaker was traveling outside of the record, the actions of the legislatures not having been presented to the House.

Mr. Stephens admitted this fact, and addressed himself to the remarks of Mr. Campbell. He denied that it was the province of Congress to interfere in the case of morals.

Sir, the Constitution of the United States has guarded this point. Congress has no power to establish any religion—none at all. Congress has no power to touch the question of morals, which lie at the foundation of all systems of religion. Congress can rightfully exercise no power which looks to the establishment of any particular tenets of any religion or any religious sect, or to the putting down of any such religion or sect, either in the States, Territories, or anywhere else. Congress can interfere only with such actions in a criminal point of view as come within the class of "*mala prohibita.*" Congress has no right to look to those actions designated by ethical writers as "*mala in se.*" None whatever.

The gentleman says that this practice of polygamy is regarded as a great moral crime in every one of the States of the Union. I am not going to discuss before this House the question whether that practice is moral or not. Congress has no right to set up a standard of morals for the people of any portion of this country. I meet this question at the threshold—I stand upon principle. I stand upon the Constitution of the United States. I will do the same justice to the people of Utah that I will to people of other Territories, without inquiring into their ecclesiastical polity.

I am in favor of granting lands to the people of the Territory of Utah in the same manner, and upon the same terms, as we do to the people of other Territories of the Union. I would make no discrimination. If we discriminate to-day against *Mormons,* to-morrow, perhaps, we shall be asked to discriminate against Baptists, Methodists, Presbyterians, or Catholics. The evils of such discriminations, or even the attempt to make them, have been wisely provided against in the Constitution. Let us stand by the Constitution. Let us strike out this proviso, and let the people of Utah, amenable to their own laws, civil as well as ecclesiastical, have the rights and privileges of this bill, just as the people of all the other Territories within our jurisdiction. The power which will be exercised in this proviso will, if ever brought in full operation, break down the only safeguard we have for religious freedom.

Mr. Smith [N. Y.] thought that no subject had come before the House involving more important principles than this question, and therefore that it should be discussed temperately and acted upon deliberately and wisely. He was in favor of retaining the proviso.

In reply to Mr. Smith [Va.] he would say that Congress should discuss questions in their legal aspect. We are not to accept concessions in place of rights. Kind masters might concede marriage to their slaves, but this was not granted the slaves by law. Wives could be sold away from husbands, and a new mate forced upon either of the separated parties.

He agreed that government went outside of its province either in promoting or protecting morals. Its function was limited to protection of persons and property.

The office of government is to hold a shield over the great essential natural rights of its subjects. Now, sir, I hold that polygamy invades a great natural right, and that it is, therefore, the duty of civil government to suppress it.

I suppose it will not be denied that polygamy prevails in Utah. But it is said that polygamy is a part of the religion of the Mormons; and that, as we would keep ourselves clear of the offense of invading the religion of our subjects, we must not strike at polygamy. I admit, sir, that the reformation of religion cannot be a legitimate object of legislation. But, sir, that legislation may be sound and justifiable which incidentally affects religious systems. If a religious system tramples on any of those great rights which it is the office of government to protect, then, at just those points where such system offends, government is to meet it and overcome it.

I argue the duty of government to suppress polygamy on just the principles that I argue the duty of government to suppress land monopoly. I believe that all persons have an equal right to the soil. The Maker of the earth has provided one home, not two homes, for each person; not two farms, but one farm, for each farmer. The right to the soil is natural and equal.

So, sir, the right of each man to one wife, and each woman to one husband, is a natural right; and for one man to get more than one wife, or for one woman to get more than one husband, is to violate this natural right, which it is the duty of government to protect.

The word of God shows that nature provides but one wife for one man, and one husband for one woman. That word teaches us that He "made them male and female"—not male and females, nor female and males. And if there are any present who do not bow to the authority of that word I would point such to the census. The census, in every country, and in every age, shows that the sexes are numerically equal, and that the arrangements of Providence forbid polygamy.

I have proceeded in my argument for sustaining this proviso on the ground that this Government has as full power and authority over the people and institutions of its Territories as a State government has over the people and institutions within its jurisdiction. Now, I ask the gentleman from Georgia [Mr. Stephens] whether the government of his State should or would permit the dark-haired men of his State to press and practice upon their claim to a hundred wives each, and thus to shut out the light-haired men from marriage?

Mr. Disney claimed that the bill did not interfere with the religious belief or existing institutions of the people of Utah. The proviso simply provided that in making these grants of lands a particular class of persons should not be entitled to them. It was a *donation*, and so differed *in toto* from the payment of an officer's salary for services rendered, to which Mr. Letcher would apply the proviso.

The Government might pay one who practices polygamy for discharging the duties of surveyor-general for services rendered, and yet might esteem it impolitic to make donations of land—gifts to parties on condition of settlement, and thus settle that country with person practicing polygamy.

Now, with regard to the Mormons themselves, I have to state the fact that polygamy is a legal institution in the Territory of Utah. I have a volume of the statutes of Utah before me, and I have examined it carefully.

Mr. MILLSON.—Really, I am somewhat astonished at that declaration of the gentleman from Ohio. Do I understand the gentleman to say that polygamy is a legal institution in the Territory of Utah?

Mr. DISNEY.—Yes.

Mr. MILLSON.—Has the law legalizing it ever been revised by the Committee on Territories? And, if so, are the Committee on Territories prepared to—what I take it for granted they will promptly do—report a bill annulling such a law?

Mr. DISNEY.—There is no statute in the Territory of Utah expressly allowing polygamy as such, although it recognizes its existence. The statutes recognize the issue of marriages under such a system there as heirs-at-law, and make provisions in re-

gard to estates, and in every way and form recognize the existence of polygamy as a legal institution. I desire merely to
make one more remark in addition to what I have already said.
It is proper for me, in justice to the Mormons, to state that their
statute-books are filled with provisions against incontinence of
a most severe character.

Mr. Simmons was opposed to striking out the proviso
for the reason that it would repudiate the whole ante-
cedent policy of the Government, which was to control
absolutely the Territories, including the subject of
morals. The Ordinance of 1787, organizing the Northwest Territory, specifically stated that:

"*Religion, morality,* and knowledge being necessary to good government and the happiness of mankind, schools and the means of education
shall forever be encouraged."

Here, sir, *religion* and *morality* are recognized as being necessary to good republican institutions. Certainly, sir, they do not
mean by religion and morality *Mormonism* and *polygamy.*

Mr. MILLSON.—Sir, I am unwilling that the statute books of
this Confederacy shall contain the admission that anywhere,
within the reach of our laws, an institution exists under which
a man is allowed to be at one time the husband of more than one
wife. Sir, this proviso would be a confession of the weakness
and powerlessness of Congress. Have we no further control
over those who would establish this profligate institution in a
Territory belonging to the United States than by withholding
from them largesses and benefits? Have we not the right to
apply to them our criminal legislation?

But how can a man be truly said to be the husband of more
than one wife? Our laws acknowledge the right to have but
one; and every second and further matrimonial contract, the
wife being still alive, is simply null, and does not raise the
female to the dignity of a wife. No man, then, in any Territory
subject to our laws, can have more than one wife; and if, in the
Territory of Utah, a man may, as this proviso seems to suppose,
have more than one wife, it is only because Congress establishes
or consents to such a law. We have reserved to ourselves the
right to revise the statutes of the territorial assembly of Utah,
and have declared that all acts disproved by us shall be null
and void. There can be no statute in Utah allowing a plurality
of wives, except by the consent of Congress; and until Congress

gives that assent—and it has not done it yet—there can be only one wife who can legally hold that relation.

Now, Mr. Chairman, I was surprised to hear just now, what I learned then for the first time, from the gentleman from Ohio [Mr. Disney], that the legislative assembly of Utah has already provided, or attempted to provide, for the legalization of polygamy. I beg leave to call the attention of the Committee on Territories to this act of the legislature of Utah. It devolves upon the Committee on Territories to lose no time in bringing this subject to the notice of the House. I trust they will act promptly and decidedly.

I, for one, have never surrendered, and I will not agree to surrender, the control of Congress over the legislation of the Territories. And the gentleman from Ohio [Mr. Giddings] made an incorrect statement this morning, when he said that no Southern gentleman in this House had yet spoken who had not ridiculed the right of Congress to interfere with the domestic institutions of a Territory.

MR. GIDDINGS.—I stand corrected.

MR. MILLSON.—I know many Southern gentlemen who, in the recent debate, have, as I myself have done, protested against this doctrine—a doctrine which was, only a very little while ago, known as "squatter sovereignty," but which, in the more euphonious and refined vocabulary of the present day, is designated as "popular sovereignty." I believe that this Government has full control over the legislation of the territorial assembly, and full authority to annul any law which the people of the Territory, in their legislative capacity, may undertake to enact. I do not pretend to say that we can deprive them of any of their natural or personal rights; but such powers as they derive from us are always subject to our supervision and control. All their political power—all their legislative authority—is derived from Congress, and it can be derived from no other source. And I, for one, will never abandon these principles.

Sir, if it be true, as I was grieved to hear the gentleman from Ohio [Mr. Disney] say it is, that it has been attempted to legalize this licentiousness in the Territory of Utah, then we shall be partakers of the shame and of the disgrace, if we fail to discountenance and repress it. If we, either directly or indirectly, give it our sanction, we shall be held responsible for it. May not the very language of the proviso be construed as an indirect sanction of it? I ask gentlemen who have spoken upon this subject, and who, as I infer from their remarks, agree with me in sentiment, I ask them if there is not some reason for apprehending that if this proviso be adopted, declaring that land shall not be given to those having more than one wife, some judicial authority, I know not where, may torture it into a sanction by Congress of the crime of polygamy in the Territory of Utah, by recognizing the possession, in one man, of more wives than one? For these reasons I shall vote to strike out this proviso.

MR. PARKER.—Does the gentleman mean to say that Virginia could not make polygamy legal within the limits of that State?

MR. MILLSON.—I do not.

MR. PARKER.—Then the gentleman would confine his action exclusively to the Territories. Now, sir, how can we go to the Territory of Utah to prevent polygamy? How can we prevent it by any direct legislation? Who will enforce the law if you make one? Here, then, is a great, if not an insurmountable, difficulty. I am, therefore, in favor of retaining this proviso in the bill, for the purpose of discouraging the evil there. I am in favor of refusing to grant to men who practice polygamy any portion of the public domain. It is perfectly legitimate and proper, in my view of the case, that the proviso should be retained.

My friend from Georgia [Mr. Stephens] thinks that, by retaining this provision, we infringe upon the Constitution; for we have no right to adopt any legislation which may look to a religious test. Sir, what religious test is there here? If there be a religious test here, there are other religious tests in the bill. Go back to the preceding section of the bill, and you will find that we make a discrimination between married and unmarried men. Why that discrimination? It is simply because we wish to invite to those Territories men with their families. If that be the case, and it be a legitimate object, cannot we discourage the population of these Territories by those who have two, or a dozen, or twenty wives, and rebuke the practice of the crime of polygamy? It seems to me to be perfectly legitimate. No provision of the Constitution is infringed.

Polygamy can exist in fact, and the question is, shall we countenance it in this law, or not? I am against it tooth and nail; and I will go with the gentleman, when the laws of Utah are submitted to us, to put a quietus on this feature of them to the full extent of our power. It is our duty as a moral and Christian people to do so.

MR. BENSON.—We have been told by the gentleman from Ohio [Mr. Disney] that the laws of Utah recognize the right to have more than one wife. Now, I want the committee to look, for a single moment, at the act organizing the Territory of Utah, and see how the law stands on this subject.

"All the laws passed by the legislative assembly and governor shall be submitted to the Congress of the United States, *and, if disapproved, shall be null and of no effect.*"

Now, I ask the lawyers of this House whether, when a law has gone through the regular course of enactment in the Territory of Utah, it is not the law of the land in Utah until it is disapproved by Congress?

SEVERAL MEMBERS.—Certainly.

MR. BENSON.—Then if such is the fact, I ask if it is not legal in the Territory of Utah for a man to have more than one wife? I agree entirely with what the gentleman from Virginia [Mr. Millson] has said. But I ask if you are going to shut your eyes to the fact that there are such laws existing in the Territory of Utah, and strike out this proviso because you are not willing to acknowledge, by implication, that there are any such laws in existence? Sir, we know the fact; the world knows it; the Congress of the United States knows it, for it has been proclaimed upon this floor again and again that there are such laws in Utah. And, with your eyes wide open to this fact, are you going to strike out this proviso, and say to the people of Utah, of every other Territory, and to the world, especially with this new doctrine of squatter sovereignty which seems to be prevailing in some quarters, though, I desire to be thankful, not in others, that you regard such laws and such a practice, in this Republic, of no sort of consequence?

MR. MILLSON (interrupting).—The gentleman from Maine and myself evidently aim at the same end. We have the same views. We merely differ as to the proper mode of accomplishing a common object.

MR. BENSON.—Yes, sir.

MR. MILLSON.—I merely wish to make a suggestion to him. I am aware, and it was for that reason that I said what I did, that the act organizing the territorial government of Utah provides that the acts passed by the territorial legislature shall be transmitted to Congress, and, if disapproved, shall be null and void. If disapproved, then they are null and void, not only from the moment when they are disapproved, but the disapproval dates back and declares those laws to have been null and void.

MR. BENSON.—Oh, no, that would be a kind of *ex post facto* legislation. They are laws until disapproved by Congress.

Mr. Millson.—I think not.

Mr. Benson.—The statute says so. That is all I can say about it.

Mr. Lane [Ore.].—It has been so decided with reference to our Territory.

Mr. Benson.—Let me ask the gentleman from Virginia one question. Suppose Congress should declare that polygamy, or a plurality of wives, should not be allowed, by disapproving of the laws of Utah which now allow it, could you go back and punish for bigamy, or polygamy, those persons who have had more than one wife under the laws existing in Utah?

I wish simply to say to the committee that I hold it to be the duty of Congress to put their hands upon crime of this kind wherever they can find it. But we have been told by certain gentlemen upon the floor that we are not to punish crime, and that we are to close our eyes to its commission. I do not believe in any such thing. We punish, most assuredly, piracy; and there has been, if I am informed aright, in the other branch of Congress, a proposition to confer upon the President power to suspend certain laws for the punishment of crime.

Mr. Stephens, of Georgia.—I certainly advocated no such doctrine. Power is conferred upon Congress by the Constitution of the United States to punish certain specified crimes. Congress may define any line of duty upon subjects within its constitutional limits, and point out what shall be the penalty for a violation of it; and such a violation would be an offence coming within the class of which I spoke. I deny that Congress can go beyond that.

Mr. Benson.—One line of duty in which Congress may punish crime—and I call that crime which is held so in the thirty-one States of this Union—is by withholding its donations. This bill says "donate."

Mr. Stephens.—Can there be any crime where there is no law? If there be no law in Maine against bigamy, would it be just to punish for a violation of the principle? And if there be no law in Utah against polygamy, is it not manifestly unjust to make such an unjust discrimination as is proposed? There is no law there against polygamy, and hence there is no legal crime of which your courts can take jurisdiction.

Mr. Benson.—Congress should administer this Government according to those principles which shall promote the morals of the country. Now, I ask, where there are thirty-one States of this Union that punish this multiplicity of wives as a crime, will you treat those who practice this in Utah so tenderly, and *donate* to them your public lands? I will agree with the gentleman from Georgia [Mr. Stephens], if there is no law in Utah against a multiplicity of wives, that it is not a crime by law there—that is a self-evident proposition. At the same time the practice is to be discountenanced in all proper ways—and I hold this to be one—do not give them your public lands according to the provisions of this bill. Let them first conform to the laws upon this subject, so important to the common welfare, which prevail in every State in the Union, and then it will be time to confer upon them the gift of your public domain.

We have not been officially informed of it, but it is universally conceded that polygamy exists among the citizens of Utah. Now, then, I ask, again, are we to shut our eyes to this fact, and make a donation to those who live in violation, not of the law of Utah, but of the law of every State in the Union, and I may add, of the law of God? I would make no such donation as that —nor am I willing to close my eyes to the fact which exists, while I know that it does exist—and I therefore am opposed to the striking out of this proposition.

MR. WALSH.—The best, and, in my estimate, the most effectual method of preventing polygamy, is for every young man, at the earliest opportunity after he finds that he can support a wife, to procure one. [Laughter.] Now, sir, if my friend on the opposite side of the House [Mr. Simmons]—for I believe he still remains a bachelor, and, therefore, he ought to be the last man in the world to grumble about other men taking two or more wives, as he has not yet taken one himself—if, I say, my colleague and others had pursued that course, there would have been no such thing as an opportunity afforded to any man to monopolize wives. [Laughter.]

Mr. Chairman, in reference to the provision under consideration, I am in favor, most emphatically, of striking it out of the bill. I think the gentleman from Georgia [Mr. Stephens] has given incontrovertible reasons why it should be stricken out. And I see no propriety at this time, when this flourishing Territory is progressing toward the condition of a populous State, in creating a state of feeling there which may tend to produce irritation and injury. The history of this people, from the earliest period of their settlement, has been one of outrage, wrong, bloodshed, and oppression; and now that they have removed far beyond reach of the narrow prejudices and bigotry of those surrounding them, the system of oppression and wrong under which they suffered should not be revived. I believe that, with the single exception of this conventional idea of theirs, of their right to have more wives than one—and that is only a simple difference of opinion between them and us—the Mormons are as good citizens, and as faithful to the Constitution and the Republic, as the citizens of any other State or Territory in this Republic.

Sir, time, example, good precepts, and persuasion will do more to remove polygamy from that Territory than all the laws you can pass here. Do nothing. I would impress upon the members of this House the propriety of doing nothing to insult the prejudices of a people already goaded into madness by the wrongs and oppressions which they suffered before they reached their present location. They are rapidly gaining in strength and numbers. They will soon become one of the most powerful sects —you must not shut your eyes to the fact—in this country; and I trust that the liberality of this House will not disgrace itself by indorsing so narrow and so contemptible a species of legislation.

Mr. Kerr.—Polygamy has been acknowledged in the Territory of Utah ever since the organization of the Territory. It was known at the time of its organization that it did exist, and then was the time for Congress to meet the question directly, and take the necessary measures for its prevention. But, sir, Congress did not meet the question in that form at that time. And I say it is our manifest duty to meet it directly—now. Congress possesses the power of supervising all laws made by a territorial legislature; and I say it is clearly the duty of Congress to exercise that power by annulling any law which may exist in that Territory that countenances or sanctions such a crime.

But I am in favor of striking out this provision for another reason. Congress knew of the existence of polygamy among these people when they organized the Territory, and used no means for its suppression. These people, when they took possession of a portion of the territory of this Republic, practiced polygamy openly as no crime; and I say that, under these circumstances, it is unjust to exclude them from the benefits of this provision when they are extended so freely to outcasts from Europe and fugitives from justice.

When we are taking hold of this crime I propose to take hold of it directly, as we should of any other crime. By the laws, I believe, of some of the States of this Union polygamy is a crime punishable with death. I believe that punishment suited to the crime, and I believe it the duty of this Government to prescribe that penalty for its committal, wherever it exists in the Territories over which the Federal Government has jurisdiction.

MR. CAMPBELL.—This land proposed to be donated is the public domain, and belongs to the people of the States in common. If, then, we give it to actual settlers who will cultivate, we have a right to impose the terms; and we have the power, I hold, to say that "you shall not have this public domain as a gift if you intend to use it to perpetuate that system which is recognized throughout all the States as a high offence against public morals."

The gentleman from Georgia [Mr. Stephens] assumes the ground that Congress is undertaking to define such acts as shall be regarded as crimes, and to punish them as such in the Territory of Utah. Such is not the fact. I do not know that I should disagree with him very much as to the power of Congress to enact a criminal code for Territories, but I do contend that the people of that Territory, or those who would settle on our lands, have no right to ask of us a bonus in favor of extending a system of wrongdoing or revolting crimes, in the shape of donation of public lands. If we donate the lands we have the right, and it is our duty, to impose such terms and restraints as will lay deep and strong in that far distant land the foundation of sound morals.

I will never agree, as one of the Representatives of the people who own the soil, to give it as a bonus for settlement to those who disregard all the moral restraints which they themselves enforce in their own State governments, through the instrumentality of strong penal enactments.

MR. GOODRICH.—Strike at this crime as directly as you may, you will not reach it so effectually as you will by retaining this proviso in the bill. Annul by law the act authorizing polygamy, and how will you secure the practical enforcement of your law? Annulled as that act may be by the law of Congress, the people of Utah will still practice polygamy. I therefore want this proviso retained for the purpose of reaching that people, if they are not already beyond the reach of moral considerations, by carrying the moral power of this Government there, so far as we have the power of legislating on the subject. We derive that power just as we derive the power in the States to reach any evil. Polygamy, as all agree, is a great moral, social, and political evil. I am ready to strike it down in any way, directly or indirectly. I would reach it by carying the moral power of this nation out to Utah Territory, and saying to the people of that Territory that any man who practices this crime of polygamy shall not receive the Government bounty—shall not have the land which we give to other people. I would touch them through their interests in that way. I would reach this evil just as we reach the great evil of intemperance in the States. We legislate in the States upon the subject of intemperance, some by the application of the Maine law, and others by other means. I am for the Maine law; others are in favor of other measures. But we strike down intemperance as an evil, and so would I strike down this evil, if these people are not beyond the power and influence of moral considerations. I wish to put into this bill a moral power against polygamy. I want to say to the people of Utah that they shall not receive grants of the public lands as other people receive them if they continue in the practice of this crime.

MR. TAYLOR [Tenn.].—I regard the proposition to strike out the whole proviso as offering a premium to the polygamists of the whole world to settle in that Territory. In a very few years, under the operation of the proposition to strike out this proviso, you will have that Territory peopled by polygamists, who will inevitably outnumber those who may settle there opposed to polygamy. What then? The first step will be to apply for admission into the Union. If you admit them, what then? By your action, your initiatory action, in encouraging settlements in that country, you, the American Congress, have virtually established there polygamy—this crime and vice of the dark ages. Is the American Congress prepared, for the sake of technicalities, to establish this principle? I cannot vote for the proposition to strike out this proviso.

MR. MILLSON.—The question is one which demands the solemn consideration of Congress; and the best way to effect this would be the introduction of a joint resolution or bill, having one single object only in view; and that, the annulling of any such laws or regulations in the Territory of Utah. A bill to this end, and not connected with any other measure of legislation, will therefore command the almost unanimous assent of every member, perhaps, in both Houses of Congress.

MR. READY.—I move to amend by adding at the end of the proviso the following:

And that any person who shall at any time have more than one living wife shall forfeit all right to any lands acquired under this act.

My object in presenting that amendment, sir, is to eradicate the evil of polygamy by the roots. [Great laughter.] I regard it as an excrescence on the body-politic. [Renewed laughter.]

The proviso to this bill does not reach the evil. You may pass the bill with the proviso, and still the polygamist may indulge in this practice with impunity, afterward as well as before. What is he to do? You say that if he has more than one wife he shall not be entitled to the benefit of this act. You permit him to avail himself of the benefits of this act, having but one wife, and when he has obtained his three hundred and twenty acres of land from the Government—when he has perfected his title, then you allow him to go and marry fifty wives, if he can find so many to have him. Therefore, I propose this amendment with a view of making a forfeiture of his right to the land which he may have acquired by his grant from the Government, if he shall afterward indulge in this unlawful practice.

Mr. Chairman, I differ with the gentlemen who seem to be of the opinion that Congress has no right or power to interfere with this subject. Certainly, so far as the constitutional right of this body is concerned, there can be no question. The Constitution declares that "Congress shall have power to dispose of and make all needful rules and regulations respecting the territory or other property belonging to the United States." What are we doing here? Are we not proposing, by legislation, to make certain needful rules and regulations respecting the territory of the United States?

The question was then taken on Mr. Ready's amendment, and it was adopted.

Mr. Keitt.—I merely desire to throw out some suggestions for the consideration of the committee. You propose now to interfere in the domestic relations of these Territories. You say that no man shall have two wives. Where do you get the power to do that? In fact, where do you get the power to legislate at all for the Territories? The right to acquire carries with it the right to govern, you say. But to what limitations is the right to govern subjected? To all the restrictions and limitations contained in the Federal Constitution. The power to legislate is, at best, an implied power; and all such powers should be used with great caution. Now, if Congress has a right to say that no man in the Territories shall have more than one wife, may it not say that no man shall have a wife at all? If it can prescribe the number of wives, may it not altogether abrogate the marital relation?

I ask the question for information. If Congress can determine that there shall be no polygamy, may not Congress also determine that there shall be no marriage union whatever? Cannot Congress go a step further, and say that there shall be no parental relation? What power is involved in the decision of this question? Is not sovereignty involved? Is not sovereignty necessarily implicated in the right to arrange and manipulate the vital relations of a community? If so, where is sovereignty lodged? In the inhabitants of the Territory? Sir, I have scarcely even contempt for the piebald doctrine of "squatter sovereignty." Is it in the Federal Government? This assumption of power would aggrandize this Government with a ruthless, overshadowing, and awing central despotism. Where is it, then? In the *people of the several sovereign States.*

If, then, this exercise of power appertains to sovereignty, how will you reach the evil alluded to? The declamation of gentlemen may bubble up, but it will never moisten the roots of any constitutional right. In truth, sir, an exigency has arisen which was never contemplated by the framers of the Constitution. To meet this you propose to swell the powers of Congress by construction. Do this, and you will soon burst the bands of our federative union, and weld the fragments of the Constitution into a consolidated despotism. The first step in this always is an amplification of power by construction. Sir, I think polygamy a burning shame upon any community. I abhor all trifling with the marital tie; all conjugal licentiousness; and I will extirpate this disgraceful evil as quickly and as sharply as any man, if I can but see the power in Congress to do it. All I ask is for gentlemen to show me this power.

Again, how do gentlemen propose to accomplish this purpose? By the enactment of laws? How will they be executed? By a jury of the vicinage? Why, every inhabitant is a Mormon. He will screen the accused, instead of aiding in the execution of your laws. Government can only scourge out this evil by military tyranny. Sir, "to this complexion" your acts must come at last. Now, sir, will this justify an assumption of power? I again ask for the power of Congress in this matter; and if it is shown to me I will cheerfully act. I cannot legislate in blindness, both as to power and the mode of reaching an end. I advise gentlemen to look to these, and not to moral and social enormities, in the character of which we all agree.

MR. DAVIS [R. I.].—I would ask the gentleman where Congress gets the power to insert the word "white" in this bill? I should like to have the gentleman answer that question.

MR. KEITT.—I have an immitigable scorn, sir, for abolitionism and all its offshoots; but I will answer the question——

[Here the hammer fell.]

MR. SEWARD.—It is too late now, after the Government of the United States has sanctioned the existence of this law of polygamy, and given to these people a territorial organization, to fix upon them as a crime that which has been sanctioned by your Government. I hold that the only way to treat this matter is to bring up the question directly, and assert the power, if we possess it, of repealing the organic law under which polygamy is sanctioned in this Territory. What right have we to fix upon these people as a crime that which has been sanctioned by law? The very highest authority we have declares that there can be no offence where there is no law. Such is the language of the Bible; and it is useless to talk about the existence of crime when it receives the sanction of your laws. The marriages which have taken place under territorial law are valid; and the rights of these parties cannot be disturbed by the action of Congress. All that we can do is to look to the future, and prevent these marriages, if we consider them immoral.

MR. KERR.—I do not see that anything in the world is to be accomplished by the fling that is now being made at the Mormons. Supposing polygamy to be a crime, as all of us pronounce it to be, what will be the effect of an attempt, at the present time, to strike at it? It will drive off the Mormons from Utah to some other portions of the Union, where the homestead bill that we have passed during the present session of Congress will enable them to settle down again comfortably and securely. Congress will thus aid and abet in establishing them elsewhere by the authority given them to go there, and thus indirectly sanction this very institution of polygamy, and do injustice to other communities.

If Congress has not got the fearless independence and determination to make a bold and direct onslaught on the institution of polygamy, by providing penalties for the punishment of those guilty of that crime—so long as Congress does not aim at its total suppression—then I say let it stay where it is. Let it be confined to Utah; and do not interpose any enactment of legislation here, the direct tendency of which will be to unsettle again that migratory horde of people—for they are a migratory people, start at a very short notice, and go a very great distance, in order to secure a place where they can enjoy the exercise of their religious rights. I am in favor of giving these Mormons a title in the land, instead of having them cut off as they are by the restriction of this territorial bill.

MR. BERNHISEL.—I desire simply to remark that there is no

statute in the Territory of Utah on the subject of polygamy. It is a matter of ecclesiastical law.

Mr. Walbridge.—If this practice rests upon ecclesiastical law, and this House has not the power to strike it down, I shall then sustain this proviso, that being the only manner of reaching the evil. I am therefore decidedly in favor of standing by the proviso.

Mr. Lyon.—Against the striking out of this proviso I most earnestly protest. This subject is too lightly considered, I fear, by this enlightened committee. Its great consequence as a precedent makes it needful that our investigation should be thorough, worthy of Christian statesmen and Christian lawgivers. I would appeal to the hearty patriotism of every member present, educated, as they have been, in the principles of the Pilgrim fathers, Cavaliers, and the Huguenots—the descendants of men who fled from profligate, libidinous, and licentious courts to enjoy a virtuous quiet in the unbroken wilderness of the West —if they are willing to see this Government disgrace itself by express or implied legislation in any way sanctioning the practice of polygamy in this country. Its enormity as a crime has been made the subject of stringent statutes in every State in the Confederacy. Is a premium to be paid, in fertile lands, for the debauching of our daughters and the deluding of our wives? Is this Congress so weak as basely to stoop to such a purpose, reversing all the cherished associations and instructions of our childhood? Is this black cancer sore, this creeping leprosy, to be encouraged?

When the people of Utah are placed on the same basis as the people of other Territories, is not that sufficient, is not that enough? Strike out the clause, and what will be its actual consequences? Individuals will go there whose senses are stronger than their sentiments, whose passions override their principles, and avail themselves of Government bounty, and, like Persians, Hindoos, and Mussulmen, fill their houses with the blooming beauties of the North, and the witching women of the South, provided they have wealth or personal attractions to induce such a painful and horrid sacrifice. It has been demonstrated clearly by all political economists, Dr. Franklin, Malthus, and Miss Martineau, that one man is just enough for one woman, the very state the Lord originally intended when he created Adam and Eve—that there should be no monopoly of the fair sex. Yet, when polygamy is tacitly *respectablized* by an American Congress, it may not be so difficult to fill with sisters and daughters —those whom God destined for a nobler domestic sphere—an

American harem, a Mormon seraglio. Sir, there is but one way to kill the cockatrice. *It is to break the egg.*

Here the speaker described the degradation of women in polygamous Islam:

And, sir, do you think things are different among the "Latter-Day Saints" in the Mormondom of Utah? No, sir; just as bad. Amid the jealousies of a plurality of wives the respect of parental authority is lost, the gentleness of fireside instruction and hearthstone memories is destroyed. Crime of the most revolting character ensues; infanticide follows as a matter of course as soon as the husband finds he is getting more children than he can support. Sir, human nature is just the same in every land. Do you think Abdul Medjid, with three hundred and seventy wives, has been the father of only five children? It is impossible. [Applause and laughter.] The bodies of dead infants float on the sapphire tide of the Bosphorus, and the light of many a harem, from the destruction of her offspring, has been lost among the dark shadows of the cypress of Scutari. There is not a drug shop in an Oriental city but sells the means of destroying the new-born. And, being warned of these things, let us not fix this plague-spot upon the route to the golden gate of the Pacific, the western pathway of empire. Posterity, sir, will anathematize this kind of legislation to the latest years of the Republic. We all shall die, crumble to dust, our names be lost in oblivion, but the principle we establish by implication, as the ghost of Hamlet's father, will evidence against us when we have passed away. Let us meet this subject, discourage it, condemn it, reject it. And, sir, it will be an honorable precedent, *not for a day, but for all time.*

The Mormons have been spoken of as a persecuted people—a martyred people, driven from State to State. With their sorrows I sympathize, for their griefs I grieve; but it seems a curious way to console them for the past by asking Congress to sanction polygamy in the future. It is said that this practice existed in the days of Solomon. True. The running after the strange women of Egypt, the falling from grace in the service of God, was the great reason of Solomon's reign, after a glorious day, ending with a lurid sunset. And from his loins issued that undutiful heir, whose unjust acts were the scourge of Israel; for plurality of wives destroys young men, as well as debases the old. The light of the Prophets went out the night Jesus was crucified. Let us, as Christians, follow and legislate in the doctrines of Christ, not of Joe Smith; let us take the holy Gospel, not the book of Mormon.

It has been doubted by gentlemen whether this clause is constitutional; yet, with the following words in relation to the powers of Congress, tender must be their scruples if they doubt it. Section third of the Constitution of the United States reads as follows:

> "Congress shall have power to dispose of, and make all needful *rules* and *regulations* respecting, the Territories."

This is one of the necessary *regulations*—one of the wholesome *rules*. We are told by the Delegate from Utah [Mr. Bernhisel] that it is an "ecclesiastical establishment," a religious law, and over such many strict constitutional constructionists believe we have no control. Then the thugs or stranglers of men, the Phansegars, the Buddhists, who worship Juggernaut, the Seftis, who perform every year human sacrifices, would all have a right to practice their abominations under the territorial government of the United States, if once settled here. They would all have an equal claim to their "religious establishment," no matter how demoralizing or inhuman, over which it is said Congress has no right to interfere or to control; but that we have power to prevent giving a bounty for its encouragement I think I have fairly shown. If the many-wifed demoralizers get outnumbered by the virtuous single-wifed, a wise State government may yet be formed that will do honor and credit to the Union. Let us nip this evil in the bud, for the sake of morality, religion, and Christianity.

Polygamy, sir, is a

> "Monster of so frightful mien
> As, to be hated, needs but to be seen;
> Yet, seen too oft, familiar with her face,
> We first endure, then *pity*, THEN EMBRACE."

By the blessed memory of those virtuous spirits who battled for liberty, not licentiousness, it should be blotted out, as a stigma, a dishonor, a disgrace, from existence on the soil of North America. [Sensation, and cries of "Good!" "Good!" "Well done!"]

MR. HUGHES.—I move to strike out of the proviso all after the word "hereafter," and to insert in lieu thereof the words "live with or have more than one woman as his wife, under color of law."

The provision, as I propose to amend it, would do away altogether with the idea of legality. It merely involves the idea that there is a custom prevailing in the Territory—a claim that, under the color of law, a man may have more than one woman as a wife.

The question was then taken on Mr. Hughes's amendment, as modified; and it was agreed to.

MR. PERKINS.—I have seen recently in the newspapers a statement declaring that no law shall be cited, except the statutes of the United States, in any court whatever in the Territory of Utah. Then the common law is not recognized there, and the spiritual law is recognized, if this statement in the newspapers is true, which gives the privilege and right to a person there to have as many wives as he can get. It seems to me utterly preposterous, and will be disgraceful to this Congress, to allow the governors, judges, and other officers appointed by the Government of the United States, to hold their offices, at large salaries, and have just as many wives as they please, as their salaries will enable them to support, and yet prohibit the poor men from enjoying the benefit of land there, if they happen to have only two wives. [Laughter.]

MR. BOYCE.—What right has this Government to interfere with the religious relations of the people of this Territory? The whole power which this Government exercises over the Territory is simply that of a constructive character. Where is it derived from? There is no express clause in the Constitution in relation to this matter. The authority which is derived from that clause which prescribes the right of making all needful rules and regulations for the Territories clearly does not authorize a governmental power. It is said by the best writers on constitutional law to be derived as an incident to the treaty-making power; they lay down the principle thus: because you have the right to acquire territory, you have also the right to govern it.

Well, Mr. Chairman, the right to govern the Territory is not an unlimited power of Government. It is subject to all the express limitations of the Constitution that may be applicable to the subject; and the subject is liable to all the implied limitations derivable from the nature of this Government. Sir, what is the object of the government of the Territory? The governments of Territories are organized merely for the purpose of protecting the Territories in their infant state, until they are able to become States. The whole power of the Government over the Territories should be confined to that narrow sphere of protecting the rights of persons and things until they are able to become States. It by no means implies that Congress has a right to interfere with the domestic, the social, or the religious relations of the people. Their religious relations, I say, are not to be interfered with. This is a religious subject; and because it is a religious subject it is one of great magnitude.

But, Mr. Chairman, if there is one thing clear in reference to the power of Congress, it is that it has no right to interfere with the subject of religion. That is the very first of the amendments to the Constitution; it stands at the head of all the amendments. Congress shall pass no law upon this subject. But it may be said that this religion of the Mormons is not a true religion—that it is a false religion. But I do not think that Congress has any right to say that this or that religion is true or false. Who made us judges over this matter? Who appointed us apostles, or bishops, or priests? Why, Mr. Chairman, if there is any one subject which this Congress does not understand practically I expect it is this very subject of religion.

I ask you, sir, who set us up to be judges of other people's religion? Who gave us authority to legislate for them on the subject of religion? But it may be supposed that it is no great violation of the principles of the Constitution to interfere with the religion of the Mormons; but once you break in upon that principle, once you violate it in any regard, where will you stop? I am opposed to any infraction at all of the Constitution on this point. Let all religions be free. Let every man worship God according to his own heart and conscience.

MR. CAMPBELL.—I wish to put a case to the honorable member from South Carolina.

Suppose that, in the wildness of religious fanaticism in Utah, the Mormons should imagine that they had received a revelation from the prophet Joe Smith which required them to enact an ecclesiastical law to the effect that the eldest born of every woman in that Territory should, when it was one month old, be sacrificed and slaughtered; and suppose, further, that, under such circumstances, that people should come here and ask Congress to make a grant of lands to encourage settlement under a system of that kind, would not the honorable gentleman, acting in the capacity of a guardian, and representing a people having a joint interest with all the rest of the people of this land in that domain, deem it proper and advisable to provide that no person who subscribed to, and practiced upon, the principles of such a religion, or rather *fanaticism*, should have a grant of land? Now, I will yield to the gentleman from South Carolina [Mr. Boyce] to answer my question.

MR. BOYCE.—I propose to ask the gentleman from Ohio——

MR. CAMPBELL.—I propose that you answer the question, which I have already propounded, first.

MR. BOYCE.—You put an extreme case, and I believe it is customary to answer one question by asking another.

MR. CAMPBELL.—Answer the question first, and then propound yours.

MR. BOYCE.—Then I will say that I would do nothing to recognize such a state of things.

Now, I will ask the gentleman whether Congress has the right to declare, in this bill, that no Presbyterian should have the privilege of taking a portion of this land?

MR. CAMPBELL.—If a Presbyterian church in Utah, actuated by a wild fanaticism, should declare, by an ecclesiastical provision, the allowance of polygamy, or any other crime, as a tenet of its faith, I should say that no person subscribing to such a provision, or practicing under it, should have any portion of the public domain, and that it would clearly be the duty of Congress so to declare.

MR. PHILLIPS.—If, through the exercise of the power "to dispose of" the public lands, Congress is to take this incidental control over this particular crime, why not over every other? And, if in this mode, why not in every other mode of disposing of the territory? Why not extend the proviso so as to exclude from the benefit of the act all persons who are guilty of murder, arson, piracy, forgery, and, I might add, theft of slaves, if I were not afraid of shocking the sensibilities of some gentlemen, and thus bring the influence of the Government to bear upon the whole dark catalogue of crime?

Sir, these considerations are not answered by sophomoric declamation as to the heinousness of the offence. That, sir, is not the question, but whether we shall, for the first time in the history of our legislation, link into our acts the discouragement or punishment of crimes which are appropriately referred to the local legislatures.

If Congress possesses any power, acting as the legislature of this Territory, then let them exert it in a direct manner, by virtue of that power, and we could then meet the question fairly when it is presented; but let us not smuggle into this bill a jurisdiction not warranted by the clause of the Constitution under which it is framed.

MR. TAYLOR, of Ohio.—My friend from Alabama [Mr. Phillips] said that we might as well insert a provision here to exclude any man guilty of murder, perjury, or any other crime. I understand that the territorial legislature of Utah denounce those crimes, and hold them to be crimes as they do in the States of this Union, whereas they tolerate the other crime, that of polygamy.

And here we have a beautiful specimen of this squatter sovereignty, so ably advocated by gentlemen in Congress; the leaving of the Territories to do as they please; the Territorial legislatures to do what they please; establish any crime they choose. Whether we approve or not, we are to pass the laws unnoticed.

If I had the time I would read from the law organizing the Territory of Utah, a law for which I take this occasion to say I did not vote. I felt indisposed to give the people of Utah (whom I conceived at that time to be a set of strolling squatters, who had seized the public land, and defied the authority of the United States, a territory twelve times as large, I am informed, as that of the State of New York) the power to set up and to justify a crime in defiance of the Congress of the United States.

MR. BOYCE.—I am opposed to this wholesale legislation against a whole community. It reminds me of our revolutionary struggle. Sir, I well recollect what Burke said, when Lord North and his servile majority attempted to proscribe a whole province. He said, "I do not know how to draw up an indictment against a whole nation." And so with me. I do not know how to draw up an indictment against this whole people. I am for letting them alone.

It seems to me that this proviso is at war with that provision of the Constitution which says that no man shall be bound to answer for any criminal offence unless upon the presentment of a grand jury. Here you require this whole people to answer for a criminal offence, and on what presentment? The presentment of the Congress of the United States. Is that in consonance with the Constitution? Again: Every man has a right to a trial by jury when he is charged with crime. Do you give the people of Utah this right? No, you do not. To whom do you give the power to decide this question? You give it to this surveyor-general.

Sir, these people are entitled to our pity. Look at their history. It is a history of misfortune and persecution, of disaster and suffering. They have never been permitted to live in

peace and security in any community. They were driven from
Missouri and from Illinois. Their beautiful city of Nauvoo was
devastated, and they were compelled, with bleeding hearts, to
bid adieu to the graves of their people and to their beautiful
temple. Their prophet was taken and placed in jail in Carthage,
and while there was brutally murdered by assassins. They were
then driven into the wilderness. They went up on the western
side of Iowa, and there at mid-winter, while they were in the
midst of suffering, the United States called upon them to go and
fight the battles of the country. And how did they respond to
that call? They responded to it better than the people of many
parts of the United States. They sent almost their whole military force; and that people rallied around the star-spangled
banner, and went out to fight the battles of our country. And
yet you will not now permit those men to enjoy a home in that
wilderness which they have rescued from barbarism and from
the Indians.

Mr. Perkins moved that the committee [of the whole]
rise and report the bill to the House with the recommendation that it be rejected. Carried.

The Republican party, in the presidential campaign
of 1856, coupled polygamy with slavery as a "relic of
barbarism." On February 24, 1857, Justin S. Morrill
[Vt.], speaking in the House of Representatives, denounced the practice and upheld the constitutional power
of the Federal Government to abolish it.

POLYGAMY A NATIONAL REPROACH

BY JUSTIN S. MORRILL, M. C.

We are told, because our Constitution declares that "Congress shall make no law respecting an establishment of religion, or prohibiting the free exercise thereof," that we must
tamely submit to any burlesque, outrage, or indecency which
artful men may seek to hide under the name of religion! But
it is impossible to twist the Constitution into the service of
polygamy by any fair construction. The fullest latitude of
toleration in the exercise of religion could not be understood to
license crimes punishable at common law; and, if Congress is
prohibited from making an established religion, a Territory must

be equally prohibited, for a Territory is the creature of Congress, and Congress cannot authorize a Territory to authorize an incorporated company of priests to do what it may not do itself. The practice under our Constitution has been, and is specially provided for in the organic act of Utah, that territorial laws are annulled and void the moment they are *disapproved* of by Congress. We cannot shirk the responsibility by creating a territorial government to do that which the Constitution inhibits to ourselves. If the laws of Utah are in our judgment such as are "not fit to be made," it is our duty to annul them; and if they create an establishment of religion, then it is clearly an open and palpable violation of the Constitution, and not too sacred to go untouched.

The general assembly of the Territory of Utah has incorporated a church, over which one man presides with an insolent and all-grasping power, with authority to establish the practice of polygamy, and *not be legally questioned* therefor. Now, I submit that we not only have the power, but it is eminently proper that we exercise it by disapproving of and annulling this act.

From all these statutes, from all the teachings set forth in the Mormon tabernacle, from all the evidences within our reach, it is clear that an ecclesiastical hierarchy exists in Utah, with a plenitude of power greater than that which can to-day be exercised by the Pope of Rome.

Commencing with tithings, not to be evaded by the poorest day-laborer; continued by monopoly of land and water privileges; swelled in its current by the waifs, estrays, and escheats incident and contrived as to the rights of property; the whole wealth of the Territory of Utah, present and future, threatening to be finally and wholly absorbed by the church and its dignitaries; the system ends in the foul abomination of spiritual wifery.

This hierarchy is clearly repugnant to the Constitution of the United States, which guarantees to every State a republican form of government. The republican form of government in Utah is a dead letter, existing only *pro forma,* and only so much of the tattered remains are exhibited as will secure the largesses of the national Government; while the real *bona fide* government is that of the Mormon priesthood. The obligations of the Constitution cannot be held in abeyance or postponed, nor have the people of Utah the right to evade them. A republican form of government in substance, and not the shadow, is required at the hands of the United States at all hazards. How can this be complied with if we suffer our Territories, while in a state of pupilage, so to educate the people, mold their habits, fix their affections and their antipathies—so to control the rights of persons and property, as to make a republican form of government unprofitable, sinful, hated, and impossible?

All human experience proves that it is in vain to undertake to regulate men's views of God and eternity by human legislation. All such attempts are resolved into persecution, and there are no sects which are not blessed with memb?rs ambitious of martyrdom. The blood of foolish saints is not less the seed of some churches than the blood of wiser saints. In this regard, it makes no difference whether Joseph Smith was an imposter, a vulgar, fiddling tavern-keeper or not—his followers believe, or affect to believe, that he was a prophet of God (the brother of Moses and Christ) with equal power to work miracles, to raise the dead, and heal the sick, grant forgiveness of sins, to interpret and pronounce new divine revelations, and that Brigham Young, as the successor of Smith, is also a prophet and a "lion of the Lord." This may be lamentable, but it cannot be cured by law. Faith is intangible. But when the works of such a religion, in its overt acts, exhibit the grossest immorality and debauchery, and covertly asserts civil and criminal jurisdiction over all its members, it is questionable whether legislators should remain neutral, or whether the "livery of heaven" should screen men from criminal courts, because they have the impudence to give their crimes the privileges of a sacred name.

Could a man, charged with burglary or rape, find privilege and excuse before any of our courts on a plea that it was an act done in accordance with the religion of the prophet Mercury, or the prophet Priapus, and that our Constitution permits the *free exercise* of religion? And, if individuals could not thus shelter their villainy, where is there a chance for Territories to creep in for similar grace?

The test which Brigham Young requires as the sole dispenser of the "blessings of Abraham" is subserviency to the priesthood, as will be seen in one of his published discourses of February 27, 1853:

"The elders of Israel frequently call upon me—'Brother Brigham, a word in private, if you please.' 'Bless me, this is no secret to me. I know what you want; it is to get a wife!' 'Yes, brother Brigham, if you are willing.'

"I tell you here, now, in the presence of the *Almighty God*, it is not the privilege of *any elder* to have even *one wife* before he has *honored* his *priesthood,* before he has *magnified* his *calling.* If you *obtain one* it is by *mere permission,* to see *what* you will *do, how* you will *act,* whether you will *conduct yourself* in *righteousness* in that *holy estate.''*

This power, held in the hands of one man, and that man Brigham Young, is one which may be wielded with tremendous effect. When Judge Brandenbury was upon the point of leaving the Territory, in order, if possible, to change his purpose, Brigham Young went and urged him to remain, telling him that ''he would even black his boots, and that he might have as many wives as he chose, if he would only stay.'' If such a license is granted in one case as a bribe, doubtless it is in others. If the license is a powerful temptation to some men when granted, the refusal of it is a not less fearful vengeance to others.

That the women in Utah would escape from their miserable fate if it were in their power is shown by the escape of the fourteen traitors to polygamy who fled with Colonel Steptoe, and also by reported cases where women have preferred—''a dinner of herbs rather than the stalled ox''—to seek the protection and undivided affection of the Indian rather than to remain in Mormon seraglios.

One plan of ridding the Territory of polygamy—and the idea derives some pungency from having been suggested by one himself a Mormon—is to make some regulation by which those who have more wives than one shall be *compelled to live under the same roof with them!*

From the discourse of President Young, to put down the embryo rebellion among the women, on the afternoon of the 21st of September, 1856, I make a single extract:

''My wives have got to do one of two things—either round up their shoulders and endure the afflictions of this world and live their religion, or they may leave; for I will not have them about me. I will go into heaven alone, rather than have scratching and fighting around me. I will set all at liberty. What! first wife too? Yes, I will liberate you all.''

The remarks by President J. M. Grant, Sunday, September 21, 1856, as reported in the *Deseret News,* shows that even sterner threats are made against the rebellious women.

''We have women here who like anything but the celestial law of God; and if they could break asunder the cable of the Church of Christ, there is scarcely a mother in Israel but would do it this day. And they talk it to their husbands, to their daughters, and to their neighbors, and say they have not seen a week's happiness since they became acquainted with that law, or since their husbands took a second wife. They want to break up the Church of God, and to break it from their husbands and family connections.

"We have been trying long enough with this people; and I go for letting the sword of the Almighty be unsheathed, not only in word, but in deed."

Whether these bloody threats ever have been or ever will be put in execution is not for me to say; but they certainly do *not* tend to allay the suspicions widely entertained, as I am informed, by gentlemen who, having been United States officers of the territorial government, have resided there (Major Holman and Judge Brandenbury). They suppose that there is a secret society existing there called *Danites, Shanpips,* or *Destroying Angels,* whose mission is to fulfill the dark and unwritten prophecies of the heads of the Mormon church. There is a mystery hanging over this subject that it would be well for all "good Mormons" to have cleared up.

There have been many strange murders and disappearances in Utah, which have been charged to the Danites. All these charges may be slanderous stories; but the cases are surrounded with many circumstances tending to arouse suspicion. It is almost incredible to suppose the doings of the Thugs can find a parallel in the history of any portion of America; but these Mormon prophets and apostles, if they do not mean anything (and they claim for themselves and all revelation a literal interpretation) should be more wary about talking of unsheathing the *sword,* fixing the *place,* and the shedding of *blood in word and deed.*

I have no desire to make party capital by making any issues touching Utah. It is a subject requiring the deliberate attention of statesmen. It is quite within the power of gentlemen to throw the question into the pool of partisan politics by giving "aid and comfort" to the wildest theories to which any religious imposture ever gave birth. The president and rulers of the Mormon Church have already sought shelter in the bosom of the Democratic party by their proclamation of the 14th August, A. D. 1856. They find fault with the Republican party for including their "sacred institution" in the phrase of "the twin relics of barbarism." They also declare:

"The Democratic convention in Cincinnati, which nominated James Buchanan for President, passed the following resolution:

"*Resolved,* That Congress has no power under the Constitution to interfere with or control the domestic institutions of the several States, and that all such States are the sole and proper judges of everything appertaining to their own affairs not prohibited by the Constitution.

"This is the principle of the Democratic party, which they have extended to Territories as well as States, and the doctrines of sovereignty apply to us in the desert as well as to the settlers in Kansas or Nebraska.

"The Democratic party is the instrument, in God's hand, by which is to be effected our recognition as a sovereign State, with the domestic institution of slavery and polygamy, as established by the patriarchs and renewed to the saints of latter days, through God's chosen rulers and prophets."

There is, I hope, room to doubt whether the Democratic party will allow itself to be used for any such purpose. Their political necessities must be great when they accept of such coadjutors upon the conditions indicated.

It may be very properly asked, supposing it should be shown that a state of things exists in Utah which all would admit to be wrong, what are you going to do about it? The subject is not without its difficulties, but they are not altogether insurmountable. For one, I should greatly prefer that the people of Utah would, upon a calm reconsideration of their own affairs, remove by their own action all just matters of complaint. But, if they choose to refuse, or neglect so to do, we have only to say by our silence and non-action that we will acquiesce, or to constitutionally express our disaproval.

1. We may "disapprove" of all the laws of the Territory that we please, and thereby annul them, and for such reasons as may appear proper.

2. We may circumscribe the boundaries of the Territory, and give the inhabitants much narrower limits.

3. If the second proposition be adopted, we may then abandon them, and leave them to fight out their own independence and salvation, spiritually and temporarily, in their own good time.

4. We may cut up the Territory and annex it to the various adjoining Territories.

5. We may organize a territorial government on the old plan of a Council, consisting of a governor and judges—not Mormons; and with a military force sufficient to maintain it.

I cannot but hope enough of earnest men will ere long be found in Congress ready to devise some action—not of persecution—whereby our common country may be rescued from the great reproach of a barbaric age.

Others than Republican statesmen made political capital out of the question of polygamy.

Senator Stephen A. Douglas [Ill.] made it a point against James Buchanan, in his war with that President, that he had not removed Brigham Young from office. To this the President replied, in his annual message of 1857, that there was no longer any Government in Utah but Brigham Young. Nevertheless, on the report that the Mormons had destroyed records of the Federal court in Utah the Government dispatched 1,500

MORMON BREASTWORKS AND U. S. TROOPS
From the collection of the New York Historical Society

troops to Utah. Young, declaring that he asked "no odds of Uncle Sam or the devil," organized a "Nauvoo Legion" and halted the approach of the troops by setting fire to the grass (forage), stampeding their draft cattle, and burning their supply trains, and so compelling the force to winter near Fort Bridger.

On May 2, 1858, A. Cumming, Governor of Utah, reported to the Federal Government that the judicial records were intact; thereupon the troops were recalled.

An anti-polygamy bill, introduced by Representative Justin S. Morrill [Vt.], was passed in February, 1860, but as the severest punishment was the statutory penalty for bigamy, the act was ineffective.

During the Civil War, because treasonable tendencies were suspected of the Mormons, Utah was put under military supervision. In view of the more crucial problems of the war no anti-polygamy legislation was passed.

CHAPTER XII

Polygamy: Crime, or Religious Practice?

[DEBATE ON THE CULLOM BILL]

Shelby M. Cullom [Ill.] Introduces Bill in the House to Punish Polygamists in Utah—Debate: in Favor, Mr. Cullom; Opposed, William H. Hooper [Utah]; Bill Passed by House, but Not Acted upon by Senate—President Grant on Polygamy—Enactment of the Poland Anti-Polygamy Bill; It Is Upheld by the Supreme Court Decision That Religious Belief Is not a Valid Plea against an Act Made Criminal by Law; the Act Is Ineffectual.

I T was not until five years after the war that the Republican party attempted to execute its pledge of 1856.

On February 17, 1870, Shelby M. Cullom [Ill.] brought forward in the House of Representatives from the Committee on Territories a bill "in aid of the execution of laws in Utah," which, among other provisions, excluded from grand and petit juries all believers in polygamy; made the lawful wife in prosecutions for this offense a competent witness to prove her husband's first and second marriages; made cohabitation and kindred acts a proof of the original and subsequent marriages, there being no public official Mormon marriage ceremony or record; and declared plural marriage to be concubinage, punishable by fine and imprisonment, the concubines to be competent witnesses; authorized the use of United States troops to enforce the act; excluded alien polygamists from citizenship, and native polygamists from voting or holding office or preëmpting homesteads; prescribed that an office-holder qualify by swearing he is not a polygamist or will become one; prescribed that marriages be solemnized as in other parts of the country;

439

debarred marriage within specified degrees of consanguinity; required divorce from former spouse in case of a marriage of a person whose former spouse was living, etc.

In support of this bill Mr. Cullom made a long speech explaining its provisions. In it he said in part:

As to the qualification to hold any office of trust or profit in the Territory it seems to me that there can be no question that these leading Mormons, openly and defiantly violating law and practicing crime in the face of Federal authority, should be rendered ineligible to hold office; they are criminals, running at large because the Government has not had the courage to arrest them, and are unfit to hold office of honor or trust.

This being shown by the testimony of all who are acquainted with the condition of things existing in that Territory, and, as we have already adopted this principle in regard to certain classes of men lately in rebellion against the Government, I see no good reason why these wicked and vile men should be shielded from the operation of such a law as applied to them. I maintain that men practicing bigamy and polygamy in defiance of law are no better qualified to hold office than those lately in rebellion whom we have deprived of this right by statute and constitutional amendment.

As to the clause in regard to voting, my opinion is that the time has come when stringent, positive, and even severe legislation should be resorted to for the purpose of uprooting and destroying the iniquity that exists everywhere in that Territory; and this enactment, by depriving them of the right to vote and hold office, will take the power out of the hands of these leaders and tend to prevent the election of men sworn to defend the interests of the church at all hazards. This is a matter concerning which there should be no hesitation or timidity; and I contend that these people should neither be entitled to vote, to hold office, nor to have their aliens naturalized so long as they persist in the violation of the laws against bigamy and polygamy. The same as regards the right to preëmpt lands. Some may say that is too severe a hardship on these people. Sir, it is not a new thing in the history of our Government that persons should be prevented from the right to take possession of the public domain who are living in violation of its laws. It is but a short time since we passed a general law upon this subject as regards the public lands of the South, wherein, while inviting law-abiding men to come forward and partake of the benefits derived under it, we made a proviso that any person so desiring to preëmpt any portion of the public domain should first swear that he had not taken up nor voluntarily borne arms against the Government of the United States, and that he would support the Constitution. I regard, then, this provision as in entire harmony with the previous legislation of Congress and think it ought to become a part of the law.

Mr. Cullom answered the objection that the bill would "too suddenly break down the system of polygamy and leave the women and children of the Territory helpless and dependent, and, perhaps, in a starving condition."

Sir, I do not believe that any such result will be likely to follow the passage of this bill and the destruction of the institution of polygamy. The testimony before the committee, and which has been presented to the House, shows that the women of that Territory, in many instances, support not only themselves, but their children and their husbands. I could cite many cases where prominent Mormons have been supported by their numerous wives, made rich by their labors, and, instead of being dependent upon their husbands for their own and their children's support, the husbands are dependent upon the women.

In conclusion he asked:

Are we to have any legislation that will effectually crush out this bold and defiant iniquity, or are we to go on as we have been for over thirty years, allowing the practice of bigamy and polygamy to flourish in violation of human and divine laws, cloaked by the title of "Latter-day Saints" and a pretended system of religion? Shall we continue to temporize any longer with it and allow its defenders and abettors to go unpunished?

The great mass of the Mormons are either actively or passively in hostility to the Government of the United States. A great majority of them are of foreign birth, brought from their homes by persons assuming the garb of bishops or apostles of the church, and have never known, and never would know under the present system, anything of the institutions of this country. The power of these priests and presidents and apostles and bishops over them must be destroyed, so that the light of Christianity and civilization may reach their benighted understand-ings. They know nothing of the glorious principles of our Declaration of Independence. They have no impressions in regard to our people except as they are taught by Mormon teachers. They are led to believe the American people are the most infamous and bloodthirsty people on the face of the earth, and they hear from their pulpits, in their workshops, in their fields, nothing but the denunciations by their leaders against the American people. Under such a system of things it is not to be wondered at that these ignorant and deluded people come finally to regard us as their worst enemies, and become passive or active agents in the hands of their leaders to carry out their infamous designs.

Under almost any other system of religion or ethics we might hope that, in time, they would be divested of their prejudices and partake of the influences of enlightenment and civilization which are spread throughout this great country. And upon this theory the argument is raised that we had better do nothing now, that the system will die out, especially since the completion of the Pacific railroad, which will bring them more and more under the influence of our civilization and our modes of life. I confess that I had some hope that such would be the case upon the completion of the Pacific railroad. But, sir, the testimony shows that, since the completion of that great work, there has been a greater degree of proscription on the part of the leaders of that people than ever before. Within the last few months many men, Gentiles, who had been in business there, and who in years past have been favored with some degree of prosperity, latterly these men have been hunted and persecuted and in every way thwarted in their enterprises until they have been compelled, in order to protect their persons and their property, to leave the Territory and return among people where liberty and freedom prevail.

Sir, Brigham Young stands at the head of all affairs, spiritual and temporal. He has the power of "sealing." He is a "revealer"; he is prophet, priest, seer-revelator, first president, and trustee of the church of Latter-day Saints. He holds the keys of the kingdom; unfolds to the people the will of God as revelator. As seer he warns the people of danger, and as priest seals men and women for time and eternity. The testimony shows that, while there is no law upon the statute-books of the Territory in relation to marriages in any way whatever, yet there is a law in relation to divorces. Brigham Young seals the people in wedlock and divorces them at pleasure. But of late, since it has become apparent to him that perhaps a little observance of law would be necessary in order to save his head, while he divorces his people one from another in secret, yet, after it is done by him, and not until then, do they ever approach a court of justice to have the bonds of matrimony broken? To show the power as well as the supreme authority claimed and exercised by him I will call your attention to a sentence or two from a sermon recently delivered by him in that Territory.

"I have never yet preached a sermon and sent it out to the children of men that they may not call Scripture. Let me have the privilege of correcting a sermon and it is as good Scripture as they deserve."

Such, Mr. Speaker, is the manner in which he speaks to those benighted and ignorant people, and I suppose it is true that the great mass of them believe he speaks as from God.

Polygamy has been declared a criminal offence by every State and Territory in the Union, and is regarded by the civilized world as opposed to law and order, decency and Christianity, and the prosperity of the State. Polygamy has gone hand in hand with murder, idolatry, and every secret abomination. Misery, wretchedness, and woe have always marked its path. Instead of being a holy principle, receiving the sanction of Heaven, it is an institution founded in the lustful and unbridled passions of men, devised by Satan himself to destroy purity and authorize whoredom. It is not enough to say that it was practiced by many of the ancients and has been mentioned in the Bible. While it is true that such practices did prevail to some extent in ancient times, yet in no single instance does Holy Writ approbate it.

On March 22 and 23 William H. Hooper. Delegate from Utah, opposed the bill.

Mr. Speaker, I wish to make a few remarks concerning the extraordinary bill now under consideration. While so doing I crave the attention of the House; for I am here not alone as one of the people sought to be cruelly oppressed, not only as the delegate representing Utah, but as an American citizen, to utter my solemn protest against the passage of a bill that aims to violate our dearest rights and is fraught with evil to the Republic itself.

I do not propose to occupy the time of the House by dwelling at length upon the vast contributions of the people of Utah to the wealth of the nation. There is no member of this House who does not recollect in his schoolboy days the vast regions west of the Rocky Mountains characterized in the geographies as the "great American desert." There, said those veracious textbooks, was a vast arid region wherein no man could live, around the borders of which roamed the painted savages, only less cruel and remorseless than the desert itself.

In the midst of this inhospitable waste to-day dwell an agricultural, pastoral, and self-sustaining people, numbering one hundred and twenty thousand souls. Everywhere can be seen the fruits of energetic and persistent industry. The surrounding mining Territories of Colorado, Idaho, Montana, Arizona, and Nevada in their infancy were fed and fostered from the surplus stores of the Mormon people. The development of the resources of these mining Territories was alone rendered possible by the existence at their very doors of an agricultural people who supplied them with the chief necessities of life at a price scarcely above that demanded in the old and populous States. The early emigrants to California paused on their weary journey in the redeemed wastes of Utah to recruit their strength and that of their animals, and California is to-day richer by thousands of lives and millions of treasure for the existence of this halfway house to El Dorado.

This, however, is but a tithe of our contributions to the nation's wealth. By actual experiment we have demonstrated the practicability of redeeming these desert wastes. When the Pacific slope and its boundless resources shall have been developed; when beyond the Rocky Mountains forty million people shall do homage to our flag, the millions of dwellers in Arizona, Nevada, Idaho, Colorado, and Montana, enriched by the products of their redeemed and fertilized deserts, shall point to the valley of Great Salt Lake as their exemplar, and accord to the sturdy toilers of that land due honor, in that they inaugurated the system and demonstrated its possible results. These results are the offering of Utah to the nation.

For the first time in the history of the United States, by the introduction of the bill under consideration, a well-defined and positive effort is made to turn the great law-making power of the nation into a moral channel, and to legislate for the consciences of the people.

Here, for the first time, is a proposition to punish a citizen for his religious belief or unbelief. To restrain criminal acts, and to punish the offender, has heretofore been the province of the law, and in it we have the support of the accused himself. No man comes to the bar for trial with the plea that the charge upon which he is arraigned constitutes no offence. His plea is "Not guilty." He cannot pass beyond and behind the established conclusions of humanity. But this bill reaches beyond that code into the questionable world of morals, the debatable land of religious beliefs; and, first creating the offence, seeks, with the malignant fury of partisan prejudice and sectarian hate, to measure out the punishment.

The bill before us declares that that system which Moses taught, which God allowed, and from which Christ, our Savior, sprung, is a crime, and that any man believing in it and practicing it shall not be tried, but shall be convicted, and his children shall be declared bastards, his wives turned out to starve, and his property confiscated—in fact, for the benefit of the moral reformers who, as I believe, are the real instigators in this matter.

The honorable member from Illinois, the father of this bill, informs us that this is a crime abhorred by men, denounced by God, and prohibited and punished by every State in the Union. I have a profound respect for the motives of the honorable member. I believe he is inspired by a sincere hostility to that which he so earnestly denounces. No earthly inducement could make him practice polygamy. Seduction, in the eyes of thousands, is an indiscretion, where all the punishment falls upon the innocent and unoffending. The criminal taint attaches when the seducer attempts to marry his victim. This is horrid. This is not to be endured by man or God, and laws must be promulgated to prevent and punish.

While I have this profound regard for the morals and motives of the honorable member, I must say that I do not respect to the same extent his legal abilities. Polygamy is not denounced by every State and Territory, and the gentleman will search in vain for the statute or criminal code of either defining its existence and punishment. The gentleman confounds a religious belief with a criminal act. He is thinking of bigamy when he denounces polygamy, and, in the confusion that follows, blindly strikes out against an unknown enemy. Will he permit me to call his attention to the distinction? Bigamy means the wrong done a woman by imposing upon her the forms of matrimony while another wife lives, rendering such second marriage null and void. The reputation and happiness of a too confiding woman are thus forever blasted by the fraudulent acts of her supposed husband, and he is deservedly punished for his crime. Polygamy, on the contrary, is the act of marrying more than one woman, under a belief that a man has the right, lawfully and religiously, so to do, and with the knowledge and consent of both the wives.

Suppose, Mr. Speaker, that in proclaiming the old Jeffersonian doctrine that that government is best which governs least, I would not have even a minority upon this floor. But, when I say that in a system of self-government such as ours, that looks to the purest democracy, and seeks to be a government of the people, for the people, and by the people, we have no room for the guardian, nor, above all, for the master, I can claim the united support of both parties. To have such a government, to retain such in its purest strength, we must leave all questions of morals and religion that lie outside the recognized code of crime to the conscience of the citizen. In an attempt to do otherwise than this the world's abiding places have been washed with human blood, and its fields made rich with human bones. No government has been found strong enough to stand unshaken above the throes of religious fanaticism when driven to the wall by religious persecution. Ours, sir, would disappear like the ''baseless fabric of a vision'' before the first blast of such a convulsion. Does the gentleman believe, for example, that, in aiming this cruel blow at a handful of earnest followers of the Lord in Utah he is doing a more justifiable act than would be, in the eyes of a majority of our citizens, a bill to abolish Catholicism because of its alleged immorality? Let that evil door once be opened; set sect against sect; let the Bible and the school-books give place to the sword and the bayonet, and we will find the humanity of to-day the humanity of the darker ages, and our beautiful Government a mournful dream of the past.

This is not only philosophically true, but, sir, it is historically a fact. In making the appeal I stand upon the very foundation-stone of our constitutional Government. That they might worship God in accordance with the dictates of conscience the fathers fled from their homes in Europe to the wilds of America. For this they bore the fatigues or perished in the wilds of a savage-haunted continent; for this they poured out their blood in wars, until every stone in the huge edifice that shelters us as a nation is cemented by the blood of the martyr.

In our Constitution, still perfect and fresh as ever, we have a clause that cannot be changed and leave a vestige of a free government. In the original instrument we find this language: ''No religious test shall ever be required as a qualification to any office or public trust under the United States.'' But this was not considered sufficiently comprehensive for a free people, and subsequently we find it declared: "Congress shall make no law respecting an establishment of religion or prohibiting the free exercise thereof."

Upon the very threshold of my argument, however, I am met by the advocates of this extraordinary bill with the assumption that polygamy is not entitled to be considered as a portion of our religious faith; that, under the Constitution, we are to be protected and respected in the enjoyment of our religious faith, but that we are not entitled to consider as a portion thereof the views held by us as a people in reference to the marriage relation. One eminent disputant, as an argument, supposes a case where a religious sect might claim to believe in the rightfulness of murder, and to be protected in the enjoyment of that right. This is not in any sense a parallel case. Murder, by all law, human and divine, is a crime; polygamy is not. Not only by the authority of the Old Testament writers, but by numerous leading writers of the Christian and Jewish churches, the doctrine of polygamy is justified and approved. The only ground upon which any argument can be maintained that our views of the marriage relation are not to be considered as a portion of our religious faith is that marriage is a purely civil contract, and therefore outside the province of religious doctrine. No sect of Christians can, however, be found who will carry their beliefs to this extent. The Catholic church, the most ancient of the Christian churches, and among the most powerful in numbers of the religious denominations of our country, upon this point is in accord with the Mormon church.

Marriage, according to the faith of the Catholic church, is one of its sacraments; is not in any sense a civil contract but a religious ordinance, and the validity of a divorce granted by a civil court is denied. And not in any Christian church is the marriage contract placed on a par with other civil contracts, with a swap of horses, or a partnership in trade. It is a civil contract, in that a court of equity for certain specified causes may dissolve it; but not otherwise. To most intents and purposes with every Christian denomination the marriage ceremony is regarded as a religious ordinance. Upon this point, therefore, and a vital point in the discussion of the question before us, the Catholic church in fact, and the other religious denominations in theory and usual practice, are with the Mormons in their position, that the supervision and control of the marital relation are integral and essential portions of their religious faith and practice, in the enjoyment of which they are protected by the Constitution.

The Mormon people are a Christian denomination. They believe fully in the Old and New Testaments, in the divinity of Christ's mission, and the upbuilding and triumph of His church. They do not believe, however, that light and guidance from above ceased with the crucifixion on Calvary. On the other hand, they find that in all ages, whenever a necessity therefor existed, God has raised up prophets to speak to the people and to manifest to them His will and requirements. And they believe that Joseph Smith was such a prophet; that the time had arrived when there was a necessity for further revelation, and, through Joseph Smith, it was given to the world.

Upon this point of continuous revelation, which is really one of the turning points of the controversy, we are in accord with many of the most eminent divines of the Christian church, and with the most earnest and vigorous thinkers of our own day.

Says Ralph Waldo Emerson, in one of his most golden utterances:

"I look for the hour when that supreme beauty which ravished the souls of those Hebrews, and through their lips spoke oracles to all time, shall speak in the West also. The Hebrew and Greek Scriptures contain immortal sentences that have been the bread of life to millions. But they have no epical integrity; are fragmentary; are not shown in their order to the intellect. I look for the new teacher that shall follow so far those shining laws that he shall see them come full circle; shall see their rounding, complete grace; shall see the world to be the mirror of the soul."

Ours is a religious sect; it has to-day vindicated its right to live by works and sacrifices which are the admiration even of its enemies. It brings forward certain new doctrines; of church government; of baptism, even for their dead; of the marriage relation. Upon what point is it more probable that light from above would be given to our race than upon the marriage relation? The social problem is the question of the age. The minds of many of the foremost men and women of our day are given to the study of the proper position and relations of the sexes. The wisest differ—differ honestly and unavoidably. Endless are the dispute and clamor of those honestly striving to do away with the social evil, to ameliorate the anomalous condition of the wronged and suffering women of to-day. And, while this is so, while thousands of the good and pure of all creeds and parties are invoking the divine guidance in their efforts for the good of our fallen humanity, is it strange that the divine guidance thus earnestly besought should come; that the prayers of the righteous be answered? The Mormon people believe that God has thus spoken; that, through Joseph Smith,

He has indicated the true solution of the social questions of our day; and, while they persecute or question no man for differing honestly with them as to the Divine authority of such revelation, they firmly insist that in their following of what they believe to be the will of God they are entitled to the same immunity from persecution at the hands of the Government, and to the same liberty of thought and speech, wisely secured to other religious beliefs by the Constitution.

Upon the point whether polygamy can properly be considered as a part of our religious faith and practice I beg leave humbly further to submit, sir, that the decision rests solely on the conscience and belief of the man or woman who proclaims it to be a religious belief. My people proclaim polygamy as a part of their religious belief. If they are honest in this, however much they may be in error, they stand on their rights under the Constitution, and to arrest that error you must appeal to reason and not to force. I am here not to argue or demonstrate the truthfulness of their faith; but if I can convince you that this belief is honorably and sincerely entertained my object is accomplished.

It is common to teach, and thousands believe, that the leaders of the sect of Latter-day Saints, popularly known as Mormons, are hypocrites, while their followers are either ignorant, deluded men and women or people held to their organization by the vilest impulses of lust. To refute these slanders I can only do as the earlier Christians did: point to their sufferings and sacrifices, and I may add the unanimous testimony of all, that, aside from what they consider the objectionable practice of polygamy, my constituents are sober, moral, just, and industrious in the eyes of all impartial witnesses. In this community, removed by long reaches of wastes from the moral influences of civilization, we have a quiet, orderly, and Christian community. Our towns are without gambling-hells, drinking-saloons, or brothels, while from end to end of our Territory the innocent can walk unharmed at all hours. Nor is this due to an organized police, but to the kind natures and Christian impulses of a good people. In support of my argument of their entire sincerity I with confidence appeal to their history.

Here the speaker recounted the early history of the Mormons, ending with their expulsion from Missouri.

The annals of religious persecution, so fruitful of cruel abuse, can give nothing more pitiable and heartrending than the scenes which followed this last expulsion. Aged men and women, the sick and feeble, children of tender years, and the wounded, driven into the flats of the river, yet in sight of their once happy houses, to perish from exposure and starvation. While over our broad land the churchbells of Christian communities were ringing out peace and good-will to men; while to the churches thronged thousands to hear preached the Gospel of charity and forgiveness, these poor, heart-sick followers of the same Redeemer were driven in violence from their houses to perish like wild beasts in the swamps and wilderness.

Word went out to the world that Mormonism had finally been annihilated. But again the scattered hosts were gathered together, and set out on a pilgrimage that since that of the children of Israel has been without parallel in the history of the human race. They had no stores; they were beggared in the world's goods, yet with earnest religious enthusiasm they toiled on through unknown deserts, over unexplored mountain ranges, and across plains haunted by savages only less cruel than the white Christians who had driven them forth in search of that promised land where at last they could worship God in accordance with the dictates of their own consciences and find unbroken that covenant of the Constitution which guards this sacred right. Ragged, foot-sore, starving, and wretched they wandered on. Delicately nurtured women and their little children dug roots, or subsisted on the bark of trees or the hides of animals. From Nauvoo to Salt Lake, the valley of their promised land—fifteen hundred miles—there is to-day scarce a mile along that dreary and terrible road where does not repose the body of some weary one whom famine or sickness or the merciless savage caused to perish by the way.

It was while on this pilgrimage that an order came from the Government for five hundred men to serve as soldiers in the Mexican war. The order was promptly obeyed. These devoted men who had received only cruel persecution from the people they were called upon to protect on the field of battle dedicated their poor, helpless wives to God and themselves to their country. Leaving their families to struggle on as best they could these brave, patriotic men followed our flag into New Mexico and California, and were at last disbanded at San Diego with high praise from their officers, but with scanty means to return to those they loved, and whom they had left to suffer, and perhaps to perish on the way.

Mr. Speaker, is this shining record that of a community of lustful hypocrites? What other Christian denomination of our country can show higher evidences of earnestness, of devoted self-sacrifice for the preservation of their religious faith?

Mr. Hooper here reverted to his claim that the Christian and Jewish churches had endorsed polygamy.

At the period of the Reformation in Germany, those great reformers, Luther, Melancthon, Zuringli, and Bucer, held a solemn consultation at Wittenberg on the question "whether it is contrary to divine law for a man to have two wives at once?" and decided unanimously that it was not, and upon the authority of this decision Philip Landgrave, of Hesse, married a second wife, his first being still alive.

Dr. Hugo Grotius states that "the Jewish laws allow a plurality of wives to one man."

The Evangelical Christian missionaries in India, in a conference at Calcutta, decided that having more wives than one should not debar a man from membership in the church.

These facts prove that one of its main charges, that polygamy is abhorrent to every Christian nation, is false; for the British empire is a Christian nation, and Hindustan is an integral part of that empire. Hindustan is a civilized country, with schools and colleges and factories and railroads and telegraphs and newspapers. Yet the great mass of the people, comprising more than eighty millions, are polygamists, and, as such, they are recognized and protected by the laws of the British Parliament and the courts of the queen's bench; and the English and American missionaries of the Gospel who reside there, and have resided there many years, and who know the practical working of polygamy, have assembled together in solemn conference, and unanimously pronounced it to be right, and in accordance with the practice of the primitive Christian churches; and the French, the Spanish, the Dutch, the Portuguese, and other Christian nations are known to pursue a similar policy, and to allow the different peoples under their governments the free and unmolested enjoyment of their own religions and their own marriage system, whether they are monogamous or polygamous.

Polygamy is a doctrine the practice of which, from the precedents cited, is clearly not inconsistent with the highest purity of character and the most exemplary Christian life. My opponents may argue that it is unsuited to the civilization of the age, or is the offspring of a religious delusion; but, if so, its remedy is to be sought through persuasion and not by the exercise of force; it is the field for the missionary and not for the jurist or soldier. So soon, however, as the Luthers, the Melancthons, the Whitfields of to-day have wiped out the immorality, licentiousness, and crime of the older communities, and have made their average morality equal to that of the city of Salt Lake, let them transfer their field of labor to the wilds of Utah, and may God forever prosper the right.

Mr. Hooper then addressed himself to the subject of prostitution, stating that polygamy had been presented as a remedy for it long before the days of Joseph Smith.

Rev. Martin Madan, relative of the poet Cowper, and an accomplished scholar, was chaplain of the Lock Hospital in London during the latter part of the eighteenth century. By his exertions the first chapel for the use of the unfortunate inmates of that hospital was built, and then, perhaps for the first time in the history of England, the gospel was preached for the special benefit of fallen women. The sympathies of their benevolent chaplain were so deeply enlisted in their behalf that he published a book upon the subject in 1780 entitled ''Thelyphthora; or, a Treatise on Female Ruin, in Its Cause, Effects, Consequences, Prevention, and Remedy'' which remedy he discovers to be polygamy, and which he discusses in a very thorough manner in three octavo volumes. I submit copious extracts from this learned work.

Here the speaker read the extracts.
Mr. Hooper then arraigned the bill as a reversion, in these days of religious toleration, to the days of the Holy Inquisition and the persecution of New England Quakers and witches.

It is but a short time since the country hailed with satisfaction a treaty negotiated on the part of a pagan nation through the efforts of a former member of this body [Anson Burlingame], and whose recent death has filled our hearts with sadness, whereby the polygamous Chinese emigrants to our shores are protected in the enjoyment of their idolatrous faith, and may erect their temples, stocked with idols, and perform their (to us) heathenish worship in every part of our land unquestioned. And, while the civilized nations of Europe have combined to sustain and perpetuate a heathen nation practicing polygamy in its lowest form, and are hailing with acclamation the approach of its head, the American Congress is actually deliberating over a bill which contemplates the destruction of an industrious people and the expulsion of the great organizer of border civilization.

Mr. Hooper spoke of the "countless lies which had been circulated for years" about his people.

These falsehoods have a common origin—a desire to plunder the treasury of the nation. They are the children of a horde of bankrupt speculators anxious to grow rich through the sacrifice even of human life.

Here the speaker charged that the "Mormon War" in Buchanan's Administration, costing twenty or thirty million dollars, had been promoted by army contractors, who spread the report that the Mormons had destroyed the official records of the Federal court in Utah; this report was subsequently proved false, and the troops were withdrawn.

These contractors, and numerous would-be imitators, long for the return of that golden age. They fill the ears of the public with slanders and with falsehoods; that murders are rife; that life and property are unsafe in Utah without the presence of large armies. They have even sometimes induced Federal territorial officers, through ignorance or design, to become their tools to help forward their infamous work. But since the railroad was completed many of the American people have looked for themselves. They see in Utah the most peaceful and persistently industrious people on the continent. They judge the tree by its fruits. They read that a community given up to lust does not build factories and fill the land with thrifty farms. That a nation of thieves and murderers do not live without intoxicating liquors and become famous for the products of their dairies, orchards, and gardens. A corrupt tree bringeth not forth the fruits of temperance, Christianity, industry, and order.

Mr. Speaker, those who have been so kind and indulgent as to follow me thus far will have observed that I have aimed, as best I might, to show—

1. That, under our Constitution, we are entitled to be protected in the full and free enjoyment of our religious faith.

2.   That our views of the marriage relation are an essential portion of our religious faith.

3.   That, in considering the cognizance of the marriage relation as within the province of church regulations we are practically in accord with all other Christian denominations.

4.   That, in our views of the marriage relation as a part of our religious belief, we are entitled to immunity from persecution under the Constitution if such views are sincerely held; that, if such views are erroneous, their eradication must be by argument and not by force.

5.   That of our sincerity we have, both by words and works and suffering, given for nearly forty years abundant proof.

6.   That the bill in practically abolishing trial by jury, as well as in many other respects, is unconstitutional, uncalled for, and in direct opposition to that toleration in religious belief which is characteristic of the nation and age.

It is not permitted, Mr. Speaker, that any one man should sit as the judge of any other as regards his religious belief. This is a matter which rests solely between each individual and his God. The responsibility cannot be shifted or divided. It is a matter outside the domain of legislative action. The world is full of religious error and delusion, but its eradication is the work of the moralist and not of the legislator. Our Constitution throws over all sincere worshipers, at whatever shrine, its guaranty of absolute protection. The moment we assume to judge of the truthfulness or error of any creed the constitutional guaranty is a mockery and a sham.

Three times have my people been dispersed by mob violence, and each time they have arisen stronger from the conflict; and now the doctrine of violence is proposed in Congress. It may be the will of the Lord that to unite and purify us it is necessary for further violence, suffering, and blood. If so, we humbly and reverently submit to the will of Him in whose hands are all the issues of human life. Heretofore we have suffered from the violence of the mob; now the mob are to be clothed in the authority of an unconstitutional and oppressive law. If this course be decided upon I can only say that the hand that smites us smites the most sacred guaranties of the Constitution, and the blind Samson, breaking the pillars, pulls down upon friend and foe alike the ruins of the State.

On March 23 the House passed the bill by a vote of 94 to 32. It was discussed in the Senate, but not acted upon.

In his fourth annual message [of December, 1872] President Grant called the attention of Congress to the Cullom Bill against polygamy at the previous session, and inferentially recognized the impossibility of crushing out the abuse at once by asking for the passage of this or a similar law looking to "the ultimate extinguishment of polygamy."

His recommendation was not acted upon.

In 1874 an anti-polygamy bill, introduced by Representative Luke P. Poland [Vt.], was enacted. It was along the lines of the Cullom bill. Convictions under it being appealed, the Supreme Court decided that religious belief cannot be accepted as justification for an overt act made criminal by the law of the land.

Nevertheless the act was an ineffectual one, polygamy continuing to flourish in the Mormon settlements, not only in Utah, but in other Territories.

CHAPTER XIII

DEBARRING POLYGAMISTS FROM CIVIL RIGHTS

[DEBATES ON THE EDMUNDS BILL]

George F. Edmunds [Vt.] Moves an Anti-Polygamy Bill in the Senate, with a Provision for a Commission to Declare Persons Polygamists and so Ineligible to Vote, Hold Office, or Serve on Juries—Debate on the Commission Feature: in Favor, Augustus H. Garland [Ark.], Mr. Edmunds; Opposed, George G. Vest [Mo.], John T. Morgan [Ala.], Wilkinson Call [Fla.]; Bill Is Passed by Congress and Approved by the President—President Cleveland on the Execution of the Law— Federal Dissolution of the Mormon Church Corporation—Manifesto of the Mormon President, Wilford Woodruff, against Practicing Polygamy—President Harrison's Comment on the Manifesto: "The Doctrine Is Not Abjured"—Admission of Utah into the Union with Polygamy Forbidden.

I N his third annual message [December, 1879] President Hayes struck at the root of the matter by declaring that polygamy could be suppressed only by taking away the political power of the sect which practiced it. Like remarks of Presidents Garfield and Arthur in 1881 led to the passage of an act in which this principle was embodied. This, with supplementary legislation, finally proved effective.

On December 12, 1881, George F. Edmunds [Vt.] introduced in the Senate a bill to amend the statute relating to bigamy, so as better to prohibit polygamy in the territories. It was referred to the Committee on Judiciary. It was reported from the committee on January 24, 1882, by Senator Edmunds. The bill provided that practice of or *belief in* polygamy disqualified a juror in a case under the statute, and gave the President power to grant amnesty to persons guilty of

"bigamy, polygamy, or unlawful cohabitation" before the passage of the act.

It further provided that no polygamist should be eligible to vote or hold office, and that the question of this eligibility be determined by a bi-partisan board of five persons appointed by the President.

The bill came forward for discussion on February 15.

THE EDMUNDS ANTI-POLYGAMY BILL

SENATE, FEBRUARY 15-16, 1882

George G. Vest [Mo.] objected to the last provision of the bill as "establishing an anomaly in the jurisprudence of the United States, and striking down the fundamental principle of American liberty."

If there is one single clause in our Constitution or bill of rights dear to the American heart, it is that no citizen shall be deprived of life, liberty, or property without the judgment of his peers or of a competent tribunal. The idea that any citizen can have taken from him a right conferred by law, without the judgment of a competent tribunal and without a trial, is abhorrent to every principle of personal liberty and constitutional right. It is the very essence of good government and of freedom and of constitutional right that every man should be tried and convicted before punishment. The seventh section of this bill takes away from a citizen of the United States the right to vote or hold office before conviction by his peers of any crime.

The Senator from Delaware [Thomas F. Bayard] is pleased to say that this case is analogous to that of a Territory applying for admission into the Union, when Congress has the right under the Constitution to impose its own terms and form of government under the Constitution. But, sir, there is no analogy. The people of Utah to-day are voters; the people of Utah to-day are officeholders; they have had this right from the organization of the Territory.

SENATOR BAYARD.—By act of Congress.

SENATOR VEST.—By act of Congress under the Constitution; and under the Constitution I say that no man can be deprived of the right to vote or to hold office except after conviction. I announce that proposition to-day. If Utah were here apply-

ing for admission into the Union then we could say to her:
"Accept certain conditions"; and, if they were within the
limitations of the Constitution, those conditions of course must
be accepted or rejected. But here these rights have been conferred; they are already given; and we propose by a commission
which is outside of the law, outside of the Constitution, to give
to its members the power to say absolutely who shall be elected
and what shall be the returns, to canvass the returns, and to
declare who shall be the voters and who shall be elected. Such
power inside of American legislation was never known before.

But, Mr. President, I say as a lawyer that the principle
of taking away the right of suffrage or the right to hold office
before conviction for crime is unknown in the legislation of
this country or in its jurisprudence. In the case of Barker, in
3 Cowen, this doctrine was announced by the Supreme Court
of New York by John Savage, a man who graced the bench and
the tribunal over which he presided. The legislature of New
York undertook to stamp out dueling, and provided that any
man who should fight a duel should be deprived of the right
to vote or to hold office. The case was taken to the highest
tribunal in the State and adjudicated. I wish I had time to
read it all, for every word of it is applicable to the case now
before the Senate. I will simply read as much of it as constitutes the syllabus:

> But, while many rights are consecrated as universal and inviolable, the
> right of eligibility to office is not so secured. It is not one of the express
> rules of the Constitution, and is not declared as a right or mentioned in
> terms as a principle in any part of the instrument. Important as this
> right is, it stands, as the right to life itself stands, subject to the general
> power of the legislature over crimes and punishments.

I call the attention of the Senate to the fact that this bill
inflicts a punishment for crime on any man guilty of polygamy,
or any person cohabiting with more than one woman, etc., by
providing that he shall be deprived of the right to vote and
the right to hold office. A subsequent section provides that
five gentlemen, constituting a commission, shall determine the
question of guilt. I say that this bill comes within the meaning of this decision, for it is the infliction of a punishment for
crime.

> As a right flowing from the Constitution, it cannot be taken away by
> any law declaring that classes of men, or even a single person not con-
> victed of a public offence, shall be ineligible to public stations.

The Territories of the United States are peopled by citizens of the United States, and I say to-day that the highest judicial declaration, in my judgment, ever made by the Supreme Court of the United States was made by the late Chief-Justice Taney when he declared that the Constitution of the national Government and the citizen walked into the Territories side by side under the Constitution of our common country. This idea that the Territories are absolute creatures to be governed by Congress as they please, without reference to the Constitution or law or right is, in my judgment, abhorrent to every principle of American freedom.

Much as I detest polygamy, much as I believe it to be utterly subversive of all pure society and good morals, I shall never vote for a provision which, in my judgment, subverts the highest and dearest rights of every American citizen.

Augustus H. Garland [Ark.].—Mr. President, the argument of the Senator from Missouri [Mr. Vest] goes somewhat to the foundation of this bill. He has said that the provisions of section 7 and section 8 are severe provisions. They were intended to be severe. They have been said to be rough provisions. They were intended to be rough. Desperate cases need desperate remedies, and I am of the opinion that every provision in this bill is as well sanctioned by the organic law and precedents under the organic law of this country as any bill that has ever received the sanction of Congress.

Mr. President, what are we undertaking to do? We are undertaking to provide for a government in the Territory of Utah. What Territory? One of the Territories of the United States. We are not undertaking to legislate for a State; we are not undertaking to reconstruct a State that has already been rehabilitated; but we are undertaking to legislate for the government of a distant Territory of the United States. Where do we get that power? We get it under the following provision of the Constitution:

The Congress shall have power to dispose of and make all needful rules and regulations respecting the territory or other property belonging to the United States.

The Senator from Missouri is correct when he says that the Constitution goes into the Territories. It goes in and enters into the Territories by virtue of this very provision in the Constitution which gives Congress power to make all needful rules and regulations respecting the Territories. What now has the highest tribunal of the land said is the relative position of these

Territories to the United States under that grant of power?
A case that has been followed repeatedly by no divided court,
by no individual opinion merely, but followed repeatedly—it is
the fountain of the authority as construed by the Supreme
Court—the case of Gratiot *vs.* The United States, in 14 Peters:

> The term territory as here used—

That is, as used in the clause of the Constitution I have just
read—

> is merely descriptive of one kind of property, and is equivalent to the
> word "lands." And Congress has the same power over it as over any
> other property belonging to the United States, and this power is vested in
> Congress without limitation, and has been considered the foundation upon
> which the territorial governments rest.

And no other. You cannot place your hand upon this Territory without this grant of power; you cannot legislate for it in
one form or another without this grant of power or some similar grant; and, upon this grant of power, says the Supreme
Court, rests your territorial government. That is the law of
this land. That being so, what are your territorial governments? Under a law that has been in force for many years,
section 1850 of the Revised Statutes, it is provided:

> All laws passed by the legislative assembly and governor of any ter-
> ritory except in the territories of Colorado, Dakota, Idaho, Montana, and
> Wyoming shall be submitted to Congress, and, if disapproved, shall be null
> and of no effect.

And on several occasions since I have been in the Senate
Congress has disapproved of acts of the Territories and set them
aside under this section 1850.

So the legislative acts of the Territories have no force and
effect save and only as Congress acquiesces in them. They are
operative laws only because Congress does not see proper to
repeal them or to disapprove of them. Ten thousand people in
Utah Territory vote. They vote by the sanction of Congress;
they vote by reason of the non-repeal, the non-disapproval by it
of the Territorial acts giving them the franchise. Certainly, if
that be the case, it is within the power of Congress to repeal
them whenever it sees proper, and that is what we are undertaking to do in this bill.

The difficulty in Utah is not because a man has one, two, or
ten wives; it arises not merely upon the morality or the virtue

of that peculiar proceeding; but it is because he has a government there at war with the spirit and theory of the Government under which we live; he has a government there that bids defiance and stands not in awe of the laws passed by the Congress of the United States. Probably no law will ever be effective to prevent polygamy or polyandry there if you please, probably no law can ever be passed that can effectually prevent cohabitation; but yet I have in my hand the laws of every State and Territory of this Union except that one, and there is a severe penalty against that crime of cohabitation, bigamy, or whatever name you may choose to call it by. If they had a law there that the other Territories and the States have against these crimes, probably nothing need be said on this subject; but, as stated by the honorable Senator from Delaware, there is no republican government there, there is a hierarchy, a theocracy; it is a government bred and brought into life by an inspiration, according to the report of Mr. Cullom submitted in 1870, "by an independent revelation of God to Brigham Young." The marriages are held within the bosom of the church there, all the property goes through the church, the lands and the wills and everything else go through the same sanction of the church. Will you tell me, then, that there is a republican government there?

The theory of our Government is that church and State shall not be commingled, shall not be made to run together; and, in the case of the United States *vs.* Reynolds, in 98 U. S. Supreme Court Reports, where Reynolds pleaded that he was only practicing his religion there and was not committing an indictable offence, the Supreme Court told him in plain language that the plea would not do in this country to shield a man under his religion to perpetuate these crimes which the civilized world denounces. It was from an inspiration, I believe, that Guiteau said he was impelled to take the life of the Chief Magistrate of this country and plunge this people in woe. Yes, you may have your religion, but you cannot have it as a cloak to commit crimes that the laws of the country say must be punished and put down and suppressed. Let it go to the world that that Territory is organized on the theory that a man can govern himself because he is inspired by God to a certain course, and you may as well abolish all your statute-books and dispense with your law-making power. When the Constitution spoke and when the theory of this Government spoke, and when Jefferson and the men of his day spoke on this subject, declaring that Church and State should not be mixed, it was not meant to give an authority to commit crime under the cloak and guise of religion by whatever name it might be called.

Our Constitution says that the United States shall guarantee to each State a government republican in form. What is the object and purpose of your Territories? They are now in their chrysalis state, marching on to full sisterhood and to admission into the Union. Suppose, now, Utah was to be presented for admission into the Union, is there a Senator here present who could say that there is a republican form of government there? That is the test of this question. Suppose Utah now were to knock at the doors of Congress for admission, let us see what your constitution says and what your practice under the Constitution is; let us see what you would say in reference to it. Its people might say: "We only have four or five or six or ten wives apiece; we live in this kind of business at large, and everybody knows it is according to law; nobody can be punished for it; our property comes through the Church, and our rules and regulations are all from the church." That is not a government carried on by the people through their representatives, which means a republican government—people who are guilty of crimes, as suggested to me by the Senator from Texas [Samuel B. Maxey], which were punishable at common law at the time of the adoption of the Constitution and by all the States at the time they adopted it.

Now, it is in the power of Congress to say to these people "You shall not vote at all." We have seen that our power in that regard is ample, that it is plenary. When we speak of a man forfeiting a right, it is not a right of voting secured by the laws of the country, because that right is conferred by the law-making power and it is changed repeatedly by a change of law or constitution. That is not one of those guaranteed rights (as decided repeatedly by the Supreme Court) of which a man cannot be deprived without the intervention of a jury; but every State and every Territory in this Government disqualifies persons for certain things from sitting upon a jury. Aliens and felons shall not sit upon juries; persons under twenty-one years of age shall not, and yet they are taxed. True a felon is convicted; but look at all the laws of your different States and you will find that provisions as severe and as far-reaching as these apply to making up your jury boxes.

We cannot afford to stand here speaking of the rights of a Territory in these matters. Nor is it novel for the Congress of the United States to provide for a commission government in the Territories. Have we not provided a commission govern-

ment for this District which is no more under the control of
Congress than are the Territories by the Constitution of the
United States and the decisions of the Supreme Court under
the Constitution? Have you not taken away the right of suffrage from the people here in this District?

SENATOR EDMUNDS.—If the Senator will allow me to add to
his suggestion about this District, he will remember that in three
or four instances of the Territories in the Northwest we governed them entirely by commission composed of the governor
and judges.

SENATOR GARLAND.—Here we have a Territory, anomalous as
it may appear, directly at war and directly antagonistic to all
the theories of our Government and at war with the principles
of our Government. It is a Territory subject to our own control,
under the needful rules and regulations we may think proper
to make. Shall we hesitate to adopt this proposed law? If it is
extreme, it is an extreme case upon which it is to operate.

On February 16 John T. Morgan (Ala.) opposed the
mooted sections as unconstitutional.

Whatever you may choose to declare a crime in this country,
I do not care what it may be, that moment the Constitution
comes in and guarantees to that citizen that no punishment for
that crime can be inflicted upon him of any character whatsoever
unless it is done according to the due process of law and through
the judicial tribunals of the country.

The elective franchise is a right which was guaranteed at
the time we enacted the law organizing this Territory; for the
moment we put the citizens in Utah in possession of the rights
of American citizens within that Territory by the act of 1850,
we gave them then the guaranties of the Constitution of the
United States, which would follow them in all cases and in all
places for the protection of their personal rights, secured to
them under the law by the community at large, and to all men
who are described in the fifth section of the act of 1850 as
being citizens and settled in that Territory.

A case came up in the Supreme Court of the United States
which I think clearly establishes the doctrine for which I am
contending now as against this section of the bill. The first
was the Cummings vs. The State of Missouri. An attempt
was made in the constitution of that State to deprive a number
of persons of certain rights and privileges of a similar character
because they refused to take what was called there the iron-

clad oath, who refused to exculpate themselves for having participated in the then recent rebellion. It is not necessary to
read all the statement of the case in order to get before the
Senate the part of it which I think is applicable to this particular matter. The court say:

> The disabilities created by the constitution of Missouri must be re-
> garded as penalties—they constitute punishment. We do not agree with
> the counsel of Missouri that ''to punish one is to deprive him of life,
> liberty, or property, and that to take from him anything less than these
> is no punishment at all.'' The learned counsel does not use these terms—
> life, liberty, and property—as comprehending every right known to the law.
> The deprivation of any rights, civil or political, previously enjoyed, may
> be punishment, the circumstances attending and the causes of the depriva-
> tion determining this fact. Disqualification from office may be punish-
> ment, as in cases of conviction upon impeachment.

After having considered the *ex post facto* nature of this
enactment, its operation on existing rights, emoluments, honors,
privileges, and trusts, the court proceeded to discuss the other
feature to which I now desire to call the special attention of
the Senate:

> No State shall pass any bill of attainder, *ex post facto* law, or law
> impairing the obligation of contracts.

It will be observed, of course, that that language is made
applicable by this section of the Constitution to States, but not
to States alone. The Supreme Court of the United States has
repeatedly held that these restrictions are just as obligatory
upon the Congress of the United States as they are upon the
States themselves.

> A bill of attainder is a legislative act which inflicts punishment with-
> out a judicial trial.

A more perfect definition could not be given. You can
neither contract it, nor can you enlarge it, without depriving
it of its proper force. But is this bill before us to-day a bill
which by legislation inflicts punishment without judicial process? What is the object of disfranchising a man because he is
a polygamist or a bigamist? It is not to preserve the purity
of the ballot-box, but it is to inflict a punishment upon him for
that crime which the Congress feels may be at work destroying
the foundations of society.

Mr. President, I venture to say that there is no gentleman
on this floor who has a more profound abhorrence of that Mor-

mon hierarchy that exists in Utah and some of the neighboring Territories, and no one who feels greater anxiety for its being trodden down than I do. No one has considered the necessity as more imminent than I do that we should take all proper and legitimate steps for the purpose of crushing out this bane of all civil society in those Territories, this growing evil, which it seems to me if tolerated much longer must overwhelm that Western country, beautiful as it is, with the pall of destruction and despair. But, sir, I am not willing to persecute a Mormon at the expense of the Constitution of the United States. I am not willing to go to the Indian tribes where polygamy is practiced and take up those men and inform them that they shall not have the right to life or liberty because they are polygamists; and we have just the same right to tell an Indian that he shall not live because he is a polygamist as we have to tell a Mormon that he shall not vote because he is a polygamist, provided we make that the penalty of the crime and give the power to a legislative tribunal to declare his crime and punish it. We must be cautious in times like these how we employ our power. It is the power of a people who have a written constitution, but they should be careful when the circumstances arouse them to anger, as in that time we are apt to do something that may sap the foundations of our liberties. This is not the time for us to permit transgressions of the Constitution of the United States; it is a time when we should hold up the standard of the Constitution and ask all men to respect it.

Senator Wilkinson Call [Fla.] opposed the provision.

With all this argument and discussion, here is the Constitution of the United States, and here is the Fourteenth Amendment which the honorable Senator from Vermont was himself largely instrumental in passing, which declares that every person subject to the jurisdiction of the United States is a citizen and entitled to the equal protection of the laws. What equal protection of the laws is it between those men in Utah when five men say that ''We believe, without evidence, without trial, without notice, without hearing, that you have been guilty of an act of impropriety with a female, and we deny you the right to that franchise, that eligibility to office, which you now possess. We deny you the right to a trial by a jury of your peers. We require you to be tried by men who are unfriendly to you, and we believe that your religious faith is an enemy of the country and ought to be suppressed with fire and the sword.'' Your faith, says the Senator from Vermont, is a shame to Christianity and therefore must be destroyed by these cruel methods. Mr. President, I have not so learned the precepts of our Christianity —I have not so learned our Constitution. I have been taught that the Christian religion was one of peace and good-will, and that ''no religious test'' for office in the Constitution forbids the exclusion of Jew or Gentile because of his belief. Mr. President, it is useless to attempt to govern and control this question in this way. The honorable Senator from Delaware [Mr. Bayard] speaks of the Mormons as a theocratic government. Why? What right is there for that allegation here? What is the argument? Because the organization of the Mormon church rests in religious matters and in social, an absolute power in the head of the church. Does not another church do that? Does not our Christian church in one of its leading bodies, which is not to be spoken of anywhere except with the profoundest veneration, the ecclesiastical body that witnessed the beginning of Christianity, that certainly contributed no small part to its early history and its struggles with paganism and maintained it all through the generations of the past, assert the absolute infallibility of the head of the church upon all religious and social matters, and, when it speaks *ex cathedrâ*, command the absolute obedience of its millions of votaries?

There is nothing theocratic in the government of the Mormon church that is exhibited to the world. It does not claim to govern the Territory of Utah. It acknowledges the authority of the Government of the United States. You cannot assail it by declaring as a matter of opinion on the part of the American Congress that for a man to worship God according to his belief, as Mormons do (however contrary to our opinions and our wishes), is a theocracy to be suppressed with fire and sword. But, if you will make war upon it, let it not be by striking down the liberties of your people and doing violence to your own holy faith; but assail it with the red right hand of war, with the sword to stab it out, and say to them: ''Proclaim your heresies and conduct your rites beyond the limits of this territory of the United States.'' Sir, this is worse than open, flagrant war. This is asserting to the people that what our fathers, acting under the teachings of the Christian religion, fought for more than a hundred years to accomplish, shall be thrown away. This is an assertion by the Congress of the United States that there may be a trial by a packed and prejudiced court, and by partial jurors—by a man's foes, and not his friends; and that, in defiance of the principles which control our whole political system, a government shall be constructed through penal provisions and verdicts of courts selected and organized to try and convict, by which one-tenth of the people shall rule nine-tenths.

Mr. President, I would go to any constitutional extent necessary to suppress polygamy, and I believe that the way is open and easy to suppress this evil. I think that the women of the country, having a right, as I believe they have, to every occupation and every employment consistent with their health and their strength, and having a free and vigorous thought that is quite equal to that possessed by our own sex, when protected by the laws, will assert for themselves freedom and right without the use of unconstitutional and, I think, wicked processes for the accomplishment of public objects.

Give them the aid of the laws and the protection of the courts and juries fairly constituted. Enact your laws declaring what shall be crime, and, if necessary, change your place of trial in conformity to established law wherever and whenever proof is made before your court that the state of public feeling is such that a fair trial cannot be had. Make the way to the writ of *habeas corpus* easy and sure; make provision for the support of those women who, with their children, desire to leave the polygamous relation.

If the situation is so grave as to require extraordinary methods, these would seem to be the proper ones. Protect individuals in their freedom and choice in leaving this state of polygamy; provide for their support, and, above all, educate them and their children, and send among them ministers of the Gospel. Why seek to build up a local despotism in the name and under the false pretence of law to accomplish objects which are easily accomplished by lawful means?

Senator Edmunds defended his bill.

We take out by this bill from the present government of Utah all of its essential powers, because the statistics and the information that we have demonstrate that the government of the Territory of Utah from top to bottom now is and has been for a long time—I do not know but all the time—including both houses of its territorial assembly, in the hands of the polygamists. Every member of its council but one is a polygamist glorying in from two to six wives. Every one but two or three of the twenty-six members of its House of Representatives is also adorned with that distinction. And, when you go into the executive offices of that Territory, much the same thing exists.

Now this act, if it has no other effect, will have the effect of displacing from political supremacy all the persons whom the laws of the United States for twenty years have said were people who ought not to be allowed to carry on a government. It will have that effect provided the President of the United States and the Senate of the United States, his constitutional advisers, select for the administrative and judicial offices of that Territory men who are wise enough and able enough to enforce the laws; and that, I may say, has been the great difficulty for the last twenty years that the Government of the United States is far from being free from criticism upon that point. It will do so much.

Now, if there be in this Mormon church a body of people, as we believe there are, who have no more faith in this idea of polygamy than any Senator who hears me has, as a fact, and who wish to discourage it and who wish to emancipate themselves from the tyranny of this hierarchy that now has its foot on their necks, there will be a chance for them to assert themselves.

Now I come back to the precise point that we have before us; the essential substance of this bill is that the distinction between the power of the people to regulate political rights and their power to deny civil rights is as plain as anything can be. In the case of the constitution of every State in this Union almost, there has always been the provision that no man who is an idiot, a pauper, or a lunatic shall be entitled to vote; and that question of whether he is entitled to vote is not submitted to a judicial tribunal to decide whether he is a pauper or an idiot; but it is decided in the first instance (subject, as in every case, and as it is here, to an appeal to a judicial tribunal) by the political authority of the State in which the question arises. That has existed in, I presume, every State constitution. Upon what principle does it stand? It stands upon the principle that the body of the people—and that for the Territories is the Congress of the United States and nobody else, for we might abolish them to-morrow—have the right to determine who shall exercise a political franchise as distinct from a private or civil right.

The Supreme Court of the United States, in the woman suffrage case, have recognized and affirmed exactly the same proposition that the right to vote or to hold office is not an inherent right of a citizen, but it is a conventional right dependent upon the will of the majority of the community in which the right is claimed to exist. That is just what this does.

The Committee on the Judiciary recognize to the fullest extent all that has been said touching the right of every man and every woman to believe precisely what he or she likes. He may be an infidel and believe in nothing; he may be of any sect; he may believe that a hundred wives or no wives are right; he may believe in horse-stealing or whatever he likes; but, when it comes to what he has to do in the government of the country, it is a different thing. The horse-thief may not sit on the jury where a horse-thief is on trial, if he says on being asked that he thinks horse-stealing is a Christian duty; and yet some people have talked to us the idea that if you exclude horse-thieves from a jury that is to try a horse-thief you have packed the jury. That is not the case unless it be that every jury is packed in a sense. As I said some time ago, each jury, like every other agency of government, must believe in the law that they are called upon to enforce; otherwise the law itself becomes a mere mockery, and trial by jury a sham. You must, in that sense, pack it upon one side or the other; and upon which side? If you are to have a government at all, you must pack it on the side of the people who believe in the law that they are sworn when they take their places in the jury-box that they will faithfully and impartially execute. That has existed without statute at the common law; it is the common law now; it is the law of the United States in Utah now, and this jury clause that we have in this bill only puts into form and provides convenient methods of carrying out exactly what the Supreme Court of the United States has decided that the law now is.

This is not a question of religion at all—for there is no clause in the bill that can be tortured into affecting any man's faith; but there are clauses in the bill that deal with his conduct; and it is an essential principle of every organized community that conduct, be it of faith or of practice without faith, is subject to be dealt with by the authority of that community. Nobody questions that; and, when you deprive the pauper in Illinois or Georgia or Vermont of the right to vote, you do not say that he must be convicted of pauperism by a judicial trial in advance. You say that the political authority must decide in the first instance whether he is a pauper or not. If that political authority decides wrongfully against him, and his vote turns the question of how that election is to go, the judicial authorities come into play and put the right man in his place. That is exactly the effect of this bill.

Polygamy is not alone an evil in itself, but it happens to be an inherent and controlling force in a society which is the most intense and anti-republican hierarchy, as well as the most thoroughly organized and systematic government that has ever existed on the face of the earth. The Church of the Latter-day Saints, a corporation organized under the authority of law, controls in every respect every step in the territorial operations of that community. The three first presidents, as they are called—but I believe that the last one of those is the absolute ruler in point of fact—control the destiny and the fate of that people: polygamists, Mormons who are not polygamists, and Gentiles. Is that republican? Can you tolerate in the heart of this continent of republics the building up of a State of that character? If you cannot tolerate it, and have the power to dispose of it, are you willing to exert that power? This bill is only one step to that end. The Committee on the Judiciary have under consideration other and further measures, which I hope we shall report in due time, which will make up and supplement this measure, to eradicate, as far as just government may, not any man's faith or opinion, but to bring the political community that exists within the boundaries of that Territory into its republican relations with the great Republic that surrounds it. That is all.

You can always find reasons and flaws and difficulties for not doing a thing if you do not wish to do it, and the Committee on the Judiciary do not suppose that this measure alone is sure to have the effect that some people imagine it is to have; but we hope that this Senate, before it is through with this business, will do all—and that will be sufficient—that the absolute political power of this Government has within its reach to accomplish the purpose, not of breaking down any man's faith or his opinions, but making the practice of the government of the Territory of Utah and of its inhabitants conformable to what is essential to the republican safety of every one of the States of this Union and the republican safety of them all under the Union of the United States.

The bill was passed *viva voce,* the passage being greeted with applause in the galleries. It was passed by the House on March 13 by a vote of 199 to 42. It was approved by President Arthur on March 23, 1882.

The manner in which the law was executed during the first few years after its passage may be gathered from the reference to it in the first annual message of President Cleveland, December 8, 1885.

In the Territory of Utah the law of the United States passed for the suppression of polygamy has been energetically and faithfully executed during the past year, with measurably good results. A number of convictions have been secured for unlawful cohabitation, and, in some cases, pleas of guilty have been entered and a slight punishment imposed upon a promise by the accused that they would not again offend against the law, nor advise, counsel, aid, or abet, in any way, its violation by others.

The Utah Commissioners express the opinion, based upon such information as they are able to obtain, that but few polygamous marriages have taken place in the Territory during the last year. They further report that, while there cannot be found upon the registration lists of voters the name of a man actually guilty of polygamy, and while none of that class are holding office, yet at the last election in the Territory all the officers elected except in one county were men who, though not actually living in the practice of polygamy, subscribe to the doctrine of polygamous marriages as a divine revelation and a law unto all higher and more binding upon the conscience than any human law, local or national. Thus is the strange spectacle presented of a community protected by a republican form of government to which they owe allegiance, sustaining by their suffrages a principle and a belief which sets at naught that obligation of absolute obedience to the law of the land which lies at the foundation of republican institutions.

There should be no relaxation in the firm but just execution of the law now in operation, and I should be glad to approve such further discreet legislation as will rid the country of this blot upon its fair fame.

Since the people upholding polygamy in our Territories are reënforced by immigration from other lands, I recommend that a law be passed to prevent the importation of Mormons into the country.

The recommendation of the President was not acted upon.

However, on March 3, 1887, a law was enacted to terminate the Mormon corporations known as the Perpetual Emigrating Fund Company and the Church of Jesus Christ of Latter-Day Saints, which was upheld by the Supreme Court in 1890, the charters of the corporations being forfeited and their property, amounting to $800,000, being escheated. Upon the decision of the court, Brigham Young's successor to the presidency of the church, Wilford Woodruff, issued a manifesto in which he advised the Latter-Day Saints to "refrain from contracting any marriage forbidden by the law of the land."

President Harrison, in his second annual message (December 1, 1890), commented upon this manifesto as follows:

The advice of President Woodruff has attracted wide attention, and it is hoped that its influence will be highly beneficial in restraining infractions of the laws of the United States. But the fact should not be overlooked that the doctrine or belief of the church that polygamous marriages are rightful and supported by Divine revelation remains unchanged. President Woodruff does not renounce the doctrine, but refrains from teaching it, and advises against the practice of it because the law is against it. Now, it is quite true that the law should not attempt to deal with the faith or belief of anyone; but it is quite another thing, and the only safe thing, so to deal with the Territory of Utah as that those who believe polygamy to be rightful shall not have the power to make it lawful.

Utah was admitted into the Union on January 4, 1896, with the following articles, among others, in its constitution:

Polygamy is forever prohibited.
Perfect toleration in religious matters is guaranteed, and the separation of church and state is decreed.